LIVES of AMERICAN WOMEN

A History with Documents

JOYCE D. GOODFRIEND
University of Denver

CLAUDIA M. CHRISTIE
Formerly, Wellesley College

Little, Brown and Company
Boston □ Toronto

For Our Parents

Library of Congress Catalog Card No. 80-84681

ISBN 0-316-320056

9   8   7   6   5   4   3   2   1

MV

Published simultaneously in Canada
by Little, Brown & Company (Canada) Limited

Printed in the United States of America

CREDITS

The authors gratefully acknowledge permission to use the following photographs: Valerie Christie, courtesy of Valerie Jane Christie; Maud Rittenhouse, courtesy of Richard L. Strout; Joyce Maynard, photo © Alex Gotfryd; Sarah Hill Fletcher, Indiana Historical Society; Ellen Birdseye Wheaton, courtesy of Crawford Gordon; Anne Lasoff, photo by Diane Michener; Maria Brown, courtesy of Constance Kuhn; Hannah Lambertson, from *Hannah's Daughters: Six Generations of an American Family, 1876–1976* by Dorothy Gallagher (Thomas Y. Crowell Company), page 3, copyright © 1976 by Dorothy Gallagher, reprinted by permission of Harper & Row, Publishers, Inc.

Preface

In this book we have examined the lives of American women from the seventeenth century to the present, using the concept of the life cycle as an organizing principle. Our primary focus has been on women themselves and the ways in which they have evaluated their experiences, relationships, and choices at each stage of life. Our goal has been to build a sturdy historical foundation for the study of contemporary women's lives.

Through our work we have sought to demonstrate that the life cycle concept can enhance historical studies of American women by furnishing a means for integrating two levels of analysis, the individual and the societal. Studying women's lives in terms of developmental as well as historical guideposts has enabled us to clarify the relationship between individual and social change. This approach should make the text particularly useful for courses in women's history, women's studies, and American social history.

The book consists of a general introduction and five chapters that correspond to five basic life stages: childhood, adolescence, young adulthood, middle age, and old age. The introduction sets the stage for the chapters that follow by reviewing the varied applications of the life cycle concept. Each period of life is then explored from historical, psychological, and sociological viewpoints. After identifying the major theoretical issues pertaining to the life stage, we outline the dominant and alternative experiences of the life stage from the colonial era to the present. This historical narrative supplies a framework for interpreting the detailed case studies in each chapter.

Personal documents composed by women form an integral part of every section of the book. In addition to illustrating the historical trends and patterns delineated in the comprehensive discussion, they highlight fundamental aspects of personal development. However revealing the documents are of the complexity of individual lives, these fragments of personal history are designed to illuminate experiences and attitudes common to women over the centuries.

Certain criteria guided our choice of documents. We preferred writings such as diaries and letters that revealed an individual's immediate interpretation of events, rather than accounts composed from hindsight. We felt that lengthy selections from the writings of a small number of women would produce greater insight into women's lives than would brief excerpts from the testimonies of a wider sample. It was essential, however, that the documents chosen reflect the variety of experience and take into account differences in social class, race, ethnicity, religion, and regional background, as well as personality, temperament, and talents. Above all, we sought authentic voices, women who truly represented their peers. Our subjects, then, are by definition ordinary women rather than exceptional women.

ACKNOWLEDGMENTS

Many people at Little, Brown have aided us in creating this book. We want to thank our sponsoring editors, Katherine Carlone and Marian Ferguson, as well as their assistants, Viki Merrick and Nano Chatfield, for their continuing support. We also express our appreciation to our book editor, Cynthia Chapin, for efficiently guiding the manuscript through the production process, and to our copy editor, Susan Brown, for her meticulous reading of the manuscript. In addition the careful and constructive reviews of various drafts of the manuscript by Mary Kelley, Juanita Williams, Nancy Cott, Gladys Beckwith, Mary Anne Sedney, Anne Firor Scott, Patricia Cline Cohen, Barbara Brackney, and Nancy Weiss were most helpful.

We also wish to express our appreciation to colleagues, friends, and family whose contributions were many and diverse. Throughout the preparation of the manuscript we have been aided immeasurably by the staff of the University of Denver Department of History, and, in particular, Claudia Price. We are indebted to Valerie Christie for allowing us to publish a portion of her private childhood diary, and to Debra Shoemaker for her careful research on the Adelaide French diary.

Joyce Goodfriend is grateful for Irvine Slater Goodfriend's astute comments on the manuscript and for the counsel of Sarah Nelson during the long period of composition. Claudia Christie thanks Elizabeth Rock, Rodney Morrison, Maud Chaplin, Robert Kelly, and Ethel Brown for being there when it counted most, and Mario and Ida Petino for their innumerable kindnesses. Most important, we are grateful to our parents for their unshakable faith in all of our work.

Contents

Four: Middle Age   261

Five: Old Age   313

Introduction

Inaccurate images of women's lives abound in American culture. Like the reflections in a fun-house mirror, these images convey a semblance of truth but in a form so exaggerated that all sense of proportion is lost. The perfect housewife, the devoted mother, the frustrated spinster, the sex object, the ruthless career woman, the "uppity" woman — all of these stereotypes have proved exceedingly durable because they offer simplified, yet believable, versions of the life experience of American women. Indeed, it is their idealized quality that has made these images so influential in molding our perceptions of female existence. Nevertheless, it is widely recognized that such stereotypic representations distort the reality of women's lives. By reducing women to embodiments of particular attributes, they conceal the ambiguities inherent in female identity and mask the contradictory impulses with which women have perennially struggled. Unquestionably, the actuality of female experience in America has always been far more complex than is suggested by prevalent characterizations.

In recent years historians have made considerable headway in correcting the simplistic images of women embedded in popular culture. Spurred by the changing climate of opinion concerning woman's role in society, feminist scholars have mounted an impressive research effort designed to ferret out the salient facts of American women's lives, past and present. Assessment of newly unearthed documents, as well as standard sources, in the light of modifications in social and psychological theory has produced an ongoing reinterpretation of the female experience in America. Although the emergent scholarship is diverse in character, it is possible to categorize current research efforts under two broad methodological approaches.[1]

One major thrust of recent work is directed toward delineating the framework of female life in America, or what might be called the objective

[1] For useful reviews of recent works on the history of American women, see Barbara Sicherman, "American History — Review Essay," *Signs* 1 (Winter 1975): 461–485; and Mary Beth Norton, "American History — Review Essay," *Signs* 5 (Winter 1979): 324–337. Insight into the field of women's history can be gained from Gerda Lerner, *The Majority Finds Its Past: Placing Women in History* (New York: Oxford University Press, 1979).

1

circumstances of women's lives. The aim of such studies is to provide an analysis of the social and economic conditions as well as the cultural imperatives that have defined women's lives. Resourceful investigators have accumulated an enormous body of information through studies of demographic processes, employment patterns, household technology, medical care, and voluntary organizations. In addition, surveys of ideas and attitudes have clarified the cultural norms that guide female behavior. Researchers have combed obvious as well as obscure sources, ranging from sermons, magazine articles, and works of fiction, to films, television programs, and advertising, to ascertain the messages being transmitted to women about the ideals of femininity. All of this work has finally made it possible to place American women in the context of their times.

A different, but complementary, approach to the study of American women's lives takes as its starting point the individual female rather than the society and culture. Biographies not only document the personal history and public career of a particular woman but, more importantly, attempt to explain the reasons for her behavior at critical junctures in her life. The most illuminating studies in this vein focus on the subjective reality of female life, probing women's mental and emotional states, and draw conclusions about their psychological makeup.[2] The value of this perspective on women's lives is evident, since it alone affords readers the opportunity to scrutinize a woman's inner self.

Nevertheless, biographical studies, no matter how ably conceived and executed, do not provide an adequate basis for generalizing about the life course of the majority of American women. With few exceptions, biographers have written about notable or notorious women, women who stood out from the mass because of their distinctive accomplishments or their defiance of convention. What makes a woman a likely candidate for an in-depth profile is the fact that she led an unusual life or played a decisive role in shaping public events. In other words, the rationale for the selection of an appropriate subject is her singularity, not her typicality. Consequently, the findings of biographers, however enlightening with respect to individual careers, have limited applicability. There remains a significant gap in our knowledge of the female experience in America that can only be filled when scholars are convinced of the necessity of examining the subjective dimension of the average woman's life.

The personal histories of ordinary women merit investigation for a purpose other than that underlying traditional biographies. A particular female life can be dissected for the light it sheds on representative patterns of female development rather than, as in the traditional biographical approach, for its own sake. Instead of laboring to discern those qualities that make their subjects unique, researchers examine the lives of ordinary women to identify commonalities in experience and outlook. They begin with the premise that although few American women have had the resources to

---

2 See, for example, Allen F. Davis, *American Heroine: The Life and Legend of Jane Addams* (New York: Oxford University Press, 1973); and Kathryn Kish Sklar, *Catharine Beecher: A Study in American Domesticity* (New Haven: Yale University Press, 1973).

challenge the norms of their culture directly, countless women have dealt with the manifold problems posed by their daily existence in creative and meaningful ways. These women very definitely did make their own history, even if they were hemmed in by the proscriptions of society. Their legacy to us will be lost unless we devise an effective strategy for analyzing their life experiences.

Collecting and evaluating personal documents is one means of answering this call. Gathering such data presents a real, but not insurmountable, problem. Diaries, letters, and autobiographies of undistinguished women are available in plenitude to the diligent researcher, but, not surprisingly, white, middle-class, Protestant women are clearly overrepresented in these sources. This bias must be consciously compensated for in the presentation and interpretation of documents.

A more knotty problem concerns the elaboration of a methodology that facilitates generalization about the full spectrum of female experience in America without sacrificing the personal element so crucial to biographical works. In essence, what is needed is a mode of analysis that preserves the focus on the individual, which is the sine qua non of biography, but at the same time allows us to reconstruct representative female experiences for different historical periods. We believe that the concept of the life cycle, employed by developmental psychologists to study processes of cognitive growth and identity formation, can be used fruitfully to structure a historical study of the temporal dimension of female life. In this book, life cycle categories supply a matrix for organizing personal documents produced by American women over the centuries. We do not assume that each life stage embodies any one specific psychosocial task, but we do believe that there are certain theoretical issues that are critical for understanding each life stage and that these issues must be explored before historical analysis can proceed. Although this application of the life cycle concept lacks the theoretical rigor customary in the social sciences, it promises to increase our understanding of the nature of individual development in both the past and present.

Processes of aging as well as the progression of changing roles people assume from childhood through old age have long been popularly perceived as movement through stages in life.[3] The emergence of a scientific model of life stages to describe the many facets of human development,

---

[3] This is not to imply, however, that those stages have been uniformly or universally understood in the past, or to say that what is defined as a separate stage at any historical period has always been recognized as such. Many factors shape a society's classification of people at all ages. Recent scholarship investigating how conceptions of childhood, adolescence, and adulthood have been profoundly influenced by social forces and how they reflect demographic circumstances includes: Philippe Ariès, *Centuries of Childhood: A Social History of Family Life,* trans. Robert Baldick (New York: Alfred A. Knopf, 1962); Joseph F. Kett, *Rites of Passage: Adolescence in America, 1790 to the Present* (New York: Basic Books, 1977); Winthrop D. Jordan, "Searching for Adulthood in America," and Tamara K. Hareven, "The Last Stage: Historical Adulthood and Old Age," *Daedalus* 105 (Fall 1976): 1–11, 13–27; David Hackett Fischer, *Growing Old in America* (New York: Oxford University Press, 1977); and W. Andrew Achenbaum, *Old Age in the New Land: The American Experience Since 1790* (Baltimore: Johns Hopkins University Press, 1978).

however, is a relatively recent phenomenon. Originating in the biological sciences in the nineteenth century, the life cycle concept has become a potent analytical tool for psychologists, sociologists, anthropologists, and historians.

Charles Darwin's biological theory of evolution — a gradual, continuous process beginning with single-cell organisms and advancing through higher stages to the most complex species, human beings — dramatically transformed conceptions of the physical and psychological nature of individual development. Among the first to explore the psychological implications of Darwin's ideas was G. Stanley Hall. Constructing an evolutionary psychological system, Hall delineated a series of biogenetic stages of individual development, linking each to a particular stage in the evolution of the whole species.

Hall postulated that physiological factors, which were genetically determined, controlled human consciousness and behavior. Minimizing the role that environment plays in shaping personality, he described natural patterns of physical and psychological development as they unfolded during different periods of life. Although Hall explained both male and female development in terms of biology, he maintained that physiology controlled females to a greater extent than it did males. Because a woman's sex organs constituted a "far larger proportion of her body than those of man," he wrote, "their psychic reverberations" were "more all pervasive." The natural course of development for females thus led inevitably to marriage and motherhood.[4]

Early in the twentieth century Sigmund Freud proposed his general theory of human sexual development, which he expanded and revised throughout his life. Freud described how the unconscious and its mechanisms function at various psychosexual stages of development and serve as a source of motivation and behavior. He hypothesized that the course of development diverged for males and females during the phallic stage, between the ages of four and seven, when children discover that the genitals of the sexes are different.

According to Freud, the girl's discovery that she lacks a penis makes her envious of males and has profound psychological consequences for her later personality formation and behavior. If she follows a "normal" path of development she resolves her penis envy, becomes reconciled to her anatomical inferiority, and accepts her position in life. Freud also saw the psychosexual conflicts characteristic of each life stage as largely unaffected by environmental influences. Thus, anatomy determines personality, emotions, interests, and character and explains differences between the sexes.[5]

---

[4] Hall (1846–1924) began his research on developmental processes in children in the 1880s, later exploring adolescence and old age. A discussion of his contributions to developmental psychology can be found in Howard Gardner, *Developmental Psychology: An Introduction* (Boston: Little, Brown, 1978), pp. 148–151. Quote is from Hall, *Adolescence* (New York: D. Appleton, 1904), 2:562.

[5] For a lucid discussion of psychoanalytical theories and criticisms from feminist writers, see Juanita H. Williams, *Psychology of Women: Behavior in a Biosocial Context*

Interest in the stages of life development waned after 1920, as environmental learning theories began to dominate the field of psychology. Reacting against both the methodology and assumptions of early developmental psychologists, environmental learning theorists emphasized the role of environment in conditioning personality and behavior and turned their attention to creating experimental situations where variables could be precisely defined and controlled.[6] The resurgence of interest in the life cycle idea in recent decades is directly attributable to the original research and writings of Jean Piaget and Erik Erikson.

In his investigations of how children learn to reason, Piaget identified a sequence of cognitive stages through which children pass, each reflecting different modes of organizing knowledge and understanding the world. Piaget held that all children move through cognitive stages in sequence, proceeding from the simple, reflex behavior of infancy to the development of logical thought processes. By linking these stages of cognitive development to levels of maturation, which define the nature and limitations of intellectual functioning at any particular phase, Piaget offered a cognitive-structuralist framework of analysis.[7]

Without a doubt the best-known general theorist of the life cycle today is Erik Erikson. His research and writings in the 1950s and 1960s extended psychoanalytical insights about human development by emphasizing the importance of societal influences on personality formation. Erikson divided life development into eight stages, postulating that growth depends on how successfully each person resolves specific psychological crises, in sequence and through interaction with one's environment. Subsequent achievements depend on past accomplishments, and how an individual resolves each crisis directs future identity development. For Erikson, certain periods in life are critical for an individual's social and emotional growth. They are seen as times when specific life experiences can shape individual personality for life. The eight stages are thus defined in terms of particular psychological tasks an individual is attempting to master.[8]

(New York: W. W. Norton, 1977), pp. 17–62. A full-length account of the life cycle from a psychoanalytical perspective is provided by Theodore Lidz, *The Person* (New York: Basic Books, 1968).

[6] Gardner, *Developmental Psychology*, pp. 150–151.

[7] Ibid., pp. 62–80. The ideas of Piaget and anthropologist Claude Lévi-Strauss and the creation of a structuralist movement in the social sciences are thoroughly discussed in another book by Gardner, *The Quest for Mind: Piaget, Lévi-Strauss, and the Structuralist Movement* (New York: Alfred A. Knopf, 1973).

[8] Erikson's major writings include *Identity and the Life Cycle: Selected Papers*, Psychological Issues, no. 1 (New York: International Universities Press, 1959), which was revised in *Identity: Youth and Crisis* (New York: W. W. Norton, 1968), and *Childhood and Society* (New York: W. W. Norton, 1963). The literature on childhood and adolescent development is extensive, and not all of it is systematically related to Eriksonian concepts and theories. Development during adulthood has received increasing attention in recent years. See the work of Bernice L. Neugarten, *Personality in Middle and Late Life: Empirical Studies* (New York: Atherton Press, 1964) and Neugarten, ed., *Middle Age and Aging* (Chicago: University of Chicago Press, 1968). On male development during adulthood, see Daniel J. Levinson, et al., *The Seasons of a Man's Life* (New York:

At Stage I, during infancy, the newborn is totally dependent on others for physical and emotional support and feels both trust and mistrust toward the surrounding environment. In resolving those feelings, the presence or absence of a nurturing environment is a crucial factor in determining how trustful or mistrustful the infant will become.

The child at ages two to three begins discovering new abilities and creating a sense of individuality. The psychological task at Stage II is to gain a sense of autonomy. If this is unsuccessful, for example, if parents are too permissive or too strict, a child may become inhibited, feel shame or doubt. During Stage III, the preschool years, the child is learning to be assertive and is testing the limits of initiative. This is the time for acquiring a sense of conscience and responsibility; failure to do so results in feelings of guilt. The next critical period comes for the school-aged child at Stage IV. The psychological task is to develop feelings of competence. Through the performance of school activities, the child can either gain a sense of accomplishment or inferiority. Cognitive development is particularly important during the years from ages six to twelve.

Achieving an integrated sense of self is the task which confronts the individual during adolescence and characterizes Stage V. At this period a young person is questioning future roles and making decisions with long-term ramifications. Failure to create a strong sense of identity at this stage can result in identity diffusion.

The last three crises that Erikson describes occur during adulthood. At Stage VI the young adult is developing the capacity for intimacy in personal relationships and preparing to make decisions about marriage and family life. Failure in relationships at this stage can result in a sense of isolation and self-absorption. Middle adulthood, Stage VII, can be a time of generativity or of stagnation. Erikson defines generativity as "concern in establishing and guiding the next generation." This impulse can be satisfied in various ways, such as working or having children. Failure to become generative results in stagnation — accomplishing nothing creative and setting no new goals in life. The last psychological problem is faced during old age, Stage VIII. At this point the individual reflects upon past accomplishments and must accept them. Failure to do so can lead to feelings of despair and futility.

Although Erikson's model of human development has been enormously influential in molding both popular and scholarly conceptions of the life cycle, it has not been totally immune to criticism. While paying homage to the originality and perceptiveness of Erikson's formulations, researchers have been frustrated by the resistance of his concepts to empirical testing.

Ballantine Books, 1979). A popularized account of crises in adult life is Gail Sheehy, *Passages* (New York: E. P. Dutton, 1976).

Erikson's theories have been summarized in many places. This discussion draws on material in Gardner, *Developmental Psychology*, pp. 528–532, 545–546; Williams, *Psychology of Women*, pp. 49–51; and Diane E. Papalia and Sally Wendkos Olds, *Human Development* (New York: McGraw-Hill, 1978), pp. 106–107, 164–165, 227–228, 262, 342, 379, 426.

Until the issues of each life stage are defined more precisely, they contend, the entire Eriksonian schema will remain in the realm of the speculative.

Another criticism leveled at Erikson is that there is not enough evidence to support the idea that any one psychological characteristic is definitively achieved at any particular stage or by any specific time. It has been hypothesized that each quality that Erikson defines — trust, autonomy, identity, and so on — has different meanings at various age levels. Furthermore, there exist many individual and group exceptions to Erikson's sequential pattern.[9]

Perhaps the most trenchant criticism of Erikson's model has been advanced by feminist scholars who note that his research subjects have been predominantly male; when women are mentioned in his works they are discussed primarily in terms of their roles as mothers. Once more, the female reproductive function emerges as the main determinant of identity.[10] In essence, these critics argue that the Eriksonian model of psychological development is premised exclusively on male life experiences and is therefore, in fact, a theory of male development. As psychologist Juanita Williams aptly puts it, "If women are an exception to the theory, then it is not a theory of human development." [11]

Whether or not the psychosocial stages identified by Erikson can be verified using female subjects is not yet clear. Research now in progress on female development over the life span will shed much-needed light on this question and may ultimately lead to the creation of new psychological theories.[12]

Sociologists have suggested that Erikson's fixed sequence of psychological stages implies an orderliness in people's lives that is not realistic in light of the frequency with which social roles and relationships change. Since personality is expressed through the roles and relationships an individual experiences, when these change substantially, so too does the person.[13]

[9] These criticisms are discussed in an essay by John A. Clausen, "The Life Course of Individuals," in *Aging and Society*, eds. Matilda White Riley, Marilyn Johnson, and Anne Foner (New York: Russell Sage Foundation, 1972), 3:457–514, and Erikson himself has acknowledged them.

[10] These problems in the relationship between Erikson's theories and the psychology of women are raised by Williams in *Psychology of Women*, pp. 50–62. Williams points out that Erikson addressed the issue of female personality development per se late in his career in two papers, "The Inner and the Outer Space: Reflections on Womanhood" (1964) and "Once More the Inner Space" (1975). Erikson analyzed differences in play activities of boys and girls, ages ten to twelve, which he then linked to differences in male and female anatomy. His conclusion, that anatomy determines identity, has been strongly attacked.

[11] Ibid., p. 57.

[12] Carol Gilligan discusses the ways in which theories of the life cycle, by failing to take into account experiences of women, promote imbalanced conceptions of human development. See "Woman's Place in Man's Life Cycle," *Harvard Educational Review* 49 (November 1979): 431–446. Mary Brown Parlee reviews the current state of psychological research and theory about and for women in an essay in *Signs* 5 (Autumn 1979): 121–133.

[13] Clausen, "The Life Course of Individuals," p. 505. The complex questions of to what extent identity is comprised of one's roles and in what ways it is independent of

By conceptualizing the life cycle in terms of sequences of roles that individuals assume within the family, in school, at work, and in the community at large, sociologists offer an alternative approach, one that is more flexible in studying female development. For sociologists, investigations of the nature of human interactions within social and economic structures is central to understanding individual development over the life cycle. Sociological theories identify stages in family, marital, and career cycles that highlight important developments in people's lives.

Each stage in the family life cycle — being newly married, becoming a parent, living alone with one's spouse after the children have left home, and, finally, living alone after the death of a spouse — is characterized by very different personal involvements and interests. Changing marital and parental roles and responsibilities within the family profoundly affect people's life patterns and thus influence the ways they see themselves, as well as how others perceive them.[14]

By compiling data on the experiences of successive birth cohorts as they pass through the stages of life, researchers can discern dominant and alternate patterns of role sequences. Analysis of statistics on marriage, divorce, fertility, mortality, and labor-force participation enables social scientists to depict changing life patterns as well as to pinpoint variations according to sex, race, and nativity.[15]

Historians as well as sociologists have recognized the value of the life cycle concept for their work. In his pioneering study of family life in seventeenth-century Plymouth, John Demos utilized Eriksonian theory to probe the inner life of Puritan colonists in family settings. Applying Erikson's definition of each life stage to historical data, Demos analyzed the

---

them are dealt with in Peter Berger and Thomas Luckmann, *The Social Construction of Reality* (Garden City, New York: Doubleday, 1966) and in Erving Goffman, *The Presentation of Self in Everyday Life* (Garden City, New York: Doubleday, 1959).

14 Clausen, ibid., pp. 482–500. Interpreting findings that reveal that women today are having fewer children, spending fewer years raising them, and living longer than in previous times, Roxann A. Van Dusen and Eleanor Bernert Sheldon hypothesize that the importance of the marital life cycle has declined in the total life cycle of females, and the effects of this development will be profound with respect to changing sex roles and bases of self-identification in the decades ahead. See their article, "The Changing Status of American Women, A Life Cycle Perspective," *American Psychologist* (February 1976), pp. 106–116. See also the writings of Jessie Bernard, *The Future of Motherhood* (New York: Dial Press, 1974) and *Women, Wives, Mothers: Values and Options* (Chicago: Aldine, 1975). Another sociological view is provided by Bernice Neugarten and N. Datan, "Sociological Perspectives on the Life Cycle," in *Life Span Developmental Psychology: Personality and Socialization*, eds. P. B. Baltes and K. W. Schaie (New York: Academic Press, 1973), pp. 53–69.

15 See, for example, Glen H. Elder, Jr., *Children of the Great Depression: Social Change in Life Experience* (Chicago: University of Chicago Press, 1974). This long-range study on the family, educational, marriage, and employment experiences of a cohort born in 1920 and 1921 in Oakland, California, uses data gathered from the 1930s through the early 1960s. Also, two articles by Peter Uhlenberg, "A Study of Cohort Life Cycles: Cohorts of Native Born Massachusetts Women, 1830–1920," *Population Studies* 23 (1969): 407–420, and "Cohort Variations in Family Life Cycle Experiences of United States Females," *Journal of Marriage and the Family* 36 (May 1974): 284–292.

psychological development of the typical colonist from birth, through youth, to adulthood, and into old age.[16]

Sociologically oriented historians have forged new theoretical and methodological approaches to studying stages of family development throughout history. Although this work focuses on the family, rather than the individual, studies employing concepts such as the family life cycle and the life course, which have their roots in sociology, clearly can enhance our understanding of individual life patterns. The demographic findings of these historians have illuminated different patterns of female behavior at different historical periods.[17]

Two recent major works in women's history offer limited applications of the life cycle concept: Mary Ryan's *Womanhood in America from Colonial Times to the Present* and Gerda Lerner's *The Female Experience: An American Documentary*.[18] As part of her wide-ranging, chronologically organized overview of womanhood in America, Ryan presents a series of composite pictures of typical female life cycle patterns during key historical periods. In contrast to that of Ryan, the primary focus of Lerner's work is on the personal dimension of women's lives. Lerner uses the life cycle concept as the organizing principle of one major section in an innovative documentary history compiled from the female point of view. That the life cycle concept provides an invaluable framework for structuring inquiries into American women's lives is no longer in doubt. What remains to be seen is how profoundly its implementation will transform our understanding of the history of American women.

[16] John Demos, *A Little Commonwealth: Family Life in Plymouth Colony* (New York: Oxford University Press, 1970). And also, Demos, "Developmental Perspectives on the History of Childhood," *Journal of Interdisciplinary History* 2 (Autumn 1971): 315–327. Historian David Hunt has also applied the Eriksonian model in his work on family life in seventeenth-century France, *Parents and Children in History: The Psychology of Family Life in Early Modern France* (New York: Basic Books, 1970). Hunt limited his analysis to the stages of infancy and childhood.

Erikson himself has written psychobiographies of Luther and Gandhi, following the course of their lives through various sequences of development and exploring the relationships between their inner and public selves. In her psychobiography of Thomas Jefferson, Fawn Brodie acknowledges the influence of Erikson's writings and draws on his ideas throughout the work. Erikson, *Young Man Luther* (New York: W. W. Norton, 1968) and *Gandhi's Truth* (New York: W. W. Norton, 1969). Brodie's book is *Thomas Jefferson: An Intimate History* (New York: W. W. Norton, 1974).

[17] For a sampling of this work, see Tamara Hareven, ed., *Transitions: The Family and the Life Course in Historical Perspective* (New York: Academic Press, 1978). Other methodological articles by Hareven include, "The Family As Process: The Historical Study of the Family Cycle," *Journal of Social History* 7 (1973–1974): 322–329, and "Cycles, Courses and Cohorts: Reflections on Theoretical and Methodological Approaches to the Historical Study of Family Development," in ibid., 12 (Fall 1978): 97–109.

See also the work of Robert V. Wells, "Women's Lives Transformed: Demographic and Family Patterns in America, 1600–1970," in *Women of America: A History*, eds. Carol Ruth Berkin and Mary Beth Norton (Boston: Houghton Mifflin, 1979), pp. 16–33; and his article, "Demographic Change and the Life Cycle of American Families," *Journal of Interdisciplinary History* 2 (Autumn 1971): 273–282.

[18] Mary P. Ryan, *Womanhood in America from Colonial Times to the Present*, 2nd ed. (New York: New Viewpoints, 1979); Gerda Lerner, *The Female Experience: An American Documentary* (Indianapolis: Bobbs-Merrill, 1977).

ONE

Childhood

Children are studied and loved, protected and respected in special ways today. Judging by the sales of Dr. Benjamin Spock's *Baby and Child Care* alone (over 22 million copies since it was first published in 1946), parents are probably better informed than ever before about their children's growth and development. Heightened concern for children's welfare and rights is reflected by recent efforts to deal with the problem of child abuse and by the landmark 1969 Supreme Court decision that defined children as "persons" under the law, entitled to the same constitutional protection and privileges as adults. Legions of specialists in the biological and social sciences systematically scrutinize and publicize children's distinctive physical, emotional, and intellectual requirements and abilities.

Researchers distinguish infancy, a period of total physical and emotional dependency on others, from the years of childhood, and they employ the nearly universal experience of schooling to differentiate preschoolers, those about ages three to six, from schoolchildren, those ages six to twelve. In chronological terms then, the years from around age three to the onset of puberty — anywhere from age ten to thirteen — currently mark the boundaries of childhood. Growth in size and strength of skeletal, muscular, and nervous systems, so rapid during infancy, continues steadily throughout childhood. Boys and girls acquire a wide range of cognitive skills as well, as they move sequentially from simple to more complex ways of perceiving, learning, thinking, and problem-solving.

From a psychological perspective, childhood is described as the time in life when a person creates a sense of self as a separate being, along with many of the components of personality that remain throughout life. An important aspect of this emerging self, and of special interest here, is the development of gender identity. Recent research indicates that gender identity is acquired early, and that by age three a child can classify his or her own sex accurately.

11

In sociological terms, childhood is the period in the life cycle when specific social behavior, including sex-typed roles and attitudes, is first learned. In studying the ways a child's behavior is influenced by the environment, sociologists examine socialization processes and social structures and delineate how adults and peers reinforce or discourage individual behavior.

Although social researchers generally agree that genetic predisposition and socialization processes interact to determine what a person is at every stage in the life cycle, they have long disagreed over exactly how the influences of biology and culture combine at any specific time. While some theorists minimize biological predisposition and focus on the ways environment makes people what they are, others see personality and behavior as primarily biologically programmed.

Whatever the differences among theoreticians, all appreciate childhood as a distinct phase in human development and perceive children as unique beings with special emotional and intellectual needs and capacities. This understanding of childhood, however, has emerged relatively recently in historical terms. Adult perceptions of children and children's actual experiences within the family and in society have undergone dramatic transformations since the seventeenth century. An assessment of these developments in the context of changing social and economic circumstances in American life should form part of any discussion of the experiences of female children, past and present.

A girl growing up in seventeenth-century America lived in a world very different from that of her counterparts today. For one thing, her very existence was precarious. Approximately 10 to 30 percent of those born did not survive beyond the first year of life, and anywhere from 30 to 50 percent of all children died before the age of ten. This high mortality rate for infants and children translated into feelings of insecurity for colonial children. Boys and girls lived with a constant awareness of death; they commonly attended the funerals of friends and siblings, not to mention those of parents and other adults. Certainly the sense of indestructibility that characterizes today's youngsters could not have flourished in such an atmosphere. The Puritans, in particular, cultivated a sensibility toward death among their offspring that heightened their already present anxiety. Parents, teachers, and ministers continually issued warnings that death could strike at any moment and provided detailed descriptions of the horrors of damnation awaiting bad children.

With the ever-present knowledge that their lives might end shortly, colonial children saw themselves as perpetually vulnerable. Consequently, they were not inclined to inflate their own self-importance. The fact that most colonial youngsters grew up in large families, surrounded by brothers and sisters, also inhibited them from thinking of themselves as singular beings. The claims of the family unit always transcended any child's quest for individual recognition.

The child's tendency toward self-abnegation was reinforced by the parental stance that children occupied a subordinate position in the family and therefore were not entitled to undue attention. Colonial parents defined a child's needs, activities, and goals with little reference to the child's own ideas or desires. Children were expected to defer to their parents' judgments in every case. In essence, this meant that children had to conform to the specifications of the adult world, since few concessions were made to the distinctive needs of childhood other than those necessary for size and physical capacity. This is not to say that children were treated exactly as "miniature adults," as some scholars have argued, but rather to suggest that in the colonial era the child's world merged imperceptibly into the world of the adult.

A seventeenth-century child's identity was forged primarily in the family. Although community standards clearly influenced the content of socialization, it was left to the parents to inculcate the proper values in their offspring. The precise manner in which colonial parents raised their children varied according to social class, geographical location, cultural background, and religious affiliation. In most instances a family's religious beliefs dictated its mode of child rearing. A girl growing up in Puritan New England underwent a particularly harsh upbringing.

The early Puritans viewed children as creatures of original sin who came into the world with instincts and impulses that were naturally evil. Without proper discipline and direction children would face damnation in the world to come. Parents defined their first responsibility as that of restraining their child's innate inclination to behave badly. The ideal child was obedient, silent until spoken to, respectful of elders, and disciplined to follow God's commandments. Idleness or wasted hours at play were not tolerated. Children were expected to participate responsibly with adults in work activities as well as religious worship. Above all, children were never to question the authority of their parents or elders.

The children of the Quakers in Pennsylvania also were exposed to an authoritarian system of child rearing. Although the religious ideals with which the Quaker young were indoctrinated differed from the Puritan teachings, both groups were alike in their determination to mold their children into the type of person valued in their faith. Thus the Quakers, as well as the Puritans, imposed rigid definitions of appropriate behavior upon their youngsters and punished transgressions with vigor. Members of the Anglican church, many of whom resided in the southern colonies, had a more relaxed approach to child rearing. Upper-class southern Anglican families were prone to indulge their children; their approach offers a marked contrast to the rigid version of child rearing practiced by their northern Puritan neighbors.

Preparation for adult roles commenced earlier and was conducted in a far more practical fashion in colonial society than it is today. By the time a child had reached the age of six or seven, his or her education as well as work life had begun. Economic activity was centered in the household during the seventeenth and eighteenth centuries, and all who were able-bodied were expected to participate in the ongoing work of the family. Young children were at first given simple tasks to perform and were gradually initiated into the more complex skills of adult workers. Although each child's contribution was valued by the family, there was a division of labor by sex from the very beginning. Boys followed their father's calling, while girls began to master the multifaceted skills of the colonial housewife under the tutelage of their mother and older sisters.

The institution of apprenticeship provided a more formal means of equipping children for their adult roles, while still perpetuating the system of familial education. Until the end of the eighteenth century apprenticeship constituted the most common form of education for white boys and girls. Whether indentured to craftsmen to learn a specific trade or bound out to neighboring farmers to provide supplementary labor, colonial children were furnished with much more than vocational training. Colonial laws charged masters with the responsibility of supplying moral and religious instruction in addition to teaching basic reading and writing skills. The major activity of girls who entered apprenticeships was domestic work, but trades such as dressmaking, embroidery, and millinery work were also open to them.

While almost all colonial children were given instruction in practical skills, only a select few male children received more than a rudimentary academic education. Girls were even less likely than boys to learn to read and write, a fact attested to by the lower rate of female literacy in the colonies.

In contrast to the majority of colonial children, the offspring of the wealthy were exempted from productive labor because their families retained servants and slaves to perform household tasks. Additionally, these privileged children possessed enhanced educational opportunities in the form of individualized instruction by tutors or attendance at private schools. Although only boys were permitted to pursue advanced studies, upper-class girls still enjoyed an advantage over their less privileged peers. At the other end of the social spectrum, impoverished children struggled merely to survive. Burdened with excessive demands for their labor from an early age, poor children, orphans, and enslaved children were denied even an elementary education.

Beginning in the eighteenth century, a new conception of childhood captured the imagination of adult Americans. Advice books for parents, most of them written by ministers, urged more gentle treatment of children and defended play as normal and healthy. Writers described the plasticity of the child's nature, rather than its inherent evilness, and called for new methods of education geared to the needs of the individual child.

Although foreshadowed in the eighteenth century, the major shift in American attitudes toward childhood did not occur until the early nineteenth century. Even then, children from families living at the margins of existence were relatively untouched by this revolution in ideas, as were those children whose parents persisted in employing the traditional repressive child-rearing methods. Nonetheless, by the mid-nineteenth century, the dominant conception of childhood in America differed significantly from colonial views on this life stage. Childhood came to be recognized as a distinct period of life, the time when a person has certain unique needs and propensities. Parents abandoned the notion that children existed to further their interests and instead developed a greater sensitivity to each child's personality. The decline in the birth rate since at least 1800 created favorable conditions for appreciating a child's individuality. The fewer the children in a family, the more attention could be lavished upon each child.

The heightened concern for children in the nineteenth century was largely a response to the massive economic and social changes America was undergoing. The expansion of industry and the growth of cities presaged a new kind of social order in which worldly achievement threatened to replace spiritual progress as the ultimate goal of human life. In this altered environment, the best safeguard against the lures of materialism and the temptations of evil was a sound moral character. Childhood was viewed as the pivotal period of life, the time when a person's character was indelibly formed. Accordingly, the child's world was deliberately set off from the adult world so that her innocence could be preserved while she was learning the fundamental moral lessons that were intended to last her for a lifetime.

The crucial figures in the child's insulated world were the mother and the teacher. Nineteenth-century mothers were led to believe that their children's destiny, and by extension, the ultimate fate of society, lay in their hands. Alerted to the critical importance of proper nurturance, mothers sought guidance on how best to fulfill their exalted mission from the host of contemporary publications on the dos and don'ts of child rearing. Writers pointed out that character development proceeded toward different ends for boys and girls. Mothers were charged with instilling qualities in young males that would guarantee success in the world outside the home. Those traits that would ensure success in the domestic sphere — submissiveness, loyalty, gentleness, and social grace — were to be implanted in young females.

Mothers were aided in their endeavors to see that their youngsters acquired the proper traits by a new institution, the public school. The organizers of public schools in the decades after 1830 stressed the importance of childhood in character formation and envisioned schools that supplemented the efforts of mothers by providing moral instruction in controlled and protective environments. Middle-class girls and boys became accustomed to going to school on a regular basis and receiving systematic instruction in academic subjects as well as a heavy dose of moral indoctrination.

Their status as children determined the activities in which nineteenth-century youngsters engaged, the people with whom they associated, the books they read, the games they played, and the places they visited. Although they were encouraged to be sober and industrious, they were not expected to undertake productive labor during their early years. In fact, their entry into the adult world of work was purposely delayed to ensure that they were thoroughly grounded in basic intellectual and moral principles.

Not all nineteenth-century youngsters were shielded from adult responsibilities and permitted the luxury of a childhood devoted to morally uplifting education and recreation. While daughters and sons of middle- and upper-class families enjoyed an increasingly privileged style of life, the children of the poor continued to face the uncertainties of a marginal existence. Girls and boys from impoverished families, many of them immigrants and blacks, were forced to toil for long hours at demanding jobs to supplement their families' meager incomes and so remained outside the scope of the educational system. Some children without homes had to roam the streets and scavenge for odd jobs, or even worse, steal in order to eat.

The specter of child labor as well as evidence of petty crimes committed by vagrant children sparked a series of reforms that restructured the world of children in ways that are familiar today. Between 1880 and 1920 virtually every state passed compulsory school attendance laws for all children between the ages of six and sixteen, as well as child labor laws specifying minimum ages for employment. Public welfare services for children were reorganized, and juvenile courts were created to separate young offenders from adult criminals. Reformers were also successful in establishing playgrounds in America's cities as recreational facilities for poor urban youngsters. As a result of these legislative initiatives, the life patterns of poor or disadvantaged children began to converge with those of their middle-class counterparts. These youngsters were brought under the control of school officials and exposed to the moralistic messages formerly transmitted only to the children of the middle class.

During the first half of the twentieth century, further modifications in child-rearing advice and elementary education altered the context of childhood in America. The emergence of a scientific approach to the study of childhood in the late nineteenth century augured a change in parental attitudes. Given the intense interest in child nurture evident in the early nineteenth century, it was predictable that middle-class parents would seek out the latest scientific wisdom regarding children. In giving credence to the opinions of psychologists and other researchers, parents were implicitly rejecting the moralistic schemes of child rearing promulgated by earlier generations.

American parents were prepared to place their confidence in men such as G. Stanley Hall, John B. Watson, and later Arnold Gesell and Benjamin Spock, who, on the basis of clinical and experimental research, formulated various theories of child development. Each expert enjoined parents to follow a certain set of scientific principles in raising their offspring instead of trusting to maternal instinct or religious precepts. A child was to be evaluated according to absolute scales developed under controlled conditions and then subjected to a prescribed regimen. It should be noted that the scientists were careful to specify what was appropriate for girls and for boys. Thus twentieth-century parents grew accustomed to consulting specialists in child care, whether directly, in the form of physicians or child psychologists, or indirectly, in the form of advice literature.

Professionals also played a major part in reshaping the child's early educational experience. Mandatory school attendance, along with increases in the length of the school day and the school year, gave educators a wide canvas on which to test their theories. Around the turn of the century classrooms were organized in a highly structured fashion and the curriculum was correspondingly inflexible. A child exposed to this method of teaching was expected to learn facts and to imbibe universal moral principles. Reformer John Dewey challenged this system with his philosophy of progressive education. In essence, Dewey endorsed a less authoritarian, child-centered education in which materials and methods were specifically geared toward the special needs of young girls and boys. The classroom was more congenial to the child, with books, toys, and activities all designed to harmonize with the child's own sense of self. By mid-century, Dewey had left his mark on the majority of American schoolrooms.

In the second half of the twentieth century another powerful force shaping children's lives appeared: television. Today, watching television is a nearly universal experience for American children, whatever their backgrounds. Preschoolers spend an estimated thirty-three hours a week, about one-third of their waking hours, viewing programs and commercials. An average sixth grader watches about thirty-one hours weekly. Television, reinforced by movies and other media, furnishes contemporary youngsters with new ways of seeing the world and thus, in large measure, molds their view of reality. Since in many homes television functions as a baby-sitter in lieu of direct parental supervision, its potential impact on children's attitudes is magnified.

By the late twentieth century, then, children have become increasingly subject to agencies other than the family — scientific experts, the school, and television. Concomitantly, children are spending less time with their families. Since great numbers of children now come from homes in which both parents are employed, or from single-parent families in which the only parent works, they are on their own from an early age, moving from day-care centers to the public schools. Moreover, when conditions arise in their homes that endanger children's well-being, they are protected from their families. In these instances, the state intervenes to preserve children's rights.

Still, the kind of family in which a child grows up exerts a powerful influence over her development. In the middle-class family, the child occupies a position of prominence and also carries the burden of high parental expectations. Parents often make sacrifices to ensure more plentiful opportunities for their offspring in the form of enriched educational experiences, travel, and material possessions. Working-class youngsters have narrower horizons than their more privileged peers. Their parents, many of whom are poor or minority people, adhere to the traditional notion that the interests of the family as a whole take precedence over the special needs of any child. Consequently, children from a working-class background must seize the initiative if they are to strike out in new directions, whereas their affluent counterparts are inundated with choices.

Changes in the context of childhood in the twentieth century have had an impact on both girls and boys. Yet, it is clear that a child's sex still plays a major part in determining the nature of childhood experience. Throughout American history, female children have been expected to conform to more restrictive definitions of suitable behavior than those imposed on males. The contemporary movement for nonsexist child rearing is a reaction to centuries of sex-specific socialization and education. Whether or not such efforts can counteract the sexual stereotypes that pervade American culture, their mere existence suggests that the experience of this generation of female children is qualitatively different than that of its predecessors.

The changing environments in which children have developed, adult concepts of childhood, and the different expectations for boys and girls are all germane topics in a discussion of what it has been like to be a female child in American society. Exploring this stage of the life cycle from the perspective of the child herself is perhaps a more difficult task, but it is one that should yield even deeper insights. How have girls perceived themselves as different from boys? What have been their own expectations for themselves as children? What have they envisioned for themselves as adults? Which sex-specific values and modes of behavior have they accepted and which did they reject in their childhood socialization?

G irls in colonial America began preparing for their prescribed roles as wives and mothers during childhood, but the social context of an individual's upbringing largely determined how her socialization proceeded. Among the privileged classes in the late eighteenth century, an ideal of "genteel education" that emphasized the development of social graces and ornamental domestic arts was promoted in the home, in classes, and through social activities. The financial resources of their families afforded upper-class girls the leisure time as well as the means to keep up with the latest fashions, attend music and dancing lessons, and enjoy teas and parties during their late childhood years.

In the selection here, twelve-year-old Anna Green Winslow, daughter of a well-established and wealthy New England family, describes her day-to-day activities and concerns growing up in Boston in 1771 and 1772. Anna's parents were fifth-generation descendants of Massachusetts colonists. Joshua Winslow, her father, was a professional officer in the British army who remained a loyalist during the Revolutionary War. In 1770, sensing that conflict would soon erupt between the colonies and England, Winslow took a post in Nova Scotia and moved there with his wife and son.

Anna, age ten, remained behind in Boston with her father's sister, Sarah Deming, to finish her schooling. Aunt Deming had no children of her own, but she regularly took in young female boarders while they attended school in Boston. At her father's urging Anna kept a diary, which was actually a series of letters about events in her life written to her parents.

With her aunt and in school, Anna learned to sew, knit, and embroider. She sewed some of her own clothing, made gifts for her friends, and regularly spent her allowance from her parents on the newest fashions. Anna's household responsibilities were light — tedious housekeeping chores were handled by Lucinda, a black slave purchased at the age of seven by Mrs. Deming.

In addition to her training in the finer domestic crafts, Anna worked conscientiously at improving her penmanship, a highly respected art in the eighteenth century. For girls, however, fine penmanship served as a mark of accomplishment, and was not related to preparation for any vocation. Anna also took dancing lessons and put her skills into practice at the rounds of parties she described as "genteel well regulated assembl[ies]." Typical was her twelfth birthday party to which she invited eight girl friends to enjoy country dancing. Such occasions prepared young girls for the mixed social events they would attend during their teen years and provided opportunities for developing poise and practicing conversational skills.

Anna not only socialized with her age peers, she also felt comfortable in social situations with adults. Her diary describes numerous visits, teas, and dinners with relatives and friends of all ages. Anna's mother was one of twelve children, and references to her many aunts, uncles, and cousins appear throughout Anna's writings.

Following Puritan tradition, Anna tried earnestly to be a pious child, dutifully reading the Bible every morning, attending catechism classes, and carefully recording her thoughts about the sermons she listened to in church — even if at times she missed some of the finer points. She strove also to be industrious and diligent in her studies, and often in her letters home, Anna expressed a desire to please her parents and her aunt and make them proud of her.

Anna felt comfortable, happy, and loved in her Aunt Deming's home. Her aunt guided her with patience and gentleness; she even made allowances whenever one of Anna's "egregious fit[s] of laughterre" — a giggling fit — overcame her. Within this relaxed atmosphere, nevertheless, a keen awareness of death runs throughout the diary. Anna mentioned the deaths of friends and relatives and her attendance at funerals. Her feelings about the precarious nature of life are expressed in such comments as "if I live a few years longer" and "if he lives so long."

Although no official record of Anna's death exists, family records state that she died of tuberculosis in 1779 in Marshfield, Massachusetts. Her short life ended at the age of twenty.

—— 1 ——

Anna Green Winslow

NOVEMBER THE 29TH, 1771. — My aunt Deming gives her love to you and says it is this morning 12 years since she had the pleasure of congratulating papa and you on the birth of your scribling daughter. She hopes if I live

SOURCE: From *Diary of Anna Green Winslow: A Boston School Girl of 1771* (Boston: Houghton Mifflin, 1894).

12 years longer that I shall write and do everything better than can be expected in the *past* 12. I should be obliged to you, you will dismiss me for company.

30TH NOV. — My company yesterday were

> Miss Polly Deming,
> Miss Polly Glover,
> Miss Peggy Draper,
> Miss Bessy Winslow,
> Miss Nancy Glover,
> Miss Sally Winslow,
> Miss Polly Atwood,
> Miss Hannah Soley.

Miss Attwood as well as Miss Winslow are of this family. And Miss N. Glover did me honor by her presence, for she is older than cousin Sally and of her acquaintance. We made four couple at country dansing; danceing I mean. In the evening young Mr. Waters hearing of my assembly, put his flute in his pocket and played several minuets and other tunes, to which we danced mighty cleverly. But Lucinda was our principal piper. Miss Church and Miss Chaloner would have been here if sickness, — and the Miss Sheafs, if the death of their father had not prevented. The black Hatt I gratefully receive as your present, but if Captain Jarvise had arrived here with it about the time he sail'd from this place for Cumberland it would have been of more service to me, for I have been oblig'd to borrow. I wore Miss Griswold's Bonnet on my journey to Portsmouth, & my cousin Sallys Hatt ever since I came home, & now I am to leave off my black ribbins tomorrow, & am to put on my red cloak & black hatt — I hope aunt wont let me wear the black hatt with the red Dominie — for the people will ask me what I have got to sell as I go along street if I do, or, how the folk at New guinie do? Dear mamma, you dont know the fation here — I beg to look like other folk. You dont know what a stir would be made in sudbury street, were I to make my appearance there in my red Dominie & black Hatt. But the old cloak & bonnett together will make me a decent bonnett for common ocation (I like that) aunt says, its a pitty some of the ribbins you sent wont do for the Bonnet. — I must now close up this Journal. With Duty, Love, & Compliments as due, perticularly to my Dear little brother (I long to see him) & Mrs. Law, I will write to her soon.

> I am Hond Papa & mama,
> Yr ever Dutiful Daughter
> Anna Green Winslow.

N. B. My aunt Deming dont approve of my English & has not the fear that you will think her concerned in the Diction.

DEC. 6TH. — Yesterday I was prevented dining at unkle Joshua's by a snow storm which lasted till 12 o'clock today, I spent some part of yesterday afternoon and evening at Mr. Glovers. When I came home, the snow being so deep I was bro't home in arms. My aunt got Mr. Soley's Charlstown to fetch me. The snow is up to the peoples wast in some places in the street.

DEC 14TH. — The weather and walking have been very winter like since the above hotch-potch, pothooks & trammels [referring to her handwriting]. I went to Mrs. Whitwell's last wednessday — you taught me to spell the 4 day of the week, but my aunt says that it should be spelt wednesday. My aunt also says, that till I come out of an egregious fit of laughterre that is apt to sieze me & the violence of which 1 am at this present under, neither English sense, nor anything rational may be expected of me. I ment to say, that, I went to Mrs. Whitwell's to see Madam Storers funeral, the walking was very bad except on the sides of the street which was the reason I did not make a part of the procession. I should have dined with Mrs. Whitwell on thursday if a grand storm had not prevented, As she invited me. I saw Miss Caty Vans at lecture last evening. I had a visit this morning from Mrs Dixon of Horton & Miss Polly Huston. Mrs Dixon is dissipointed at not finding her sister here.

DEC 24TH. — Elder Whitwell told my aunt, that this winter began as did the Winter of 1740. How that was I dont remember but this I know, that to-day is by far the coldest we have had since I have been in New England. (N. B. All run that are abroad.) Last sabbath being rainy I went to & from meeting in Mr. Soley's chaise. I dined at unkle Winslow's, the walking being so bad I rode there & back to meeting. Every drop that fell froze, so that from yesterday morning to this time the appearance has been similar to the discription I sent you last winter. The walking is so slippery & the air so cold, that aunt chuses to have me for her scoller [scholar] these two days. And as tomorrow will be a holiday, so the pope and his associates have ordained, my aunt thinks not to trouble Mrs Smith with me this week. I began a shift at home yesterday for myself, it is pretty forward. Last saturday was seven-night my aunt Suky was delivered of a pretty little son, who was baptiz'd by Dr. Cooper the next day by the name of Charles. I knew nothing of it till noonday, when I went there a visiting. Last Thursday I din'd & spent the afternoon at unkle Joshua's I should have gone to lecture with my aunt & heard our Mr Hunt preach, but she would not wait till I came from writing school. Miss Atwood, the last of our boarders, went off the same day. Miss Griswold & Miss Meriam, having departed some time agone, I forget whether I mention'd the recept of Nancy's present. I am oblig'd to her for it. The Dolphin is still whole. And like to remain so.

DEC 27. — This day, the extremity of the cold is somewhat abated. I keept Christmas at home this year, & did a very good day's work, aunt says so. How notable I have been this week I shall tell you by & by. I spent the most part of Tuesday evening with my favorite, Miss Soley, & as she is confined by a cold & the weather still so severe that I cannot git farther, I am to visit her again before I sleep, & consult with her (or rather she with me) upon a perticular matter, which you shall know in its place. How *strangely industrious* I have been this week, I will inform you with my own hand — at present, I am so dilligent, that I am oblig'd to use the hand & pen of my old friend, who being *near by* is better than a brother *far off*. I dont forgit dear little John Henry so pray mamma, dont mistake me.

□

1 JAN 1772 — I wish my Papa, Mama, brother John Henry, & cousin Avery & all the rest of my acquaintance at Cumberland, Fortlaurence, Barronsfield, Greenland, Amherst &c. a Happy New Year, I have bestow'd no new year's gift, as yet. But have received one very handsome one, viz. the History of Joseph Andrews abreviated. In nice Guilt and flowers covers. This afternoon being a holiday I am going to pay my compliments in Sudbury Street.

JAN 4TH 1772. — I was dress'd in my yellow coat, my black bib & apron, my pompedore [silk or cotton with floral designs] shoes, the cap my aunt Storer sometime since presented me with (blue ribbins on it) & a very handsome loket in the shape of a hart she gave me — the past pin my Hond Papa presented me with in my cap, My new cloak & bonnet on, my pompedore gloves, &c, &c. And I would tell you, that *for the first time, they all lik'd my dress very much*. My cloak & bonnett are really very handsome, & so they had need be. For they cost an amasing sight of money, not quite £45 tho' Aunt Suky said, that she suppos'd Aunt Deming would be frighted out of her Wits at the money it cost. I have got *one* covering, by the cost, that is genteel, & I like it much myself. On thursday I attended my aunt to Lecture & heard Dr Chauncey preach a third sermon from Acts ii. 42. They continued stedfastly — in breaking of bread. I din'd & spent the afternoon at Mr. Whitwell's. Miss Caty Vans was one of our company.

□

JAN 11. — I have attended my schools every day this week except wednesday afternoon. When I made a setting up visit to aunt Suky, & was dress'd just as I was to go to the ball. It cost me a pistoreen [a Spanish coin worth about 20 cents] to nurse Eaton for tow cakes, which I took care to eat before I paid for them. I heard Mr. Thacher preach our Lecture last evening Heb. 11. 3. I remember a great deal of the sermon, but a'nt time to put it down. It is one year last Sept since he was ordain'd & he will be 20 years of age next May if he lives so long. I forgot that the weather want fit for me to go to school last thursday. I work'd at home.

JAN 17. — I told you the 27th Ult [of last month] that I was going to a constitution with miss Soley. I have now the pleasure to give you the result, viz. a very genteel well regulated assembly which we had at Mr Soley's last evening, miss Soley being mistress of the ceremony. Mrs Soley desired me to assist Miss Hannah in making out a list of guests which I did some time since, I wrote all the invitation cards. There was a large company assembled in a handsome, large, upper room in the new end of the house. We had two fiddles, & I had the honor to open the diversion of the evening in a minuet with miss Soley. — Here follows a list of the company as we form'd for country dancing.

Miss Soley	&	Miss Anna Greene Winslow
Miss Calif		Miss Scott
Miss Williams		Miss McCarthy
Miss Codman		Miss Winslow
Miss Ives		Miss Coffin
Miss Scolley		Miss Bella Coffin
Miss Waldow		Miss Quinsy
Miss Glover		Miss Draper
Miss Hubbard		

Miss Cregur (usually pronounced Kicker) & two Miss Sheafs were invited but were sick or sorry & beg'd to be excus'd. There was a little Miss Russell & the little ones of the family present who could not dance. As spectators, there were Mr & Mrs Deming, Mr & Mrs Sweetser Mr & Mrs Soley, Mr & Miss Cary, Mrs. Draper, Miss Oriac, Miss Hannah — our treat was nuts, rasins, Cakes, Wine, punch, hot & cold, all in great plenty. We had a very agreeable evening from 5 to 10 o'clock. For variety we woo'd a widow, hunted the whistle, threaded the needle, & while the company was collecting, we diverted ourselves with playing of pawns, no rudeness Mamma I assure you. Aunt Deming desires you would *perticulary observe,* that the elderly part of the company were *spectators* only, they mix'd not in either of the above describ'd scenes.

I was dress'd in my yellow coat, black bib & apron, black feathers on my head, my past comb, & all my past garnet marquesett & jet pins, together with my silver plume — my loket, rings, black collar round my neck, black mitts & 2 or 3 yards of blue ribbin, (black & blue is high tast) striped tucker and ruffels (not my best) & my silk shoes compleated my dress.

JAN 18. — Yesterday I had an invitation to celebrate Miss Caty's birth-day with her. She gave it me the night before. Miss is 10 years old. The best dancer in Mr Turners school, she has been his scoller these 3 years. My aunt thought it proper (as our family had a invitation) that I should attend a neighbor's funeral yesterday P. M. I went directly from it to Miss Caty's Rout & arriv'd ex . . .

JAN 31. — I spent yesterday with Aunt Storer, except a little while I was at Aunt Sukey's with Mrs Barrett dress'd in a white brocade, & cousin Betsey dress'd in a red lutestring, both adorn'd with past, perls marquesett &c. They were after tea escorted by Mr Newton & Mr Barrett to ye assembly at Concert Hall. This is a snowy day, & I am prevented going to school.

FEB. 9. — My honored Mamma will be so good as to excuse my useing the pen of my old friend just here, because I am disabled by a whitloe on my fourth finger & something like one on my middle finger, from using my own pen; but altho' my right hand is in bondage, my left is free; & my aunt says, it will be a nice oppertunity if I do but improve it, to perfect myself in learning to spin flax. I am pleased with the proposal & am at this present, exerting myself for this purpose. I hope, when two, or at most three months are past, to give you occular demonstration of my proficiency in *this art,* as well as several others. My fingers are not the only part of me that has suffer'd with sores within this fortnight, for I have had an ugly great boil upon my right hip & about a dozen small ones — I am at present swath'd hip & thigh, as Samson smote the Philistines, but my soreness is near over. My aunt thought it highly proper to give me some cooling physick, so last tuesday I took ½ oz Globe Salt (a disagreeable potion) & kept chamber. Since which, there has been no new erruption, & a great alteration for the better in those I had before.

I have read my bible to my aunt this morning (as is the daily custom) & sometimes I read other books to her. So you may perceive, I *have the use of my tongue* & I tell her it is a good thing to have the use of my tongue. Unkle Ned called here just now — all well — by the way he is come to live in Boston again, & till he can be better accomodated, is at housekeeping where Madam Storer lately lived, he is looking for a less house. I tell my Aunt I feel a disposician to be a good girl, & she pleases herself that she shall have much comfort of me to-day, which as cousin Sally is ironing we expect to have to ourselves.

FEB. 10. — This day I paid my respects to Master Holbrook, after a week's absence, my finger is still in limbo as you may see by the writeing. I have not paid my compliments to Madam Smith, for, altho' I can drive the goos quill a bit, I cannot so well manage the needle. So I will lay my hand to the distaff, as the virtuous woman did of old — Yesterday was very bad weather, neither aunt, nor niece at publick worship.

FEB. 12. — Yesterday afternoon I spent at unkle Joshuas. Aunt Green gave me a plaister for my fingure that has near cur'd it, but I have a new boil, which is under poultice, & tomorrow I am to undergo another seasoning with globe Salt....

My honor'd Grandma departed this vale of tears 1/4 before 4 o'clock wednesday morning August 21, 1771. Aged 74 years, 2 months & ten days.

Anna Green Winslow

FEB. 13. — Everybody says that this is a bitter cold day, but I know nothing about it but hearsay for I am in aunt's chamber (which is very warm always) with a nice fire, a stove, sitting in Aunt's easy chair, with a tall three leav'd screen at my back, & I am very comfortable. I took my second (& I hope last) potion of Globe salts this morning. I went to see Aunt Storer yesterday afternoon, & by the way Unkle Storer is so ill that he keeps chamber. As I went down I call'd at Mrs Whitwell's & must tell you Mr & Mrs Whitwell are both ill. Mrs. Whitwell with the rheumatism. I saw Madam Harris, Mrs Mason and Miss Polly Vans there, they all give their love to you — Last evening I went to catechizing with Aunt. Our ministers have agreed during the long evenings to discourse upon the questions or some of 'em in the assembly's shorter catechism, taking 'em in their order at the house of Mrs Rogers in School Street, every wednesday evening. Mr. Hunt began with the first question and shew'd what it is to glorify God. Mr Bacon then took the second, what rule &c. which he has spent three evenings upon, & now finished. Mr Hunt having taken his turn to show what the Scriptures principly teach, & what is God. I remember he said that there was nothing properly done without a rule, & he said that the rule God had given us to glorify him by was the bible. How miraculously (said he) has God preserv'd this blessed book. It was once in the reign of a heathen emperor condemn'd to be burnt, at which time it was death to have a bible & conceal it, but God's providence was wonderful in preserving it when so much human policy had been exerted to bury it in Oblivion — but for all that, here we have it as pure & uncorrupted as ever — many books of human composure have had much pains taken to preserve 'em, notwithstanding they are buried in Oblivion. He considered who was the author of the bible, he prov'd that God was the author, for no *good* man could be the author, because such a one would not be guilty of imposition, & an evil man could not unless we suppose a house divided against itself. he said a great deal more to prove the bible is certainly the word of God from the matter it contains &c, but the best evidence of the truth of divine revelation, every true believer has in his own heart. This he said, the natural man had no idea of. I did not understand all he said about the external and internal evidence, but this I can say, that I understand him better than any body else that I hear preach. Aunt has been down stairs all the time I have been recolecting & writeing this. Therefore, all this of own head, of consequence.

VALENTINE DAY. — My cousin Sally reeled off a 10 knot skane of yarn today. My valentine was an old country plow-joger. The yarn was of my spinning. Aunt says it will do for filling. Aunt also says niece is a whimsical child.

FEB. 17. — Since wednesday evening, I have not been abroad since yesterday afternoon. I went to meeting & back in Mr. Soley's chaise. Mr. Hunt preached. He said that human nature is as opposite to God as darkness to light. That our sin is only bounded by the narrowness of our capacity. His text was Isa. xli. 14. 18. The mountains &c. He said were unbelief, pride, covetousness, enmity, &c. &c. &c. This morning I took a walk for Aunt as far as Mr. Soley's. I called at Mrs Whitwell's & found the good man & lady both better than when I saw them last. On my return I found Mr. Hunt on a visit to aunt....

FEB. 18. — Another ten knot skane of my yarn was reel'd off today. Aunt says it is very good. My boils & whitloes are growing well apace, so that I can knit a little in the evening....

MONDAY FEB. 18. — Bitter cold. I am just come from writing school. Last Wednesday P. M. while I was at school Aunt Storer called in to see Aunt Deming in her way to Mr Inches's. She walk'd all that long way. Thursday last I din'd & spent the afternoon with Aunt Sukey. I attended both my schools in the morning of that day. I cal'd at unkle Joshua's as I went along, as I generally do, when I go in town, it being all in my way. Saterday I din'd at Unkle Storer's, drank tea at Cousin Barrel's, was entertain'd in the afternoon with scating. Unkle Henry was there. Yesterday by the help of neighbor Soley's Chaise, I was at meeting all day, tho' it snow'd in the afternoon. I might have say'd I was at Unkle Winslow's last Thursday Eve[ning] & when I inform you that my needle work at school, & knitting at home, went on *as usual*, I think I have laid before you a pretty full account of the last week. You see how I improve in my writing, but I drive on as fast as I can.

FEB. 21 THURSDAY. — This day Jack Frost bites very hard, so hard aunt won't let me go to any school. I have this morning made part of a coppy with the very pen I have now in my hand, writting this with. Yesterday was so cold there was a very thick vapor upon the water, but I attended my schools all day. My unkle says yesterday was 10 degrees colder than any day we have had before this winter. And my aunt says she believes this day is 10 degrees colder than it was yesterday; & moreover, that she would not put a dog out of doors. The sun gives forth his rays through a vapor like that which was upon the water yesterday. But Aunt bids me give her love to pappa & all the family & tell them that she should be glad of their company in her warm parlour, indeed there is not one room in this house but is very warm when there is a good fire in them. As there is in this at present. Yesterday I got leave (by my aunt's desire) to go from school at 4 o'clock to see my unkle Ned who has had the misfortune to break his leg. I call'd in to warm myself at unkle Joshua's. Aunt Hannah told me I had better not go any further for she could tell me all about him, so I say'd as it is so cold I believe aunt won't be angry so I will stay, I therefore took off my things, aunt gave me leave to call at Unkle Joshua's & was very glad I went no further. Aunt Hannah told me he was as well as could be expected for one that has a broken bone. He was coming from Watertown in a chaise the horse fell down on the Hill, this side Mr Brindley's. he was afraid if he fell out, the wheel would run over him, he therefore gave a start & fell out & broke his leg, the horse strugled to get up, but could not. unkle Ned was affraid if he did get up the chaise wheels would run over him, so he went on his two hands and his other foot drawing his lame leg after him & got behind the chaise, (so he was safe) & there lay in the snow for some time, nobody being near. at last 2 genteelmen came, they tho't the horse was dead when they first saw him at a distance, but hearing somebody hollow, went up to it. By this time there was a countraman come along, the person that hollow'd was unkle Ned. They got a slay and put him in it with some hay and a blanket, wrapt him up well as they could & brought him to Deacon Smith's in town. Now Papa & Mamma, this hill is in Brookline. And now again, I have been better inform'd for the hill is in Roxbury & poor Unkle Ned was alone in the chaise. Both bones of his leg are broke, but they did not come thro' the skin, which is a happy circumstance. It is his right leg that is broke. My Grandmamma sent Miss Deming, Miss Winslow & I one eighth of a Dollar a piece for a New Years gift. My Aunt Deming & Miss Deming had letters from Grandmamma. She was pretty well, she wrote aunt that Mrs Marting was brought to bed with a son Joshua about a month since, & is with her son very well. Grandmamma was very well last week. I have made the purchase I told you of a few pages agone, that is, last Thursday I purchas'd with my aunt Deming's leave, a very beautiful white feather hat, that is, the out side, which is a bit of white hollond with the feathers sew'd on in a most curious manner white & unsullyed as the falling snow, this hat I have long been saving my money to procure for which I have let your kind allowance, Papa, lay in my aunt's hands till this hat which I spoke for was brought home. As I am (as we say) a daughter of liberty I chuse to wear as much of our own manufactory as pocible. But my aunt says, I have wrote this account very badly. I will go on to save my money for a chip & a lineing &c.

Papa I rec'd your letter dated Jan. 11, for which I thank you, Sir, & thank you greatly for the money I received therewith. I am very glad to hear that Brother John papa & mamma & cousin are well. I'll answer your letter papa and yours mamma and cousin Harry's too. I am very glad mamma your eyes are better. I hope by the time I have the pleasure of hearing from Cumberland again your eyes will be so well that you will favor me with one from you.

FEB. 22. — ...Last saturday morning we had a snow storm come on, which continued till four o'clock P.M. when it turned to rain, since which we have had a warm air, with many showers of rain, one this morning a little before day attended with thunder. The streets have been very wet, the water running like rivers all this week, so that I could not possibly go to school, neither have I yet got the bandage off my fingure. Since I have been writing now, the wind suddenly sprung up at N W and blew with violence so that we may get to meeting to-morrow, perhaps on dry ground. Unkle Ned was here just now & has fairly or unfairly carried off aunt's cut paper pictures, tho' she told him she had given them to papa some years ago. It has been a very sickly time here, not one person that I know of but has been under heavy colds — (all laid up at unkle Storer's) in general got abroad again. Aunt Suky had not been down stairs since her lying in, when I last saw her, but I hear she is got down. She has had a broken breast. I have spun 30 knots of linning yarn, and (partly) new footed a pair of stockings for Lucinda, read a part of the pilgrim's progress, coppied part of my text journal (that if I live a few years longer, I may be able to understand it, for aunt sais, that to her, the contents as I first mark'd them, were an impenetrable secret) play'd some, tuck'd a great deal (Aunt Deming says it is very true) laugh'd enough, & I tell aunt it is all human *nature*, if not human reason. And now, I wish my honored mamma a very good night.

SATURDAY NOON FEB. 23. — Dear Pappa, do's the winter continue as pleasant at Cumberland as when you wrote to me last? We had but very little winter here, till February came in, but we have little else since. The cold still continues tho' not so extreme as it was last Thursday. I have attended my schools all this week except one day, and am going as soon as I have din'd to see how Unkle Ned does. I was thinking, Sir, to lay up a piece of money you sent me, but as you sent it to me to lay out I have a mind to buy a chip & linning for my feather hatt. But my aunt says she will think of it. My aunt says if I behave myself very well indeed, not else, she will give me a garland of flowers to orniment it, tho' she has layd aside the biziness of flower making.

FEB. 25. — This is a very stormy day of snow, hail & rain, so that I cannot get to Master Holbrook's, therefore I will here copy something I lately transcribed on a loose paper from Dr. Owen's sermon on Hab. iii, 1, 2, 3, 4, 5, 6, 7, 8, 9. "I have heard that a full wind behind the ship drives her not so fast forward, as a side wind, that seems almost as much against her as with her; & the reason they say is, because a full wind fills but some of her sails."

WEDNESDAY. — Very cold, but this morning I was at sewing and writing school, this afternoon all sewing, for Master Holbrook does not in the winter keep school of afternoons. Unkle Henrys feet are so much better that he wears shoos now.

MONDAY NOON FEB. 25. — I have been to writing school this morning and Sewing. . . .

MARCH 9. — After being confined a week, I rode yesterday afternoon to & from meeting in Mr Soley's chaise. I got no cold and am pretty well today. This has been a very snowy day today. Any body that sees this may see that I have wrote nonsense but Aunt says, I have been a very good girl to day about my work however — I think this day's work may be called a piece meal for in the first place I sew'd on the bosom of unkle's shirt, mended two pair of gloves, mended for the wash two handkerchiefs, (one cambrick) sewed on half a border of a lawn apron of aunts, read part of the xxist chapter of Exodous, & a story in the Mother's gift.

Now, Hon'd Mamma, I must tell you of something that happened to me to-day, that has not happen'd before this great while, viz My Unkle & Aunt both told me, I was a very good girl. Mr Gannett gave us the favour of his company a little while this morning (our head). I have been writing all the above gibberish while aunt has been looking after her family — now she is out of the room — now she is in — & takes up my pen in *my* absence to observe, I am a little simpleton for informing my mamma, that it is *a great while* since I was prais'd because she will conclude that it is *a great while* since I deserv'd to be prais'd. I will henceforth try to observe their praise & yours too. I mean deserve. It's now tea time — as soon as that is over, I shall spend the rest of the evening in reading to my aunt. It is near candle lighting.

MARCH 10, 5 O'CLOCK P. M. — I have finish'd my stent of sewing work for this day & wrote a billet to Miss Caty Vans, a copy of which I shall write on the next page. To-morrow if the weather is fit I am to visit. I have again been told I was a good girl. My Billet to Miss Vans was in the following words. Miss Green gives her compliments to Miss Vans, and informs her that her aunt Deming quite misunderstood the matter about the queen's night-Cap. Mrs. Deming thou't that it was a black skull cap linn'd with red that Miss Vans ment which she thou't would not be becoming to Miss Green's light complexion. Miss Green now takes the liberty to send the materials for the Cap Miss Vans was so kind as to say she would make for her, which, when done, she engages to take special care of for Miss Vans' sake. Mrs. Deming joins her compliments with Miss Green's — they both wish for the pleasure of a visit from Miss Vans. Miss Soley is just come in to visit me & 'tis near dark.

MARCH 11. — Boast not thyself of tomorrow; for thou knowest not what a day may bring forth. Thus king Solomon, inspired by the Holy Ghost, cautions, Pro. xxvii. 1. My aunt says, this is a most necessary lesson to be learn'd & laid up in the heart. I am quite of her mind. I have met with a disappointment to day, & aunt says, I may look for them every day — we live in a changing world — in scripture call'd a vale of tears. Uncle said yesterday that there had not been so much snow on the ground this winter as there was then — it has been vastly added to since then, & is now 7 feet deep in some places round this house; it is above the fence in the coart & thick snow began to fall and condtinu'd till about 5 o'clock P. M. (it is about 1/4 past 8 o'clock) since which there has been a steady rain — so no visiting as I hoped this day, & this is the disappointment I mentioned on t'other page....

MARCH 14. — Mr. Stephen March, at whose house I was treated so kindly last fall, departed this life last week, after languishing several months under a complication of disorders — we have not had perticulars, therefore cannot inform you, whether he engag'd the King of terrors with christian fortitude, or otherwise.

> Stoop down my Thoughts, that use to rise,
> Converse a while with Death;
> Think how a gasping Mortal lies,
> And pants away his Breath.

Last Thursday I din'd with unkle Storer, & family at aunt Sukey's — all well except Charles Storer who was not so ill but what, *that* I mean, he din'd with us. Aunt Suky's Charles is a pretty little boy & grows nicely. We were diverted in the afternoon with an account of a queer Feast that had been made that day in a certain Court of this town for the Entertainment of a number of Tories — perhaps seventeen. One contain'd three calves heads (skin off) with their appurtinencies anciently call'd pluck [heart, liver, lungs, and windpipe] — Their other dish (for they had but two) contain'd a number of roast fowls — half a dozen, we suppose, & all roosters at this season no doubt. Yesterday, soon after I came from writing school we had another snow storm begun, which continued till after I went to bed. This morning the sun shines clear (so it did yesterday morning till 10 o'clock.) It is now bitter cold, & such a quantity of snow upon the ground, as the Old people don't remember ever to have seen before at this time of the year. My aunt Deming says, when she first look'd abroad this morning she felt anxious for her brother, & his family at Cumberland, fearing lest they were covered up in snow. It is now 1/2 after 12 o'clock noon. The sun has been shineing in his full strength for full 6 hours, & the snow not melted enough anywhere in sight of this house, to cause one drop of water.

MARCH 17. — Yesterday, I went to see aunt Polly, & finding her going out, I spent the afternoon with aunt Hannah. While I was out, a snow storm overtook me. This being a fine sun shine (tho' cold) day I have been to writing school, & wrote two pieces, one I presented to aunt Deming, and the other I design for my Honor'd Papa, I hope he will approve of it. I sent a piece of my writing to you Hon'd Mamma last fall, which I hope you receiv'd....

My aunt gives her love to you & directs me to tell you that she tho't my piece of linnin would have made me a dozen of shifts but she could cut no more than ten out of it. There is some left, but not enough for another. Nine of them are finish'd wash'd & iron'd; & the other would have been long since done if my fingers had not been sore. My cousin Sally made three of them for me, but then I made two shirts & part of another for unkle to help her. I believe unless something remarkable should happen, such as a *warm day*, my mamma will consent that I dedicate a few of my next essays to papa. I think the second thing I

said to aunt this morning was, that I intended to be *very good all day.*
To make this out,

> Next unto *God,* dear Parents I address
> Myself to you in humble Thankfulness,
> For all your Care & Charge on me bestow'd;
> The means of Learning unto me allow'd,
> Go on I pray, & let me still pursue
> Those Golden ARTS the Vulgar never knew.

> Yr Dutifull Daughter
> Anna Green Winslow.

MARCH 19. — Thursday last I spent at home, except a quarter of an hour
between sunset and dark, I stepped over the way to Mr. Glover's with
aunt. Yesterday I spent at Unkle Neddy's & stitched wristbands for aunt
Polly. By the way, I must inform you, (pray dont let papa see this) that
yesterday I put on No 1 of my new shifts, & indeed it is very comfortable.
It is *long* since I had a shift to my *back.* I dont know if I ever had till
now — It seem'd so strange too, to have any linen below my waist — I
am going to dine at Mrs. Whitwell's to day, by invitation. I spent last
evening at Mrs Rogers. Mr Hunt discoursed upon the doctrine of the
Trinity — it was the second time that he spoke upon the subject at that
place. I did not hear him the first time. His business last evening was
to prove the divinity of the Son, & holy Ghost, & their equality with the
Father. My aunt Deming says, it is a grief to her, that I don't always
write as well as I can, *I can write pretily.*

MARCH 21. — I din'd & spent the afternoon of Thursday last, at Mrs
Whitwell's. Mrs Lathrop, & Mrs Carpenter din'd there also. The latter
said she was formerly acquainted with mamma, ask'd how she did, &
when I heard from her, — said, I look'd much like her. Madam Harris &
Miss P. Vans were also of the company. While I was abroad the snow
melted to such a degree, that my aunt was oblig'd to get Mr Soley's chaise
to bring me home. Yesterday, we had by far the gratest storm of wind
& snow that there has been this winter. It began to fall yesterday morning & continued falling till after our family were in bed. (P. M.) ...

MARCH 26. — Yesterday at 6 o'clock, I went to Unkle Winslow's, their
neighbor Greenleaf was their. She said she knew Mamma, & that I look
like her. Speaking about papa & you occation'd Unkle Winslow to tell
me that he had kiss'd you long before papa knew you. From thence we
went to Miss Rogers's where, to a full assembly Mr Bacon read his 3d
sermon on R. iv. 6, I can remember he said, that, before we all sinned
in Adam our father, Christ loved us. He said the Son of God always did
as his father gave him commandment, & to prove this, he said, that above
17 hundred years ago he left the bosom of the Father, & came & took
up his abode with men, & bore all the scourgings & buffetings ...

... inflicted on him, & then was hung upon the accursed tree — he died, was buried, & in three days rose again — ascended up to heaven & there took his seat at the right hand of the Majesty on high from whence he will come to be the supream and impartial judge of quick & dead — and when his poor Mother & her poor husband went to Jerusalem to keep the passover & he went with them, he disputed among the doctors, & when his Mother ask'd him about it he said "wist ye not that I must be about my Father's business," — all this he said was a part of that wrighteousness for the sake of which a sinner is justafied — Aunt has been up stairs all the time I have been writeing & recollecting this — so no help from her. She is come down now & I have been reading this over to her. She sais, she is glad I remember so much, but I have not done the subject justice. She sais I have blended things somewhat improperly — an interruption by company.

MARCH 28. — Unkle Harry was here last evening & inform'd us that by a vessel from Halifax which arriv'd yesterday, Mr H Newton, inform'd his brother Mr J Newton of the sudden death of their brother Hibbert in your family 21 January ult. (Just five months to a day since Grandmamma Sargent's death.) With all the circumstances relating to it. My aunt Deming gives her love to Mamma & wishes her a sanctified improvement of all God's dealings with her, & that it would please him to bring her & all the family safe to Boston. Jarvis is put up for Cumberland, we hope he will be there by or before Mayday. This minute I have receiv'd my queen's night cap from Miss Caty Vans — we like it. Aunt says, that if the materials it is made of were more substantial than gauze, it might serve occationally to hold any thing measur'd by an 1/2 peck, but it is just as it should be, & very decent, & she wishes my writing was *as* decent. But I got into one of my frolicks, upon sight of the Cap.

APRIL 3. — Yesterday was the annual Fast, & I was at meeting all day. Mr Hunt preach'd A. M. from Zac. vii. 4, 5, 6, 7. He said, that if we did not mean as we said in pray's it was only a compliment put upon God, which was a high affront to his divine Majesty. Mr Bacon, P. M. from James v. 17. He said, "pray's, effectual & fervent, might be, where there were no words, but there might be elegant words where there is no prayr's. The essence of pray's consists in offering up holy desires to God agreeable to his will, — it is the flowing out of gracious affections — what then are the pray'rs of an unrenewed heart that is full of enmity to God? doubtless they are an abomination to him. What then, must not unregenerate men pray? I answer, it is their duty to breathe out holy desires to God in pray's. Prayer is a natural duty. Hannah pour'd out her soul before the Lord, yet her voice was not heard, only her lips moved. Some grieve and complain that their pray's are not answered, but if *thy will be done is,* as it ought to be, in every prayer; their prayers are answer'd." ...

My aunt Deming says, that if my memory had been equal to the memory of some of my ancestors, I might have done better justice to Mr.

Bacon's good sermon, & that if hers had been better than mine she would have helped me. Mr Bacon *did* say what is here recorded, but in other method.

APRIL 6. — I made a shift to walk to meeting yesterday morning. But there was so much water in the streets when I came home from meeting that I got a seat in Mr Waleses chaise. My aunt walk'd home & she sais thro' more difaculty than ever she did in her life before....

APRIL 9. — ... Yesterday afternoon I visited Miss Polly Deming & took her with me to Mr Rogers' in the evening where Mr Hunt discours'd upon the 7th question of the catechism viz what are the decrees of God? I remember a good many of his observations, which I have got set down on a loose paper. But my aunt says that a Miss of 12 year's old cant possibly do justice to the nicest subject in Divinity, & therefore had better not attempt a repetition of perticulars, that she finds lie (as may be easily concluded) somewhat confused in my young mind. She also says, that in her poor judgment, Mr Hunt discours'd soundly as well as ingeniously upon the subject, & very much to her instruction & satisfaction. My Papa inform'd me in his last letter that he had done me the honor to read my journals & that he approv'd of some part of them, I suppose he means that he likes some parts better than other, indeed it would be wonderful, as aunt says, if a gentleman of papa's understanding & judgment cou'd be highly entertain'd with *every little* saying or observation that came from a girl of my years & that I ought to esteem it a great favour that he notices any of my simple matter with his *approbation.* ...

APRIL 14. — I went a visiting yesterday to Col. Gridley's with my aunt. After tea Miss Becky Gridley sung a minuet. Miss Polly Deming & I danced to her musick, which when perform'd was approv'd of by Mrs Gridley, Mrs Deming, Mrs Thompson, Mrs Avery, Miss Sally Hill, Miss Becky Gridley, Miss Polly Gridley & Miss Sally Winslow. Col Gridley was out o' the room. Col brought in the talk of Whigs & Tories & taught me the difference between them. I spent last evening at home. I should have gone a visiting to day in sudbury street, but Unkle Harry told me last night that they would be full of company. I had the pleasure of hearing by him, that they were all well. I believe I shall go somewhere this afternoon for I have acquaintances enough that would be very glad to see me, as well as my sudbury street friends.

APRIL 15. — Yesterday I din'd at Mrs. Whitwell's & she being going abroad, I spent the aftternoon at Madam Harris's & the evening at home, Unkle Harry gave us his company some part of it. I am going to Aunt Storer's as soon as writing school is done. I shall dine with her, if she is not engaged....

APRIL 16. — I dined with Aunt Storer yesterday & spent the afternoon very agreeably at Aunt Suky's. Aunt Storer is not very well, but she drank tea with us, & went down to Mr Stillman's lecture in the evening. I spent the evening with Unkle & Aunt at Mrs Rogers's. Mr Bacon preach'd his fourth sermon from Romans iv. 6. My cousin Charles Storer lent me Gulliver's Travels abreviated, which aunt says I may read for the sake of perfecting myself in reading a variety of composures. she sais farther that the piece was desin'd as a burlesque upon the times in which it was wrote, — & Martimas Scriblensis & Pope Dunciad were wrote with the same design & as parts of the same work, tho' wrote by three several hands.

APRIL 17. — You see, Mamma, I comply with your orders (or at least have done father's some time past) of writing in my journal every day tho' my matters are of little importance & I have nothing at present to communicate except that I spent yesterday afternoon & evening at Mr Soley's. The day was very rainy. I hope I shall at least learn to spell the word *yesterday*, it having occur'd so frequently in these pages! (The bell is ringing for good friday.) Last evening aunt had a letter from Unkle Pierce, he informs her, that last Lords day morning Mrs Martin was deliver'd of a daughter. She had been siezed the Monday before with a violent pluritick fever, which continued when my Unkle's letter was dated 13th instant. My Aunt Deming is affraid that poor Mrs Martin is no more. She hopes she is reconcil'd to her father — but is affraid whether that was so — She had try'd what was to be done that way on her late visits to Portsmouth, & found my unkle was placably dispos'd, poor Mrs Martin, she could not then be brought to make any acknowledgements as she ought to have done.

APRIL 18. — Some time since I exchang'd a piece of patchwork, which had been wrought in my leisure intervals, with Miss Peggy Phillips, my schoolmate, for a pair of curious lace mitts with blue flaps which I shall send, with a yard of white ribbin edg'd with green to Miss Nancy Macky for a present. I had intended that the patchwork should have grown large enough to have cover'd a bed when that same live stock which you wrote me about some time since, should be increas'd to that portion you intend to bestow upon me, should a certain event take place....

Pray mamma, be so kind as to bring up all my journal with you. My Papa has promised me, he will bring up my baby house with him. I shall send you a droll figure of a young lady, in or under, which you please, a tasty head Dress. It was taken from a print that came over in one of the last ships from London....

BOSTON APRIL 20, 1772. — Last Saterday I seal'd up 45 pages of Journal for Cumberland. This is a very stormy day — no going to school. I am learning to knit lace.

APRIL 21. — Visited at uncle Joshua Green's. I saw three funerals from their window, poor Captain Turner's was one.

□

APRIL 24. — I drank tea at Aunt Suky's. Aunt Storer was there, she seemed to be in charming good health & spirits. My cousin Charles Green seems to grow a little fat pritty boy but he is very light. My aunt Storer lent me 3 of cousin Charles' books to read, viz. — The puzzeling cap, the female Oraters & the history of Gaffer too-shoes.

APRIL 25. — I learn't three stitches upon net work to-day.

APRIL 27. — I din'd at Aunt Storer's & spent the P. M. at aunt Suky's.

APRIL 28. — This P. M. I am visited by Miss Glover, Miss Draper & Miss Soley. My aunt abroad.

□

AUG. 18. — Many avocations have prevented my keeping my journal so exactly as heretofore, by which means a pleasant visit to the peacock, my Papa's & mamma's journey to Marshfield &c. have been omitted. The 6 instant Mr Samuel Jarvis was married to Miss Suky Peirce, & on the 13th I made her a visit in company with mamma & many others. The bride was dress'd in a white satin night gound.

27. — Yesterday I heard an account of a cat of 17 years old, that has just recovered of the meazels. This same cat it is said had the small pox 8 years ago!

*A*mericans are accustomed to believe that all children grow up in nuclear families composed of parents and their offspring. But this has not been the case for countless boys and girls. Prior to the twentieth century, the high incidence of mortality resulted in many children living in households lacking one or both parents. Although the death of a parent during a child's early years is uncommon today, high divorce rates ensure that, again, large numbers of youngsters will spend much of their childhood without a mother or father close at hand. A child's development is greatly influenced by the nature of her interactions with parents or other adults who serve as her primary caretakers.

Caroline Cowles Richards was seven years old when her mother died, and she, her sister, Anna, who was three years younger, and her two older brothers, James and John, went to live with her mother's parents in Canandaigua, New York, a village in the western part of the state. Her grand-parents, the Bealses, had already raised eleven children of their own.

When she began her diary in 1852, Caroline was ten. Her brothers had already moved away to boarding school, and her father, a Presbyterian minister, had remarried, although why Caroline and Anna did not live with him and his second wife is not clear. Reverend Richards's occasional visits to his daughters were always special events in their lives, and Caroline corresponded with him regularly. But the relationship between the two seemed distant compared with that which Caroline enjoyed with her grandparents. Grandfather and Grandmother Beals fulfilled the role of parents in Caroline's and Anna's lives.

In some ways Caroline's childhood experiences were similar to those of Anna Green Winslow. Puritan values strongly prevailed in the Beals household, and like Anna Winslow, Caroline read the Bible daily, attended catechism classes, and faithfully recorded her notes on Sunday sermons. Comparing her own conduct and that of her sister to accounts she heard about girls in the past, Caroline concluded that they must have been more pious and disciplined. She and Anna sometimes forgot when it was Sabbath Day and joked and laughed and had to be corrected by their grandparents.

Caroline expressed the love she felt toward and from Grandmother and Grandfather Beals throughout the diary. They were gentle and patient with their granddaughters, and by their own example they sought to instill proper moral and religious values. Their grandparents shared in activities with Caroline and Anna. Grandmother Beals told them stories and care-fully selected their readings, suggesting moral stories addressed specifi-cally to young girls. Grandfather Beals took them on walks, rides in his carriage, and picnics.

Caroline's education was less self-consciously genteel than Anna Wins-low's, and it proceeded in more informal ways. At home she helped her grandmother with little chores — running errands, threading needles, get-ting her room ready to be cleaned. The Bealses could afford hired help for cleaning and maintenance work. Caroline's grandparents were cer-tainly concerned that their granddaughters learn social manners, in school and at home, but the processes were more relaxed in the small community setting. Caroline was aware of impoverished children who lived in New York City and of the poverty of the segregated black community in the nearest town. At first puzzled as to why her grandmother would invite a poor, black woman to dinner, she later concluded that her grandmother was right and wondered if she would ever be so good.

Caroline and Anna had much freedom at play. Their father bought them hoops, sticks, and jump ropes, and Grandfather Beals put swings and a seesaw in the backyard. Although Caroline participated in games popular among boys, such as snap-the-whip and mumblety-peg, she ex-pressed the feeling that the former was so rough it was "not a very good game for girls," and that the latter was "dangerous." Caroline was quite certain that her grandmother would not give her a knife of her own with which to play mumblety-peg, and she herself felt that some games were appropriate for boys and not girls.

From Caroline's description, the district school that she and Anna attended was typical of those in nineteenth-century rural America. She and her sister mixed with boys and girls of all ages to learn their lessons. This range of ages existed in the private girls' school that they later attended as well.

Speculating about her future, Caroline thought of becoming a writer, one of the few professions open to women in the nineteenth century. Noting the success of a well-known female author of children's books, Caroline thought she could succeed also. A stronger female role model in her life, however, seemed to be one of her teachers, who was "pretty and good," and who was probably going to be married soon.

At age twenty-four Caroline married and soon after gave birth to a daughter. She kept her diary intermittently for twenty years, and in 1911, at the age of sixty-nine, she added and edited later entries. It seems likely that at the same time she may have edited some of her childhood reflections as well.

—— 2 ——
Caroline Cowles Richards

CANANDAIGUA, N.Y.

NOVEMBER 21, 1852. — I am ten years old to-day, and I think I will write a journal and tell who I am and what I am doing. I have lived with my Grandfather and Grandmother Beals ever since I was seven years old, and Anna, too, since she was four. Our brothers, James and John, came too, but they are at East Bloomfield at Mr Stephen Clark's Academy. Miss Laura Clark of Naples is their teacher.

Anna and I go to school at District No. 11. Mr James C. Cross is our teacher, and some of the scholars say he is cross by name and cross by nature, but I like him. He gave me a book by the name of "Noble Deeds of American Women," for reward of merit, in my reading class. To-day, a nice old gentleman, by the name of Mr William Wood, visited our school. He is Mrs Nat Gorham's uncle, and Wood Street is named for him. He had a beautiful pear in his hand and said he would give it to the boy or girl who could spell "virgaloo," for that was the name of the pear. I spelt it that way, but it was not right. A little boy, named William Schley, spelt it right and he got the pear. I wish I had, but I can't even remember now how he spelt it. If the pear was as hard as the name, I don't believe any one would want it, but I don't see how they happened to give such a hard name to such a nice pear. Grandfather says perhaps Mr Wood will bring in a Seckle pear some day, so I had better be ready for him.

Grandmother told us such a nice story to-day. I am going to write it down in my journal. I think I shall write a book some day. Miss Caroline Chesebro did, and I don't see why I can't. If I do, I shall put this story in it. It is a true story and better than any I found in three story books Grandmother gave us to read this week, "Peep of Day," "Line Upon Line," and "Precept Upon Precept," but this story was better than them all. One night Grandfather was locking the front door at nine o'clock, and he heard a queer sound, like a baby crying. So he unlocked the door and found a bandbox on the stoop, and the cry seemed to come from inside of it. So he took it up and brought it into the dining-room and called the two girls, who had just gone upstairs to bed. They came right down and opened the box, and there was a poor little girl baby, crying as hard as could be. They took it out and rocked it and sung to it and got some milk and fed it and then sat up all night with it, by the fire. There was a paper pinned on the baby's dress with her name on it, "Lily T. LaMott," and a piece of poetry called "Pity the Poor Orphan." The next morning, Grandfather went to the overseer of the poor and he said it should be taken to the county house, so our hired man got the horse and buggy, and one of the girls carried the baby and they took it away. There was a piece in the paper about it and Grandmother pasted it into her "Jay's Morning and Evening Exercises," and showed it to us. It said, "A Deposit After Banking Hours." "Two suspicious looking females were seen about town in the afternoon, one of them carrying an infant. They took a train early in the morning without the child. They probably secreted themselves in Mr Beals' yard and if he had not taken the box in they would have carried it somewhere else." When Grandfather told the clerks in the bank about it next morning, Mr Bunnell, who lives over by Mr Daggett's, on the park, said, if it had been left at some people's houses it would not have been sent away. Grandmother says they heard that the baby was adopted afterwards by some nice people in Geneva. People must think this is a nice place for children, for they had eleven of their own before we came. Mrs McCoe was here to call this afternoon and she looked at us and said: "It must be a great responsibility, Mrs Beals." Grandmother said she thought "her strength would be equal to her day." That is one of her favourite verses. She said Mrs McCoe never had any children of her own and perhaps that is the reason she looks so sad at us. Perhaps some one will leave a bandbox and a baby at her door some dark night.

SATURDAY. — Our brother John drove over from East Bloomfield to-day to see us and brought Julia Smedley with him, who is just my age. John lives at Mr Ferdinand Beebe's and goes to school and Julia is Mr Beebe's niece. They make quantities of maple sugar out there and they brought us a dozen little cakes. They were splendid. I offered John one and he said he would rather throw it over the fence than to eat it. I can't understand that. Anna had the faceache to-day and I told her that I would be the doctor and make her a ginger poultice. I thought I did it exactly right but when I put it on her face she shivered and said: "Carrie, you make lovely poultices only they are so cold." I suppose I ought to have warmed it.

TUESDAY. — Grandfather took us to ride this afternoon and let us ask Bessie Seymour to go with us. We rode on the plank road to Chapinville and had to pay 2 cents at the toll gate, both ways. We met a good many people and Grandfather bowed to them and said, "How do you do, neighbour?"

We asked him what their names were and he said he did not know. We went to see Mr Munson, who runs the mill at Chapinville. He took us through the mill and let us get weighed and took us over to his house and out into the barn-yard to see the pigs and chickens and we also saw a colt which was one day old. Anna just wrote in her journal that "it was a very amusing site."

SUNDAY. — Rev. Mr Kendall, of East Bloomfield, preached to-day. His text was from Job 26, 14: "Lo these are parts of his ways, but how little a portion is heard of him." I could not make out what he meant. He is James' and John's minister.

WEDNESDAY. — Captain Menteith was at our house to dinner to-day and he tried to make Anna and me laugh by snapping his snuffbox under the table. He is a very jolly man, I think.

THURSDAY. — Father and Uncle Edward Richards came to see us yesterday and took us down to Mr Corson's store and told us we could have anything we wanted. So we asked for several kinds of candy, stick candy and lemon drops and bulls' eyes, and then they got us two rubber balls and two jumping ropes with handles and two hoops and sticks to roll them with and two red carnelian rings and two bracelets. We enjoyed getting them very much, and expect to have lots of fun. They went out to East Bloomfield to see James and John, and father is going to take them to New Orleans. We hate to have them go.

FRIDAY. — We asked Grandmother if we could have some hoop skirts like the seminary girls and she said no, we were not old enough. When we were downtown Anna bought a reed for 10 cents and ran it into the hem of her underskirt and says she is going to wear it to school to-morrow. I think Grandmother will laugh out loud for once, when she sees it, but I don't think Anna will wear it to school or anywhere else. She wouldn't want to if she knew how terrible it looked.

I threaded a dozen needles on a spool of thread for Grandmother, before I went to school, so that she could slip them along and use them as she needed them. She says it is a great help.

Grandmother says I will have a great deal to answer for, because Anna looks up to me so and tries to do everything that I do and thinks whatever I say is "gospel truth." The other day the girls at school were disputing with her about something and she said, "It is so, if it ain't so, for Calline said so." I shall have to "toe the mark," as Grandfather says, if she keeps watch of me all the time and walks in my footsteps.

We asked Grandmother this evening if we could sit out in the kitchen with Bridget and Hannah and the hired man, Thomas Holleran. She said we could take turns and each stay ten minutes by the clock. It gave us a little change. I read once that "variety is the spice of life." They sit around the table and each one has a candle, and Thomas reads aloud to the girls while they sew. He and Bridget are Catholics, but Hannah is a member of our Church. The girls have lived here always, I think, but I don't know for sure, as I have not lived here always myself, but we have to get a new hired man sometimes. Grandmother says if you are as good to your girls as you are to yourself they will stay a long time. I am sure that is Grandmother's rule. Mrs McCarty, who lives on Brook Street (some people call it Cat Alley but Grandmother says that is not proper), washes for us Mondays, and Grandmother always has a lunch for her at eleven o'clock and goes out herself to see that she sits down and eats it. Mrs McCarty told us Monday that Mrs. Brockle's niece was dead. who lives next door to her. Grandmother sent us over with some things for their comfort and told us to say that we were sorry they were in trouble. We went and when we came back Anna told Grandmother that I said, "Never mind, Mrs Brockle, some day we will all be dead." I am sure that I said something better than that.

WEDNESDAY. — Mr Cross had us speak pieces to-day. He calls our names, and we walk on to the platform and toe the mark and make a bow and say what we have got to say. He did not know what our pieces were going to be and some of them said the same ones. Two boys spoke: "The boy stood on the burning deck, whence all but him had fled." William Sly was one, and he spoke his the best. When he said, "The flames that lit the battle wreck shone round him o'er the dead," we could almost see the fire, and when he said, "My father, must I stay?" we felt like telling him, no, he needn't. He is going to make a good speaker. Mr Cross said so. Albert Murray spoke "Excelsior," and Horace Finley spoke nice, too. My piece was, "Why, Phoebe, are you come so soon? Where are your berries, child?" Emma Van Arsdale spoke the same one. We find them all in our reader. Sometime I am going to speak, "How does the water come down at Ladore?" Splashing and flashing and dashing and clashing and all that — it rhymes, so it is easy to remember.

We played snap the whip at recess to-day and I was on the end and was snapped off against the fence. It hurt me so, that Anna cried. It is not a very good game for girls, especially for the one on the end.

TUESDAY. — I could not keep a journal for two weeks, because Grandfather and Grandmother have been very sick and we were afraid something dreadful was going to happen. We are so glad that they are well again. Grandmother was sick upstairs and Grandfather in the bedroom downstairs, and we carried messages back and forth for them. Dr Carr and Aunt Mary came over twice every day and said they had the influenza and the inflammation of the lungs. It was lonesome for us to sit down to the table and just have Hannah wait on us. We had such lumps in our throats we could not eat much and we cried ourselves to sleep two or three nights. Aunt Ann Field took us home with her one afternoon to stay all night. We liked the idea and Mary and Louisa and Anna and I planned what we would play in the evening, but just as it was dark our hired man, Patrick McCarty, drove over after us. He said Grandfather and Grandmother could not get to sleep till they saw the children and bid them good-night. So we rode home with him. We never stayed anywhere away from home all night that we can remember. When Grandmother came downstairs the first time she was too weak to walk, so she sat on each step till she got down. When Grandfather saw her, he smiled and said to us: "When she will, she will, you may depend on't; and when she won't she won't, and that's the end on't." But we knew all the time that he was very glad to see her.

SUNDAY, MARCH 20, 1853. — It snowed so, that we could not go to church to-day and it was the longest day I ever spent. The only excitement was seeing the snowplough, drawn by two horses, go up on this side of the street and down on the other. Grandfather put on his long cloak with a cape, which he wears in real cold weather, and went. We wanted to pull some long stockings over our shoes and go too but Grandmother did not think it was best. She gave us the "Dairyman's Daughter" and "Jane the Young Cottager," by Leigh Richmond, to read. I don't see how they happened to be so awfully good. Anna says they died of "early piety," but she did not say it very loud. Grandmother said she would give me 10 cents if I would learn the verses in the New England Primer that John Rogers left for his wife and nine small children and one at the breast, when he was burned at the stake, at Smithfield, England, in 1555. One verse is, "I leave you here a little book for you to look upon that you may see your father's face when he is dead and gone." It is a very long piece but I got it. Grandmother says "the blood of the martyrs is the seed of the church." Anna learned

> In Adam's fall we sinned all.
> My Book and heart shall never part.
> The Cat doth slay and after play.
> The Dog doth bite a thief at night.

When she came to the end of it and said,

> Zaccheus he, did climb a tree, his Lord to see.

she said she heard some one say, "The tree broke down and let him fall and he did not see his Lord at all." Grandmother said it was very wicked indeed and she hoped Anna would try and forget it.

APRIL 1. — Grandmother sent me up into the little chamber to-day to straighten things and get the room ready to be cleaned. I found a little book called "Child's Pilgrim Progress, Illustrated," that I had never seen before. I got as far as Giant Despair when Anna came up and said Grandmother sent her to see what I was doing, and she went back and told her that I was sitting on the floor in the midst of books and papers and was so absorbed in "Pilgrim's Progress" that I had made none myself. It must be a good book for Grandmother did not say a word. Father sent us "Gulliver's Travels" and there is a gilt picture on the green cover, of a giant with legs astride and little Lilliputians standing underneath, who do not come up to his knees. Grandmother did not like the picture, so she pasted a piece of pink calico over it, so we could only see the giant from his waist up. I love the story of Cinderella and the poem, " 'Twas the night before Christmas," and I am sorry that there are no fairies and no Santa Claus.

We go to school to Miss Zilpha Clark in her own house on Gibson Street. Other girls who go are Laura Chapin, Julia Phelps, Mary Paul, Bessie Seymour, Lucilla and Mary Field, Louisa Benjamin, Nannie Corson, Kittie Marshall, Abbie Clark and several other girls. I like Abbie Clark the best of all the girls in school excepting of course my sister Anna.

Before I go to school every morning I read three chapters in the Bible. I read three every day and five on Sunday and that takes me through the Bible in a year. Those I read this morning were the first, second and third chapters of Job. The first was about Eliphaz reproveth Job; second, Benefit of God's correction; third, Job justifieth his complaint. I then learned a text to say at school. I went to school at quarter to nine and recited my text and we had prayers and then proceeded with the business of the day. Just before school was out, we recited in "Science of Things Familiar," and in Dictionary, and then we had calisthenics.

We go through a great many figures and sing "A Life on the Ocean Wave," "What Fairy Like Music Steals Over the Sea," "Lightly Row, Lightly Row, O'er the Glassy Waves We Go," and "O Come, Come Away," and other songs. Mrs Judge Taylor wrote one song on purpose for us.

MAY 1. — I arose this morning about the usual time and read my three chapters in the Bible and had time for a walk in the garden before breakfast. The polyanthuses are just beginning to blossom and they border all the walk up and down the garden. I went to school at quarter of nine, but did not get along very well because we played too much. We had two new scholars to-day, Miss Archibald and Miss Andrews, the former about seventeen and the latter about fifteen. In the afternoon old

Mrs Kinney made us a visit, but she did not stay very long. In dictionary class I got up sixth, although I had not studied my lesson very much....

JULY. — Every Saturday our cousins, Lucilla and Mary and Louisa Field, take turns coming to Grandmother's to dinner. It was Mary's turn to-day, but she was sick and couldn't come, so Grandmother told us that we could dress up and make some calls for her. We were very glad. She told us to go to Mrs Gooding's first, so we did and she was glad to see us and gave us some cake she had just made. Then we went on to Mr Greig's. We walked up the high steps to the front door and rang the bell and Mr Alexander came. We asked if Mrs. Greig and Miss Chapin were at home and he said yes, and asked us into the parlour. We looked at the paintings on the wall and looked at ourselves in the long looking-glass, while we were waiting. Mrs Irving came in first. She was very nice and said I looked like her niece, Julie Jeffrey. I hope I do, for I would like to look like her. Mrs Greig and Miss Chapin came in and were very glad to see us, and took us out into the greenhouse and showed us all the beautiful plants. When we said we would have to go they said good-bye and sent love to Grandmother and told us to call again. I never knew Anna to act as polite as she did to-day. Then we went to see Mrs Judge Phelps and Miss Eliza Chapin, and they were very nice and gave us some flowers from their garden. Then we went on to Miss Caroline Jackson's, to see Mrs Holmes. Sometimes she is my Sunday School teacher, and she says she and our mother used to be great friends at the seminary. She said she was glad we came up and she hoped we would be as good as our mother was. That is what nearly every one says. On our way back, we called on Mrs Dana at the Academy, as she is a friend of Grandmother. She is Mrs Noah T. Clarke's mother. After that, we went home and told Grandmother we had a very pleasant time calling on our friends and they all asked us to come again....

NOVEMBER 22. — I wrote a composition to-day, and the subject was, "Which of the Seasons Is the Pleasantest?" Anna asked Grandmother what she should write about, and Grandmother said she thought "A Contented Mind" would be a very good subject, but Anna said she never had one and didn't know what it meant, so she didn't try to write any at all.

A squaw walked right into our kitchen to-day with a blanket over her head and had beaded purses to sell....

NOVEMBER 23. — We read our compositions to-day and Miss Clark said mine was very good. One of the girls had a Prophecy for a composition and told what we were all going to be when we grew up. She said Anna Richards was going to be a missionary and Anna cried right out loud. I tried to comfort her and told her it might never happen, so she stopped crying....

SUNDAY. — Mr Tousley preached to-day. Mr Lamb is Superintendent of the Sunday School. Mr Chipman used to be. Miss Mollie Bull played the melodeon. Mr Fairchild is my teacher when he is there. He was not there to-day and Miss Mary Howell taught our class. I wish I could be as good and pretty as she is. We go to church morning and afternoon and to Sunday School, and learn seven verses every week and recite catechism and hymns to Grandmother in the evening. Grandmother knows all the questions by heart, so she lets the book lie in her lap and she asks them with her eyes shut. She likes to hear us sing:

> 'Tis religion that can give
> Sweetest pleasure while we live,
> 'Tis religion can supply
> Solid comfort when we die.

DECEMBER 1. — Grandfather asked me to read President Pierce's message aloud to him this evening. I thought it was very long and dry, but he said it was interesting and that I read it very well. I am glad he liked it. Part of it was about the Missouri Compromise and I didn't even know what it meant.

DECEMBER 8. — We are taking dictation lessons at school now. Miss Clark reads to us from the "Life of Queen Elizabeth" and we write it down in a book and keep it. She corrects it for us. I always spell "until" with two l's and she has to mark it every time. I hope I will learn how to spell it after a while.

SATURDAY, DECEMBER 9. — We took our music lessons to-day. Miss Hattie Heard is our teacher and she says we are getting along well. Anna practiced her lesson over sixty-five times this morning before breakfast and can play "Mary to the Saviour's Tomb" as fast as a waltz.

We chose sides and spelled down at school to-day. Julia Phelps and I stood up the last and both went down on the same word — eulogism. I don't see the use of that "e." Miss Clark gave us twenty words which we had to bring into some stories which we wrote. It was real fun to hear them. Every one was different.

1854 . . . TUESDAY. — A gentleman visited our school to-day whom we had never seen. Miss Clark introduced him to us. When he came in, Miss Clark said, "Young ladies," and we all stood up and bowed and said his name in concert. Grandfather says he would rather have us go to school to Miss Clark than anyone else because she teaches us manners as well as books. We girls think that he is a very particular friend of Miss Clark. He is very nice looking, but we don't know where he lives. Laura Chapin says he is an architect. I looked it up in the dictionary and it says one who plans or designs. I hope he does not plan to get married to Miss Clark and take her away and break up the school, but I presume he does, for that is usually the way.

MONDAY. — There was a minister preached in our church last night and some people say he is the greatest minister in the world. I think his name was Mr Finney. Grandmother said I could go with our girl, Hannah White. We sat under the gallery, in Miss Antoinette Pierson's pew. There was a great crowd and he preached good. Grandmother says that our mother was a Christian when she was ten years old and joined the church and she showed us some sermons that mother used to write down when she was seventeen years old, after she came home from church, and she has kept them all these years. I think children in old times were not as bad as they are now.

TUESDAY. — Mrs Judge Taylor sent for me to come over to see her to-day. I didn't know what she wanted, but when I got there she said she wanted to talk and pray with me on the subject of religion. She took me into one of the wings. I never had been in there before and was frightened at first, but it was nice after I got used to it. After she prayed, she asked me to, but I couldn't think of anything but "Now I lay me down to sleep," and I was afraid she would not like that, so I didn't say anything. When I got home and told Anna, she said, "Caroline, I presume probably Mrs Taylor wants you to be a missionary, but I shan't let you go." I told her she needn't worry for I would have to stay at home and look after her. After school to-night I went out into Abbie Clark's garden with her and she taught me how to play "mumble te peg." It is fun, but rather dangerous. I am afraid Grandmother won't give me a knife to play with. Abbie Clark has beautiful pansies in her garden and gave me some roots.

WEDNESDAY. — Grandmother sent Anna and me up to Butcher Street after school to-day to invite Chloe to come to dinner. I never saw so many black people as there are up there. We saw old Lloyd and black Jonathan and Dick Valentine and Jerusha and Chloe and Nackie. Nackie was pounding up stones into sand, to sell, to scour with. Grandmother often buys it of her. I think Chloe was surprised, but she said she would be ready, to-morrow, at eleven o'clock, when the carriage came for her. I should hate to be as fat as Chloe. I think she weighs 300. She is going to sit in Grandfather's big arm chair, Grandmother says.

We told her we should think she would rather invite white ladies, but she said Chloe was a poor old slave and as Grandfather had gone to Saratoga she thought it was a good time to have her. She said God made of one blood all the people on the face of the earth, so we knew she would do it and we didn't say any more. When we talk too much, Grandfather always says N. C. (nuff ced). She sent a carriage for Chloe and she came and had a nice dinner, not in the kitchen either. Grandmother asked her if there was any one else she would like to see before she went home and she said, "Yes, Miss Rebekah Gorham," so she told the coachman to take her down there and wait for her to make a call and then take her home and he did. Chloe said she had a very nice time, so probably Grandmother was all right as she generally is, but I could not be as good as she is, if I should try one hundred years....

SATURDAY. — Grandfather took us down street to be measured for some new patten leather shoes at Mr Ambler's. They are going to be very nice ones for best. We got our new summer hats from Mrs Freshour's millinery and we wore them over to show to Aunt Ann and she said they were the very handsomest bonnets she had seen this year.

TUESDAY. — When we were on our way to school this morning we met a lot of people and girls and boys going to a picnic up the lake. They asked us to go, too, but we said we were afraid we could not. Mr Alex. Howell said, "Tell your Grandfather I will bring you back safe and sound unless the boat goes to the bottom with all of us." So we went home and told Grandfather and much to our surprise he said we could go. We had never been on a boat or on the lake before. We went up to the head on the steamer "Joseph Wood" and got off at Maxwell's Point. They had a picnic dinner and lots of good things to eat. Then we all went into the glen and climbed up through it. Mr Alex. Howell and Mrs Wheeler got to the top first and everybody gave three cheers. We had a lovely time riding back on the boat and told Grandmother we had the very best time we ever had in our whole lives.

MAY 26. — ... There is a Mr Packer in town, who teaches all the children to sing. He had a concert in Bemis Hall last night and he put Anna on the top row of the pyramid of beauty and about one hundred children in rows below. She ought to have worn a white dress as the others did but Grandmother said her new pink barege would do. I curled her hair all around in about thirty curls and she looked very nice. She waved the flag in the shape of the letter S and sang "The Star Spangled Banner," and all the others joined in the chorus. It was perfectly grand....

SUNDAY. — I almost forgot that it was Sunday this morning and talked and laughed just as I do week days. Grandmother told me to write down this verse before I went to church so I would remember it: "Keep thy foot when thou goest to the house of God, and be more ready to hear than to offer the sacrifice of fools." I will remember it now, sure. My feet are all right any way with my new patten leather shoes on but I shall have to look out for my head....

Grandmother always comes upstairs to get the candle and tuck us in before she goes to bed herself, and some nights we are sound asleep and do not hear her, but last night we only pretended to be asleep. She kneeled down by the bed and prayed aloud for us, that we might be good children and that she might have strength given to her from on high to guide us in the straight and narrow path which leads to life eternal. Those were her very words. After she had gone downstairs we sat up in bed and talked about it and promised each other to be good, and crossed our hearts and "hoped to die," if we broke our promise. Then Anna was afraid we would die, but I told her I didn't believe we would be as good as that, so we kissed each other and went to sleep....

WEDNESDAY. — I got up this morning at twenty minutes after five. I always brush my teeth every morning, but I forget to put it down here. I read my three chapters in Job and played in the garden and had time to read Grandmother a piece in the paper about some poor children in New York. Anna and I went over to Aunt Ann's before school and she gave us each two sticks of candy apiece. Part of it came from New York and part from Williamstown, Mass., where Henry goes to college. Ann Eliza is going down street with us this afternoon to buy us some new summer bonnets. They are to be trimmed with blue and white and are to come to five dollars. We are going to Mr Stannard's store also, to buy us some stockings. I ought to buy me a new thimble and scissors for I carried my sewing to school to-day and they were inside of it very carelessly and dropped out and got lost. I ought to buy them with my own money, but I haven't got any, for I gave all I had (two shillings) to Anna to buy Louisia Field a c[a]rnelian ring. Perhaps Father will send me some money soon, but I hate to ask him for fear he will rob himself. I don't like to tell Grandfather how very careless I was, though I know he would say, "Accidents will happen."

THURSDAY. — I was up early this morning because a dressmaker, Miss Willson, is coming to make me a new calico dress. It is white with pink spots in it and Grandfather bought it in New York. It is very nice indeed and I think Grandfather was very kind to get it for me. I had to stay at home from school to be fitted. I helped sew and run my dress skirt around the bottom and whipped it on the top. I went to school in the afternoon, but did not have my lessons very well. Miss Clark excused me because I was not there in the morning. Some girls got up on our fence to-day and walked clear across it, the whole length. It is iron and very high and has a stone foundation. Grandmother asked them to get down, but I think they thought it was more fun to walk up there than it was on the ground.... I made the pocket for my dress after I got home from school and then Grandfather said he would take us out to ride, so he took us way up to Thaddeus Chapin's on the hill....

FRIDAY, MAY. — Miss Clark told us we could have a picnic down to Sucker brook this afternoon and she told us to bring our rubbers and lunches by two o'clock; but Grandmother was not willing to let us go; not that she wished to deprive us of any pleasure for she said instead we could wear our new black silk basks and go with her to Preparatory lecture, so we did, but when we got there we found that Mr Daggett was out of town so there was no meeting. Then she told us we could keep dressed up and go over to Aunt Mary Carr's and take her some apples, and afterwards Grandfather took us to ride to see old Mrs Sanborn and old Mr and Mrs Atwater. He is ninety years old and blind and deaf, so we had quite a good time after all.

Rev. Mr Dickey, of Rochester, agent for the Seaman's Friend Society, preached this morning about the poor little canal boy. His text was from the 107th Psalm, 23rd verse, "They that go down into the sea in ships," He has the queerest voice and stops off between his words. When we got home Anna said she would show us how he preached and she described what he said about a sailor in time of war. She said, "A ball came — and struck him there — another ball came — and struck him there — he raised his faithful sword — and went on — to victory — or death." I expected Grandfather would reprove her, but he just smiled a queer sort of smile and Grandmother put her handkerchief up to her face, as she always does when she is amused about anything. I never heard her laugh out loud, but I suppose she likes funny things as well as anybody. She did just the same, this morning, when Grandfather asked Anna where the sun rose, and she said "over by Gen. Granger's house and sets behind the Methodist church." She said she saw it herself and should never forget it when any one asked her which was east or west. I think she makes up more things than any one I know of.

□

SUNDAY. — Rev. Mr. Tousley preached to-day to the children and told us how many steps it took to be bad. I think he said lying was first, then disobedience to parents, breaking the Sabbath, swearing, stealing, drunkenness. I don't remember just the order they came. It was very interesting, for he told lots of stories and we sang a great many times. I should think Eddy Tousley would be an awful good boy with his father in the house with him all the while, but probably he has to be away part of the time preaching to other children.

□

SUNDAY, AUGUST 10, 1854. — Rev. Mr. Daggett's text this morning was, "Remember the Sabbath day to keep it holy." Grandmother said she thought the sermon did not do us much good for she had to tell us several times this afternoon to stop laughing. Grandmother said we ought to be good Sundays if we want to go to heaven, for there it is one eternal Sabbath. Anna said she didn't want to be an angel just yet and I don't think there is the least danger of it, as far as I can judge. Grandmother said there was another verse, "If we do not have any pleasure on the Sabbath, or think any thoughts, we shall ride on the high places of the earth," and Anna said she liked that better, for she would rather ride than do anything else, so we both promised to be good. Grandfather told us they used to be more strict about Sunday than they are now. . . .

AUGUST 21. — Anna says that Alice Jewett feels very proud because she has a little baby brother. They have named him John Harvey Jewett after his father, and Alice says when he is bigger she will let Anna help her take him out to ride in his baby carriage. I suppose they will throw away their dolls now.

TUESDAY, SEPTEMBER 1. — I am sewing a sheet over and over for Grandmother and she puts a pin in to show me my stint, before I can go out to play. I am always glad when I get to it. I am making a sampler, too, and have all the capital letters worked and now will make the small ones. It is done in cross stitch on canvas with different colour silks. I am going to work my name, too. I am also knitting a tippet on some wooden needles that Henry Carr made for me. Grandmother has ravelled it out several times because I dropped stitches. It is rather tedious, but she says, "If at first you don't succeed, try, try again." Some military soldiers went by the house to-day and played some beautiful music. Grandfather has a teter and swing for us in the back yard and we enjoy them usually, but to-night Anna slid off the teter board when she was on the ground and I was in the air and I came down sooner than I expected. There was a hand organ and monkey going by and she was in a hurry to get to the street to see it. She got there a good while before I did. The other day we were swinging and Grandmother called us in to dinner, but Anna said we could not go until we "let the old cat die." Grandmother said it was more important that we should come when we are called.

OCTOBER. — Grandmother told us a story to-day, how when she was a little girl, down in Connecticut, in 1794, she was on her way to school one morning and she saw an Indian coming and was so afraid, but did not dare run for fear he would chase her. So she thought of the word sago, which means "goodmorning," and when she got up close to him she dropped a curtesy and said "Sago," and he just went right along and never touched her at all. She says she hopes we will always be polite to every one, even to strangers.

□

DECEMBER. — There was a moonlight sleighride of boys and girls last night, but Grandfather did not want us to go, but to-night he said he was going to take us to one himself. So after supper he told Mr Piser to harness the horse to the cutter and bring it around to the front gate. Mr Piser takes care of our horse and the Methodist Church. He lives in the basement. Grandfather sometimes calls him Shakespeare to us, but I don't know why. He doesn't look as though he wrote poetry. Grandfather said he was going to take us out to Mr Waterman Powers' in Farmington and he did. They were quite surprised to see us, but very glad and gave us apples and doughnuts and other good things. We saw Anne and Imogene and Morey and one little girl named Zimmie. They wanted us to stay all night, but Grandmother was expecting us. We got home safe about ten o'clock and had a very nice time. We never sat up so late before.

*A*ll children need nurturing, supportive environments in which to grow and develop in positive ways. The material and psychological obstacles that black families have faced in American society in their efforts to create such conditions for raising children have been enormous.

Under slavery, black families had no legal status and could be broken up by order of their white owners at any time. Parents and children lived with the constant fear that their families would be dispersed, as many thousands were. Frequently parents and children were sold separately and never saw each other again.

Annie Louise Burton's childhood, described here, presents a stark contrast to what has been presented in the previous documents. Born about 1860 on a plantation in Alabama, Annie wrote her reminiscences about her slave childhood in an autobiography that was published in 1909.

Annie's father was a white plantation owner who lived nearby, and, as was commonly the case in the antebellum South, he never acknowledged that she was his child. Her mother was a cook on the plantation where Annie lived and had served as childhood companion to the white girl who became her mistress. After a whipping by her mistress, Annie's mother ran away, leaving behind her three children, Annie, age three; her younger half-brother, Henry; and her older half-sister, Caroline.

The Civil War had already begun. As Annie recalled, slave children listened as adult slaves discussed the conflict, although the youngest were not able to grasp the full significance of what was happening. She remembered her earliest years as carefree and happy. Slave and white children roamed freely and played together; awareness of their oppressed status came later for black children, generally around age six or seven. In many slave autobiographies, authors vividly recall a specific incident that marked the beginning of this understanding; for example, watching a parent get whipped or being told they were strong enough to begin working in the fields. The carefree days of a slave's childhood were short.

Conditions of life for Annie were harsh, and as the war continued, they grew more so. She and the other slave children sneaked extra food at harvest time to supplement their meager rations. Her provision of clothes did not include a pair of shoes. Violence pervaded her world. Annie heard stories about the execution of two black men and got whipped for falling asleep and knocking over a churn.

When the Civil War ended, Annie's mother returned to the plantation to reclaim her children. After the former owner refused to release them, Annie, Henry, and Caroline ran away with their mother to set up a new home for themselves. As Annie's narrative describes, conditions after the abolition of slavery continued to be oppressive.

While women of all class, racial, and ethnic backgrounds have been restricted by cultural beliefs about female inferiority, black women have carried a twofold burden: they have been judged inferior on the basis of their sex and of their color. That Annie, with the love and support of her mother, was able to create a positive sense of herself and the inner strength to better the conditions of her life is testimony to her strong character and determination. There have been many black women like her.

Soon after being reunited with her mother, Annie, then about seven years old, went to work for a white family as a nursemaid. There she learned to read and write. At the age of twenty she moved to Macon, Georgia and attended high school for a short time. During the next ten years she managed a restaurant, a boardinghouse, and some other small business enterprises.

After marrying at age thirty, Annie worked with her husband in resort hotels. They eventually moved to Boston where Annie enrolled in evening classes at the Franklin Institute. She was then forty-four years old. With the assistance of one of her teachers she wrote *Memories of Childhood's Slavery Days* from which these excerpts are taken.

— 3 —

Annie Louise Burton

The memory of my happy, care-free childhood days on the plantation, with my little white and black companions, is often with me. Neither master nor mistress nor neighbors had time to bestow a thought upon us, for the great Civil War was raging. That great event in American history was a matter wholly outside the realm of our childish interests. Of course we heard our elders discuss the various events of the great struggle, but it meant nothing to us.

On the plantation there were ten white children and fourteen colored children. Our days were spent roaming about from plantation to plantation, not knowing or caring what things were going on in the great world outside our little realm. Planting time and harvest time were happy days for us. How often at the harvest time the planters discovered cornstalks missing from the ends of the rows, and blamed the crows! We were called the "little fairy devils." To the sweet potatoes and peanuts and sugar cane we also helped ourselves.

Those slaves that were not married served the food from the great house, and about half-past eleven they would send the older children with food to the workers in the fields. Of course, I followed, and before we got to the fields, we had eaten the food nearly all up. When the workers returned home they complained, and we were whipped.

The slaves got their allowance every Monday night of molasses, meat,

SOURCE: Annie L. Burton, *Memories of Childhood's Slavery Days* (Boston: Ross Publishing, 1909).

corn meal, and a kind of flour called "dredgings" or "shorts." Perhaps this allowance would be gone before the next Monday night, in which case the slaves would steal hogs and chickens. Then would come the whipping-post. Master himself never whipped his slaves; this was left to the overseer.

We children had no supper, and only a little piece of bread or something of the kind in the morning. Our dishes consisted of one wooden bowl, and oyster shells were our spoons. This bowl served for about fifteen children, and often the dogs and the ducks and the peafowl had a dip in it. Sometimes we had buttermilk and bread in our bowl, sometimes greens or bones.

Our clothes were little homespun cotton slips, with short sleeves. I never knew what shoes were until I got big enough to earn them myself.

If a slave man and woman wished to marry, a party would be arranged some Saturday night among the slaves. The marriage ceremony consisted of the pair jumping over a stick. If no children were born within a year or so, the wife was sold.

At New Year's, if there was any debt or mortgage on the plantation, the extra slaves were taken to Clayton and sold at the court house. In this way families were separated.

When they were getting recruits for the war, we were allowed to go to Clayton to see the soldiers.

I remember, at the beginning of the war, two colored men were hung in Clayton; one, Caesar King, for killing a blood hound and biting off an overseer's ear; the other, Dabney Madison, for the murder of his master. Dabney Madison's master was really shot by a man named Houston, who was infatuated with Madison's mistress, and who had hired Madison to make the bullets for him. Houston escaped after the deed, and the blame fell on Dabney Madison, as he was the only slave of his master and mistress. The clothes of the two victims were hung on two pine trees, and no colored person would touch them. Since I have grown up, I have seen the skeleton of one of these men in the office of a doctor in Clayton.

After the men were hung, the bones were put in an old deserted house. Somebody that cared for the bones used to put them in the sun in bright weather, and back in the house when it rained. Finally the bones disappeared, although the boxes that had contained them still remained.

At one time, when they were building barns on the plantation, one of the big boys got a little brandy and gave us children all a drink, enough to make us drunk. Four doctors were sent for, but nobody could tell what was the matter with us, except they thought we had eaten something poisonous. They wanted to give us some castor oil but we refused to take it, because we thought that the oil was made from the bones of the dead men we had seen. Finally, we told about the big white boy giving us the brandy, and the mystery was cleared up.

Young as I was then, I remember this conversation between master and mistress, on master's return from the gate one day, when he had received the latest news: "William, what is the news from the seat of war?" "A great battle was fought at Bull Run, and the Confederates won," he replied. "Oh, good, good," said mistress, "and what did Jeff Davis say?" "Look out for the blockade. I do not know what the end may be soon," he answered. "What does Jeff Davis mean by that?" she asked. "Sarah Anne, I don't know, unless he means that the niggers will be free." "O, my God, what shall we do?" "I presume," he said, "we shall have to put our boys to work and hire help." "But," she said, "what will the niggers do if they are free? Why, they will starve if we don't keep them." "Oh, well," he said, "let them wander, if they will not stay with their owners. I don't doubt that many owners have been good to their slaves, and they would rather remain with their owners than wander about without home or country."

My mistress often told me that my father was a planter who owned a plantation about two miles from ours. He was a white man, born in Liverpool, England. He died in Lewisville, Alabama, in the year 1875.

I will venture to say that I only saw my father a dozen times, when I was about four years old; and those times I saw him only from a distance, as he was driving by the great house of our plantation. Whenever my mistress saw him going by, she would take me by the hand and run out upon the piazza, and exclaim, "Stop there, I say! Don't you want to see and speak to and caress your darling child? She often speaks of you and wants to embrace her dear father. See what a bright and beautiful daughter she is, a perfect picture of yourself. Well, I declare, you are an affectionate father." I well remember that whenever my mistress would speak thus and upbraid him, he would whip up his horse and get out of sight and hearing as quickly as possible. My mistress's action was, of course, intended to humble and shame my father. I never spoke to him and cannot remember that he ever noticed me, or in any way acknowledged me to be his child.

My mother and my mistress were children together, and grew up to be mothers together. My mother was the cook in my mistress's household. One morning when master had gone to Eufaula, my mother and my mistress got into an argument, the consequence of which was that my mother was whipped, for the first time in her life. Whereupon, my mother refused to do any more work, and ran away from the plantation. For three years we did not see her again.

Our plantation was one of several thousand acres, comprising large level fields, upland, and considerable forests of Southern pine. Cotton, corn, sweet potatoes, sugar cane, wheat, and rye were the principal crops raised on the plantation. It was situated near the P—— River, and about twenty-three miles from Clayton, Ala.

One day my master heard that the Yankees were coming our way, and he immediately made preparations to get his goods and valuables out of their reach. The big six-mule team was brought to the smoke-house door, and loaded with hams and provisions. After being loaded, the team was put in the care of two of the most trustworthy and valuable slaves that my master owned, and driven away. It was master's intention to have these things taken to a swamp, and there concealed in a pit that had recently been made for the purpose. But just before the team left the main road for the by-road that led to the swamp, the two slaves were surprised by the Yankees, who at once took possession of the provisions, and started the team toward Clayton, where the Yankees had head-quarters. The road to Clayton ran past our plantation. One of the slave children happened to look up the road, and saw the Yankees coming, and gave warning. Whereupon, my master left unceremoniously for the woods, and remained concealed there for five days. The niggers had run away whenever they got a chance, but now it was master's and the other white folks' turn to run.

The Yankees rode up to the piazza of the great house and inquired who owned the plantation. They gave orders that nothing must be touched or taken away, as they intended to return shortly and take pos-session. My mistress and the slaves watched for their return day and night for more than a week, but the Yankees did not come back.

One morning in April, 1865, my master got the news that the Yankees had left Mobile Bay and crossed the Confederate lines, and that the Emancipation Proclamation had been signed by President Lincoln. Mis-tress suggested that the slaves should not be told of their freedom; but master said he would tell them, because they would soon find it out, even if he did not tell them. Mistress, however, said she could keep my mother's three children, for my mother had now been gone so long.

All the slaves left the plantation upon the news of their freedom, except those who were feeble or sickly. With the help of these, the crops were gathered. My mistress and her daughters had to go to the kitchen and to the washtub. My little half-brother, Henry, and myself had to gather chips, and help all we could. My sister, Caroline, who was twelve years old, could help in the kitchen.

After the war, the Yankees took all the good mules and horses from the plantation, and left their old army stock. We children chanced to come across one of the Yankees' old horses, that had "U.S." branded on him. We called him "Old Yank" and got him fattened up. One day in August, six of us children took "Old Yank" and went away back on the plantation for watermelons. Coming home, we thought we would make the old horse trot. When "Old Yank" commenced to trot, our big melons dropped off, but we couldn't stop the horse for some time. Finally, one of the big boys went back and got some more melons, and left us eating what we could find of the ones that had been dropped. Then all we six, with our melons, got on "Old Yank" and went home. We also used to hitch "Old Yank" into a wagon and get wood. But one sad day in the fall, the Yankees came back again, and gathered up their old stock, and took "Old Yank" away.

One day mistress sent me out to do some churning under a tree. I went to sleep and jerked the churn over on top of me, and consequently got a whipping.

My mother came for us at the end of the year 1865, and demanded that her children be given up to her. This, mistress refused to do, and threatened to set the dogs on my mother if she did not at once leave the place. My mother went away, and remained with some of the neighbors until supper time. Then she got a boy to tell Caroline to come down to the fence. When she came, my mother told her to go back and get Henry and myself and bring us down to the gap in the fence as quick as she could. Then my mother took Henry in her arms, and my sister carried me on her back. We climbed fences and crossed fields, and after several hours came to a little hut which my mother had secured on a plantation. We had no more than reached the place, and made a little fire, when master's two sons rode up and demanded that the children be returned. My mother refused to give us up. Upon her offering to go with them to the Yankee headquarters to find out if it were really true that all negroes had been made free, the young men left and troubled us no more.

The cabin that was now our home was made of logs. It had one door, and an opening in one wall, with an inside shutter, was the only window. The door was fastened with a latch. Our beds were some straw.

There were six in our little family: my mother, Caroline, Henry, two other children that my mother had brought with her upon her return, and myself.

The man on whose plantation this cabin stood, hired my mother as cook, and gave us this little home. We children used to sell blueberries and plums that we picked. One day the man on whom we depended for our home and support, left. Then my mother did washing by the day, for whatever she could get. We were sent to get cold victuals from hotels and such places. A man wanting hands to pick cotton, my brother Henry and I were set to help in this work. We had to go to the cotton field very early every morning. For this work, we received forty cents for every hundred pounds of cotton we picked.

Caroline was hired out to take care of a baby.

In 1866, another man hired the plantation on which our hut stood, and we moved into Clayton, to a little house my mother secured there. A rich lady came to our house one day, looking for some one to take care of her little daughter. I was taken, and adopted into this family. This rich lady was Mrs. E. M. Williams, a music teacher, the wife of a lawyer. We called her "Mis' Mary."

Some rich people in Clayton who had owned slaves, opened the Methodist church on Sundays, and began the work of teaching the negroes. My new mistress sent me to Sunday school every Sunday morning, and I soon got so that I could read. Mis' Mary taught me every day at her knee. I soon could read nicely, and went through Sterling's Second Reader, and then into McGuthrie's Third Reader. The first piece of poetry I recited in Sunday school was taught to me by Mis' Mary during the week. Mis' Mary's father-in-law, an ex-judge, of Clayton, Alabama, heard me recite it, and thought it was wonderful. It was this:

> I am glad to see you, little bird
> It was your sweet song I heard.
> What was it I heard you say?
> Give me crumbs to eat today?
> Here are crumbs I brought for you.
> Eat your dinner, eat away.
> Come and see us every day.

After this Mis' Mary kept on with my studies, and taught me to write. As I grew older, she taught me to cook and how to do housework. During this time Mis' Mary had given my mother one dollar a month in return for my services; now as I grew up to young womanhood, I thought I would like a little money of my own. Accordingly, Mis' Mary began to pay me four dollars a month, besides giving me my board and clothes. For two summers she "let me out" while she was away, and I got five dollars a month. . . .

Right after the war when my mother had got settled in her hut, with her little brood hovered around her, from which she had been so long absent, we had nothing to eat, and nothing to sleep on save some old pieces of horse-blankets and hay that the soldiers gave her. The first day in the hut was a rainy day; and as night drew near it grew more fierce, and we children had gathered some little fagots to make a fire by the time mother came home, with something for us to eat, such as she had gathered through the day. It was only corn meal and pease and ham-bone and skins which she had for our supper. She had started a little fire, and said, "Some of you close that door," for it was cold. She swung the pot over the fire and filled it with the pease and ham-bone and skins. Then she seated her little brood around the fire on the pieces of blanket, where we watched with all our eyes, our hearts filled with desire, looking to see what she would do next. She took down an old broken earthen bowl, and tossed into it the little meal she had brought, stirring it up with water, making a hoe cake. She said, "One of you draw that griddle out here," and she placed it on the few little coals. Perhaps this griddle you have never seen, or one like it, I will describe it to you. This griddle was a round piece of iron, quite thick, having three legs. It might have been made in a blacksmith's shop, for I have never seen one like it before or since. It was placed upon the coals, and with an old iron spoon she put on this griddle half of the corn meal she had mixed up. She said, "I will put a tin plate over this, and put it away for your breakfast." We five children were eagerly watching the pot boiling, with the pease and ham-bone. The rain was pattering on the roof of the hut. All at once there came a knock at the door. My mother answered the knock. When she opened the door, there stood a white woman and three little children, all dripping with the rain. My mother said, "In the name of the Lord, where are you going on such a night, with these children?"

The woman said, "Auntie, I am travelling. Will you please let me stop here to-night, out of the rain, with my children?" My mother said, "Yes, honey, I ain't got much, but what I have got I will share with you." "God bless you!" They all came in. We children looked in wonder at what had come. But my mother scattered her own little brood and made a place for the forlorn wanderers. She said, "Wait, honey, let me turn over that hoe cake." Then the two women fell to talking, each telling a tale of woe. After a time, my mother called out, "Here, you, Louise, or some one of you, put some fagots under the pot, so these pease can get done." We couldn't put them under fast enough, first one and then another of us children, the mothers still talking. Soon my mother said, "Draw that hoe cake one side, I guess it is done." My mother said to the woman, "Honey, ain't you got no husband?" She said, "No, my husband got killed in the war." My mother replied, "Well, my husband died right after the war. I have been away from my little brood for four years. With a hard struggle, I have got them away from the Farrin plantation, for they did not want to let them go. But I got them. I was determined to have them. But they would not let me have them if they could have kept them. With God's help I will keep them from starving. The white folks are good to me. They give me work, and I know, with God's help, I can get along." The white woman replied, "Yes, Auntie, my husband left me on a rich man's plantation. This man promised to look out for me until my husband came home; but he got killed in the war, and the Yankees have set his negroes free and he said he could not help me any more, and we would have to do the best we could for ourselves. I gave my things to a woman to keep for me until I could find my kinsfolk. They live about fifty miles from here, up in the country. I am on my way there now." My mother said, "How long will it take you to get there?" "About three days, if it don't rain." My mother said, "Ain't you got some way to ride there?" "No, Auntie, there is no way of riding up where my folks live, the place where I am from."

We hoped the talk was most ended, for we were anxiously watching that pot. Pretty soon my mother seemed to realize our existence. She exclaimed, "My Lord! I suppose the little children are nearly starved. Are those pease done, young ones?" She turned and said to the white woman, "Have you-all had anything to eat?" "We stopped at a house about dinner time, but the woman didn't have anything but some bread and butter-milk." My mother said, "Well, honey, I ain't got but a little, but I will divide with you." The woman said, "Thank you, Auntie. You just give my children a little; I can do without it."

Then came the dividing. We all watched with all our eyes to see what the shares would be. My mother broke a mouthful of bread and put it on each of the tin plates. Then she took the old spoon and equally divided the pea soup. We children were seated around the fire with some little wooden spoons. But the wooden spoons didn't quite go round, and some of us had to eat with our fingers. Our share of the meal, however, was so small that we were as hungry when we finished as when we began.

My mother said, "Take that rag and wipe your face and hands, and give it to the others, and let them use it, too. Put those plates upon the table." We immediately obeyed orders, and took our seats again around the fire. "One of you go and pull that straw out of the corner and get ready to go to bed." We all lay down on the straw, the white children with us, and my mother covered us over with the blanket. We were soon in the "Land of Nod," forgetting our empty stomachs. The two mothers still continued to talk, sitting down on the only seats, a couple of blocks. A little back against the wall my mother and the white woman slept.

Bright and early in the morning we were called up, and the rest of the hoe cake was eaten for breakfast, with a little meat, some coffee sweetened with molasses. The little wanderers and their mother shared our meal, and then they started again on their journey towards their home among their kinsfolk, and we never saw them again. My mother said, "God bless you! I wish you all good luck. I hope you will reach your home safely." Then mother said to us, "You young ones put away that straw and sweep up the place, because I have to go to my work." But she came at noon and brought us a nice dinner, more satisfactory than the supper and breakfast we had had. We children were delighted that there were no little white children to share our meal this time....

F or some girls childhood, in comparison with later stages in life, has been a time for enjoying the greatest amount of freedom. Through a broad range of activities and behavior they have stretched prevailing definitions of how female children ought to behave.

Adelaide French, the author of the following document, is one such example. When she began writing her diary in 1890 at the age of eleven, Adelaide and her family lived on a ranch in Valverde, Colorado, an area that is now part of Denver. In 1890, however, Valverde was a small community of 400 people at the end of the streetcar line on the outskirts of the city. Adelaide's father commuted to Denver daily to run a real estate business.

Adelaide was the oldest child and only daughter in the French family. Her brothers, who are mentioned frequently in her diary, ranged in age from ten to three. Frank was about one year younger and Dick two years younger than Adelaide. Sid was seven and the baby, George, age three when the diary opened.

In this rural setting Adelaide spent much of her time in outdoor activities — jumping on haystacks, swinging in hammocks, engaging in snowball fights, walking to and from the schoolhouse. There appear to have been few restrictions on her behavior compared with those placed on Anna Green Winslow and Caroline Cowles Richards. Adelaide herself relished her freedom to move around and commented in her diary, "I should not like to live in town much, because you must be prim and proper for if you were not, people would be shocked."

Although the older children helped with chores around the ranch, their responsibilities were light. The Frenches hired help to take charge of the heavy work involved with raising cattle and horses and inside the house. The children's activities at home were not rigidly defined on the basis of sex. Dick attempted to mend his own trousers, and Frank sewed his own watch pocket. Adelaide tried to start the kitchen fire one morning after the boys' effort failed, and George played with a paper doll that Adelaide had given to him. With her girl friends, Adelaide played with and dressed her dolls — but she had her own penknife too.

Yet, it is also clear that certain responsibilities fell to Adelaide because she was the only girl in the family. She was expected to take care of her younger brothers and help with small housekeeping tasks. Certain chores, such as washing dishes, were definitely considered women's work.

Outside of their family, school provided the major source of social contact for Adelaide and her brothers, offering an opportunity for amusement as well as learning. The informality of schooling in this setting is revealed in many ways. Mothers frequently sent younger children to school with older brothers and sisters; the curriculum was less structured, and the children did not know that the school term was finished for the year until recess of the last day. Adelaide would enroll in high school when she, her parents, and her teacher felt that she was ready to go.

As a young woman Adelaide taught school for a few years but did not enjoy the experience. Supported by family income, she traveled extensively and spent a considerable amount of time in volunteer community work and women's club activities throughout her life. She never married. Adelaide French died in Denver in 1974 at the age of ninety-six.

—— 4 ——
Adelaide A. French

FEBRUARY 9, 1890. June stayed all night last night. This morning we played in bed quite a while before we got up. then after we ate our breakfast, we played on the old hay racks, made the beds for Mamma then went down to the brook. had lots of fun running around on steep places, and jumping around. We then ate raw turnips, cold fried pork, bread and butter, some cookies and eggs. When June went in [returned to Denver], Mamma gave her a piece of the umbrella plant. June also left a hatpin, and a little gold-beaded-pin....

SOURCE: Excerpted by permission from the diary of Adelaide A. French, 1890, Adelaide A. French Collection, Western History Department, Denver Public Library.

FEBRUARY 10. This morning when we started to school, it was [so] warm, and clear that Sid took his jacket. Frank and Dick took nothing and I took my cape. But about noon the wind began to blow, so when Willie went to town, Mamma sent us some extra things, and soon after it grew colder and began to snow so near four o'clock she sent Pete over with the big ranch-wagon and a pair of horses to bring us home. I lost my little pen-knife yesterday. Doctor Wheeler was out here when we got home. Mama says Mrs. Morris is sick.

FEBRUARY 11. This morning I was up before six o'clock. I went out in the kitchen and found Frank and Dick trying to start the fire, before the[y] began milking, but the wood was wet and they could not do much with it, then I tried but succeeded no better than the boys. So when the boys got through milking, I went over to the Morris' to get warm. when we went in Laura popped her head out of the door, and told us to come in there, so we went in and were showed Mrs. Morris' baby. it is a little girl. They have named it "Musadora." The roof leaked on the boys beds so, that Frank, Dick and Sid are going to sleep in my room, and I am going to sleep with Miss Benneson.

FEBRUARY 12. The girls, or some of them, are going skating this evening at the lake if the ice is strong enough. I did not sleep with Miss Benneson last night, but in a little cot-bed, at the foot of Miss Benneson's bed, and I am going to sleep there again to-night. When I get home from school, I go in and visit Mrs. Morris, until about dinner-time. I am going to take a book into her to-morrow, so I can read to her. The snow is melting a little, so as to make the roads muddy in some places. Mamma finished George's new dress today, so he put it on but before he had worn it two hours, he had got a grease spot on it.

FEBRUARY 13. The Willets came out here the afternoon and stayed to dinner. Tomorrow will be St. Valentine's day and Mamma got some Valentines for us to give away. I did not go in to see Mrs. Morris to-day because the Willets came out. June, George, and I ate at the little table. June and I had lots of fun together. . . .

FEBRUARY 14. I gave three Valentines away to-day, one to Carlos Hall, one to George Ashton, and one to Eva Holford [a]nd received three, one from Edith Ashton, one from George Ashton, and I think that the other was from the little Hardy Children. I went over to visit Mrs. Morris, and took one of Miss Alcott's books and read a story out of it to Mrs. Morris, and the little baby began to cry when I was over there, so Mrs. Morris let me take it up, hold it and rock it. Lyla Kyte, Carrie Kyte, Edith Ashton, and some of the other school children went skating last night on our lake and several of the boys went in once or twice, about up to their knees, but Carrie Kyte was the only girl that went, and she only ran the toe of her skate into the ice a little bit.

FEBRUARY 15. Mamma says I must write Goodnight [and] finish in the morning, but I don't want to do that very [much] and It makes me cry. . . . Edith, George, and Edwin came up here yesterday and we snow balled. Sam, Peter, and Willie and Pete snow-balled back. Such fun as we did have! such running, dodging, laughing and what a hard time we did have when Willie got our basket (a bushel basket) which contained our snow balls. And when Pete got after Frank, Edith, George and I, how we did have to run up one side of the stack and down the other. Even then I got some snow down my neck. Edith lost her cap, somewhere on the straw-stack.

FEBRUARY 16. Mamma Papa and George went in town to-day in the big carriage and brought Miss Williams out to dinner.... Mrs. Morris was sick, worse this afternoon so Mamma took Miss Williams in[. S]he called for Doctor Wheeler but he was not in, ...

FEBRUARY 17. We walked to school and home again. I found Edith's cap (the one she lost on the strawstack Saturday) this evening when I went down to hunt for eggs. I got two valentines to-day[. O]ne was a cute little book called "Woodland Voices by Wordsworth" the other was a lovely card, and a box of paper and envelopes. The paper was very pretty[. I]t had two little birds sitting on one fourth of the paper[. T]hey were purple, on another one gray, on a third pink, and on the last (but not least) light blue. I think the book was from Cousin Emilie, and the others from Miss Phillips. Delia has ha[d] a very bad headache and toothache, which makes her almost crazy.

FEBRUARY 18. My "Youths Companion" did not come tonight as usal. Mrs. Morris got a nurse yesterday. Madge McDowell and Lottie Bennett have made an alphabet so that they can write notes to each other without any one else being able to read it. But Edith found our alphabet and theirs right under it so she copied it and now we can read theirs if we can only get hold of theirs. thus $-+X\mathbb{L}$ means dear.

FEBRUARY 19. My Youths Companion did not come to-day. Richard was very naught[y] in school to-day. he began it by pulling my apronstrings, and when I succeeded in getting them away from him and tied them around in the front Miss McClure made him untie them though he did not want to at first. Mamma went to Mrs. Herbert Hutchings funeral to-day. Mrs. Morris had a little fever this evening, and Morris is not feeling very well. The horse medicine (for the horse distemper) is gone. The Cosmopolotian came. We have to learn the Star-spangled Banner at school, so I am cop[y]ing the words for us.

FEBRUARY 20. My Youths Companion did not come to-day. Edith Ashton is playing that she is a man and I am playing that I am a lady. Mamma sent me over to the Morris' this evening, and as the boys were with me I summoned up courage enough to stay a little while. We have our exercises tomorrow for George Washington's birthday, as it comes on Saturday. Miss Benneson has been helping the boys (Frank and Dick) with their examples in Arithmetic. Madge and Lottie Bennett are geting another alphebet, up and as Madge sits in front of me I can copy a very little by looking over her shoulder....

FEBRUARY 23. Today was Laura's birthday, and she was eighteen years old and I gave her such a whipping she said I made her back sore and blistered it. But I guess she exaggerated it a little bit. ... The Willets were out here to-day[. W]e teased Mrs. Willets to let June stay all night but she would not let her. The wind is blowing, and sounds very dreary indeed.

FEBRUARY 24. Miss Benneson came out to-night. My "Youth's Companion" came for last week, from the looks (it's very much torn and very dirty) I should think it some body had got it by mistake, where there were nine or ten children and kept it until each one had read it through several times. The "Harpers Bazar," "Harpers Magazine" and the "Scribners" [came.] Mamma got Frank, Dick Sid and George a pair of shoes to-day....

FEBRUARY 25. It was very cold this morning when we started to school [. T]his morning the thermometer was seven degrees above zero. When we started I had my cape over my head, but after a little while Sidney began crying with the cold, so I let him have my cape over his head and even then he said his ears were cold, so I took his head and made him lean against my hip, and with one hand I carried my things[. T]he other held his head and I guided him. It was so cold this afternoon in school, some of the girls (of which I was one) had their cloaks on and Miss McClure had her shawl on. Mrs. Morris is very, very sick. They are afraid that she will not live.

FEBRUARY 26. This morning when we started to school it was two above zero,... Mamma went to town to-day, so when it came near time to send for us, if they should send[,] Miss Benneson sent Will over after us. Mrs. Morris is a little better, Mamma says. Mrs. Morris Mother came this morning. We play proverbs this way. We make as many little dashes, (like this —) as there are letters in the proverb, then mark off words, by a line like this / . It is storming.

FEBRUARY 27.... Papa went out to look at the thermometer about quarter past eight, and said it [was] four below zero. Nice weather for making ice for skating, but it don't help me for I have no skates and don't know how to skate. At school this noon, some of the girls fixed up their cloaks for dolls. [W]hen the boys saw them, they (the boys) did the same.

FEBRUARY 28. Mrs. Morris is very much worse. The girls, or some of them went skating last night, but did not stay long. The men have to wash their dishes,... because they have no girl, but they expect one to-morrow morning. The horses are getting over the distemper very well indeed.... We got fifteen eggs, to-day. We found that some or all of the potatoes were frozen. Dick is sitting up in his night gown to mend his trousers. I am afraid he will make a bad job of it.

MARCH 1. Mrs. Morris is dead. She died about five o'clock. Mr. Morris feels dreadfully about it, and I should think he would. Mamma had to help lay her out. A new girl came this morning, her name is Bessie, but she she won't stay. Mrs. Ashton came up this evening, and is up yet, I believe. The boys went skating this after-noon. Mamma had the doctor look at Sidney's eyes while he (the doctor) was here. Mamma and I both have colds....

MARCH 2. Mrs. Morris' funeral is to be to-morrow. She is to be buried at Golden. Oh my! I can scarcely realize that Mrs. M. is dead. I saw her this evening in the casket. She [looked] very natural indeed. But oh how pale and yellow. I don't beleive I shall ever forget it. they had some lovely flowers. They don't know who will take the baby. They have changed its name, from Musa Dora, to Musa Dillie. Mrs. Morris' name was Dillie. Bessie left to-day....

MARCH 4. ... Papa got Frank a watch to-day, and when Dick has the money, Papa will let him have one just like Frank's. I ironed all of the handkerchiefs for Delia, to-day. My Youth's Companion came to-night, and is more than usually interesting. Miss Benneson came out to-night. Frank is trying to make a watch-pocket for his watch, as Mamma is sick, and very tired.

MARCH 5. ... I took my baby-doll to school to-day. her name is Lilly. Frances is going to take her doll to-morrow. ... Frank, Dick, Sid and I tried to see who could get the most words out of "Constantinople." I got one hundred and two[.] I think I could get more. I don't know how many the others got. Mr. Morris started to-day with Musa Dillie, to take her to his Aunt....

MARCH 6. June Willits came out to-day, and I wanted her to stay all night and sleep with me, but her mother would not let her, which made me mad, but not so very mad. Frances Ogilvie said her father and her little brother, Rob, are coming, and will arrive to-morrow morning. I took my doll to school to-day, and she took hers. Miss Whittlesey was sick, so at noon she excused all the scholars in her room, then she went home herself. Papa told Frank not to [illeg.] the regulator of his watch but he did and the penalty is that he can't have it for two days. Frank don't like it. Had plenty of fun this eve!

MARCH 7. ... Alfred Walters walked part way home from school with Lyla, this afternoon. He teased, us, and plagued us, and Lyla said "he was a horrid boy." We got thirty eggs to-day....

MARCH 8. To-day has been a very busy day for all of us, and Mamma is about sick, while I am very tired. I gave George, the older of my two paper dolls, and he takes great delight, in putting on the different hats, dresses, capes, aprons, and jackets, of which it has quite a number. Miss Benneson did not come out to-night, (when we need her most she stays in town).... Grace, (the colt,) is a little sick, she will not eat, at all. Papa gave Dick his watch and Frank received his also, the two days having expired....

MARCH 9. The school-house is burned. We saw the flames, Sam said that he saw the cover of Sid's book, but Sid has his book at home. Sid lost a slate and some pencils, Dick, his reader, slate, paper, pen, pencils, and copy-book, Frank his reader, Arithmetic, Geography, and writing book, while I lost my Reader, Arithmetic, Language, Mental Arithmetic, Geography, copy-book and Spelling blank.... Mr. and Mrs. Alexander, with Lucy and their little boy came out to-day. Lucy and I had lots of fun, on the straw-stack....

MARCH 10. They shot poor old Ben [a horse] to-day. Franklin and I washed all of the men's break-fast and dinner things, also the milk-things, or rather Frank wiped the things, and I washed them. I skimmed the milk, to-day for Mamma. I made some molasses candy this after-noon, by cousin Emelie's receipt [recipe], which is real good. Mamma has got a girl engaged for the other side, who is to come to-morrow morning.... We don't have school until about a week, the teachers don't know exactly when or where we are going to have it, but they say they'll let us know in time. I have a loose tooth.

MARCH 11. Mamma got a girl, (or rather she was a woman, for she had gray in her hair) for the other side, but I don't think she will stay long, as she is, or seems a little superstitious, and won't sleep in the room where Mrs. Morris died, or even in the next room, unless some one of the men sleep in the little room. so Mr. Morris says he is going to have Andy sleep there to-night. Miss Benneson came out, and we made some molasses candy but it did not get boiled quite enough, therefore, it is quite soft. Mamma made a pair of stockings for my doll out of a pair of hers....

MARCH 12. Mamma and Papa went into the Willets this evening. I am just full of "The very old Nick" to-night, cutting up, and teasing most every body....

□

JUNE 1. June and I had a nice ride on her tricycle this morning before breakfast. After breakfast we went up in the attic, and while one swung in the hammock, the other swung in the swing. I should not like to live in town much, because you must be prim and proper for if you were not, people would be shocked. The Willets brought me out after dinner, and as some of the ice cream was left, we each had a saucerful.... Coming home I saw 22 people with white dresses on.

JUNE 5. Papa, Mamma, Cathie, Frank and Dick went to the races to-day.... They all enjoyed it. Bismark won his race. Sidney, George and I went down to Ashton's where we had lots of fun by dressing up with hop vines, roses and evening lilly. George and Sid rode home with Susie, but I stayed a little longer and walked. The Ashton's 2 kittens have disappeared and are not to be found. Their black cat was walking by the new building by the railroad when Mr. Parker shot at her, but didn't hurt her much.

JUNE 6. To-day was the last day of school, though we didn't know it until after recess, and we did not have any visitors or have a chance to get dressed up, or fix the school-house, just rehearsed and came home. Not any fun....

JUNE 10. ... I washed 12 handkerchiefs this morning to get the starch out but did not succeed very well. I trimmed the edge of some embroidery Mamma got to trim my dress with, and varnished the little table and washstand over at Mrs. Crabtree's. Mamma went to town this afternoon, and while away, got lovely wild roses and red cypress. This evening I was see-sawing with Sidney. and was down while he was up when he leaned forward very suddenly and crashed the board. . . .

JUNE 15. To-day is June's birthday. Mr., Mrs., and June Willets came out to dinner. Mamma gave June a pin with a little bead on it, and I gave her the picture and frame with rice on it gilded. We had lots of fun. After dinner June and I had a swing in Papa's swing chair, then we seesawed and had lots of fun bumping, and coming near being pitched off. June said she wasn't going out doors, but was going to stay in the house and behave like a young lady 16 yrs old. It was hard getting her out, but when she was out, she was, — well she was out. . . .

JUNE 21. . . . Mamma went to town for about [illeg.] hours this morning, and while there, bought some satin for a dress for me. She did not get the peacock blue, for it didnot look pretty in the piece, but an electric blue with [illeg.] white figures, which is very pretty. Papa got home quite early and did some irragating. . . .

JUNE 22. To-day is my birthday. I am 12 years old, and guess I am the happiest girl alive. This morning when I awoke I heard the boys voices and thought I would try to get up before they knew it, but pretty soon Dick came in with a penknife. [T]hen came Sid with a blue Autograph Album and then George with some light blue ribbon and said Mamma and Papa wished to see me when I got dressed. My present from Mamma was my dress she got yesterday and I like it very much. from Papa a breast pin (solid silver) of 4 little birds. Bennie [Miss Benneson] sent a collar for me. Frank gave me a pin to fasten my hair with. The Willits came out and June gave me a lovely little bowl, plate and jug. They are very nice.

□

SEPTEMBER 2. Frank, Dick and I went to school to-day. There are quite a lot of scholars that came last term but did not come this. We have 3 new scholars 1 girl and 2 boys. . . . Edith Ashton started in the high school to-day but as she came home this afternoon she came up with me. I wonder if I shall be ready for High school next term — I'm afraid not. Lyla Kyte and I have one seat to gether but [it] is a very big one. The boys need some new books. I have just lots of books to carry, and have not got straightened out yet.

SEPTEMBER 4. We got to school about one hour before school began. Miss McClure had not got there but John Dodg and Bert Mills were there and they rang the bell, whistled and made a dreadful racket, then they locked the door but opened it when Miss McClure came. . . . We had some fun in German Class. Mr. Ripley came and took our books home but I walked as Edith Ashton was there. Mamma and Papa went out to the big pasture this after-noon.

SEPTEMBER 5. Mamma, Papa and Dick went up to Loveland this morning, so we took Georgie to school with us. Mr. Ripley took us over and came for us when school was done. We took Miss McClure home then went for Bennie and she came. Georgie was very good. After we got home he got hurt on his gums but he was very good. He had just gone to bed. Bennie is *so* peticular. It made me cry trying to get George to bed, (we were getting along all right) she pulled him out of his chair and hurt his head, and then did not seem to mind it, but walked away. It just made me cry. I don't know what's the matter. I feel lonely. I think "Gentleness is better than force."

SEPTEMBER 6. Mamma, Papa and Dick got home this evening. They had a lovely time. Dick was up at 1/2 past 12 last night hunting for his clothes, for he wanted to [illeg.] the boys milk. Georgie has been sick today but is better now.... I am so glad Mamma is home for now I don't have all the responsibility on my shoulders. . . .

SEPTEMBER 10. After I got to school this morning I sat down against the wood-shed and took a sun-bath.... I could not get the 31st example at school but I got it this evening. I did not get my Geography very well to-day but intend to do better to-morrow. Minnie asked me to bring my doll to-morrow and I guess I will take Lily. Doctor Lamb was out, and intended dehorning the bulls but the saw snapped so he had to give it up.

SEPTEMBER 11. Doctor Lamb came out this afternoon and dehorned Odeecodee, Mountain Boy, and Pansy Boy. Now, Mamma feels safer. I took my doll, Lily to school with me this morning and Minnie, Grace, and Ollie each brought a doll.... The boys teased us about our dolls and took Ollie's doll once but Miss McClure rescued it. then they took mine and Miss McClure got it then they got it again and Miss McClure got it and put it away. . . .

SEPTEMBER 12. Eva Holford brought her doll to school and I took Lily and a little rag-doll which I gave to Herbert Millington when he got Eva's doll. Now some of the other boys want me to make them dolls and Frank, Dick and Georgie want me to make them each one. The girls played "Pullaway!" on their own side to day, for the boys are so rough.... Mamma made grape jelly to-day and got 7 glasses out of less than a basket of grapes.

SEPTEMBER 13. Mamma went [to] town to-day and took Sid with her. Sid stayed at Willets. Georgie and I went down to Ashton's this afternoon and Edwin, Arthur and Harry Ashton came up to see the boys. Edith still likes High School and Lyla Kyte is going to start on Monday. This morning I made George a rag doll which he named Nelle Grace, and took down to Ashton's with him this afternoon.

□

SEPTEMBER 17. ... School went on about as usual to-day but I missed 1 word it was Wallace. I spelled it: Wallece which is wrong. We ate our lunch on the hill. 3 of the boys followed us up and ate their lunch there and kept plaguing us girls. Mr. Ripley brought me home with Gypsey. She goes real nicely. Papa had the dogs put up.... Lilly Roeschlaub brought her little brother, Jesse to school to-day.

SEPTEMBER 18. Miss McClure changed my seat to-day, to the long seat where Franklin sits. We played Pullaway, to-day. It rained a little this afternoon. Papa got a telegram for him to start east and he has to start to-morrow evening. Mamma is feeling so badly she is crying over it, So I must try to comfort her, but I can't do any good I'm afraid. I sent my doll in Saturday to be mended and got her home this evening. . . .

SEPTEMBER 26. Mr. Ripley took us to school this morning with the ranch buggy. We had lots of fun at school to-day. Edwin Ashton brought his rope and at noon the boys got on their side of the walk and took hold of one end of the rope while the girls got on their side and got hold of the other end of the rope and pulled and the girls came out ahead, then we just shouted and Miss McClure stood in the doorway and laughed. We got a letter from Papa this evening. . . .

NOVEMBER 11. We have a new school teacher, her name is Miss Hansen. She wears glasses. I think that the scholars will mind her. I like her pretty well. Mamma and Papa came home by the new school-house and got out and went in. Dick had to stay in after school, and so did Leo Shupe and George Ashton. . . . Miss Hansen does not teach German therefore the german class will have to skip it, for a little while at least.

NOVEMBER 12. This morning when we got to school we found we had 25 minutes till school so Mr. Ripley and I drove up to Miss McClure's to see how she was and she said she was better. . . . Bennie came out this evening. I made a little candy-box this evening, Frank and Dick are working bookmarks. Bennie and Papa are partners and Mamma and Lalla are partners and all are playing cribbage. When Georgie crys either Mamma or Lalla goes into him so I am kind of a substitute [in] her place.

NOVEMBER 13. We got to school this morning before Miss Hansen. At noon we children had just lots of fun the girls and boys snowballing each other and trying to wash each others faces. We, that is the girls and myself, washing some of the boy' faces. I didn't get my face washed once though I came pretty near it. . . .

NOVEMBER 19. This has been a very eventful day. . . . At school there was trouble also for Miss McClure was sick so Miss Hansen taught to-day. The boys threw gravel, rolled marbles and whispered. Miss Hansen could not manage them. At noon she whipped Joe Roeschlaub. At last she sent for Mr. Asenour. He came and brought Miss McClure. They sent away all those who would not come in school. There are 11 girls and 7 boys in school. June came out with Papa to-night and is going to school with me to-morrow.

NOVEMBER 20. June came to school with us to-day. As Carlos was absent (I believe the boys say he is sick) June sat in his seat and we had just lots of fun. She has been just overwhelmed with questions regarding her things, such as: "How many bracelets have you?" "How do you keep your hair braided?" "What do you call that?" etc. Miss McClure was there to-day. She made the boys that played truant yesterday say they were sorry and etc. We tried to get in the school-house to see how it was getting on but could not as all the outside doors and windows were locked.

NOVEMBER 21. June had to go home this morning and as we were going to school at the very same time we rode over to school with her. Mr.

Ripley took her to the cable cars. Just after I got to school I stood at the stove to get warm but got too near and burned my dress in two places. At noon Grace and I tied our feet together and tried to run but we fell down and I fell undermost, on my knee, and this afternoon I had a toothache....

NOVEMBER 28. This morning I washed 15 pieces [of] doll clothes, little cradle spreads, and a couple of my aprons. Right after lunch Frank went down to Ashton's and I went down to Kyte's. Lyla and Carrie had company, and had gone up the track, so I walked up there and walked around with them and had lots of fun and then came home. I put my room to rights and fixed it up generally. Mamma made some of her salve to-day....

NOVEMBER 29. I went to town to-day. Mr. Ripley took me to the cars with Captain. I just caught the Electric. I got to town before Mamma. When she did come, we walked down to a shoe store to look for some slippers that were advertised, but what she wanted were all gone. We then got some ginger snaps for lunch, ate them at the office, went up to Doctor Wheeler's then up to see Mrs. Rickard and Amy, but Amy wasn't at home so we visited Mrs. Rickard who was sick abed. then we went to call on Mrs. Hart but she wasn't at home then to Willits and they were absent, so I came on the Cable and Electric and walked to Ashton's and after Papa got home Will came down for me.

NOVEMBER 30. This morning I ironed my doll's clothes. Mamma, Papa, Lalla, Sid, and Georgie went to ride this morning, but I stayed at home. They have put a flag upon the pole on top of the new school-house. I don't know as it's finished, but I hope so. When we went to gather the eggs we saw a large rat in the hen house. I suppose it carries off the eggs. We also found a dead pig in the pen but don't know what killed it. I climed up in the hay loft to play with the little kittens. Their mother was with them and let me pat her....

DECEMBER 2. The new school-house will not be ready until next Monday, Mr. Dodge says.... Mamma went to town to-day. I[n] school Miss McClure asked me to stay after school and look over a piece for the boys. But she happened to have to keep quite a number of children in, so I waited, and waited and at last all but Murry Bennett was left. then I went in. I told her I had been waiting and as I was nervous, began to cry. Then she hugged me and kissed me, and I thought she was getting nervous too. Will left to-day....

DECEMBER 5. It snowed last night but though it was not much, it did not melt for the [sun] did not come out once to-day. It was rather cold so the boys did not play marbles but played Pullaway. We played at recess this A.M. noon and recess this afternoon. It was lots of fun. I worked the 6 and 7 examples in partial payments to-day. We are expected to go in the new school-house Monday. This evening I spoke my piece for Papa. It is still snowing and I hope there will be quite a lot by to-morrow morning....

DECEMBER 15. It has been very windy to-day and the new ice-house in Manchester got blown down. Mamma went to town to-day.... The churn broke down to-day. I do so try to be good and I do my best, but it seems as though I never could succeed. I expect I have been lazy, but I *do* try to be good.

I f children are growing up faster these days, a phenomenon often linked to the pervasive influence of the mass media, then females may be feeling some of the pressures of adolescence at an earlier age. The evidence from a diary written by a girl growing up in the 1960s indicates that this may well be the case.

The diary begins in 1963 when the author, Valerie Jane Christie, was seven years old and ends in 1965 when she was ten. Like Adelaide French, Valerie grew up in Colorado, although the environment that she describes is very different from Adelaide's world. Valerie's family lived in a suburb of Denver, and in many ways her experiences typified those of girls from affluent families who grew up in suburban surroundings across the country in the 1960s and 1970s. The material circumstances of her childhood were comfortable, and her requests for toys, clothes, records, and jewelry were fulfilled, as can be seen in the description of her birthday presents and in her account of a visit to her father's office to ask for spending money for an afternoon's shopping.

Valerie grew up the youngest of three children. She has a sister, one of the coauthors of this book, and a brother, ten and eight years older respectively. Although she made a few references to family activities, most of her diary focuses on relations and incidents with her peers. Their interactions and activities defined a special world apart from her home, one filled with its own intrigues and adventures. The powerful role of age-peers in determining how children learn what is expected of them as boys and girls is vividly illustrated in the excerpts that follow. Valerie and her girl friends spent the night at one another's houses, celebrated birthdays, shopped, and saw movies together. Boys and girls attended the same classes, played softball, and drenched one another in water fights.

With respect to her behavior around boys, Valerie demonstrated contradictory impulses. On the one hand, she relished competing with them as an equal in class and in sports activities. She expressed pride in her "tomboy" skills, challenged boys to softball hitting contests, and considered giving a "pounding" to one who annoyed her. At the same time she worried about her appearance and popularity with boys and contrived situations where she could talk and flirt with her "boyfriend" Bart. She measured herself against another girl who was vying for Bart's attention, in terms of her looks, sense of humor, and charm.

There are dramatic changes in Valerie's attitudes and ways of expressing her interest in boys as the diary progresses. By age ten she was eagerly anticipating her first boy-girl party and wondering about what making out would be like.

The onset of puberty, used to mark the boundary between childhood and adolescence, occurs earlier today. The age at menarche has declined steadily in the last one hundred years, for reasons to be explained in the next chapter. Valerie expresses her mixed reaction to the arrival of her first period when she is ten, concluding that on balance the experience has made her feel even more grown-up.

After graduation from high school and college in Colorado, Valerie moved to Boston to attend law school. She graduated in 1980 and plans to practice law in Denver. She is also contemplating marriage in the near future — although the young man's name is not Bart.

—— 5 ——
Valerie Jane Christie

JANUARY 13, 1963. Dear Diary, Today was Barts birthday. He was nine years old. Instead of spanking him I felt like kissing him.

Change!!! I hate his guts. [added later]

JANUARY 18. Dear Diary, Today was D'Anne's birthday. She had me eat dinner with her. That night we went to play Bingo and I won $3.50¢. That was not very much but it was something. When we got home we were tired so we went to bed. And we giggled all night.

JANUARY 19. Dear Diary, Today was Barbara ———— and Paula's birthday, and I went to Barbara's party.

JANUARY 25. Dear Diary, Today I had Jan spend the night. We had so much fun. We twisted to crazy records til after 1200 o'clock and we knitted for a wayle. Finally we went to bed[. I]n the morning we woke up early and we jumped on beds and broke both of the beds but we got them fixed and went up stairs for breakfast. thankgoodness no one found out.

JANUARY 26. Dear Diary, Today was my fathers birthday.

JANUARY 27. Dear Diary, Today was the day after my father's birthday.

FEBRUARY 2. Dear Diary, I'm very sad the groundhog saw his shadow so that means no spring until March 23, Boo-Boo.

FEBRUARY 14. Dear Diary, Today was Valentines day. At school we watched a film on Disney land and had a party.

MARCH 7. Dear Diary, Today i was sick. It is not very fun. When I heard we had a speed test I was about to cry. I can't think of anything more to tell so good night.

SOURCE: Excerpted from the diary of Valerie Jane Christie, 1963–1965, by permission of the author. Copyright © 1981 by Valerie Jane Christie.

Valerie Jane Christie

MARCH 8. Dear Diary, Mrs. Flinstone and Mrs. Benter both got a baby. Mrs. Benter called her baby Caora and Mrs. Flinstone called her baby Pebbles.

MARCH 11. Dear Diary, Today is the day before my birthday. Tonight we had sptgitty for dinner. D'Anne ate dinner with us today. I got my presents early and this is what I got, leartedds [leotards], a new blouse, a diary, and a dress for Barbie [her doll]. It was also Beacky's... birthday. And Miss Esheshlman left to teach her own class. Boo Who.

MARCH 12. Dear Diary, Today was my birthday. I got many knew thing[s]. her are some — a new braclet, a pink beautiful blanket, a new neaklece, a stationary, a nee sweater, 4 new head bands, a new ring, a lauerandry basket, and a barbie dress.

MARCH 16. Dear Diary, Today I learned Pearl stitch, bind off. How to brotder [embroider]. I finish[ed] Pee Wee's [a stuffed animal] blanket. Now I am starting Timothy's [her dog] and Pee Wee's sweter.

MARCH 17. Dear Diary, Today was saint Pactroc's day. Boo Who we didant get to pinch each other because it was on a Sunday.

MARCH 27. Dear Diary, To day my girlfriend told me a joke and hears how it gos: I'm a little tea pot short and stout, hear is my handall and hear is my spout. I'm a little tea pot short a spout, hear is my handle, oh Hell, I'm a sugar bowl! Good-By.

MARCH 28. Dear Diary, Today I made a diorama for school. I hope It will be in the exabit.

MARCH 31. Tooth out can't write

APRIL 1. Tooth out cant write

APRIL 2. Boy that tooth was a bumb. And it was a moler.

APRIL 3. Dear Diary, We had 3 false airraids today and I had to run in the closet.

JUNE 6. Dear Diary, Today many things happened. first of all we got out of school and got our report cards and this is what I got 6 A's and 1 B. Second of all we or rather I should say Kathy & Rita & Susan & I went over to High school and ran relays against other schools. Darnit I didn't win. Well By By.

[No entries all summer]

SEPTEMBER 4. Dear Diary, Ick Ick Ick Ick. Today school started (uhg) I almost barfe because I don't like school very much. I have this teacher and her name is Mrs. Frandsen.

Change I like school! [added later]

SEPTEMBER 26. Dear Diary, Today was Timothy my dog's birthday.

OCTOBER 8. Dear Diary, Boy was I mad today. In school my old slip tore. I couldent read.

OCTOBER 31. Dear Diary, Today was Hallowenne. D'Anne was Ragedie Andy & I was Ragdie Ann.

NOVEMBER 1. Dear Diary, Today I & D'Ann & Magret & Cindy & Judy & Toni were elected for flag patrol.

NOVEMBER 2. Dear Diary, The very first day on flag patrol we got the flag up sighdown. Gulp.

NOVEMBER 22. Dear Diary, President Kenedy got shot in the head. President Kennedy died today. Toni, Susan, Jan were crying today and we had to lower the flag at half mast.

[No diary for 1964]

JANUARY 2, 1965. Dear Diary, I have to make a dam for school. It's due the 4 of this month. I'd better get busy.

JANUARY 3. Dear Diary, Today I made my dam and when I was done I went and played with Rhonda.... (that creep)....

JANUARY 5. Dear Diary, Nothing happened except D'Anne I think started her periods.

(nope) [added later]

I'm glad! [added later]

JANUARY 6. Dear Diary, Today in P.E. we played kickball. I smacked a homerun (almost) I smacked one almost as high as Jim Klingenmere which is pretty good.

JANUARY 15. Today was D'An's birthday. she asked me to her slumber party but my shitty parents would not let me go. Paula, me or Kathy ——— could go.

JANUARY 23. Dear D. Today was Bart's birthday. I love him very much.

JANUARY 25. Dear Diary, Today when I went to Jimmy's ——— he taught me this secret language where you say "oung" after every consonant & you say every vowel like vong o uong e rone i e. (Valerie) Just some of the boys know the language. I was the first girl to know it. Jimmy said "I only teach it to my good friends." Love Valerie

JANUARY 26. Dear Diary, Today was Dad's birthday. As usual his line this year was "Don't worry 'bout me, just a pair of sox." Then when he sees all his presents he says... damn! Why did you do this?" Our reply, "Because we love you, now shut up & open your gifts! Love, Val

FEBRUARY 2. Dear D. Today I was eating in the cafeteria & Bart made his sign to call me (cleared his throat) & I turned around and he smiled at me. I almost fainted. I love him.

FEBRUARY 3. Dear Diary: Tonight I went to Jean's house for a birthday dinner party. We played "Murder in the dark." When I got murdered I screamed under my breath *"Rape Rape Rape"* instead of "Murder, Murder." Rhonda called me & told me about some ideas she had about a boy-girl (M.O.) [make-out] party for Valentine's party. Sounds like a good, Good, Good idea. Love, Val

FEBRUARY 14. Today was Valentines Day. I got a valentine from Bart. It showed an elephant. stupid but I still love him, his sense of humor & his blue eyes. I wish he loved me. Val

MARCH 13. D. D. Today Patty and I went up to the store. We saw Spike and I smiled at him and visa versa....

MARCH 18. Dear Diary, Today we were playing softball with the boys. Spike hit the ball and if I had not have blocked it he would have had a homerun, well anyway I grabbed it & tore off to 1st base like a "bat out of hell" because Rhonda would never catch it. All the boys were tense but I ran & got him out by a split second. Edward was stunned & then said "Christie, I've seen TOMBOYS but you take 1st place." He's jealous & I'm proud!

MARCH 20. Today M̶r̶ *"Joe"!* gave us a test on central [America?] & what countries and bodies of water border it. My desk was a mess & I tried to get my book, paper, & pencil out in a hurry. Somehow my *mirror* got under my books & when I shut my desk fast all the books crashed down & broke the mirror into smitherines. It just shattered on the bottom of my desk. I still haven't cleaned out my desk. 7 years bad luck!

MARCH 28. D. D. Tonight I played softb. at Rita's. And John . . . (Craig's cousin) squirted me with water. I was soaked & I almost pounded him. Tonight I fell right on top of Spike (hep hep) Love Val

MARCH 29. Tonight Rita told me that she & Bart made out this year. I almost cried. I hope its not true. *I love Bart.* Val

MARCH 30. Today Spike walked in front of me on the way home from school & we talked. Today I was in the room with Bart all alone. I asked him if he would like Claudia J. if she didn't wear her glasses. He said he couldn't stand her. . . .

APRIL 4. Today I was over at Jean's house & we had a bet that I could jump off her roof. If I could she would pay for my way at "My Fair Lady." If I couldn't, I would have to pay her way. I got up there & could not get down! (We are going to pay our own way). I finally got down. (I love Bart) Love Val.

APRIL 5. Dear Diary, Today I went to D'Anne's house. I saw a little of her diary and it said some cruddy things about me, so she can "go to hell." Then we went Downtown Denver on 16th St. I went & visited Dad & I asked for $14.00 but that went over like a lead balloon so I got $5.00 & blew it on a $1.50 box of carmel popcorn & a Barbra Streisand album for $3.69. I might, I'm not sure, exchange it tomorrow. Val

APRIL 9. D. D. Today Mary & I went downtown Denver. . . . Man she's *stacked!* I bought a Granny nightgown. Just darling. She bought a dress. I went over to M's house tonight. I dyed Easter eggs. . . .

APRIL 13. Today Bart and I had to do a science project together! The question was: What is your regular body temperature? I said 96° & he said 98°. So we went up & looked in the encyclopedia. We hardly got any work done because we talked, talked, talked about different things. . . .

APRIL 16. Today I got straight A's on my report card. Bart told me he thought he did not deserve a "C" in reading so he made a chart of ME & HIM! Taking all of my grades and all his grades & he's going to average them up at the end of the year to see if he's been cheated. I love him.

AUGUST 3. Dear Diary, Today was Mom's and John's birthday. Went to Neusteters tonight for dinner. It was very nice. . . . Great Aunt Florence is here. I tried to make a cake today, I[t] was a complete flop, it was dry, fell in the middle, and when I tried to put icing on, the top peeled off. thank goodness they made a cake at Neusteters. After we came home we watched Square Dancing at the park. Love, Val

AUGUST 22. Dear Diary, There are nine days till we go to school. Yetch Love, Val

AUGUST 23. Dear Diary, If I can get 8 books done before the 15 of September I win $5.00 from Claudia. (Read, Read Read!) Love Val

AUGUST 26. Dear Diary Today was Mom and Dads Anniversary. We went to dinner.

AUGUST 27. Dear Diary A lot of things happened today. First of all 5 nuns were at dinner tonight. They were very nice. Their names were Sister Margaret Sister Ann Louise, Sister Frances, Sister Agnes Regina and Sister Patricia Ann. And also I went to a drive in and saw Love & Kisses and Father Goose. I liked Father Goose better. And I also spent the night at Jeane's ———— and didn't get to bed till 2:00 A.M. Love & Kisses, Val

AUGUST 28. Tonight we ate dinner a[t] Sylvia's house. I[t] was delicious. I had to play dolls with Sylvia all night. And to thinke she was 16 Monday. Oh well she's a nice kid. (I guess).... Love Stuffed Val

SEPTEMBER 1. 6th Grade. Today we go back to school (ick) Love Val

OCTOBER 15. Dear Diary, Today I discovered I was in love! ! ! ! ! ! The darling boy is Bart.... [When] I was up at the map today he came up and looked on the same map I did (he got so close! !) I couldn't find Cape Breton Island so he and I looked together, and also he got so close we almost kissed! I like him very much.... I am going to the School Carnival tomorrow night. I am going to buy a million bottles of coke between 6:30 P.M. and 7:00 P.M. The reason: Bart is working the coke machine from 6:30–7:00 P.M. ...

OCTOBER 24. Dear Diary, Today I played softball for 3 hrs. I chose this boy to a "hitting the softball the hardest" contest. Of course I won. (brag, brag). Love Val

NOVEMBER 15. Dear Diary, Today I washed and rolled my hair. When I took it out I look[ed] ridiculous (bad enough to go on Fred & Fae). Watched some T.V. and I saw a terrific show on the "Young Man From Boston" it was the story about President Kennedys life. It's almost 2 years since he [was] ass. and I'm still not used to the Texan. Love Val

NOVEMBER 19. Dear Diary, WOW! ! ! Today I started my Periods! (Groan). (It's not to bad) I suppose

NOVEMBER 20. Dear Diary, I thought menstrating would be fun but I hate it. That big bulky pad, ick. Theres one advantage to it, it makes you feel more grown up. Jan and I are the only ones who have started. I like Jan a lot. I hope she likes me as much as I like her.

DECEMBER 11. Dear Diary, Wow! ! ! ! ! ! ! ! Today I found out that I'm going to be invited to Jimmy's boy girl party. Bill ———— said that he wouldn't mind *making out* with me at the party. We will probably play *spin the bottle*. I like Bill as a friend but Bart and Spike as ! ! ! ! ! ! !

R ecent research shows that by the age of two, children already know whether they are boys or girls, an awareness of gender that remains a central component of personality throughout life. In every century society has associated particular characteristics with maleness and femaleness and has held different expectations for children regarding temperament, talents, and intelligence on the basis of sex. Aggressiveness, dominance, and analytical abilities have been traditionally labeled masculine traits, while submissiveness, dependency, and emotionalism have been considered feminine. Starting in childhood those qualities have been nurtured in boys and girls respectively through experiences and relationships at home, in school, and in the broader community. Through observing and interacting with parents, teachers, other adults, siblings, and peers, children learn sex-specific roles and acquire sex-typed attitudes at young ages.

The girls studied in this chapter grew up in various regions of the United States and at different times over the course of three centuries. Although differences in geographic location, class, racial background, and historical period account for variations in their particular experiences, conventional beliefs about the nature of girls and assumptions about what they would do as adults explain some common elements in the lives of four of the five presented here.

White and from upper- and middle-class families, Anna Green Winslow, Caroline Cowles Richards, Adelaide A. French, and Valerie Jane Christie all enjoyed fortunate childhood circumstances. Parents, grandparents, and others freely expressed their love in comfortable home environments. None of the girls was disciplined harshly, and only minor conflicts surfaced between parental standards and their own desires. None was required to work as a child to help with the financial support of her family.

The conditions of Annie Louise Burton's childhood contrast sharply with those of the other girls. As a black slave girl on a large plantation, Annie had barely enough to feed and clothe herself and faced the continual threat of punishment for not completing her chores. She lived without her mother, under the direct control of her white owners, for four years of her childhood, and she had to cope emotionally with the fact that her white father, who lived nearby, refused to acknowledge her existence.

The force of Puritan tradition in defining the moral education of Anna Winslow and Caroline Richards is evident. Bible readings at home, church attendance, discussions of sermon topics, and catechism classes were all a part of the daily routine. In the 1850s Caroline and her sister believed that girls were more pious in previous times, and they even dared to make fun of the stories they read about good girls dying of "early piety." The religious climate in the home and community was more relaxed for Caroline and Anna Richards compared with what Anna Winslow described, although the aim of educating girls to be pious, obedient, and industrious remained the same.

Neither Adelaide French, who was probably of Protestant religious background, nor Valerie Christie, who was raised as a Catholic, discussed formal religious instruction or attendance at church services. The values and standards transmitted to them at home and in school were not directly linked to theology but were cast in secular terms.

The day-to-day activities among the girls vary in their different settings and change over the centuries. Anna Winslow in the 1770s was receiving a "genteel" education typical for girls of her class, one that was obviously geared to prepare her for housewifery and motherhood. At home and in private schools in Boston, she practiced her sewing and knitting, and through social events with girls her own age and with adults, she developed poise and social manners. She tried earnestly to control her "whimsical" nature and conduct herself in ways that would please her aunt and her parents — to be obedient and diligent in her religious and domestic studies.

Caroline Richards was slightly younger than Anna Winslow when she wrote her diary in the 1850s, and that fact, along with differences in class background and the more casual atmosphere in the small village in upstate New York where Caroline lived, explains some of the variations in their experiences. Caroline and her sister attended the local district school before enrolling in a nearby private girls' academy to learn "manners as well as books." Their education, both in school and at home, was less self-consciously and formally "genteel," however. Although Caroline helped her grandmother with small household tasks, it is clear that she and her sister enjoyed a great amount of time for play and exercise. In contrast to Adelaide French and Valerie Christie, though, Caroline and her sister Anna faced greater restrictions on the types of games and activities in which they could participate. Among all of the girls presented in this chapter, Caroline was the only one to express a specific career ambition: to be a writer of stories for children. She was aware, however, of what the assumed life course was for women when she wrote that she expected her teacher would soon be resigning to get married because "that is usually the way."

Annie Burton's childhood remained a struggle even after slavery ended, and her labor was necessary to the daily survival of her family. In rural environments, poor children worked as unskilled farm laborers or in domestic service. Like millions of impoverished black and immigrant girls in the nineteenth century, Annie had no choice but to work. The luxury of schooling and playtime was not hers to enjoy. The determination and generosity of her mother in the face of great hardship was an important source of strength and inspiration for Annie.

The final selections in the chapter were written by two girls who grew up in the West about seventy-five years apart. Adelaide French, who lived on a ranch in a small community outside of Denver, Colorado, described a childhood filled with play activities with boys and girls of all ages. Despite the greater freedom Adelaide enjoyed, different parental expectations for her and her brothers were expressed in a number of ways. Adelaide helped out with small housekeeping tasks considered women's work, and as the oldest and only daughter she was primarily responsible for the care of her youngest brother when her parents traveled out of town. She indicated her awareness of behavior deemed appropriate to each sex when she related how on one occasion a friend "play[ed] the man" and she "play[ed] the lady." In a somewhat disgusted tone, she commented that her sixteen-year-old friend June was trying "to behave like a young lady" and would not come out and play. Adelaide was not looking forward to the time when she would have to adhere more strictly to the rules of conduct for young ladies.

By contrast, Valerie Christie, who lived in a suburb of Denver in the 1960s, seemingly could not wait to be more grown-up. At seven years of age when her diary began, she was the youngest of the authors in the chapter, and her writings illuminate some dramatic changes in the concerns of girls in recent decades. Valerie focused almost exclusively on daily activities with her peers, and their powerful influence, along with that of the media, in shaping her sex-role development is apparent. At early ages she and her friends were discussing boyfriends and make-out parties, and wondering what their periods would be like. Although Valerie enjoyed competing with boys in classes and in sports, she was equally concerned about how boys perceived her physical appearance and personality. She mentioned learning traditional female crafts — knitting, sewing, and embroidery — yet there is no sense that she was expected to follow a formal regimen in developing those skills, either at home or in school.

The revived feminist movement of the 1960s and 1970s brought the question of the validity of preparing girls for traditional female roles into sharp focus. Demands for educational programs that would train girls at young ages to think in terms of choosing among options in later life — and for making those options a reality — have increased.

There are some indications that more parents, teachers, and guidance counselors are aware of the ways that different expectations for girls and boys limit the development of individual talent. There is current concern about how toys, children's books, and television programs reinforce narrow, sex-typed behavior and attitudes at an early age. If society expects girls to be passive and boys to be active, then socialization will, as a matter of course, produce those characteristics.

Studies show that boys and girls are more alike than different in their intellectual and psychological needs and capacities during childhood. If seriously considered, the implications of these findings could have an enormous impact on the freedom to develop *human* potential in all girls and boys.

Bibliography

Beales, Ross W., Jr. "In Search of the Historical Child: Miniature Adulthood and Youth in Colonial New England." *American Quarterly* 27 (1975): 379–398.

Bronfenbrenner, Urie. "The Changing American Child: A Speculative Analysis." *Journal of Social Issues* 17 (1961): 6–18.

Cable, Mary. *The Little Darlings: A History of Child Rearing in America.* New York: Charles Scribner's Sons, 1975.

Coles, Robert. *Children of Crisis: A Study of Courage and Fear.* New York: Dell, 1964.

Demos, John. "Developmental Perspectives on the History of Childhood." *Journal of Interdisciplinary History* 2 (1971): 315–327.

Demos, John. *A Little Commonwealth: Family Life in Plymouth Colony.* New York: Oxford University Press, 1970.

Earle, Alice Morse. *Child Life in Colonial Days.* New York: Macmillan, 1899.

Elkin, Frederick, and Handel, Gerald. *The Child and Society: The Process of Socialization.* 2nd ed. New York: Random House, 1972.

Erikson, Erik H. *Childhood and Society.* New York: W. W. Norton, 1950.

Frost, J. William. *The Quaker Family in Colonial America.* New York: St. Martin's Press, 1973.

Greven, Philip. *The Protestant Temperament: Patterns of Child-Rearing, Religious Experience, and the Self in Early America.* New York: Alfred A. Knopf, 1977.

Illick, Joseph. "Child-Rearing in Seventeenth-Century England and America." In *The History of Childhood,* edited by Lloyd de Mause. New York: Harper & Row, 1975, pp. 303–350.

Kuhn, Anne L. *The Mother's Role in Childhood Education: New England Concepts, 1830–1860.* New Haven: Yale University Press, 1947.

Mechling, Jay. "Advice to Historians on Advice to Mothers." *Journal of Social History* 9 (1975): 44–63.

Rapson, Richard. "The American Child as Seen by British Travelers, 1845–1935." *American Quarterly* 18 (1965): 520–534.

Rothman, David J. "Documents in Search of a Historian: Toward a History of Childhood and Youth in America." *Journal of Interdisciplinary History* 2 (1971): 367–377.

Stannard, David E. "Death and the Puritan Child." *American Quarterly* 26 (1974): 456–476.

Steere, Geoffrey H. "Freudianism and Child Rearing in the Twenties." *American Quarterly* 20 (1968): 759–765.

Sunley, Robert. "Early Nineteenth-Century American Literature on Child-Rearing." In *Childhood in Contemporary Cultures,* edited by Margaret Mead and Martha Wolfenstein. Chicago: University of Chicago Press, 1955, pp. 150–167.

Walzer, John. "A Period of Ambivalence: Eighteenth-Century American Childhood." In *The History of Childhood,* edited by Lloyd de Mause. New York: Harper & Row, 1975, pp. 351–382.

Weiss, Nancy Pottisham. "Mother, the Invention of Necessity: Dr. Benjamin Spock's *Baby and Child Care.*" *American Quarterly* 29 (1977): 519–546.
Wishy, Bernard. *The Child and the Republic: The Dawn of Modern American Child Nurture.* Philadelphia: University of Pennsylvania Press, 1968.

TWO

Adolescence

Contemporary society recognizes adolescence as a separate stage in the life cycle that spans the years between childhood and adulthood. Although no single event marks the end of childhood, some very dramatic physical changes in the second decade of life herald the transition to adolescence. With the exception of fetal development and the first two years of infancy, at no other time does the human body change so rapidly in size and shape. Between ages ten and thirteen for girls and ages twelve and fifteen for boys, individuals experience spurts of growth in height and weight and begin to acquire adult male and female body shapes. These changes intensify individual awareness of being male or female as well as sensitivity to how one's gender is perceived by others.

An important aspect of the adolescent developmental process is reaching puberty — achieving the capacity to reproduce children. For females, this is signaled by first menstruation, which today usually occurs around age twelve. Puberty can trigger many different feelings — embarrassment or resentment, confusion or a new sense of being grown-up — which change throughout adolescence. How a young woman responds is influenced to a great extent by the specific context in which she achieves sexual maturity, although in all situations what an individual knows about menstruation before it happens is an important factor in determining her reactions. With more open and straightforward discussion of sexuality through the mass media and through the promotion of sex education courses in recent decades, female adolescents are better informed about sexual maturation than ever before, and feelings of embarrassment or shame are more rare.

In terms of psychological development, adolescence is characterized as the stage in the life cycle when a person endeavors to create a stable inner identity. Assessments of changing physical appearance, intelligence, and personality, as well as the long-range goals a young person sets, constitute the total sense of self. During adolescence all aspects of identity come under self-scrutiny. It is a time for testing one's talents and personality and for defining what qualities and skills one values in oneself and wants to develop.

Cultural context and social values play a central role in directing the process of self-definition, and how each person handles this developmental task also varies according to temperament, abilities, and interests. In general, however, feelings of confidence or inferiority have been connected to very different aspects of the self for males and females. Traditionally, males in their teens have been expected and encouraged to establish a sense of self-worth based on their vocational talents. Adolescence has been a period to prepare for or actually begin the work they would do as adults. For females, identity has been more directly linked to feelings about physical appearance and relationships with others. Society has assumed that marriage and motherhood provided the only means to self-fulfillment for women, and consequently female adolescence has been a time for concentrating on developing skills and qualities bound to the tasks of homemaking and child rearing.

Laws and programs created in the 1960s and 1970s to end sex discrimination in education and employment have expanded young women's opportunities for self-development. Yet, as the idea that young women as well as young men should be able to define what they want to be gains acceptance, many female adolescents find themselves in *double bind* situations. Encouraged to express their intelligence and abilities as fully as young men do, many still face pressure from parents, peers, or society at large to demonstrate traditional feminine qualities — passivity and submissiveness — and to build their primary sense of self-worth around meeting the needs of others.

In sociological terms, adolescence is a period of moving away from childhood dependence on parents and preparing for adult roles and responsibilities. Teenagers are expected to assume more control over their own actions and to begin to establish their own personal and professional goals and values. For some, becoming more independent of parents is a relatively smooth process, while for others it is an experience fraught with tension and conflict.

As emotional dependence on parents lessens, adolescents develop closer relationships with their peers. Teenagers spend a greater portion of their time with those their own age now than in earlier centuries, a phenomenon directly attributable to the expansion of secondary and postsecondary education since 1900. An estimated 90 percent of those in their teens are currently enrolled in high school, compared to less than 10 percent at the turn of the century, and a large proportion continue their education today in postsecondary institutions. The extent to which peers influence each other regarding their social activities, sexual behavior, tastes in clothing, food, and music, and attitudes toward school and drugs is profound. It is primarily through interaction with people their own age that adolescents begin relating in adult ways and acting out sex roles.

Sexuality is a major concern among teenagers. With respect to young women especially, sexual attitudes and experiences have been radically transformed in recent decades. The availability of more reliable birth control methods coupled with more permissive attitudes among parents and adolescents alike has weakened the constraints on young women to remain "pure" until marriage. Indeed, many now face intense pressure from their peers to experiment with premarital sex. Although experiences differ according to class, ethnic, and regional background, about half of all females have sexual intercourse by age nineteen. In addition, nearly one million — or one in every ten American females aged fifteen to nineteen — become pregnant each year. Despite improvements in birth control technology, some young women are unaware of this information, some do not choose to use contraceptives, and others feel that birth control is too much trouble.

The physiological, psychological, and sociological dimensions of adolescent development all need to be considered in evaluating individual female experiences. Examining the various historical contexts within which women in their teen years have lived provides another perspective on this stage in the life cycle. How young women have proceeded with the sociological and psychological tasks commonly associated with adolescence has differed over the centuries. Indeed, only in the past one hundred years has adolescence itself been clearly defined as a unique developmental stage.

Colonial Americans did not perceive the teen years as comprising a separate stage of life. During the seventeenth and eighteenth centuries, preparing for adulthood began in earnest during childhood. At age six or seven children began participating in adult social and economic activities, even dressing in adult styles of clothing. In an agrarian setting, where the family functioned as a cohesive economic unit, youngsters and teenagers were required to perform productive labor. Teenage daughters as a rule worked beside their mothers manufacturing household goods — food, clothing, soap, candles, fuel, and other necessities — and caring for younger siblings.

Not only the context of individual development, but also the actual rate of physical change and sexual maturation among teenagers was different from that of today. Physical growth was less rapid and less dramatic during the colonial era. Today most young men and women attain their full height by age eighteen, while in previous centuries this did not occur until the midtwenties. The average age at menarche is presently around twelve, contrasted with age fifteen or sixteen in the seventeenth and eighteenth centuries. Its decline of approximately four months per decade since 1850 is attributed to better nutrition and overall health. The important point is that rate of physical development did not affect the social definition of those in their teens — or the ways they understood themselves — as directly as it does now. Society did not identify those in their teens as "teenagers," nor did young men and women feel part of a separate youth culture.

During the colonial era virtually all white females in their teens prepared to marry, and in the seventeenth century many did wed before they were twenty. Although young white women at this time played only a limited role in the marriage-making process, their black counterparts, most of whom were enslaved, were permitted little latitude with respect to the choice of a spouse.

In the 1600s the consent of parents, or masters in situations where individuals were apprenticed, to a marriage was required by custom, and in some colonies by law. Practical concerns such as wealth, status, and religion frequently took precedence over a daughter's own preference. In the eighteenth century the direct involvement of parents in selecting spouses for their children lessened. During the revolutionary era relations between parents and children began to alter as traditional patterns of deferential behavior weakened and new expectations about upward mobility were articulated. Modern attitudes toward marriage, in part an indirect social consequence of the American Revolution, began to emerge, although the idea of marrying primarily for romantic love was not widespread until the nineteenth century.

Not many young women in their teens made a conscious choice to remain single in the seventeenth and eighteenth centuries, as few socially approved alternatives to marriage existed. Even though females participated in the apprenticeship system of education, their opportunities were limited almost exclusively to learning domestic crafts. In rare instances in the seventeenth century young women attended secondary school, but although their numbers increased in the eighteenth century, females constituted only a small proportion of the students.

In the 1780s and 1790s private female academies were organized in urban areas throughout the states and enrolled young women from the upper classes whose families did not require their labor and could afford the tuition and board costs. In general, the curricula in these institutions were more advanced than those in primary schools, but they were not comparable to what was offered in male academies. Their purpose can be seen in their content: classes and social activities for developing domestic skills and social graces. Speculations at the end of the eighteenth century about whether or not female intelligence could or should be cultivated presaged heated debates in the nineteenth century. Opponents of advanced education for women were already expressing fears in the 1780s and 1790s that too much schooling would be defeminizing and lead to the abandonment of domestic responsibilities.

An ideology of domesticity in the nineteenth century justified women's relegation to the home by exalting the uniquely feminine qualities of submissiveness and self-sacrifice. Female biology was increasingly cited to explain woman's character, intelligence, behavior, and social place. In this context the physiological changes of puberty acquired heightened importance. Sexual maturation came to be viewed as the most significant facet of female adolescent life. Hosts of physicians, educators, and psychologists described puberty as a critical point in a woman's life and warned that too much exertion, mental or physical, during adolescence could lead to sterility, insanity, or even early death. Preparing for adulthood meant getting ready for the task of reproducing children, and young women were advised to turn their full attention to the proper regulation of menstrual functions.

Although daughters of the privileged classes were subject to these strictures, most adolescent women had neither the time nor the inclination to heed such advice. Teenage daughters of working-class families, which included the majority of black and immigrant populations, spent their days working at menial jobs in factories or as domestic servants. By 1890 factories employed about one million female workers, most of them unmarried immigrants or the daughters of immigrants. Nearly 25 percent were girls under the age of fifteen. Girls and women worked long hours for low wages under oppressive physical conditions. Impoverished young black women, denied access to factory employment, generally worked at unskilled farm labor or domestic service.

With the expansion of secondary and postsecondary education in the last decades of the nineteenth century, opportunities for advanced schooling began to open up for young women, in large part because of the demands and efforts of women themselves. Although few working-class families could afford the luxury of keeping either teenage sons or daughters off the job market, increased numbers of middle-class youth were experiencing some schooling beyond the elementary level by the turn of the century. Of the roughly 7 percent of the teenage population graduating from high school in 1900, the majority, about 57 percent, were females. In terms of higher education, private women's colleges were organized in the East in response to the protests of women who had been denied admission to male institutions such as Yale, Princeton, and Harvard. Public universities in the Midwest and West adopted coeducational admissions policies in the 1870s and 1880s as well.

The growth of secondary and higher education affected the lives of young men and women in different ways, however. Additional schooling did not lead to better employment opportunities for women or challenge the traditional idea that marriage and motherhood were the only paths to feminine fulfillment. Although some young women attended high school, and perhaps college, to prepare for a job prior to marriage in teaching, nursing, or social work — virtually the only jobs considered respectable for middle-class females — for the majority such schooling simply provided enjoyable activities before marriage and raising children.

The first students at private women's colleges in the period from 1880 to 1910, imbued with a special sense of identity and purpose, form an exception to these generalizations. But as more young women enrolled in college, the experience lost its special meaning. After 1920, going to college became expected of middle- and upper-class young women, a part of their preparation for adult roles as wives and mothers.

Attending high school, and increasingly college as well, is now a common experience for adolescent males and females of all backgrounds in modern society. Recently, educational institutions have been subjected to criticism because they shape the experiences of teenagers differently according to race, class, and sex. The feminist movement in the 1960s and 1970s directly challenged the belief that housewifery and motherhood are the inevitable or exclusive roles for women and prompted the reexamination of the objectives of schooling for both sexes. Some high school curricula include classes in parenting for males as well as females, and "shop" is now open to young women. Enrollment in academic courses in both secondary school and college is less frequently sex-typed, and women are more often included as subject matter in humanities and social science courses.

Encouraging young women to explore and express their full range of talents and abilities and providing opportunities at home, in school, and in the community to allow them to do so can drastically change the meaning of adolescence for females in American society. As sex becomes less influential in defining young women's potential, they are more able to direct the courses of their own lives.

S ocial expectations for young women were narrowly conceived and strongly imposed in past centuries. Because the roles of wife and mother offered virtually the only sanctioned means of pursuing personal happiness and fulfillment, defining future goals as a young woman meant contemplating one's place in a domestic situation.

The overwhelming majority of women are asked to marry. Although they can exercise the right to say no, women are not in the position to extend the offer. In every century, getting ready to become a wife and mother has meant preparing for an invitation to marry.

One seventeen-year-old woman, writing in 1800, expressed her thoughts on this issue in the letters that follow. The author, Eliza Southgate Bowne, discusses what options are and are not available to her as a young woman, her expectations in her relationships with young men, and her opinions on the subject of women's education. The letters, which were written to her cousin Moses Porter, provided a means for this articulate young woman to confide her innermost feelings, hopes, and doubts to a young man about her own age whom she both trusted and admired.

Eliza analyzed her attractiveness, intelligence, and worthiness in her interactions with young men and wondered about falling in love. She believed that "not one woman in a hundred marries for love," but that they rather do so out of gratitude for not having to face life as an "old maid." While examining her own criteria for choosing a husband, she also speculated about the possibility of deciding to remain single and how she would cope with the stigma attached to that choice.

Eliza grew up in a prosperous, upper-class, New England family, the third of twelve children. Her father studied medicine, then turned to law, and eventually served as judge in the Court of Common Pleas in the seaport town of Scarborough, Maine. Her mother was the daughter of wealthy Maine landowners and the sister of Rufus King, a well-known national political party leader. Like many teenage daughters of prominent families in the late eighteenth century, Eliza attended private boarding school to receive a "genteel education." The curriculum at the Young Ladies Academy in Boston where Eliza enrolled emphasized development of social graces and improvement of domestic skills through dancing classes; embroidery instruction; and attendance at chaperoned balls, musical performances, and rounds of parties.

In her letters to Moses, Eliza was quite candid about her lack of interest in academic studies and her enjoyment of social activities. She was insightful in her analysis of why she believed that most other young women she knew felt similarly. Eliza pointed to the lack of any incentive for them to take their studies seriously. Men are more analytical, she concluded, because of what they are expected and encouraged to accomplish in life. Although Eliza defended female intellectual capacity and the need for its development, she stopped short of arguing for expanding women's opportunities outside the domestic sphere. Even though she recognized the inequality of privilege between the sexes, Eliza adhered to conventional assumptions about woman's proper place. Eliza's concern for "proper conduct" and the "laws of female delicacy and propriety" reflect her upperclass background and education. That she felt a conflict, however, in asserting her own outgoing personality without violating conventional codes of feminine behavior is apparent.

Eliza married Walter Bowne, a businessman, in 1803 and gave birth to their first child in 1806. Pregnancy and the arrival of a second baby two years later proved complicated, and Eliza was advised to spend the winter in a warm climate in hopes of improving her health. Accompanied by her husband and a sister, she traveled to Charleston, South Carolina. Her condition deteriorated, however, and Eliza died there at the age of twenty-six.

— 6 —

Eliza Southgate Bowne

[c. 1800]

To Moses Porter.

My most charming Cousin! Most kind and condescending friend — teach me how I may express the grateful sense I have of the obligations I owe you; your many and long letters have chased away the spleen, they have rendered me cheerful and happy, and I almost forgot I was so far from home. — O shame on you! Moses, you know I hate this formality among friends, you know how gladly I would throw all these fashionable forms from our correspondence; but you still oppose me, you adhere to

SOURCE: *A Girl's Life Eighty Years Ago: Selections from the Letters of Eliza Southgate Bowne* (New York: Charles Scribner's Sons, 1887).

Eliza Southgate Bowne

them with as much scrupulosity as to the ten commandments, and for aught I know you believe them equally essential to the salvation of your soul. But, Eliza, you have not answered my last letter! True, and if I had not have answered it, would you never have written me again — and I confess that I believe you would not — yet I am mortified and displeased that you value my letters so little, that the exertions to continue the correspondence must all come from me, that if I relax my zeal in the smallest degree it may drop to the ground without your helping hand to raise it. I do think you are a charming fellow, — would not write because I am in debt, well, be it so, my ceremonious friend, — I submit, and though I transgress by sending a half sheet more than you ever did, yet I assure you 'twas to convince you of the violence of my anger which could *induce* me to forget the rules of politeness. I am at Wiscassett. I have seen Rebecca every day, she is handsome as ever, and we both of us were in constant expectation of seeing you for 2 or 3 days, you did not come and we were disappointed.

I leave here for Bath next week. I have had a ranting time, and if I did not feel so offended, I would tell you more about it.

As I look around me I am surprised at the happiness which is so generally enjoyed in families, and that marriages which have not love for a foundation on more than one side at most, should produce so much apparent harmony. I may be censured for declaring it as my opinion that not one woman in a hundred marries for love. A woman of taste and sentiment will surely see but a very few whom she could love, and it is altogether uncertain whether either of them will particularly distinguish her. If they should, surely she is very fortunate, but it would be one of fortune's random favors and such as we have no right to expect. The female mind I believe is of a very pliable texture; if it were not we should be wretched indeed. Admitting as a known truth that few women marry those whom they would prefer to all the world if they could be viewed by them with equal affection, or rather that there are often others whom they could have preferred if they had felt that affection for them which would have induced them to offer themselves, — admitting this as a truth not to be disputed, — is it not a subject of astonishment that happiness is not banished from this connexion? Gratitude is undoubtedly the foundation of the esteem we commonly feel for a husband. One that has preferred us to all the world, one that has thought us possessed of every quality to render him happy, surely merits our gratitude. If his character is good — if he is not displeasing in his person or manners — what objection can we make that will not be thought frivolous by the greater part of the world? — yet I think there are many other things necessary for happiness, and the world should never compel me to marry a man because I could not give satisfactory reasons for not liking him. I do not esteem marriage absolutely essential to happiness, and that it does not always bring happiness we must every day witness in our acquaintance. A single life is considered too generally as a reproach; but let me ask you, which is the most despicable — she who marries a man she scarcely thinks *well* of — to avoid the reputation of an old maid — or she, who with more delicacy, than marry one she could not highly esteem, preferred to live single all her life, and had wisdom enough to despise so mean a sacrifice, to the opinion of the rabble, as the woman who marries a man she has not much love for — must make. I wish not to alter the laws of nature — neither will I quarrel with the rules which custom has established and rendered indispensably necessary to the harmony of society. But every being who has contemplated human nature on a large scale will certainly justify me when I declare that the inequality of privilege between the sexes is very sensibly felt by us females, and in no instance is it greater than in the liberty of choosing a partner in marriage; true, we have the liberty of refusing those we don't like, but not of selecting those we do. This is undoubtedly as it should be. But let me ask you, what must be that love which is altogether voluntary, which we can withhold or give, which sleeps in dulness and apathy till it is requested to brighten into life? Is it not a cold, lifeless dictate of the head,

— do we not weigh all the conveniences and inconveniences which will attend it? And after a long calculation, in which the heart never was consulted, we determine whether it is most prudent to love or not.

How I should despise a soul so sordid, so mean! How I abhor the heart which is regulated by mechanical rules, which can say "thus far will I go and no farther," whose feelings can keep pace with their convenience, and be awakened at stated periods, — a mere piece of clockwork which always moves right! How far less valuable than that being who has a soul to govern her actions, and though she may not always be coldly prudent, yet she will sometimes be generous and noble, and that the other never can be. After all, I must own that a woman of delicacy never will suffer her esteem to ripen into love unless she is convinced of a return. Though our first approaches to love may be involuntary, yet I should be sorry if we had no power of controlling them if occasion required. There is a happy conformity or pliability in the female mind which seems to have been a gift of nature to enable them to be happy with so few privileges, — and another thing, they have more gratitude in their dispositions than men, and there is a something particularly gratifying to the heart in being beloved, if the object is worthy; it produces a something like, and "Pity melts the heart to love." Added to these there is a self-love which does more than all the rest. Our vanity ('tis an ugly word but I can't find a better) is gratified by the distinguished preference given us. There must be an essential difference in the dispositions of men and women. I am astonished when I think of it — yet — But I have written myself into sunshine — 'tis always my way when anything oppresses me, when any chain of thoughts particularly occupies my mind, and I feel dissatisfied at anything which I have not the power to alter, — to sit down and unburthen them on paper; it never fails to alleviate me, and I generally give full scope to the feelings of the moment, and as I write all disagreeable thoughts evaporate, and I end contented that things shall remain as they are. When I began this it absolutely appeared to me that no woman, or rather not one in a hundred, married the man she should prefer to all the world — not that I ever could suppose that at the time she married him she did not prefer him to all others, — but that she would have preferred another if he had professed to love her as well as the one she married. Indeed, I believe no woman of delicacy suffers herself to think she could love any one before she had discovered an affection for her. For my part I should never ask the question of myself — do I love such a one, if I had reason to think he loved me — and I believe there are many who love that never confessed it to themselves. My Pride, my delicacy, would all be hurt if I discovered such *unasked* for love, even in my own bosom. I would strain every nerve and rouse every faculty to quell the first appearance of it. There is no danger, however. I could never love without being beloved, and I am confident in my own mind that no person whom I could love would ever think me sufficiently worthy to love me. But I congratulate myself that I am at liberty to refuse those I don't like, and that I have firmness enough to

brave the sneers of the world and live an old maid, if I never find one I
can love.

[Eliza]

□

PORTLAND, MARCH 18, 1801.

Thank you for being so particular in your description of your eastern
tour. I told you that Wiscassett would delight you; ease and sociability
you know always please you. By the bye, Jewett thought *Saco* was the
land of milk and honey, such fine buxom girls! so easy and familiar.
Dorcas Stour charmed him much, her haughty forbidding manners corresponded with the dignity of her sentiments, so he says, something
congenial in their dispositions I think. But he has made his selection —
Miss Weeks is handsome, censorious, animated, violent in her prejudices,
genteel, impatient of contradiction, speaks her sentiments very freely, has
many admirers and many enemies, — on the whole a pleasant companion
amongst friends. — How think they will do together? Jewett you know.

Last evening I was out at Broads [a tavern outside Portland]; we had
only 7 in our party — a very pleasant one. Jewett, Horatio, William
Weeks, and Charles Little were our beaux. Miss Weeks, Miss Boardman
(from Exeter), and myself, the ladies. Mr. Little is engaged to Miss Boardman; he is an open, honest, unaffected, plain, *clever* fellow. She has a
pleasant face, an open guileless heart, plain unaffected manners, a
clumsy shape, easy in company — but it is rather the ease which a calm,
even temper produces, than that which is acquired in polite circles. I
think they are as much alike as possible and 'twill be a pleasant couple.
We played cards, talked and wrote crambo [a game in which one player
gives a word or phrase to be matched in rhyme by the other players];
after we had scribbled the backs of two packs of cards, cut half of them
up, and eat our supper, we set out for home, about one o'clock. You say
in your last that if reports are true, I am on the highway to matrimony,
— you know what I always said with regard to these things; if they are
true, well and good — if they are not, let them take their course, they
will be short-lived. I despise the conduct of those girls who think that every
man who pays them any attention is seriously in love with them, and
begin to bridle up, look conscious, fearful lest every word the poor fellow
utters should be a declaration of love. I have no idea that every gentleman that has a particular partiality for a lady thinks seriously of being
connected with her, and I think any lady puts herself in a most awkward
situation to appear in constant fear or expectation that the gentleman is
going to make love to her. I despise coquetry, — every lady says the same,
you will say, — but if I know myself at all — my heart readily assents
to its truth — I think no lady has a right to encourage hopes that she
means never to gratify, but I think she is much to blame if she considers
these little attentions as a proof of love; they often mean nothing, and
should be treated as such. The gentleman in question I own pays me

more attention than any other gentleman, yet I say sincerely, I don't think he means any thing more than to please his fancy for the present. I pride myself upon my sincerity, and if I ever am engaged, I trust it will be to one whom I shall not be ashamed to acknowledge. . . .

[Eliza]

□

THURSDAY, APRIL 8, [1801]

I have been thinking on that part of your letter which interests me most, respecting the propriety of conduct, opinion of the world, etc., etc. I don't exactly recollect what I wrote in my last, but I am positive you have mistaken my meaning, or at least have taken what I said on too large a scale; — as a general rule of conduct, in so extensive a sense as you talk about, such doctrine would indeed be pernicious. But whatever I said I meant to apply to this particular case, and perhaps did not express myself so clearly as I ought to have done. You have described principles which I have ever condemned — as those I now act upon. Perhaps I shall find it impossible fully to explain my sentiments on this subject — it is of a delicate nature; and many things I shall say will probably bear a misconstruction. However, I trust to your candor to judge with lenity, and to your knowledge of my heart, to believe I would not intentionally deviate from the laws of female delicacy and propriety. Reputation undoubtedly is of great importance to all, but to a female 'tis every thing, — once lost 'tis *forever* lost. Whatever I may have said, my heart too sensibly tells me I have none of that boasted independence of mind which can stand collected in its own worth, and let the censure and malice of the world pass by as the "idle wind which we regard not." I have ever thought that to be conscious of doing right was insufficient; but that it must appear so to the world. How I could have blundered upon a sentiment which I despise, or how I could have written anything to bear such a construction as you have put upon a part of my letter, I know not. When I said that I should let these reports pass off without notice or pretending to vindicate myself, 'twas not because I despised the opinion of the world, but as the most effectual method to preserve it! — *You* say as well as myself, that whatever we say in vindication of ourselves, only makes the matter worse. When I said, that I meant not to alter my conduct while my conscience did not accuse me, I had no idea that you would suppose my conduct towards him had ever been of a kind that required an alteration, or any thing more pointed than to any other gentleman. I supposed you would infer from what I said that it was such as propriety and a regard for my reputation would sanction. I know not what you think it has been, but if I can judge of my own actions, — their motives I know I can, but I mean the outward appearance, — I have never treated him with any more distinction than any other gentleman, nor have appeared more pleased with his attentions than with another's; believe me, I have kept constantly in view the opinion of the world, and if you knew every circumstance of my life, you would be convinced my feelings were "tremblingly alive" to all its slanders. But "something too much of this"; you, who know my disposition, may easily conceive how often I subject myself to the envenomed shafts of censure and malice, by that gaiety and high flow of spirits, which I sometimes think my greatest misfortune to possess, — sometimes I err in judgment — don't always see the right path, — sometimes I see it, yet the warmth and ardor of my feelings force me out of it. Yet in this affair I feel confident I have acted from right principles, — there are a thousand trifling things which at times influenced my conduct, which you cannot know, and you may be surprised when I say that his attentions were of a kind that politeness obliged me to receive, nor should I ever have suspected they meant any thing more than gallantry and politeness, had not the babbles of the world put it into my head. You have been misinformed in many respects, I am convinced. You mentioned his constant visits at Sister Boyd's. I declare to you he never was there a half dozen times the three months I was in Portland, excepting the morning after the assemblies, when the gentlemen all go to see their partners; neither was I his constant partner at assemblies. I never danced but two dances in an evening with him all winter, excepting once, and then there was a mistake, — this surely was nothing remarkable, for I always danced two with Mr. Smith at every assembly we were at. I danced as much with one as the other. True, he was my partner at 2 parties at Broads. I at the time asked Horatio, when he mentioned the party, why he would not carry me; he said if I was asked by any other, to say I was going with my brother, would be considered as a tacit declaration that I had an aversion to going with him, therefore 'twould have been folly. You cannot judge unless you know a thousand customs and every . . . which they have in Portland. But I declare to you, Cousin, I am much gratified that you told me what you thought — had you have locked it in your bosom, I should never have had an opportunity to vindicate myself. I beg of you always to write with freedom, always write with the same openness you did in your last — 'tis one of the greatest advantages I expect to derive from our correspondence — I enjoin it upon you as you value my happiness. I told you I would show you some of Martha's letters; I had one from her since I wrote you, in which she says I must on no condition whatever show her letters, — however, I will read you some passages in some of them. You *shall* see some parts; I will make my peace with — indeed I know she would not object. I love to show you her letters because you feel something as I do in reading them. You admire her or you should not be the friend of

Eliza.

□

SUNDAY, SCARBOROUGH, MAY ——, 1801.

. . . I believe I possess decent talents and should have been quite another being had they been properly cultivated. But as it is, I can never get over some little prejudices which I have imbibed long since, and which warp all the faculties of my mind. I was pushed on to the stage of action without one principle to guide my actions, — the impulse of the moment was the only incitement. I have never committed any grossly imprudent action, yet I have been folly's darling child. I trust they were rather errors of the head than the heart, for we have all a kind of inherent power to distinguish between right and wrong, and if before the heart becomes contaminated by the maxims of society it is left to act from impulse though it have no fixt principle, yet it will not materially err. Possessing a gay lively disposition, I pursued pleasure with ardor. I wished for admiration, and took the means which would be most likely to obtain it. I found the mind of a female, if such a thing existed, was thought not worth cultivating. I disliked the trouble of thinking for myself and therefore adopted the sentiments of others — fully convinced to adorn my person and acquire a few little accomplishments was sufficient to secure me the admiration of the society I frequented. I cared but little about the mind. I learned to flutter about with a thoughtless gaiety — a mere feather which every breath had power to move. I left school with a head full of something, tumbled in without order or connection. I returned home with a determination to put it in more order; I set about the great work of culling the best part to make a few sentiments out of — to serve as a little ready change in my commerce with the world. But I soon lost all patience (a virtue I do not possess in an eminent degree), for the greater part of my ideas I was obliged to throw away without knowing where I got them or what I should do with them; what remained I pieced as ingeniously as I could into a few patchwork opinions, — they are now almost worn threadbare, and as I am about quilting a few more, I beg you will send me any spare ideas you may chance to have that will answer my turn. By this time I suppose you have found out what you have a right to expect from this correspondence, and probably at this moment lay down the letter with a long sage-like face to ponder on my egotism. — 'Tis a delightful employment, I will leave you to enjoy it while I eat my dinner: And what is the result, Cousin? I suppose a few exclamations on the girl's vanity to think no subject could interest me but where herself was concerned, or the barrenness of her head that could write on no other subject. But she is a *female*, say you, with a *manly contempt*. Oh you Lords of the world, what are you that your unhallowed lips should dare profane the fairest part of creation! But honestly I wish to say something by way of apology, but don't seem to know what, — it is true I have a kind of natural affection for myself, I find no one more ready to pardon my faults or find excuses for my failings — it is natural to love our friends. . . .

Eliza.

□

SCARBOROUGH, JUNE 1ST, 1801.
As to the qualities of mind peculiar to each sex, I agree with you that sprightliness is in favor of females and profundity of males. Their

education, their pursuits would create such a quality even tho' nature
had not implanted it. The business and pursuits of men require deep
thinking, judgment, and moderation, while, on the other hand, females are
under no necessity of dipping deep, but merely "skim the surface," and
we too commonly spare ourselves the exertion which deep researches
require, unless they are absolutely necessary to our pursuits in life. We
rarely find one giving themselves up to profound investigation for amusement merely. Necessity is the nurse of all the great qualities of the mind;
it explores all the hidden treasures and by its stimulating power they are
"polished into brightness." Women who have no such incentives to action
suffer all the strong energetic qualities of the mind to sleep in obscurity;
sometimes a ray of genius gleams through the thick clouds with which
it is enveloped, and irradiates for a moment the darkness of mental night;
yet, like a comet that shoots wildly from its sphere, it excites our wonder,
and we place it among the phenomenons of nature, without searching
for a natural cause. Thus it is the qualities with which nature has endowed us, as a support amid the misfortunes of life and a shield from
the allurements of vice, are left to moulder in ruin. In this dormant state
they become enervated and impaired, and at last die for *want of exercise.*
The little airy qualities which produce sprightliness are left to flutter
about like feathers in the wind, the sport of every breeze.

Women have more fancy, more lively imaginations than men. That
is easily accounted for: a person of correct judgment and accurate discernment will never have that flow of ideas which one of a different
character might, — every object has not the power to introduce into his
mind such a variety of ideas, he rejects all but those closely connected
with it. On the other hand, a person of small discernment will receive
every idea that arises in the mind, making no distinction between those
nearly related and those more distant, they are all equally welcome, and
consequently such a mind abounds with fanciful, out-of-the-way ideas.
Women have more imagination, more sprightliness, because they have
less discernment. I never was of opinion that the pursuits of the sexes
ought to be the same; on the contrary, I believe it would be destructive
to happiness, there would a degree of rivalry exist, incompatible with
the harmony we wish to establish. I have ever thought it necessary that
each should have a separate sphere of action, — in such a case there
could be no clashing unless one or the other should leap their respective
bounds. Yet to cultivate the qualities with which we are endowed can
never be called infringing the prerogatives of man. Why, my dear Cousin,
were we furnished with such powers, unless the improvement of them
would conduce to the happiness of society? Do you suppose the mind
of woman the only work of God that was "made in vain." The cultiva-
tion of the powers we possess, I have ever thought a privilege (or I may
say duty) that belonged to the human species, and not man's exclusive
prerogative. Far from destroying the harmony that ought to subsist, it
would fix it on a foundation that would not totter at every jar. Women
would be under the same degree of subordination that they now are;

enlighten and expand their minds, and they would perceive the necessity of such a regulation to preserve the order and happiness of society. Yet you require that their conduct should be always guided by that reason which you refuse them the power of exercising. I know it is generally thought that in such a case women would assume the right of commanding. But I see no foundation for such a supposition, — not a blind submission to the will of another which neither honor nor reason dictates. It would be criminal in such a case to submit, for we are under a prior engagement to conduct in all things according to the dictates of reason. I had rather be the meanest reptile that creeps the earth, or cast upon the wide world to suffer all the ills "that flesh is heir to," than live a slave to the despotic will of another.

I am aware of the censure that will ever await the female that attempts the vindication of her sex, yet I dare to brave that censure that I know to be undeserved. It does not follow (O what a pen!) that every female who vindicates the capacity of the sex is a disciple of Mary Wolstoncraft. Though I allow her to have said many things which I cannot but approve, yet the very foundation on which she builds her work will be apt to prejudice us so against her that we will not allow her the merit she really deserves, — yet, prejudice set aside, I confess I admire many of her sentiments, notwithstanding I believe should any one adopt her principles, they would conduct in the same manner, and upon the whole her life is the best comment on her writings. Her style is nervous and commanding, her sentiments appear to carry conviction along with them, but they will not bear analyzing. I wish to say something on your *natural refinement*, but I shall only have room to touch upon it if I begin, "therefore, I'll leave it till another time." . . .

E. S.

□

PORTLAND, MAY 23, 1802.
. . . I have been pondering on your new plan of life, yet I confess it does not appear to me so delightful as to you, it sounds well, — tickles the fancy, — cuts a pretty figure on paper and would form a delightful chapter for a novel. Our novelists have worn the pleasures of rural life threadbare, every lovesick swain imagines that with the mistress of his heart he could leave the noisy tumultuous scenes of life and in the shades of rural retirement feel all the delightful serenity and peace ascribed to the golden age. . . .

I am convinced that a country life is more calculated to produce that security and happiness we are all in pursuit of than any other, but those who have ever been accustomed to it have no relish for its pleasures, and those who quit the busy scenes of life, disgusted by the duplicity or ingratitude of the world, or oppressed by the weight of accumulated misfortune — carry with them feelings and sentiments which cannot be reciprocated. Solitary happiness I have no idea of, 'tis only in the delightful sympathies of friendship, similarity of sentiments, that genuine happiness can be enjoyed. Your mind is cultivated and enlarged, your sentiments delicate and refined, you could not expect to find many with whom you could converse on a perfect equality, — or rather many whose sentiments could assimilate with yours. Were I a man, I should think it cowardly to bury myself in solitude, — nay, I should be unwilling to confess I felt myself unable to preserve my virtue where there were temptations to destroy it, there is no merit in being virtuous when there is no struggle to preserve that virtue. 'Tis in the midst of temptations and allurements that the active and generous virtues must be exerted in their full force. One virtuous action where there were temptations and delusions to surmount would give more delight to my own heart, more real satisfaction than a whole life spent in more negative goodness, he must be base indeed who can voluntarily act wrong when no allurement draws him from the path of virtue. You say you never dip't much into the pleasures of *high life* and therefore should have but little to regret on that score. In the choice of life one ought to consult their own dispositions and inclinations, their own powers and talents. We all have a preference to some particular mode of life, and we surely ought to endeavor to arrive at that which will more probably ensure us most happiness. I have often thought what profession I should choose were I a man. I might then think very differently from what I do now, yet I have always thought if I felt conscious of possessing brilliant talents, the *law* would be my choice. Then I might hope to arrive at an eminence which would be gratifying to my feelings. I should then hope to be a public character, respected and admired, — but unless I was convinced I possessed the talents which would distinguish me as a speaker I would be anything rather than a lawyer; — from the dry sameness of such employments as the business of an office all my feelings would revolt, but to be an eloquent speaker would be the delight of my heart. I thank Heaven I was *born* a woman. I have now only patiently to wait till some clever fellow shall take a fancy to me and place me in a situation, I am determined to make the best of it, let it be what it will. We ladies, you know, possess that "sweet pliability of temper" that disposes us to enjoy any situation, and we must have no choice in these things till we find what is to be our destiny, then we must consider it the best in the world. But remember, I desire to be thankful I am not a man. I should not be content with moderate abilities — nay, I should not be content with mediocrity in any thing, but as a woman I am equal to the generality of my sex, and I do not feel that great desire of fame I think I should if I was a man. Should you hereafter become an inhabitant of Boyford I make no doubt you will be very happy, because you will weigh all the advantages and disadvantages. . . .

Adieu — dinner is ready and I have nothing to say worth losing it for, write me often — I shall be at home alone these two months to come, — remember you have it in your power to amuse and gratify.

Eliza.

B lack males and females experienced the horrors of slavery in different ways. Black women, regarded as sexual objects by white men, lived with the constant threat of rape and physical violence. Actual sexual abuse of enslaved women was widespread. Under such brutal circumstances, the social and psychological ramifications of sexual maturation were extremely complicated and painful for young black women, as can be seen in the graphic account that follows. The author, Harriet Brent Jacobs, describes the suffering and frustration she endured as a fifteen-year-old slave in the 1830s, and her experiences present a dramatic contrast to those of Eliza Southgate Bowne.

Born in the South in 1818, Harriet spent her childhood with her parents and younger brother, William, in what she characterized as a "comfortable home." She remembered her first mistress as a kind woman who allowed her time to play, did not overwork her, and taught her to read and write. Her owner and her mother were half-sisters, a not uncommon situation under slavery.

After the deaths of her mother, father, and mistress, Harriet, at the age of thirteen, was bequeathed to a child of five, the niece of her former owner. Harriet's new master was the child's father, Dr. Flint, a physician who owned several farms in the country and a home in town where his practice was located. Harriet and her brother resided in the Flint's town home. The children's grandmother lived nearby and provided their only source of comfort and strength.

In her life story, Harriet describes Dr. Flint's constant reminders that she was "subject to his will in all things" and her struggles to resist his sexual advances. With no recourse under the law, Harriet had to devise day-to-day tactics for avoiding her master, such as feigning ignorance of his intentions.

Treatment of slaves varied in the nineteenth century, depending on such factors as the temperament and economic situation of individual masters and the size and location of the home, farm, or plantation where the slaves resided. Harriet was fortunate in comparison with many other slave women in that she lived in a small town. Only concern for his reputation and standing in the community restrained Dr. Flint from taking more violent action against Harriet. On isolated farms and plantations such community pressure did not operate as a deterrent.

In addition to chronicling the abuse she received from Dr. Flint, Harriet analyzed the tensions and conflicts in her relationship with Dr. Flint's wife. Her husband's sexual misconduct engendered feelings of jealousy and rage in Mrs. Flint, which she vented on Harriet.

Subjugation to the will of her owner extended to all areas of Harriet's life, including the matter of marriage. Out of vindictiveness, Dr. Flint did not allow her to marry the young black man she loved.

When she was twenty-one years old, Harriet ran away from the Flints and hid in a secret space in her grandmother's house for seven years. Finally she arranged for passage on a ship bound for Philadelphia and completed her escape. *Incidents in the Life of a Slave Girl,* from which this excerpt is taken, was published in 1861. Harriet wrote under the pseudonym Linda Brent and used fictitious names in the book to protect those who had aided in her escape.

Harriet dictated her story to the well-known nineteenth-century abolitionist Lydia Maria Child. In their efforts to end slavery, the abolitionists waged a massive propaganda campaign, making extensive use of slave narratives such as Harriet's. Although Child interjected her own comments about slavery throughout the autobiography, those additions have been deleted here to allow the harsh circumstances of Harriet's life to speak for themselves.

— 7 —

Harriet Brent Jacobs

THE TRIALS OF GIRLHOOD

During the first years of my service in Dr. Flint's family, I was accustomed to share some indulgences with the children of my mistress. Though this seemed to me no more than right, I was grateful for it, and tried to merit the kindness by the faithful discharge of my duties. But I now entered on my fifteenth year — a sad epoch in the life of a slave girl. My master began to whisper foul words in my ear. Young as I was, I could not remain ignorant of their import. I tried to treat them with indifference or contempt. The master's age, my extreme youth, and the fear that his conduct would be reported to my grandmother, made him bear this treatment for many months. He was a crafty man, and resorted to many means to accomplish his purposes. Sometimes he had stormy, terrific ways, that made his victims tremble; sometimes he assumed a gentleness that he thought must surely subdue. Of the two, I preferred his stormy moods, although they left me trembling. He tried his utmost to corrupt the pure principles my grandmother had instilled. He peopled my young mind with unclean images, such as only a vile monster could think of. I turned from him with disgust and hatred. But he was my master. I was compelled to live under the same roof with him — where I saw a man forty years my senior daily violating the most sacred commandments of nature. He told me I was his property; that I must be subject to his will in all things. My soul revolted against the mean tyranny. But where could I turn for protection? No matter whether the slave girl be as black as ebony or as fair as her mistress. In either case, there is no

SOURCE: L. Maria Child, ed., *Incidents in the Life of a Slave Girl* (Boston: Published for the Author, 1861).

shadow of law to protect her from insult, from violence, or even from death; all these are inflicted by fiends who bear the shape of men. The mistress, who ought to protect the helpless victim, has no other feelings towards her but those of jealousy and rage....

Every where the years bring to all enough of sin and sorrow; but in slavery the very dawn of life is darkened by these shadows. Even the little child, who is accustomed to wait on her mistress and her children, will learn, before she is twelve years old, why it is that her mistress hates such and such a one among the slaves. Perhaps the child's own mother is among those hated ones. She listens to violent outbreaks of jealous passion, and cannot help understanding what is the cause. She will become prematurely knowing in evil things. Soon she will learn to tremble when she hears her master's footfall.

...My master met me at every turn, reminding me that I belonged to him, and swearing by heaven and earth that he would compel me to submit to him. If I went out for a breath of fresh air, after a day of unwearied toil, his footsteps dogged me. If I knelt by my mother's grave, his dark shadow fell on me even there. The light heart which nature had given me became heavy with sad forebodings. The other slaves in my master's house noticed the change. Many of them pitied me; but none dared to ask the cause. They had no need to inquire. They knew too well the guilty practices under that roof; and they were aware that to speak of them was an offence that never went unpunished.

I longed for some one to confide in. I would have given the world to have laid my head on my grandmother's faithful bosom, and told her all my troubles. But Dr. Flint swore he would kill me, if I was not as silent as the grave. Then, although my grandmother was all in all to me, I feared her as well as loved her. I had been accustomed to look up to her with a respect bordering upon awe. I was very young, and felt shame-faced about telling her such impure things, especially as I knew her to be very strict on such subjects. Moreover, she was a woman of a high spirit. She was usually very quiet in her demeanor; but if her indignation was once roused, it was not very easily quelled. I had been told that she once chased a white gentleman with a loaded pistol, because he insulted one of her daughters. I dreaded the consequences of a violent outbreak; and both pride and fear kept me silent. But though I did not confide in my grandmother, and even evaded her vigilant watchfulness and inquiry, her presence in the neighborhood was some protection to me. Though she had been a slave, Dr. Flint was afraid of her. He dreaded her scorching rebukes. Moreover, she was known and patronized by many people; and he did not wish to have his villany made public. It was lucky for me that I did not live on a distant plantation, but in a town not so large that the inhabitants were ignorant of each other's affairs. Bad as are the laws and customs in a slaveholding community, the doctor, as a professional man, deemed it prudent to keep up some outward show of decency.

THE JEALOUS MISTRESS

...Mrs. Flint possessed the key to her husband's character before I was born. She might have used this knowledge to counsel and to screen the young and the innocent among her slaves; but for them she had no sympathy. They were the objects of her constant suspicion and malevolence. She watched her husband with unceasing vigilance; but he was well practised in means to evade it. What he could not find opportunity to say in words he manifested in signs. He invented more than were ever thought of in a deaf and dumb asylum. I let them pass, as if I did not understand what he meant; and many were the curses and threats bestowed on me for my stupidity. One day he caught me teaching myself to write. He frowned, as if he was not well pleased; but I suppose he came to the conclusion that such an accomplishment might help to advance his favorite scheme. Before long, notes were often slipped into my hand. I would return them, saying, "I can't read them, sir." "Can't you?" he replied; "then I must read them to you." He always finished the reading by asking, "Do you understand?" Sometimes he would complain of the heat of the tea room, and order his supper to be placed on a small table in the piazza. He would seat himself there with a well-satisfied smile, and tell me to stand by and brush away the flies. He would eat very slowly, pausing between the mouthfuls. These intervals were employed in describing the happiness I was so foolishly throwing away, and in threatening me with the penalty that finally awaited my stubborn disobedience. He boasted much of the forbearance he had exercised towards me, and reminded me that there was a limit to his patience. When I succeeded in avoiding opportunities for him to talk to me at home, I was ordered to come to his office, to do some errand. When there, I was obliged to stand and listen to such language as he saw fit to address to me. Sometimes I so openly expressed my contempt for him that he would become violently enraged, and I wondered why he did not strike me. Circumstanced as he was, he probably thought it was better policy to be forbearing. But the state of things grew worse and worse daily. In desperation I told him that I must and would apply to my grandmother for protection. He threatened me with death, and worse than death, if I made any complaint to her. Strange to say, I did not despair. I was naturally of a buoyant disposition, and always I had a hope of somehow getting out of his clutches. Like many a poor, simple slave before me, I trusted that some threads of joy would yet be woven into my dark destiny.

I had entered my sixteenth year, and every day it became more apparent that my presence was intolerable to Mrs. Flint. Angry words frequently passed between her and her husband. He had never punished me himself, and he would not allow any body else to punish me. In that respect, she was never satisfied; but, in her angry moods, no terms were too vile for her to bestow upon me. Yet I, whom she detested so bitterly, had far more pity for her than he had, whose duty it was to make her life happy. I never wronged her, or wished to wrong her; and one word of kindness from her would have brought me to her feet.

After repeated quarrels between the doctor and his wife, he announced his intention to take his youngest daughter, then four years old, to sleep in his apartment. It was necessary that a servant should sleep in the same room, to be on hand if the child stirred. I was selected for that office, and informed for what purpose that arrangement had been made. By managing to keep within sight of people, as much as possible, during the day time, I had hitherto succeeded in eluding my master, though a razor was often held to my throat to force me to change this line of policy. At night I slept by the side of my great aunt, where I felt safe. He was too prudent to come into her room. She was an old woman, and had been in the family many years. Moreover, as a married man, and a professional man, he deemed it necessary to save appearances in some degree. But he resolved to remove the obstacle in the way of his scheme; and he thought he had planned it so that he should evade suspicion. He was well aware how much I prized my refuge by the side of my old aunt, and he determined to dispossess me of it. The first night the doctor had the little child in his room alone. The next morning, I was ordered to take my station as nurse the following night. A kind Providence interposed in my favor. During the day Mrs. Flint heard of this new arrangement, and a storm followed. I rejoiced to hear it rage.

After a while my mistress sent for me to come to her room. Her first question was, "Did you know you were to sleep in the doctor's room?"

"Yes, ma'am."

"Who told you?"

"My master."

"Will you answer truly all the questions I ask?"

"Yes, ma'am."

"Tell me, then, as you hope to be forgiven, are you innocent of what I have accused you?"

"I am."

She handed me a Bible, and said, "Lay your hand on your heart, kiss this holy book, and swear before God that you tell me the truth."

I took the oath she required, and I did it with a clear conscience.

"You have taken God's holy word to testify your innocence," said she. "If you have deceived me, beware! Now take this stool, sit down, look me directly in the face, and tell me all that has passed between your master and you."

I did as she ordered. As I went on with my account her color changed frequently, she wept, and sometimes groaned. She spoke in tones so sad, that I was touched by her grief. The tears came to my eyes; but I was soon convinced that her emotions arose from anger and wounded pride. She felt that her marriage vows were desecrated, her dignity insulted; but she had no compassion for the poor victim of her husband's perfidy. She pitied herself as a martyr; but she was incapable of feeling for the condition of shame and misery in which her unfortunate, helpless slave was placed.

Yet perhaps she had some touch of feeling for me; for when the conference was ended, she spoke kindly, and promised to protect me. I should have been much comforted by this assurance if I could have had confidence in it; but my experiences in slavery had filled me with distrust. She was not a very refined woman, and had not much control over her passions. I was an object of her jealousy, and, consequently, of her hatred; and I knew I could not expect kindness or confidence from her under the circumstances in which I was placed. I could not blame her. Slave-holders' wives feel as other women would under similar circumstances. The fire of her temper kindled from small sparks, and now the flame became so intense that the doctor was obliged to give up his intended arrangement.

I knew I had ignited the torch, and I expected to suffer for it afterwards; but I felt too thankful to my mistress for the timely aid she rendered me to care much about that. She now took me to sleep in a room adjoining her own. There I was an object of her especial care, though not of her especial comfort, for she spent many a sleepless night to watch over me. Sometimes I woke up, and found her bending over me. At other times she whispered in my ear, as though it was her husband who was speaking to me, and listened to hear what I would answer. If she startled me, on such occasions, she would glide stealthily away; and the next morning she would tell me I had been talking in my sleep, and ask who I was talking to. At last, I began to be fearful for my life. It had been often threatened; and you can imagine, better than I can describe, what an unpleasant sensation it must produce to wake up in the dead of night and find a jealous woman bending over you. Terrible as this experience was, I had fears that it would give place to one more terrible.

My mistress grew weary of her vigils; they did not prove satisfactory. She changed her tactics. She now tried the trick of accusing my master of crime, in my presence, and gave my name as the author of the accusation. To my utter astonishment, he replied, "I don't believe it; but if she did acknowledge it, you tortured her into exposing me." Tortured into exposing him! Truly, Satan had no difficulty in distinguishing the color of his soul! I understood his object in making this false representation. It was to show me that I gained nothing by seeking the protection of my mistress; that the power was still all in his own hands. I pitied Mrs. Flint. She was a second wife, many years the junior of her husband; and the hoary-headed miscreant was enough to try the patience of a wiser and better woman. She was completely foiled, and knew not how to proceed. She would gladly have had me flogged for my supposed false oath; but, as I have already stated, the doctor never allowed any one to whip me. The old sinner was politic. The application of the lash might have led to remarks that would have exposed him in the eyes of his children and grandchildren. How often did I rejoice that I lived in a town where all the inhabitants knew each other! If I had been on a remote plantation, or lost among the multitude of a crowded city, I should not be a living woman at this day.

...My grandmother could not avoid seeing things which excited her suspicions. She was uneasy about me, and tried various ways to buy me; but the neverchanging answer was always repeated: "Linda does not belong to *me*. She is my daughter's property, and I have no legal right to sell her." The conscientious man! He was too scrupulous to *sell* me; but he had no scruples whatever about committing a much greater wrong against the helpless young girl placed under his guardianship, as his daughter's property. Sometimes my persecutor would ask me whether I would like to be sold. I told him I would rather be sold to any body than to lead such a life as I did. On such occasions he would assume the air of a very injured individual, and reproach me for my ingratitude. "Did I not take you into the house, and make you the companion of my own children?" he would say. "Have I ever treated you like a negro? I have never allowed you to be punished, not even to please your mistress. And this is the recompense I get, you ungrateful girl!" I answered that he had reasons of his own for screening me from punishment, and that the course he pursued made my mistress hate me and persecute me. If I wept, he would say, "Poor child! Don't cry! don't cry! I will make peace for you with your mistress. Only let me arrange matters in my own way. Poor, foolish girl! you don't know what is for your own good. I would cherish you. I would make a lady of you. Now go, and think of all I have promised you."

I did think of it. ...

THE LOVER

There was in the neighborhood a young colored carpenter; a free born man. We had been well acquainted in childhood, and frequently met together afterwards. We became mutually attached, and he proposed to marry me. I loved him with all the ardor of a young girl's first love. But when I reflected that I was a slave, and that the laws gave no sanction to the marriage of such, my heart sank within me. My lover wanted to buy me; but I knew that Dr. Flint was too wilful and arbitrary a man to consent to that arrangement. From him, I was sure of experiencing all sorts of opposition, and I had nothing to hope from my mistress. She would have been delighted to have got rid of me, but not in that way. It would have relieved her mind of a burden if she could have seen me sold to some distant state, but if I was married near home I should be just as much in her husband's power as I had previously been, — for the husband of a slave has no power to protect her. Moreover, my mistress, like many others, seemed to think that slaves had no right to any family ties of their own; that they were created merely to wait upon the family of the mistress. I once heard her abuse a young slave girl, who told her that a colored man wanted to make her his wife. "I will have you peeled and pickled, my lady," said she, "if I ever hear you mention that subject again. Do you suppose that I will have you tending *my* children with the children of that nigger?" The girl to whom she said this had a mulatto child, of course not acknowledged by its father. The poor black man who loved her would have been proud to acknowledge his helpless offspring.

Many and anxious were the thoughts I revolved in my mind. I was at a loss what to do. Above all things, I was desirous to spare my lover the insults that had cut so deeply into my own soul. I talked with my grandmother about it, and partly told her my fears. I did not dare to tell her the worst. She had long suspected all was not right, and if I confirmed her suspicions I knew a storm would rise that would prove the overthrow of all my hopes.

This love-dream had been my support through many trials; and I could not bear to run the risk of having it suddenly dissipated. There was a lady in the neighborhood, a particular friend of Dr. Flint's, who often visited the house. I had a great respect for her, and she had always manifested a friendly interest in me. Grandmother thought she would have great influence with the doctor. I went to this lady, and told her my story. I told her I was aware that my lover's being a free-born man would prove a great objection; but he wanted to buy me; and if Dr. Flint would consent to that arrangement, I felt sure he would be willing to pay any reasonable price. She knew that Mrs. Flint disliked me; therefore, I ventured to suggest that perhaps my mistress would approve of my being sold, as that would rid her of me. The lady listened with kindly sympathy, and promised to do her utmost to promote my wishes. She had an interview with the doctor, and I believe she pleaded my cause earnestly; but it was all to no purpose.

How I dreaded my master now! Every minute I expected to be summoned to his presence; but the day passed, and I heard nothing from him. The next morning, a message was brought to me: "Master wants you in his study." I found the door ajar, and I stood a moment gazing at the hateful man who claimed a right to rule me, body and soul. I entered, and tried to appear calm. I did not want him to know how my heart was bleeding. He looked fixedly at me, with an expression which seemed to say, "I have half a mind to kill you on the spot." At last he broke the silence, and that was a relief to both of us.

"So you want to be married, do you?" said he, "and to a free nigger."

"Yes, sir."

"Well, I'll soon convince you whether I am your master, or the nigger fellow you honor so highly. If you *must* have a husband, you may take up with one of my slaves."

What a situation I should be in, as the wife of one of *his* slaves, even if my heart had been interested!

I replied, "Don't you suppose, sir, that a slave can have some preference about marrying? Do you suppose that all men are alike to her?"

"Do you love this nigger?" said he, abruptly.

"Yes, sir."

"How dare you tell me so!" he exclaimed, in great wrath. After a slight pause, he added, "I supposed you thought more of yourself; that you felt above the insults of such puppies."

I replied, "If he is a puppy I am a puppy, for we are both of the negro race. It is right and honorable for us to love each other. The man you call a puppy never insulted me, sir; and he would not love me if he did not believe me to be a virtuous woman."

He sprang upon me like a tiger, and gave me a stunning blow. It was the first time he had ever struck me; and fear did not enable me to control my anger. When I had recovered a little from the effects, I exclaimed, "You have struck me for answering you honestly. How I despise you!"

There was silence for some minutes. Perhaps he was deciding what should be my punishment; or, perhaps, he wanted to give me time to reflect on what I had said, and to whom I had said it. Finally, he asked, "Do you know what you have said?"

"Yes, sir; but your treatment drove me to it."

"Do you know that I have a right to do as I like with you, — that I can kill you, if I please?"

"You have tried to kill me, and I wish you had; but you have no right to do as you like with me."

"Silence!" he exclaimed, in a thundering voice. "By heavens, girl, you forget yourself too far! Are you mad? If you are, I will soon bring you to your senses. Do you think any other master would bear what I have borne from you this morning? Many masters would have killed you on the spot. How would you like to be sent to jail for your insolence?"

"I know I have been disrespectful, sir," I replied; "but you drove me to it; I couldn't help it. As for the jail, there would be more peace for me there than there is here.

"You deserve to go there," said he, "and to be under such treatment, that you would forget the meaning of the word *peace*. It would do you good. It would take some of your high notions out of you. But I am not ready to send you there yet, notwithstanding your ingratitude for all my kindness and forbearance. You have been the plague of my life. I have wanted to make you happy, and I have been repaid with the basest ingratitude; but though you have proved yourself incapable of appreciating my kindness, I will be lenient towards you, Linda. I will give you one more chance to redeem your character. If you behave yourself and do as I require, I will forgive you and treat you as I always have done; but if you disobey me, I will punish you as I would the meanest slave on my plantation. Never let me hear that fellow's name mentioned again. If I ever know of your speaking to him, I will cowhide you both; and if I catch him lurking about my premises, I will shoot him as soon as I would a dog. Do you hear what I say? I'll teach you a lesson about marriage and free niggers! Now go, and let this be the last time I have occasion to speak to you on this subject." . . .

For a fortnight the doctor did not speak to me. He thought to mortify me; to make me feel that I had disgraced myself by receiving the honorable addresses of a respectable colored man, in preference to the base proposals of a white man. But though his lips disdained to address me, his eyes were very loquacious. No animal ever watched its prey more narrowly than he watched me. He knew that I could write, though he had failed to make me read his letters; and he was now troubled lest I should exchange letters with another man. After a while he became weary of silence; and I was sorry for it. One morning, as he passed through the hall, to leave the house, he contrived to thrust a note into my hand. I thought I had better read it, and spare myself the vexation of having him read it to me. It expressed regret for the blow he had given me, and reminded me that I myself was wholly to blame for it. He hoped I had become convinced of the injury I was doing myself by incurring his displeasure. He wrote that he had made up his mind to go to Louisiana; that he should take several slaves with him, and intended I should be one of the number. My mistress would remain where she was; therefore I should have nothing to fear from that quarter. If I merited kindness from him, he assured me that it would be lavishly bestowed. He begged me to think over the matter, and answer the following day.

The next morning I was called to carry a pair of scissors to his room. I laid them on the table, with the letter beside them. He thought it was my answer, and did not call me back. I went as usual to attend my young mistress to and from school. He met me in the street, and ordered me to stop at his office on my way back. When I entered, he showed me his letter, and asked me why I had not answered it. I replied, "I am your daughter's property, and it is in your power to send me, or take me, wherever you please." He said he was very glad to find me so willing to go, and that we should start early in the autumn. He had a large practice in the town, and I rather thought he had made up the story merely to frighten me. However that might be, I was determined that I would never go to Louisiana with him.

Summer passed away, and early in the autumn Dr. Flint's eldest son was sent to Louisiana to examine the country, with a view to emigrating. That news did not disturb me. I knew very well that I should not be sent with *him*. That I had not been taken to the plantation before this time, was owing to the fact that his son was there. He was jealous of his son; and jealousy of the overseer had kept him from punishing me by sending me into the fields to work. Is it strange that I was not proud of these protectors? As for the overseer, he was a man for whom I had less respect than I had for a bloodhound.

Young Mr. Flint did not bring back a favorable report of Louisiana, and I heard no more of that scheme. Soon after this, my lover met me at the corner of the street, and I stopped to speak to him. Looking up, I saw my master watching us from his window. I hurried home, trembling with fear. I was sent for, immediately, to go to his room. He met me with a blow. "When is mistress to be married?" said he, in a sneering tone. A shower of oaths and imprecations followed. How thankful I was that my lover was a free man! that my tyrant had no power to flog him for speaking to me in the street!

Again and again I revolved in my mind how all this would end. There was no hope that the doctor would consent to sell me on any terms. He had an iron will, and was determined to keep me, and to conquer me. My lover was an intelligent and religious man. Even if he could have obtained permission to marry me while I was a slave, the marriage would give him no power to protect me from my master. It would have made him miserable to witness the insults I should have been subjected to. And then, if we had children, I knew they must "follow the condition of the mother." What a terrible blight that would be on the heart of a free, intelligent father! For *his* sake, I felt that I ought not to link his fate with my own unhappy destiny. He was going to Savannah to see about a little property left him by an uncle; and hard as it was to bring my feelings to it, I earnestly entreated him not to come back. I advised him to go to the Free States, where his tongue would not be tied, and where his intelligence would be of more avail to him. He left me, still hoping the day would come when I could be bought. With me the lamp of hope had gone out. The dream of my girlhood was over. I felt lonely and desolate.

Still I was not stripped of all. I still had my good grandmother, and my affectionate brother. When he put his arms round my neck, and looked into my eyes, as if to read there the troubles I dared not tell, I felt that I still had something to love. But even that pleasant emotion was chilled by the reflection that he might be torn from me at any moment, by some sudden freak of my master. If he had known how we loved each other, I think he would have exulted in separating us. We often planned together how we could get to the north. But, as William remarked, such things are easier said than done. My movements were very closely watched, and we had no means of getting any money to defray our expenses. As for grandmother, she was strongly opposed to her children's undertaking any such project. She had not forgotten poor Benjamin's sufferings, and she was afraid that if another child tried to escape, he would have a similar or a worse fate. To me, nothing seemed more dreadful than my present life. I said to myself, "William *must* be free. He shall go to the north, and I will follow him." Many a slave sister has formed the same plans.

T he sense of who one is and what one might become develops through interactions with other people in varieties of institutional settings. During adolescence the approval or disapproval of one's values and behavior by parents and especially by peers is a tremendous force in the creation of self. In the nineteenth century, family, church, school, and community all aimed to nurture qualities of character in middle-class young women that were regarded as uniquely feminine and were thought naturally fitted for their future roles as wives and mothers. Young females were expected to obey their parents dutifully, conduct themselves properly — nonaggressively — in their activities with young men, and serve as a source of moral inspiration.

A glimpse into the day-to-day concerns and experiences of a sixteen-year-old adolescent in 1881 is provided in the diary excerpts that follow. The author, Isabella Maud Rittenhouse (she preferred to be called Maud) lived in Cairo, Illinois, a frontier steamboat town with a population of about 9,000 in the 1880s. Her father was a commission grain merchant and one of Cairo's leading citizens. Her mother was an ardent feminist and active leader in many community movements and activities. Maud was the oldest of five children and the only daughter in the Rittenhouse family. In 1881 her brothers Wood, Harry, Fred, and Robin were ages fourteen, twelve, nine, and three respectively.

Maud was among the small minority of young men and women attending high school in the 1880s, and her diary is filled with details about school and social events with her peers. The important effect that those her own age had on Maud's moods and feelings about herself is apparent. Her intense self-consciousness, a characteristic associated with modern adolescence, is revealed in her continual assessments of her physical appearance, artistic abilities, and popularity among her peers. Maud's evaluations of herself seem in constant flux — at one moment her looks and personality were a source of pride and she cheerfully described how wonderful she felt, while in the next they were a cause of despair and she thought she was "homely."

Although Maud and her friends enjoyed picnics, boat trips, dances, and visits to the ice cream saloon by themselves, they shared many social activities with parents and other adults as well. Youth culture was not segregated from the world of adults in the nineteenth century, particularly in a small, frontier town.

In discussing dating and her feelings about love and marriage, Maud indicated that she fully expected romantic love would be the basis of a partnership, although it would not be the only consideration. The importance of class position is expressed in various ways in her diary and very directly in her assessments of suitors. She wrote that one seemed to "lack ambition," and she feared he would "be content to settle down for a life as foreman of a job printing office." By contrast, she described another whom she thought she loved as "business-like, energetic, and bound to make his way in the world."

Even though dating routines seemed quite casual and relaxed in the small town environment, it is evident that certain roles and rules of conduct prevailed with respect to young women. Maud worried about being a "coquette," and about how a beau would interpret a good-night kiss from her. She believed that she must inspire her suitors, encouraging them to be successful in the work world and helping them to conquer any weaknesses of character.

Maud's parents were warm and supportive of her, and there seemed to be no conflict between how they wanted her to behave and her own inclinations. As the only daughter, Maud received special attention from her father, and her requests for clothes, a piano, a horse, and other luxuries were all met. "Papa'd let me spend every cent he has I believe if I asked him for it," she wrote. Her relationship with her mother appears to have been comfortable and close. Maud went to her for advice about marriage and discussed her feelings about the young men she was dating. It was Maud's mother who encouraged her to pursue her education beyond high school and develop her artistic talents before settling down.

Maud's domestic responsibilities were not heavy ones, although she was expected to help with traditional female tasks such as preparing meals, making beds, washing dishes, and taking care of her youngest brother. When her mother traveled out of town, Maud looked forward to taking charge of the house and showing off her skills in household management.

Two years after graduation from high school, Maud enrolled at the St. Louis School of Fine Arts for a three-year course of study in drawing and painting. Afterward she returned to Cairo and lived at home until her marriage at the age of thirty. Maud did not marry Elmer, the suitor about whom she wrote so much in the diary. He was caught embezzling money from the company that employed him, much to the shock and dismay of Maud and her parents. She met her future husband in 1889 when he was working in Cairo as an assistant engineer on the construction of the Ohio River Bridge. With Maud's encouragement, he entered and completed medical school. After six years, and many more suitors in Maud's life, they reunited, married, and moved to a town near Brooklyn, New York where Maud lived to old age.

---- 8 ----

Isabella Maud Rittenhouse

SAT. APRIL 30, 1881. My April showers are generally followed by sunshine — I feel real good to-day.

Mama is 40 to-day and her little breakfast party passed off the pleasentest kind. I love to hear refined cultivated people discuss the topics of the day.

Grandma gave Mama a pair of lovely pale-blue and bobinet [a fabric weave] pillow-shams which she made herself. Harry gave her a fuschia;

SOURCE: From *Maud*, edited by Richard Lee Strout. Copyright, 1939, by The Macmillan Company. Reprinted by permission of Richard L. Strout.

Isabella Maud Rittenhouse

Robin, a white holly fan; Fred, a hemstitched linen-cambric 'kerchief. Wood, double black-walnut picture frame. Auntie, a lovely lace kerchief which she got at Chicago, Edith, a lace double-neck-kerchief, and I gave her a large silk-lace fichu [a light triangular scarf], one of those dress affairs. Oh yes, and Papa gave her two very large oil-paintings with deep gilt frames. But I'm right mad about it, for our house is running over full of pictures as it is, and he should have gotten an elegant silver water pitcher for the same price. I wanted him to give her a watch (think of a woman of 40 with no watch) or a phaeton [a four-wheeled, horse-drawn vehicle].

I rushed downtown in a hurry to get some lace for a cretonne tidy [to protect the back and arms of a chair] last night all alone, had a real nice talk with Cousin Tom. Auntie brought Edith 2 new dresses, a silk parasol, silk mitts and new hat from Chicago....

MAY-DAY. — SUNDAY — 1881. Sang in the Episcopal Choir this A.M. Daisy Halliday had on the sweetest bonnet — shape something like mine, white, and with a soft pink ostrich plume around it, and brocaded pink satin strings tied in a knot *under the chin*. (How can she stand wearing a thing which Chicago people "hoot" at.) I guess it came from Paris or New York as she gets all her apparel at those places. How lovely to be the daughter of a millionaire.

In all my days I never saw such a madly infatuated couple as Eugene and Edith (or at least never saw a couple display their madness so extensively). At 8 we all went over to church and he took her home, walking at the rate of a mile a day. Tis as good as a novel for me to watch them. So many times this week I'd be bubbling over to write some to Robert but I won't send a word till May 26. If it takes him 15 days to answer my letter it takes me 30 to answer his. So there Mr Robert — next time you won't burn up four letters because they are uninteresting.

Supper bell is tinkling. Adieu.

THURSDAY MAY 5 — 1881. Somebody told Will WmSn that he bored me awfully and if he'd any sense he'd know it. Sunday night he asked if I'd said it, and of-course I hadn't. I'd give a dime to know who told him — I have an idea.

At this rate we'll have to charter a ferry or tug to get to church. East St. Louis is flooded, and the Mississippi rising at a terrible rate. Sipe-water [floods threatened Cairo frequently, and every spring the streets filled with "sipe-water"] nearly to the tops of the side-walks up-town, blocks and blocks covered. Its under our barn and in those low colored-folks' lots behind us.

While we were practicing at the church Tuesday night, two couples went to the parsonage — one to be married. We were invited in. Such a prosaic wedding. Heavens! The groom didn't even kiss his pale and trembling bride, or call her "Little Wifey." I'll be switched if I'd get married if I couldn't be called "Little Wifey" and have somebody's smiling eyes dancing whole acres of love upon me. But such is life, that for all I know I may marry some — well let's don't talk about it since I can't know for years to come.

SATURDAY. Papa has possession of all the corn between here and New Orleans, over 30,000 bushels shelled and is going to make an immense profit on it. His traveling agent at New Orleans is holding on to it and corn is rising every day. They can't get any more down because the elevator-spouts at St Louis are below water.

He also has another big lot at St Louis, which he can sell now at a profit of about five cents per bushel, even though it can't be gotten out at present. The reason that I speak of this to you is that I *think* he will get me a grand Steinway piano, if all goes well....

Mama and Papa have gone to hear Brigham Young's 19th wife lecture on Mormonism and Papa didn't offer to take me and I'm right mad about it. — Goodnight.

FRIDAY NIGHT MAY 13/81. I'd give all I own for one good true girl-friend who would honestly love me. There's Eva, dear Eva, she likes me well enough (when Edith isn't around) but she doesn't love me at all while she seems to worship Edith — Edith so frequently cold and sharp. But Edith is pretty, when she laughs her face lights up and her eyes sparkle, so you see it is mostly Edith's *looks*.

I compare us sometimes, we two girls and wonder how it is — Edith doesn't seem to care for their love — I am *hungry* for it, she doesn't even try to be even decently *polite* to them half the time while I always speak as kindly and pleasantly as I know how, she is no smarter than I, cannot compose as well, and is more selfish I *know* and there's only one other thing, Edith is lovely and I'm homely.

Poor little blind fool! I used to think that my mouth was small and rosy, my eyes bright and black, and my movements easy and free. Today I'm actually afraid to look in the mirror. I'm so repulsive looking, — all I can see is black hair, ugly and ill fitting in front, red eyes, swollen with crying, a sallow, freckled face, and pug-nose. Then I think of Edith's clear pretty pink and pearl complexion, her large brown eyes, and fringed, curling eye-lashes, and her nut-brown hair, with the pretty graceful curls dancing all around her forehead, and I pray even while I think it wrong, that God will make me pretty.

Yes you may laugh or think about how little beauty counts in this world, if we are only good. Good! Am I bad? Don't I try till my nerves are quivering and my head aching to be good and kind and lovable? With what reward?

The girls like me when I have them stay all night or am a convenience to them and that's as far as it goes.

I can hardly believe myself that I'm jealous of Edith and her pretty face. Yet how bitter I felt coming home from school with Eva and Edith walking slowly, lovingly together like two lovers more than anything else I can think of.

But here I'm going to hush! I'm in such a bitter resentful hurt mood tonight. I did try for a while to think of my blessings and began in this strain. Met a careworn woman and thought

"Poor thing! here *I* am strong and well" (a sharp pain in my side stopped that) "and I've dear noble Robert" — (Yes dear noble Robert who waited a month to answer my letter, and all the time I'm waiting that long to answer his don't write a word to find if I'm sick, dying or dead) and so on, so you see counting my blessings only turned them into stings.

Met a horrid impudent man down town and he winked at me, and a horrid impudent *boy* stared and then smiled.

I hate them. — Goodnight.

TUESDAY MAY 17 — 1881. Can I ever express the fun I've had since I last wrote. Saturday morning Edith and I started safely off to Villa Ridge. Elmer rode a little while with us. Reached the Villa at noon and were met by Corinne and Annie who were of course glad to see us as we them. After dinner we flew over the hills and far away, crossed a dear little brook with wild peppermint growing all around it and then climbed a rickety rail fence to find ourselves in the loveliest wood with ferns and wildflowers on all hands.

We gathered a tub-full of the loveliest and fairest. Wrote postals to Mama and Elmer (asking him to come up with Eugene Sunday, by Corinne's special request).

Elmer brought me the Sunday Bulletin with that sweet continued story in it. After dinner we sat on the porch and sang soft and sweetly till dark. Then we went in but didn't strike a light on account of the mosquitoes. Edith and Eugene were in one corner and Corinne, Annie, Elmer and I in the other. Annie says Eugene had his arm around Edith and I'll declare to goodness I believe he did. Elmer had promised to tell me the "little story" which he had put off since last December, and so with a wrap around me (for it was damp) we strolled down the path to the gate.

The story was a question which amounted to the sequel, or 2nd chapter rather, of our last winter's serious talk.

You remember my telling him he must not kiss me good-night because 'twas encouragement I could not give him knowing as I did how much better than Elmer I loved my bad boy with his merry blue eyes and sensitive heart out in the Rocky Mountains.

So he said he'd wait, "there was plenty of time yet," and he did hope I could grow to love him better than that other.

Here on one hand is Elmer, steady, business-like, pleasant, saying he loves me better than all else.

On the other, Robert, graceful, accomplished, polished and yet with a vein of seeming deep earnestness underlying it all, and he calls me "dear little sister" and says to let time show how much in earnest he is and how good he can be to win the little girl with the "big brown eyes."

Truly, my mind was never in such a state of indecision — Mama talks eternally about how good and steady and sensible Elmer is, and yet I know how she loves Robert and how kindly she kissed him goodbye.

I think how moral and kind Elmer is and then go to bed and dream of Robert calling me "Sweet little woman" and then wake up mad and wish I'd never seen a male creature in my life.

I could hardly sleep for thinking. This state of indecision seems really wicked, but I don't know how to help it.

The idea of an infant of 16 having to bother her head about lovers and sich. I'll declare its horrid. . . .

WED MAY 18 — 1881. Was up, dressed and studying at five this morning and didn't go to sleep till midnight so you see I was sleepy. Had an awful examination in Ancient History and came home at 1, laid down to sleep at 2, and slept till 5:30.

Such a glorious time as I had last night! Got my dress at 7 and you can't imagine how funny I felt in that light, regular ladies' evening dress. Mrs James just "laid herself out on it" and home it came, light and fluffy, trimmed in the loveliest satin and silk cords, with square neck and puffed sleeves. Wore my little bonnet (that I made of satin lace and flowers) and it just matched my dress, and Miss K said this morning it was lovely and so becoming that she heard several say I ought to wear bonnets all the time.

FRIDAY MAY 20 — 1881. Back must I spring to Wed night. Elmer and I loitered home and when we reached the porch he asked if I remembered the 18th of May one year ago? I did — it was the day I went to the Ft Jefferson Picnic with him.

"I've worn this ring of yours a year tonight," he said, speaking of my amethyst, "and now I want to wish a little ring upon your finger."

I hesitated but finally said "for a time only" and he placed a beautiful new amethyst much prettier than my old one, upon my finger.

It was almost 1 o'clock before I got to sleep and I was nearly dead I was so tired. My last thought before journeying to Dreamland was, "Wouldn't it be horrid if I should be serenaded tonight? I'll declare, I don't believe I'd get up at all. I'm too tired."

I seemed to have dozed about 10 minutes when I was wakened by the sounds of music. I got up, went to my room, lit the gas, threw out a card & danced to the music awhile. It was 3:30 when I crept back to bed and 5:30 got up to study, dress and take my early music lesson. Found upon the porch the remains of the serenaders, viz: a card with "Compliments of Eugene E. Ellis and Will B. Williamson" on it.

After dinner yesterday we all started for the Carnival of Authors. I fully anticipated a dull horrid time and as usual had a most superb time, ten times more pleasant than any previous evening. I found that my Maud Muller scene was to come between the tableau "Othello" and "Music by the Orchestra."

Just before the Othello tableau I went into the dressing room trembling from crown to toe.

Mrs Candee said "Scream Maud. Try to speak as loud as I did. They couldn't even hear *me* in the back part of the room." Mrs Winter helped me to the stage where "Maud Muller and the Judge" were arranging for the coming tableau, and then I heard Mr Candee's announcement and, when the bell rang, shaking like a leaf, I stepped out.

But no sooner did I set eyes on that dizzy sea of faces than I felt as cool, self-possessed, elated as a "nateral-born" actress.

I waited till every sound in the hall had ceased and then began.

Once I nearly laughed at Professor Sanders. You know how deaf he is? Well, he sat way back and with his hand at his ear was straining every nerve. I was bound he should hear and let my voice out as full and clear as I possibly could. I could see the Shakespeare Booth in the opposite end of the house, and knew by their faces that every character in it understood me.

It didn't take me long to forget the audience entirely and with only "sweet Maud Muller" the "meadow brook" and "the clover blooms" in my mind, proceeded.

When I finished and stepped back there was a perfect round of applause all over the house, and Mrs Winter caught me in her arms saying "You darling! You did splendidly! I heard every word, clear and distinct as a bell." Then Mr Silver led me out to get me a drink and the first person I ran into was a little flower-girl who exclaimed, "Oh, it was beautiful, Maud."

I had a message from Eugene, and Will (to get me away from Elmer) started me off to find him, after which we went to have some ice-cream and strawberries and so on ("so-on" means cake). While thus occupied he asked to take me to-night and I accepted his *ask*.

Hadn't got my mouth shut hardly when Elmer walked up and asked the same thing, but of-course I had to refuse him, so then he asked to take me home, which he did.

This morning Miss Krinbill at school said, "You looked lovely Maud — that dress was so pretty and becoming by gaslight." *Now* I'll let up. Of course you'll think me vain because I like to have folks say nice things about me. This is only you and I, you know, and you mustn't tell folks how silly I am over their kind encouragement.

SATURDAY NIGHT. More compliments at breakfast. Mrs Wardner — "You did look so sweet my dear. How Maud is blooming out, Mr Rittenhouse — she's growing so handsome."

"And I thought I was getting uglier all the time!"

"But you see, dear, you were in the developing age, and are now just beginning to come out in your true colors."

— I could have hugged her, as she patted me on the shoulder, looking so benevolently out from her snowy hair and cap, for it is so good to know I'm not getting uglier. Maybe people can love me sometime after all — not that I think I'm handsome. What a joke that would be!

At the Fort Jefferson picnic today Will whisked me off to a secluded nook, under a great tree with roots spreading into the bubbling brook and was inclined to be "spoony," while I, perfectly unconscious, teased him, made fun of him, and worried him generally till I tired and then went back and joined Mama and Elmer. Eugene and Edith (who'd been in the woods since dinner) soon came up. At about 6 we started home on the *Three States*, danced one quadrille on board.

Thursday is the 26th day of May when I intended writing to Robert. I shall upon that day and not sooner.

TUESDAY MAY 24 — 81. I've just finished one of the meanest letters I ever wrote in my life — its to Robert. I began it after this month of waiting —

"Rec'd your letter the other day, and now hasten to answer." Its dated May 26 — and I'll send it then.

It's 11 pages of what a gorgeously glorious time I've been having since "the other day," when I last wrote, and the other page (there are twelve) sarcasm.

How I do (in the letter) pity him for such tremendous headaches and such an immense lot of copying for "Bro. Henry" that he can't even write a line, but instead keeps me down here wondering why the family are not in deeper mourning and how it is I haven't been able to find his funeral notice in any of the papers.

I wind up with,

"I suppose you remember my address, I. Maud Rittenhouse, c/o Wood R. & Bro. Cairo, Ill."

I'll bet you he's mad as a hornet. Hope he will be. I was mad as a hornet too.

This morning I rec'd a dainty little package containing 126 toads about as big as a minute. Elmer made a standing engagement for Sunday night.

P.S. I'm pretty sure WmSn sent the toads. Mighty mean joke; if I'd happened to have opened the package in the school-room the whole place would have been alive with them. Again farewell.

WED MAY 25 — 1881. WmSn sent the toads and my conjecture proved true.

Edith was down in the afternoon and I started up with her to spend the night. We stopped in the ice cream saloon and I told Grace about the frogs and she told WmSn who was passing by. He immediately came in — denied everything. Walked up with us. Finally said, he had them caught for another party — had four hundred little darkey boys all over the commons catching frogs. You know when I went up by the Bulletin office on the day before, there were half a dozen hopping about on the crossing and I stopped and touched one with my toe and said to Mabel "Look at that cute little thing — wish I had one to examine." Smarty Will heard the remark from the window. Guess he thought he'd send me enough to examine thoroughly. I told him last night I wouldn't speak to him next time we met....

FRIDAY JULY 1 1881. Well, I've done it. Written to Elmer telling him every-thing frankly. Told him we were too young to take any decided step, that years hence were better for both, that much as I respected, esteemed, trusted him I could not say that I loved him. . . .

JULY 3 — 1881. . . . Now comes some more — this concerning Edith also. On Friday night, the 27th of May, Edith, Eugene and Will spent the evening.

Will had begun getting spoony to me, and I was disgusted, wouldn't let him take my arm when he went to the ice-cream saloon, but took his, and so on. When we got upstairs, I remarked to Edith, "What *can* be the matter with WmSn? He makes me right sick!" She made a wry face, and said, "I can't imagine. I could hardly look at him either. It's disgusting," and so on, and thus we talked as silly girls will, while we were undressing. But bear in mind that Edith said just as hateful things (if not a little worse) than I did.

Now (never mind how) I've found out the reason of Will's excessive coolness. If need be I can give my authority. Miss Edith (hypocrite) growing suddenly extremely friendly with Will, kindly told him everything I said.

Isn't she a lovely cousin — how she could stoop to such a mean little deceitful act, with our blood in her veins, I don't understand. She was jealous because Will (as he often told me) liked me so much better than her, made me little presents and so on.

Within the last few weeks, when I marveled at Will's manner, how she reveled in saying, "Oh, he just beams upon me."

How hard she worked to convince me that it was all owing to my treatment of him upon that night.

"What did I do more than refuse to let him take my arm while we were walking to the ice cream saloon?"

"Well," she said, "you know you didn't talk to him much."

"I talked to him a mighty lot more than you did."

And there the conversation dropped.

I'd no more trust to Edith Martin's honor, than I would to the lowest little street Arab's.

As for Will Williamson, my contempt for him nearly equals that I bear Edith. I don't intend to stoop so far as to even acknowledge an acquaintanceship with him.

He's so anxious not to speak. I'll not compel him to. I'll never stay all night with Edith if I can help it, nor ask her here. When I can I'll go to see Auntie, for I love her. I want to tell Edith what I think of her, and all that I know. But I can't without getting my informants into trouble. More anon.

SATURDAY JULY 16 — 1881. Our Y.P.T.C. [Young People's Temperance Committee] met at Mrs. Wheeler's on the lawn Monday night because it was too hot in the hall. Mabel, Emma and I went together and, safely ensconced behind a tall cedar in the tall grass, away from the crowd, with the stars above us, we laid around loose and told fairy stories and Greek and Roman fables and ate ice cream.

Read a book of Elmer's *No Gentleman* yesterday. It is by "Yours Truly," and I like it.

But the book I read the day before *Vashti, or Until Death do Us Part,* by Evans, was the funniest thing I ever saw. The main object of the writer seems to be to compose a book as entirely different from anything else ever written as possible and I think in that she succeeds. Her girls of 16 talk philosophy, quote poetry and the "maxims of cynical Rochefoucauld." Everybody in the book save one old maid is in love, not a person finds that love reciprocated, everybody dies but two, one the hero, whose "true love" has died, the other a glorious girl, hopelessly in love with aforesaid hero, nobody gets married, and the book stops without really ending. I suppose it did me good for it kept me running to the Dictionary or to an encyclopedia to see who Joubert is, or where the "cheerless temple of Hestia" stands or stood, or to find what "a wan Alcestis" and "a desperate Cassandra he had seen at Rome," indicated.

SAT JULY 16 — 1881. This is a big boom for Cairo, this time. I believe I told you something of it once before. Two more big companies are coming now — Singer Sewing Machine Co., worth $2,000,000 and the Dixie Oil Company. This brings us hundreds of new inhabitants — working men; and houses are booming up wherever a vacant lot can be found. The lot across the street next door to Mr Winters is being filled and a house going up on it. . . .

FRIDAY AUGUST 12 — 1881 — Its after four o'clock this afternoon and the first leisure moment I've had. Got up at 6 — dressed Robin and helped get breakfast. After breakfast helped clear off the table. Emptied slops, made beds, picked up things, and then washed the dishes and swept the dining room and kitchen, got dinner (beef stew, green-corn, water melons, ice, milk and water, bread and butter, grapes, peaches, mashed potatoes, baked pears, all by myself) churned, drew buckets and buckets of water, cleared off table, washed pots (horrid, nasty, smutty pots) and dishes, swept dining room and kitchen, fluted a skirt, pressed my lawn and came upstairs, ugh, ugh, so tired. I just dropped, and the thermometer at nine o'clock stood 100 in the shade. Of course it's higher now but I haven't had time to look again. Must stop to wash and dress Robin and myself, help get supper, wash dishes etc. Woodie went to Missouri this A.M. . . .

THURSDAY — [SEPTEMBER 22, 1881] Mother's going to Chicago. Oh, to think how dignified I must be after she leaves — for I'm to be house-keeper, treasury-department and chief-manager; must see to the pantries and closets, clothes, washes, marketing, sweeping, dusting, butter, milk etc.

Mama has a string of directions a yard long even to killing two particular roosters in the back-yard for Sunday dinner.

Finished the last two cups and saucers of my china painting today and had our first fire. I had to sit with my feet in a market-basket containing a hot iron wrapped in a *Globe-Democrat* till Julia came along with her sweet coal-scuttle and bundle of kindling. I'm going to make me some sand-bags and keep hot for my feet.

MONDAY — Friday evening Mama left. I took her to the train and then came home and cried over her slippers and things. I'm house-keeper and I keep the cook in a turmoil with my experiments and new dishes. I'm economical, though, and I'm going to save Mama $16 out of her market-money these two weeks. And I set a No 1 table, dainty, plenty and varied. In fact I'm a pearl among house-keepers, and abound in — my own praises.

But you'd call me the cream and flower could you taste my lemon-gelatine, corn-oysters, fried squirrel, etc. Mr. Aisthorpe brought me over 6 nice tender squirrels last night which Will Halliday shot. Have just finished my 2nd letter to Mama.

While Clara and I were lounging on the front porch who should saunter in but Eva and Edith. Well, they all stayed to tea and after that Clara and I started to take Eva home. We were all laughing and talking when we started across a crossing (Clara and I both had on hoops). Well, what with talking, running back and forth and general monkey-ing Clara slipped and fell full length in a muddy place.

I was directly behind her and I couldn't step out of the way fast enough for my hoops, and so I had a small scramble too, but didn't fall. How funny poor Chiq did look — plush purse, cherry hat, walking sacque [short jacket fastened at the neck], dainty kerchief — all in the mud. We "picked her up tenderly," but laughed till we nearly killed ourselves.

We went to market and I bought me some beautiful fine ribbon for this winter. Papa'd let me spend every cent he has I believe if I asked him for it. Why, he wants me to buy more nice things, lets me have a horse when I want it, and a thousand other things. One charming cherry-colored neck-bow I painted with daisies and cat-tails this morning. . . .

SUNDAY OCT 2, 1881. To-morrow — behold I shall be a proud and dignified senior — a member of the class of '82.

Yesterday we had a class meeting here. Eva and I were elected a committee of two to interview Prof. Marion Bigley, informing him of our many resolutions. You know we've decided "that open daily records" be kept and that the highest in these, together with the examinations, is to be given the valedictory and the next highest the salutary. Also that "no marks in class books are to be changed except by vote of the class and permission of teacher."

We are to be taxed .05 per week to be used at the end of our year for decorating purposes. I'm president and Jennie Wright secretary.

Early in the morning I was flying around in a big blue gingham-apron making lemon-gelatine and then devotedly scrubbed the sitting-room windows for I wanted everything to be neat and clean as I expected Mama at 11. Met Miss Jennie Pattison who is going to teach as a substitute for her sister awhile, and with her Miss Ford, our probable other teacher. She looked young, tolerably pretty and rather quiet. Hope I shall like her.

Waited on pins till 11: — Finally Mama came. Bless her dear heart!

I could have eaten her alive. She was as glad to be home as we were to have her. In these two weeks I have saved her $17.00 from her market-money. Was I not economical?

No. I mean didn't I *manage* nicely for of-course we had first class fare. . . .

MON. FEB 27, 1882. Had a very sorry time last night and am not over it yet. Elmer came last night and I read *Joan* to him for sometime, after which he began a serious talk to me. You remember that on the 12th I gave him some little encouragement and somehow it has troubled me ever since for while I know that I am fonder of him than of anyone else, I also know that I do not love him as I can (and have) loved. I told him so last night. He was awfully blue. I wanted him to try his honest best to fall in love with some other girl and it made him indignant.

Finally we came to this agreement: first, he is to try desperately to fall in love with another girl; secondly, if he can't, and if I never meet anyone I like better that way in the distant future, we may — be something a little warmer. He smiled rather bitterly and said there was poor consolation in that. He had his arms around me as he spoke and with a motion toward them I told him that we must have no more of that. He said perhaps I was right and pleaded for just one goodbye kiss. Of course he didn't plead in vain and my heart ached sadly when he left with such a hard, pained, disappointed look on his face.

MONDAY MARCH 6, 1882 — An unpleasant piece of news to-day. Edith with an air of great mystery this morning said she had something particular to say to me. She had me take dinner with her, and then gave me some information and advice. Eugene had requested her to talk to me it seems, and about *WmSn*. He has been making a "confidante" of Eugene, boldly and openly declaring to him, his absorbing love for me. Eugene says he is perfectly frantic, raving, and discussed the matter pro and con with great energy.

I exclaimed impatiently, "Oh! Why need a boy make a fool of himself. I thought Will had got over that nonsense months ago. Now he's spoiled it all. Whatever shall I do?"

"Stop going with him, give him the 'cut direct'," from Edith. "You really must Maud. WmSn is different from most boys; he's queer, and harder to deal with. He's terribly cut up and all that."

I can't go to him and say "Will I don't love you, its all nonsense this way of acting," for he's never asked for any information on the subject, or asked me to love him, nor does he do any of the said "acting" while with me.

I'm a terribly poor hand at "cutting" people unless I'm mad at them, and Will is so incessantly good natured and jolly, I *can't* get mad at him. Now isn't it a nice mess! ! . . .

TUESDAY MARCH 21, 1882. Bless that darling Elmer's heart. In spite of my note he came over Sunday night and we had a long talk. Oh! He's pretty far gone. Actually called my ear a "little pink shell." Said I was not to worry over him or have any more cries, that Edith was mistaken in calling me coquette, as I'd certainly given him no cause to hope. And he called me all the pet names in the vocabulary and stroked my hair when I tumbled it up in my abject woe. I never came so near loving him as I did Sunday night and he seemed inexpressibly happy. Wouldn't it be a joke if I should fall in love with him yet? . . .

SAT APRIL 1882. Will has come for me to go boating. . . .

LATER 6:25 P.M. Will broached upon tender topics and acted like a goose generally. Lectured him roundly about the utter aimlessness of his life. Told him it was his duty to have an object and not to spend his money faster than he made it and have no thought beyond today, *always* today.

It disgusts me to see a strong, healthy boy with no more ambition in life than he has. *Can* he be content to settle down for life as foreman of a job printing office?

He said when he found a certain girl he might settle down and make something of himself.

I assured him that unless he did the settling down first he would never find a girl fool enough to love him.

He ranted at length upon the bliss those engaged men had to look forward to, to urge them to be better; upon the beauty of early love, and even ventured to tell me how miserable a girl was who didn't know her own mind. In fact he got a little personal. I took it all down as purely supposed cases, and acted stupidity to perfection, throwing all the cold water possible on him (both theoretical water and sipe-water).

I said I hated those spoony boys who talked of love before they were old enough to tell heart-ache from colic. He said youth was the time for love. Then he said the afternoon had been unutterably happy — but why need I repeat all this stuff to you.

He asked to take me to the reception on *City of Cairo* on her maiden trip. He also wants to take me to our next dancing lesson Thursday night. . . .

JUNE, 1882. Friday night the words were spoken which make us through all eternity near and dear to each other.

I think neither of us will ever forget that night — the wood-bine vines and the stars, the lightest of Summer breezes and the completest of happiness.

When he came I was playing ball with "Papa Menager" feeling cool in my cream-colored lawn with my "graduating" cape jasmine (just arrived from the South!) at my throat; and feeling also not a little delighted at my newly acquired accomplishment of catching a high ball on the run.

We went to the Temperance Meeting together and with Mama and Robin, and didn't leave there till ten oclock.

I don't feel like telling you how it all came about but I'll remember it as long as I live. He kissed me over and over and was inexpressibly happy — but its queer as long as I didn't love him he was wretched and soon as I did, he grew nearly as wretched and said he was not worthy — indeed I believe he wanted to institute an immediate search for a perfect man for me.

I laughed at his wrinkled brow and hushed him up in a minute. We were both so bubbling over with youthfulness and joy that every trifling little incident caused us both to laugh merrily, and the next minute we were as sober as Quakers and half sad.

He can't think of waiting till I'm 25. "Why little love that is eight long years. If you love me how can you bear to wait so long?"

He says he's jealous of the little garnet ring on my third finger. It was at Mr Parsons that Eva wished it on and she said, "Shall it be for a year?" "No no not so long," I replied and Elmer looked so delighted for he knew that when my love for him was the love of my life, his diamond was to rest upon that finger (think of me — only a girl too — being able to keep that pretty solitaire which he gave me, locked up in my desk all these weeks without showing it to a soul or telling anyone about it) and my answer to Eva told him plainly that the happy time was not a year distant. The garnet comes off the day Eva leaves town.

I was so happy I wanted to crown him with laurels and cry "Eureka! I have found him — my ideal." For last night my ideal changed. Once it was founded in beauty of feature and charm of tongue with little regard for truth and high moral worth.

That was why for so long a time I saw only my good boy's defects, and because he was not graceful as a fawn, and handsome as Apollo, failed to recognize inward nobility in him.

There have been times in my life when with red eyes and heavy heart after hearing some fresh scandal I would declare, "Man, from the mightiest king to the humblest laborer is impure throughout — more animal than true man or honest love." Just as fast as I'd find some gentlemanly chivalrous pure and high-minded man on the globe and try to say, "Surely here there is no corruption" somebody older and wiser (?) than I would say I was wrong again and I'd be compelled to pull down the pedestal; I don't mean feeling in love and thinking I'd fallen in love with perfection — but any man, from the youngest and most innocent looking to the old gray haired ones which one should love to reverence.

Do you blame me for being wonderfully light-hearted and happy when I *know* Elmer to be one entirely free from such coarse dissipation of any sort.

All mankind is not depraved. When I think of Papa, Mr Spear, Mr George Fisher, and Elmer, I feel always that they ought somehow to stand way up above the rest of mankind. Of course, you wise old Journal, you're smiling sarcastically and saying, "She thinks she's in love with an angel." But indeed I don't think any-thing of the sort. I know he has faults — dozens of them; all people have. He's abrupt in manners and very outspoken, often hurting people's feelings by too strict adherence to the truth. He's not polished or what you call handsome, and he used to say "cuss-words" when I first knew him, though of-course never before me.

But he's always been pointed out to me as a model, "a boy who doesn't smoke, drink or chew, who is business-like, energetic and bound to make his way in the world"; and I would call him a "goody-goody boy" and he hated it awfully, but oh! just *am* I not glad he *is* a goody-goody boy! ! !

Corinne was down Friday and while here she said that one day when Elmer was at Villa Ridge her mother said "I think Maud is the smartest girl in Cairo" and that Elmer with an air of calm conviction replied simply "She *is*." "Oh Maud" Corinne continued "when Elmer is away from you he is silent and abstracted and answers at random with his mind seemingly miles away, but soon as you appear upon the scene he's all eyes and ears and happiness. You are the making of that boy."

The other day Elmer started to speak to Papa of me, tell him his hopes and all that, and find out his feelings on the subject, but he de-cided to wait till my answer was a more decisive one.

Yesterday while Mama and I were sewing together I told her all about it. She seems to doubt my love for Elmer, and persists in asking me if I love him as well as I did Robert three years ago, and such questions as that. She says I must make myself a fine artist and musician before I think of being married; and must also be a good house-keeper, and must have time to grow from a delicate nervous girl to a strong healthy woman. Sensible Mama!

We had a long talk about it.

Over one million immigrants a year arrived in the United States be-tween 1890 and 1915, the majority from southern and eastern Europe. Escaping economic hardship and, in some cases, religious and political persecution, most settled in ghettoes in urban, industrial centers. For a full generation, and sometimes longer, these ethnic neighborhoods remained segregated from the dominant white, Protestant culture. Different religious practices, social customs, and languages set the immigrants apart, and adjusting to life in America proved a painful and difficult process for parents and children alike.

Americanization was a highly charged subject at the turn of the century. Some, both immigrants and native-born Americans, argued that it required total abandonment of old customs and values and assimilation to dominant institutions and traditions. Others believed that a diversity of cultures was more desirable and that immigrants could gain access to equal social and economic opportunities while retaining their distinctive ethnic identity. The issue often disrupted immigrant families and created conflict between the generations.

The following selection, from an autobiographical novel, describes the psychological frustration and economic hardship of a young Jewish immigrant woman during her adolescence early in the twentieth century. Anzia Yezierska was born in a small town in Russian Poland in 1885. Her large and poor family came to America in the 1890s, locating in the Jewish ghetto on New York's Lower East Side.

Anzia's father was a talmudic scholar, a man who dedicated his life to the study of the Torah. In the Jewish orthodox tradition, the scholar was a highly respected member of the community, and when necessary, the scholar's wife and daughters were expected to take responsibility for the financial support of the family out of religious duty. In America, Anzia, her sisters, and her mother worked grueling hours in sweatshops and factories and relied on the assistance of friends for economic survival.

Feeling trapped in a conflict of cultures, Anzia decided that her only hope for a better life was separating herself from her family and the ghetto; at the age of seventeen, she left home. An unshakable faith in education as the means to her social and economic betterment and a vision of herself as a teacher, "sitting back like a lady at [her] desk," motivated her to keep on in the face of overwhelming obstacles.

Leaving New York to live in a small college town where the "real Americans enjoy life" only intensified Anzia's sense of isolation and alienation. She remained an outsider, different in class and ethnic background, physical appearance, and life experiences. Her concerns and aspirations contrasted sharply with those of her classmates who looked "as if the dirty battle of life had never yet been on them." For the young men and women of the privileged classes, college years were carefree and filled with parties, dances, and dates. Having assumed a traditional male adult role in bearing complete responsibility for her material needs, Anzia had little time for the social concerns of adolescence. Vocational identity was primary for her. Teaching offered one of the few middle-class employment opportunities for females, and for Anzia it was also the means to become an American.

The excerpts that follow are from *Bread Givers,* the autobiographical novel Anzia wrote in 1925. She gained fame in the 1920s and 1930s through her many short stories and novels about American Jewish immigrant life. Anzia's first marriage in her midtwenties was unsuccessful and was annulled within a few months. A second marriage lasted three years, and Anzia gave birth to a daughter. She continued her writings until her death at an advanced age in 1970.

—— 9 ——
Anzia Yezierska

I SHUT THE DOOR

A school teacher — I! I saw myself sitting back like a lady at my desk, the children, their eyes on me, watching and waiting for me to call out the different ones to the board, to spell a word, or answer me a question. It was like looking up to the top of the highest skyscraper while down in the gutter.

All night long I walked the streets, drunk with my dreams. I didn't know how the hours flew, how or where my feet carried me, until I saw the man turning out the lights of the street lamps. Was it already morning? The silence woke up from the block. There began the rumbling of milk wagons, the clatter of bottles and cans, and the hum of opening stores, peddlers filling their pushcarts with fruit and loaves of bread. I wasn't a bit tired, but I was starving hungry, and I walked into the nearest bakery for a cup of coffee with two rolls, for ten cents.

As I sat there, in the stillness of the morning, I realized that I had yet never been alone since I was born. This was the first time I ate by myself, with silence and stillness for my company.

At home, when they sat down to eat, all my sisters were talking everything at once. I remember one night, coming home from the shop, my bones cracking from tiredness. I crawled into the bedroom and tried to close the door.

"What is the matter? Are you sick?" they asked.

"No. I only want a little quiet in me. I only want to be alone."

"Look only the princess!" My sisters dragged me back to the noisy kitchen. "Crazy! Ain't we good enough for you any more?"

Even after my sisters were married, mealtime was when Mother let out her bitter heart of worry and Father hammered out his preaching like a wound-up phonograph. In the shop, the girls were talking all at once, clothes, styles, beaux, and dances — each one trying to out-yell the other. Perhaps in this same bakery it would be full of noise in an hour or two. But now, thank God, it was still. And I was alone in that stillness.

How strong, how full of life and hope I felt as I walked out of that bakery. I opened my arms, burning to hug the new day. The strength of a million people was surging up in me. I felt I could turn the earth upside down with my littlest finger. I wanted to dance, to fly in the air and kiss the sun and stars with my singing heart. I, alone with myself, was enjoying myself for the first time as with grandest company.

SOURCE: Excerpt from *The Bread Givers* by Anzia Yezierska. Copyright 1925 by Doubleday & Company, Inc. Reprinted by permission of the publisher and Louise Levitas Henriksen.

In this high-hearted mood I began to look for a room where I could be alone. All the room-to-let signs that I passed seemed like so many doors opening to a new life. The first house I tried, the to-let room was on the top floor. I flew up the five flights of stairs as on wings.

"You have a room?" I asked, my eyes laughing and my voice singing the joy in me.

A hard, mean look hit me in the face.

"I don't take girls." And the woman slammed the door.

In the next house, I walked up a little slower, and my voice had a quietness not like my own. A washed-out, thin-lipped woman with little suspicious eyes examined me. "No girls," snapped this one, too.

"Why no girls?" I dared ask the skinny tsarina.

"I want to keep my house clean. No cooking, no washing. Less trouble, less dirt, with men."

My heart sank to my feet. But I forced myself to hunt on. I had to find a place to live.

In the rear basement, a fat *yenteh*, in a loose wrapper, showed me a little coffin of a room, dark as the grave. "I got three girls sleeping here already. And there's yet a place for a fourth in the bed. I charge only three dollars a month."

"I want a room all alone to myself."

"You? A room alone?" She gave me one fierce look till my cheeks began to burn. "This is a decent house. I'm a respectable woman."

On and on I searched.... Each place took it out of me more and more. For the first time in my life I saw what a luxury it was for a poor girl to want to be alone in a room.

My knees bent under me. I was ready to drop from weariness when I saw a crooked sign, in a scrawling hand, "Private Room, A Bargain Cheap."

It was a dark hole on the ground floor, opening into a narrow air-shaft. The only window where some light might have come in was thick with black dust. The bed see-sawed on its broken feet, one shorter than the others. The mattress was full of lumps, and the sheets were shreds and patches. But the room had a separate entrance to the hall. A door I could shut. And it was only six dollars a month.

"This is just the thing for me," I cried. "I'll clean it up like a little palace."

Through half-shut eyes the woman examined me. "Can you pay on time?" she asked.

"Of course I can pay." I drew myself up, tall as the ceiling.

"By what you work?"

"I'm not asking for any charity that I should have to tell you my business."

"But I got to know if you're working steady, to pay me my rent."

"You won't have to worry. I'm working by day and studying for a teacher by night."

She drew back as if I was about to rob her. "My gas! My gas bill.

What I'd get from your rent, I'd lose on the gas. I already had an experience with one like you. She took out books from the library. And in the middle of the night, I could see by the crack in the door that she was burning away my gas, reading."

I looked at the room. A separate door to myself — a door to shut out all the noises of the world, and only six dollars. Where could I get such a bargain in the whole East Side?

Like a drowning person clinging to a rope, my tired body edged up to that door and clung to it. My hands clutched at the knob. This door was life. It was air. The bottom starting-point of becoming a person. I simply must have this room with the shut door. And I must make this woman rent it to me. If I failed to get it, I'd drop dead at her feet.

"Look only on me!" I commanded her. "You're a smart woman. You ought to know yourself on a person, first sight. Here, I give you a month's rent in advance." And I pushed the six dollars into her hand.

Her whole face lighted up with friendliness. She counted the money. Then kissing each dollar for good luck, she handed me the key.

At last alone, in my room. I let go everything, the weight of my body falling against the closed door. The aloneness was enough for me, and in a moment it sank me to sleep.

The first thing when I opened my eyes, I counted out the money I had left in my little knot. Only three dollars and sixty-five cents between me and hunger. A job. And I must get it at once.

It was slack season in the factories. I walked the streets, wondering where to turn for work, when I passed a laundry. A big printed sign was in the window: "Ironer wanted."

As I opened the door, a blinding wave of heat struck my face. The air was full of the sweaty smell of washing clothes. At the back, girls could scarcely be seen through the clouds of steam. Hair was sticking to their faces. Necks streamed with sweat.

A huge, bulgy-faced man sat on the counter, marking collars.

"Do you need an ironer?" I asked.

He looked at me from his big height till I felt like a speck of dust under his feet. With a grunt, he went on marking the laundry.

I put my courage into my teeth and faced him. "You got a sign out, 'Ironer wanted.'"

"Yes, but not you," he growled. "I want someone who can swing an iron." And he pointed with his thumb to a husky German woman with giant, red arms, who ironed a white dress with big, steady strokes. "That's the kind I need for an ironer."

"But let me only show you how good I can iron," I begged. "I was quicker than the big ones in my shop."

He tried me with an iron at an empty board with a small lot. But though I put all my strength into it, I was so nervous with him watching me, I thought the job was lost. But the man nodded kindly as I handed him the ironed apron. "You got guts all right," he chuckled. "I'll start you at the mangle for five a week, and later I'll break you into an ironer."

By the evening, I was so tired that I walked into the Grand Street Cafeteria for something to eat. I had read about the place in the paper. Kind, rich ladies had opened it for working girls, to have their meals in beautiful surroundings and cheap.

It was good to see flowers on the table. And the clean, educated face of the lady manager who sat by the desk. I needed something beautiful to look at after that hard day in the laundry. The portions were a little skimpy. But the white curtains and the clean, restful place lifted me with longing for the higher life.

Great dreams spurred my feet on my way to night school.

"What do you want to learn?" asked the teacher at the desk.

"I want to learn everything in the school from the beginning to the end."

She raised the lids of her cold eyes and stared at me. "Perhaps you had better take one thing at a time," she said, indifferently. "There's a commercial course, manual training ———"

"I want a quick education for a teacher," I cried.

A hard laugh was my answer. Then she showed me the lists of the different classes, and I came out of my high dreams by registering for English and arithmetic.

Then I began five nights a week in a crowded class of fifty, with a teacher so busy with her class that she had no time to notice me.

The first morning in my room, I awoke very early. My head was clear, and I looked with full eyes on the thick dirt that I had grabbed in such anxious haste. There were only a few rusty nails on the door for my clothes. The table was shaky and the one chair was patched with boards.

Against this heart-choking dinginess flashed Mashah's shining little palace. Her place was once worse than this, and she polished it up. Why can't I? A pot of paint, a little white oilcloth with brass tacks, a scrubbing brush with soap. But first of all, I thought, if only I could wash away the mud of ages from that window, it would make it lighter in the room.

When my landlady saw me start on my cleaning, she cried warningly: "I never washed the windows since I lived here, not even for the holidays, because the upstairs tenants — a black year on them — are always throwing down things. Their hands should only fall to their sides."

But I wouldn't listen to her, and began to wash the window. The minute I stuck my head out, a bunch of potato peelings fell on me. I shook off the peelings and went on with the washing. Someone began shaking a carpet. Then a shower of ashes blinded me.

I sank on the bed, all the strength out of my arms and fingers. The deadening dirt! How could I ever do anything in this airless gloom? If I open the window the dirt will be flying in. If I keep it closed, how can I breathe?

I don't ask for fancy furniture, but only a little light for the eyes, only a clean window such as Mashah has in her blackest poverty.

The sound of the factory whistle brought me to my feet. Already seven o'clock. My fussing over the window made it too late for me to start cooking my coffee for breakfast. I grabbed a slice of black bread and ate as I hurried to the car.... Fool that I am, trying to imitate Mashah, her cleanliness. Ten hours I must work in the laundry. Two hours in the night school. Two hours more to study my lessons. When can I take time to be clean? If I'm to have strength and courage to go on with what I set out to do, I must shut my eyes to the dirt.

That evening, after night school, I spread my books out on my table and began to hammer into my thick head the difference between a noun, a verb, and a preposition. Oh, the noise around me. But I tried to struggle on with the lesson.... "A noun is the name of anything...? A verb is the predicate of action...? A preposition connects words...?"

The more I repeated the definitions the more mixed up I got. It was all words, words, about words.

Maybe it was the terrible racket that was muddling my brain. Phonographs and pianolas blared against each other. Voices gossiping and jabbering across the windows. Wailing children. The yowling shrieks of two alley cats. The shrill bark of a hungry pup.

The jarring clatter tore me by the hair, stretched me out of my skin, and grated under my teeth. I felt like one crucified in a torture pit of noise.

Then I clasped my hands over my head and began talking to myself: "Stop all this sensitiveness, or you're beaten already before the fight is begun.... You've got to study. As you had to shut your eyes to the dirt, so you must shut your ears to the noise."

A quietness within me soothed my tortured nerves. I turned to my books on the table, and with fierce determination to sink myself into my head, I began my lessons again.

A PIECE OF MEAT

By the whole force of my will I could reason myself out of the dirt and noise around me. But how could I reason with my hungry stomach? How could I stretch my five dollars a week to meet all my needs?

I took a piece of paper and wrote it all down. A dollar and a half for rent. Sixty cents for carfare. I couldn't walk that long distance to work and back and have time for night school. No saving there. And I must put aside at least fifty cents a week to pay back Mother's rent money. What is there left for food? Two dollars and forty cents. That means thirty-four and two-sevenths cents a day. How could I have enough to eat from that? But that's all I can have now. Somehow, it's got to do.

But whenever I passed a restaurant or a delicatessen store, I couldn't tear my eyes away from the food in the window. Something wild in me wanted to break through the glass, snatch some of that sausage and corned-beef, and gorge myself just once.

One day in the laundry, while busy ironing a shirt, the thought of Mother's cooking came over me. Why was it that Mother's simplest dishes, her plain potato soup, her *gefülte* fish, were so filling? And what was the matter with the cafeteria food that it left me hungrier after eating than before?

For a moment I imagined myself eating Mother's *gefülte* fish. A happy memory floated over me. A feast I was having. What a melting taste in the mouth!

"Hey — there!" cried the boss, rushing madly at me.

Oi weh! Smoke was rising from under my iron.

"Oh, I'll wash it out," I gasped in fright, as I lifted the iron and saw the scorched triangle.

But the boss snatched the shirt away from me. "Three dollars out of your wages for this," he raged.

Not a word could I say. Either it was to lose my job or pay. And I could not lose my job.

Three dollars out from my wages, when every fraction of a penny was counted out where it had to go. Maybe for weeks I'd have to live on dry bread to make up the loss. I got so frightened, from weakness I longed to throw myself in some dark corner, only to weep away my bitter luck. But I dared not let go. The boss was around. I picked up the iron again, though I could hardly shift the weight back and forth.

A terrible hunger rose up in me — a hunger I had been trying to forget since my lunch of two stale slices of bread and a scrap of cheese. Just when I had to begin saving more from eating, the starvation of days and weeks began tearing and dragging down my last strength. Let me at least have one dinner with meat before I begin to starve. For that last hour of work, I saw before my eyes meat, only meat, great, big chunks of it. And I biting into the meat.

Like a wolf with hunger, I ran to the cafeteria. From the end of the line, I saw the big, printed bill of fare:

> Roast beef, 25¢
> Roast lamb, 30¢
> Beef stew, 20¢

My eyes stopped. Over the word stew, I saw big chunks of meat, carrots, and peas, with thick brown gravy. I reached for the tray, and took my place on the line. I was like a mad thing straining toward the pots of food, and the line seemed to stand for ever in one place. A big, husky, fat man stood behind me. He held his tray so that the end poked into my ribs every time he shuffled on his feet. But, thank God, the line began to move up, slowly nearer the serving table.

My anxious eyes leaped to the faces of the servers. I tried to see which one of them served the stew. My portion depended on her mood of the minute. If I'm lucky to strike her when she feels good, then the spoon will go deep down into the pot and come up heaping full. If she feels mean, then I get only from the tip of the spoon, a stingy portion. God! She holds in her hands my life, my strength, new blood for my veins, new clearness in my brain to go on with the fight. Oh! If she would only give me enough to fill myself, this one time!...

At last I reached the serving table.

"Stew with a lot of meat in it."

Breathlessly, I watched how far the spoon would go into the pot. A hot sweat broke over my face as I saw the mean hunks of potato and the skinny strings of meat floating in the starched gravy which she handed me.

"Please, won't you put in one real piece of meat?" And I pushed back the plate for more.

I might as well have talked to the wall. She did not see or hear me. Her eyes were smiling back to the fat man behind me who grinned knowingly at her.

"Stew," was all he said.

She picked up my plate, pushed the spoon deep down into the pot and brought it up heaping with thick chunks of meat.

"Oh, thank you! Thank you! I'll take it now," I cried, reaching for it with both hands.

"No, you don't." And the man took the plate from the server and set it on his tray.

Speechless, bewildered, I stood there, unable to move.

"I asked for stew — *stew!*"

"I gave you some and you didn't take it." She sniffed.

"But you didn't give me as much as you gave him. Isn't my money as good as his?"

"Don't you know they always give men more?" called a voice from the line.

"It takes a woman to be mean to a woman," piped up another.

"You're holding up the line," said the head lady, coming over, with quiet politeness.

"I want stew," came again from my tight throat.

"She gave you a fair portion."

"But why did she give more to the man just because he was a man? I'm hungry."

All the reply I got was a cold glance. "Please move on or step out of the line."

People began to titter and stare at me. Even the girl at the serving table laughed as she put on a man's plate a big slice of fried liver, twice as big as she would have given me.

"Cheaters! Robbers!" I longed to cry out to them. "Why do you have flowers on the table and cheat a starving girl from her bite of food?" But I was too trampled to speak. With tight lips, I walked out.

In the street, there was no cheap restaurant in sight. I had a dreary feeling that it was the same in every other place. Since I must starve next week, I might as well begin now. I went home boiling with hate for the whole world.

In my room, I found the tail end of a loaf of bread. Each bite I swallowed was wet with my tears.

It was so cold that night that in every tenement people huddled into their beds early and put all their clothes over themselves to keep warm. So cold it was, even the gas froze.

I stuck a candle into a bottle, took up my grammar, struggling to forget my bitterness, studying. Everything I had I wrapped around myself and, buried in my thin bedclothes, I held on to my book.

My feet were lumps of ice. How could I study? But I would. I must. I forced myself to keep to my lessons like one forcing himself awake when he's falling asleep. . . .

COLLEGE

That burning day when I got ready to leave New York and start out on my journey to college! I felt like Columbus starting out for the other end of the earth. I felt like the pilgrim fathers who had left their homeland and all their kin behind them and trailed out in search of the New World.

I had stayed up night after night, washing and ironing, patching and darning my things. At last, I put them all together in a bundle, wrapped them up with newspapers, and tied them securely with the thick clothes line that I had in my room on which to hang out my wash. I made another bundle of my books. In another newspaper I wrapped up my food for the journey: a loaf of bread, a herring, and a pickle. In my purse was the money I had been saving from my food, from my clothes, a penny to penny, a dollar to a dollar, for so many years. It was not much but I counted out that it would be enough for my train ticket and a few weeks start till I got work out there.

It was only when I got to the train that I realized I had hardly eaten all day. Starving hungry, I tore the paper open. *Ach!* Crazy-head! In my haste I had forgotten even to cut up the bread. I bent over on the side of my seat, and half covering myself with a newspaper, I pinched pieces out of the loaf and ripped ravenously at the herring. With each bite, I cast side glances like a guilty thing; nobody should see the way I ate.

After a while, as the lights were turned low, the other passengers began to nod their heads, each outsnoring the other in their thick sleep. I was the only one on the train too excited to close my eyes.

Like a dream was the whole night's journey. And like a dream mounting on a dream was this college town, this New America of culture and education.

Before this, New York was all of America to me. But now I came to a town of quiet streets, shaded with green trees. No crowds, no tenements. No hurrying noise to beat the race of the hours. Only a leisured quietness whispered in the air: Peace. Be still. Eternal time is all before you.

Each house had its own green grass in front, its own free space all around, and it faced the street with the calm security of being owned for generations, and not rented by the month from a landlord. In the early twilight, it was like a picture out of fairyland to see people sitting on their porches, lazily swinging in their hammocks, or watering their own growing flowers.

So these are the real Americans, I thought, thrilled by the lean, straight bearing of the passers-by. They had none of that terrible fight for bread and rent that I always saw in New York people's eyes. Their faces were not worn with the hunger for things they never could have in their lives. There was in them that sure, settled look of those who belong to the world in which they were born.

The college buildings were like beautiful palaces. The campus stretched out like fields of a big park. Air — air. Free space and sunshine. The river at dusk. Glimmering lights on passing boats, the floating voices of young people. And when night came, there were the sky and the stars.

This was the beauty for which I had always longed. For the first few days I could only walk about and drink it in thirstily, more and more. Beauty of houses, beauty of streets, beauty shining out of the calm faces and cool eyes of the people! Oh — too cool. . . .

How could I most quickly become friends with them? How could I come into their homes, exchange with them my thoughts, break with them bread at their tables? If I could only lose myself body and soul in the serenity of this new world, the hunger and the turmoil of my ghetto years would drop away from me, and I, too, would know the beauty of stillness and peace.

What light-hearted laughing youth met my eyes! All the young people I had ever seen were shut up in factories. But here were young girls and young men enjoying life, free from the worry for a living. College to them was being out for a good time, like to us in the shop a Sunday picnic. But in our gayest Sunday picnics there was always the under-feeling that Monday meant back to the shop again. To these born lucky ones joy seemed to stretch out for ever.

What a sight I was in my gray pushcart clothes against the beautiful gay colours and the fine things those young girls wore. I had seen cheap, fancy style, Five- and Ten-Cent Store finery. But never had I seen such plain beautifulness. The simple skirts and sweaters, the stockings and shoes to match. The neat finished quietness of their tailored suits. There was no show-off in their clothes, and yet how much more pulling to the eyes and all the senses than the Grand Street richness I knew.

And the spick-and-span cleanliness of these people! It smelled from them, the soap and the bathing. Their fingernails so white and pink. Their hands and necks white like milk. I wondered how did those girls get their hair so soft, so shiny, and so smooth about their heads. Even their black shoes had a clean look.

Never had I seen men so all shaved up with pink, clean skins. The richest store-keepers in Grand Street shined themselves up with diamonds like walking jewellery stores, but they weren't so hollering clean as these men. And they all had their hair clipped so short; they all had a shape to their heads. So ironed out smooth and even they looked in their spotless, creaseless clothes, as if the dirty battle of life had never yet been on them.

I looked at these children of joy with a million eyes. I looked at them with my hands, my feet, with the thinnest nerves of my hair. By all their differences from me, their youth, their shiny freshness, their carefreeness, they pulled me out of my senses to them. And they didn't even know I was there.

I thought once I got into the classes with them, they'd see me and we'd get to know one another. What a sharp awakening came with my first hour!

As I entered the classroom, I saw young men and girls laughing and talking to one another without introductions. I looked for my seat. Then I noticed, up in front, a very earnest-faced young man with thick glasses over his sad eyes. He made me think of Morris Lipkin, so I chose my seat next to him.

"What's the name of the professor?" I asked.

"Smith," came from his tight lips. He did not even look at me. He pulled himself together and began busily writing, to show me he didn't want to be interrupted.

I turned to the girl on my other side. What a fresh, clean beauty! A creature of sunshine. And clothes that matched her radiant youth.

"Is this the freshman class in geometry?" I asked her.

She nodded politely and smiled. But how quickly her eyes sized me up! It was not an unkind glance. And yet, it said more plainly than words, "From where do you come? How did you get in here?"

Sitting side by side with them through the whole hour, I felt stranger to them than if I had passed them in Hester Street. Wasn't there some secret something that would open us toward one another?

In one class after another, I kept asking myself, "What's the matter with me? Why do they look at me so when I talk with them?"

Maybe I'd have to change myself inside and out to be one of them. But how?

The lectures were over at four o'clock. With a sigh, I turned from the college building, away from the pleasant streets, down to the shabby back alley near the post office, and entered the George Martin Hand Laundry.

Mr. Martin was a fat, easy-going, good-natured man. I no sooner told him of my experience in New York than he took me on at once as an ironer at fifty cents an hour, and he told me he had work for as many hours a day as I could put in.

I felt if I could only look a little bit like other girls on the outside, maybe I could get in with them. And that meant money! And money meant work, work, work!

Till eleven o'clock that night, I ironed fancy white shirtwaists.

"You're some busy little worker, even if I do say so," said Mr. Martin, good-naturedly. "But I must lock up. You can't live here."

I went home, aching in every bone. And in the quiet and good air, I so overslept that I was late for my first class. To make matters worse, I found a note in my mailbox that puzzled and frightened me. It said, "Please report at once to the dean's office to explain your absence from Physical Education I, at four o'clock."

A line of other students was waiting there. When my turn came I asked the secretary, "What's this physical education business?"

"This is a compulsory course," he said. "You cannot get credit in any other course unless you satisfy this requirement."

At the hour when I had intended to go back to Martin's Laundry, I entered the big gymnasium. There were a crowd of girls dressed in funny short black bloomers and rubber-soled shoes.

The teacher blew the whistle and called harshly, "Students are expected to report in their uniforms."

"I have none."

"They're to be obtained at the bookstore," she said, with a stern look at me. "Please do not report again without it."

I stood there dumb.

"Well, stay for to-day and exercise as you are," said the teacher, taking pity on me.

She pointed out my place in the line, where I had to stand with the rest like a lot of wooden soldiers. She made us twist ourselves around here and there, "Right face!" "Left face!" "Right about face!" I tried to do as the others did, but I felt like a jumping-jack being pulled this way and that way. I picked up dumbbells and pushed them up and down and sideways until my arms were lame. Then she made us hop around like a lot of monkeys.

At the end of the hour, I was so out of breath that I sank down, my heart pounding against my ribs. I was dripping with sweat worse than Saturday night in the steam laundry. What's all this physical education nonsense? I came to college to learn something, to get an education with my head, and not monkeyshines with my arms and legs.

I went over to the instructor. "How much an hour do we get for this work?" I asked her, bitterly.

She looked at me with a stupid stare. "This is a two-point course."

Now I got real mad. "I've got to sweat my life away enough only to earn a living," I cried. "God knows I exercised enough, since I was a kid —"

"You properly exercised?" She looked at me from head to foot. "Your posture is bad. Your shoulders sag. You need additional corrective exercises outside the class."

More tired than ever, I came to the class next day. After the dumb-bells, she made me jump over the hurdles. For the life of me, I couldn't do it. I bumped myself and scratched my knees on the top bar of the hurdle, knocking it over with a great clatter. They all laughed except the teacher.

"Repeat the exercise, please," she said, with a frozen face.

I was all bruises, trying to do it. And they were holding their sides with laughter. I was their clown, and this was their circus. And suddenly, I got so wild with rage that I seized the hurdle and right before their eyes I smashed it to pieces.

The whole gymnasium went still as death.

The teacher's face was white. "Report at once to the dean."

The scared look on the faces of the girls made me feel that I was to be locked up or fired.

For a minute when I entered the dean's grand office, I was so confused I couldn't even see.

He rose and pointed to a chair beside his desk. "What can I do for you?" he asked, in a voice that quieted me as he spoke.

I told him how mad I was, to have piled on me jumping hurdles when I was so tired anyway. He regarded me with that cooling steadiness of his. When I was through, he walked to the window and I waited, miserable. Finally he turned to me again, and with a smile! "I'm quite certain that physical education is not essential in your case. I will excuse you from attending the course."

After this things went better with me. In spite of the hard work in the laundry, I managed to get along in my classes. More and more interesting became the life of the college as I watched it from the outside.

What a feast of happenings each day of college was to those other students. Societies, dances, letters from home, packages of food, midnight spreads and even birthday parties. I never knew that there were people glad enough of life to celebrate the day they were born. I watched the gay goings-on around me like coming to a feast, but always standing back and only looking on.

One day, the ache for people broke down my feelings of difference from them. I felt I must tear myself out of my aloneness. Nothing had ever come to me without my going out after it. I had to fight for my living, fight for every bit of my education. Why should I expect friendship and love to come to me out of the air while I sat there, dreaming about it?

The freshman class gave a dance that very evening. Something in the back of my head told me that an evening dress and slippers were part of going to a dance. I had no such things. But should that stop me? If I had waited till I could afford the right clothes for college, I should never have been able to go at all.

I put a fresh collar over my old serge dress. And with a dollar stolen from my eating money, I bought a ticket to the dance. As I peeped into the glittering gymnasium, blaring with jazz, my timid fears stopped the breath in me. How the whole big place sang with their light-hearted happiness! Young eyes drinking joy from young eyes. Girls, like gay-coloured butterflies, whirling in the arms of young men.

Floating ribbons and sashes shimmered against men's black coats. I took the nearest chair, blinded by the dazzle of the happy couples. Why did I come here? A terrible sense of age weighed upon me; yet I watched and waited for someone to come and ask me to dance. But not one man came near me. Some of my classmates nodded distantly in passing, but most of them were too filled with their own happiness even to see me.

The whirling of joy went on and on, and still I sat there watching, cold, lifeless, like a lost ghost. I was nothing and nobody. It was worse than being ignored. Worse than being an outcast. I simply didn't belong. I had no existence in their young eyes. I wanted to run and hide myself, but fear and pride nailed me against the wall.

A chaperon must have noticed my face, and she brought over one of those clumsy, backward youths who was lost in a corner by himself. How unwilling were his feet as she dragged him over! In a dull voice, he asked, "May I have the next dance?" his eyes fixed in the distance as he spoke.

"Thank you. I don't want to dance." And I fled from the place.

I found myself walking in the darkness of the campus. In the thick shadows of the trees I hid myself and poured out my shamed and injured soul to the night. So, it wasn't character or brains that counted. Only youth and beauty and clothes — things I never had and never could have. Joy and love were not for such as me. Why not? Why not?...

I flung myself on the ground, beating with my fists against the endless sorrows of my life. Even in college I had not escaped from the ghetto. Here loneliness hounded me even worse than in Hester Street. Was there no escape? Will I never lift myself to be a person among people?

Social attitudes and behavior concerning sex underwent tremendous change in the 1960s and 1970s during the "sexual revolution." More open discussion through the media and increased knowledge of sexuality exemplified by the research of Masters and Johnson contributed significantly to revised ideas about female sexuality. These changes did not affect all adolescent women in the same ways, however. As society began accepting female sexual freedom as readily as that of males, some young women were better able to acknowledge their own interest in sexuality. For others, changing moral standards and mores created new tensions and conflicts. With increased expectations that females as well as males would engage in premarital sex, many young women faced — and continue to face — intensified pressure from their peers to do so. "Virginity," as the author of the next selection writes, has become an "anachronism" and an "embarrassment."

The writer, Joyce Maynard, published a collection of essays entitled *Looking Back* in 1972 at the age of nineteen. In the selection reprinted here she discusses experiences during her early, middle, and late teens; describes her feelings about the women's liberation movement; and reflects on the meaning of growing up in the 1960s and 1970s.

Joyce conveys the sense of eagerness with which she and her friends awaited the physical changes that would identify them as teenagers along with the feelings of insecurity and dissatisfaction — "feeling like strangers in our own skins" — that those developments produced. Their preoccupation with sexuality began early in their teens, and the realization that they could have children seemed frightening and thrilling at the same time. At the age of fourteen classmates were going steady and "acting like married couples" in experimenting with adult sex roles.

In college Joyce found the peer pressure to have sexual relations overwhelming. In a perceptive analysis, she connects the obsession with sex among those in their teens (and in society generally) with important technological and social changes, specifically the development of safer birth control methods and the impact of mass media in shaping attitudes and offering models of sexual freedom.

Whatever the nature of Joyce's mixed emotions about the women's liberation movement, it clearly prompted her to examine her assumptions about what options she sees for the future. Her plans for marriage and children would be her own decision and not something she believed she had been "brainwashed" into accepting unquestioningly.

In her closing comments on youth in contemporary society, Joyce raises an interesting question. In a culture where the young are so much glamorized, she wonders, will enthusiasm for reaching adulthood wane? On the verge of turning twenty years old, Joyce assessed the options in adulthood already closed to her.

Joyce Maynard grew up in New Hampshire and attended private high school and Yale University. Her father is a college professor and artist, her mother a writer and consultant. Joyce's articles have appeared in *Seventeen*, *McCall's*, *Mademoiselle*, and *The New York Times Magazine*.

— 10 —

Joyce Maynard

Summertime was when the changes happened, and why the first day of school was so much fun, with everybody telling everybody how different they looked — and it was true.

Waiting for the changes to happen, though, was like watching corn grow. By August I would miss the tug of my leash and collar, with nothing, no commitments, to keep me from sleeping through the best

SOURCE: Joyce Maynard, *Looking Back: A Chronicle of Growing Up Old in the Sixties* (Garden City, New York: Doubleday, 1973). Copyright © 1972, 1973 by Joyce Maynard.

Joyce Maynard

hours of sunlight, rising late and eating soggy Cheerios by the TV set, glued there for hours (just one more program, I kept telling myself, still in pajamas) like an addict. After TV there might be waiting for the mail, then reading *TV Guide* — next week's menus — and all the advertising circulars the discount stores sent out. (Sales on men's underwear and clock radios I studied, rapt. I knew the retail price of everything, just as I came to know the stars of every TV show, the time it came on and the channel. My stores of useless summer information accumulated like algae in a swamp.) Often I'd look forward to rain — thunder storms especially — because it gave me an excuse to stay inside and make popcorn. Sometimes, when the sun was shining, I'd pull the blinds and feel guilty, or I'd rally to the weather, put on my bathing suit and bike to the town swimming pool, transplanted, in the space of half an hour, from stretched-out-on-the-couch to stretched-out-on-the-sand. Transistor radios were more in fashion then than now. (Now it is quiet we treasure. Back then it was little palm-sized boxes with wrist straps and earphones, held to the ears of teen-agers while they walked, as if without the sound of J. J. Jeffrey and his Solid Gold or Big Bud Ballou with this week's Top Ten, breathing would be impossible.)

Teen-agers seemed more *teen-age* then. They all seemed older-looking and more on top of things. It isn't true that the closer you get, the better things look. (I often think in TV jingle terms. My sentence rhythms come from Maybelline and Crest.) The closer I got to teen-age, the less grown up it seemed. Partly it was that college students came into their own during my teens (after years of isolationist scholarship, a sudden burst of *relevance*) so the action switched from us to them. It seemed unfair that I should have spent so long marking time, holding my place in line, sleeping (wake me up when I've grown up — that was my summer attitude) only to discover when finally I reached the ticket booth that no more seats were left or that, in fact, the concert had been canceled.

A perpetual summer pre-teen, always on the brink, it seemed, I spent Junes, Julys and Augusts waiting for my bathing suit to fill out, for the time when I'd lie on a "Surf's Up" towel, or one that read "Drive Slow — No Parking — Soft Shoulders Ahead," rubbing suntan lotion into some lifeguard's back while, more romantic than violins, his transistor pounded out the Beach Boys' "Surfer Girl." Annette and Fabian, transistor radios and polka-dot bikinis, were gone by my first real teen-age summer. By then I dreamed of being college age and spent my summer as a baby-sitter, changing diapers.

□

Why do looks *matter* so much?

I do not know a single girl who's really satisfied with how she looks. Some toss their hair and smooth their skirts and stride like models, and I'll start out envying them and mentally exchanging faces or shapes or hair color, but then I'll watch them looking at other girls as *they* stride by tossing *their* hair, and I'll see, in the faces I admired, the same sizing-up look that's on mine (how much does she weigh? Does she color her hair? Curl her eyelashes?) and realize that not one of us feels really *safe*. I study my reflection in every full-length mirror and window and shiny toaster I pass (less from sheer vanity, I think, than from insecurity, a dissatisfaction about the way I look) and when I do examine myself, I almost always see, reflected next to me, another insecure, dissatisfied girl doing the same thing. We put on our mirror expressions and glance hurriedly — sidelong, out of guilt — jumping a little when discovered, bent over the sink in a department store ladies' room, miming before the mirror. What we do before mirrors is an intensely private act. We are examining and repairing the illusions we're attempting to maintain (that *we* don't care about our looks, that how we look when we look good is just a lucky accident) and to be caught in mid-repair destroys the illusion. Like bald men discovered with their toupees off, women viewed early in the morning or at work before a mirror feel they can never regain, in the eyes of those who see them — *before* — the image of how they look *after*.

Why do we feel like unwelcome strangers in our own skins? I change clothes half a dozen times a day when I feel at my worst, leaving pools of discarded costumes on the floor, arranging myself in Outfit Number Nine, until, at last, I'm reasonably pleased with how I look and then, catching my image in a window two hours later, I find my shakily assembled image has disappeared — I must change again. I long for a face that I can count on; I'd like to have eyes that are never puffy, a skin that's uniformly olive (not sallow, never sallow), hair that bounces and emerges from convertibles and bike rides looking artfully tousled instead of just plain lousy. It isn't necessarily beauty I covet, but dependable attractiveness, a face I can catch off guard and be happy at the sight of.

When I talk about it, all this must sound like a casebook neurosis, but I think it's too commonplace to be labeled an abnormality. It's our culture that has put a premium on good looks — all the clothes designers and hairdressers and department store buyers and magazine editors, all aware, at least subconsciously, that we — women — will suddenly and at long last escape the tyranny of fashions on the very day we wholeheartedly *like* the way we look. While constantly creating more products to help us reach that point, they have managed to keep it always slightly beyond us. Just getting to a state of fashionable attractiveness is hard enough because fashions change so quickly. Staying there is impossible. A newer, better model is always around the corner — built-in obsolescence — so that, no sooner do we buy a pair of suede hotpants, satisfying one season's requirements, than another more pressing need is created (a patchwork skirt, an Argyle vest...). Our insecurity is what the beauty industry depends on and encourages — the constant, one-step-behind limbo we live in where each purchase, each haircut, each diet is undertaken in the hopes that it will bring us to some stable point where we can look in the mirror and smile. Sometimes, of course, we do. Never for very long. Pretty soon someone even better-looking passes by on the street, or on the TV screen or in a magazine, and the quest is on again.

Early on, magazines brought out the worst in me — greed and jealousy, wild competition. In *Seventeen* the clothes and make-up and the hairstyles fascinated me, but what really held me to the page was the models. In *Vogue* and *Glamour* they are anonymous, so the envy is at least targetless, generalized. But *Seventeen* models were, like the characters in monthly serials, old friends and sometimes enemies. We knew their names, their beauty problems ("Lucy's skin is oily, so she scrubs nightly with astringent soap and steams her face for that extra zing..."), their dieting secrets, their special touches. (Colleen would be "an individualist" one month, with a flower painted on her cheek or a tiny gold bracelet around the ankle. Next month we'd all be sporting ankle chains and cheek flowers.) What we remembered from the ads they posed in was not the brand of clothes they wore but what the girls who wore them looked like. I'd notice when a model had gained weight or when her stock seemed to be going down, when she was no longer one of the girls the magazine was on a first-name basis with, and — secretly, of course — these failures pleased me. Perhaps that's what the magazines depend on — our bitchiness and envy and our less-than-entirely joyful reaction to to New York-style model beauty. We buy the magazines, study the models, to study the competition. Then if we like the way they look and, most important, feel envy, maybe we'll buy their outfits too.

□

All of us in eighth grade knew that Sue loved Bob and vice versa. (All but me, at least. From the beginning, as I reminded my more romantic friends later, when it was all over, I had been suspicious.) Sue and Bob were no older than the rest of us — fourteen — but the permanence of their situation made them seem to us at least sixteen. As early as October, Bob had signed Sue up to go with him to every dance that year, plus the big freshman dance the next fall. She wore his ring, with tape wound around the band to keep it on her finger, and he wore on his wrist a shackle-like silver chain with a name tag on it that read SUE.

All through the school day they passed notes to each other — mushy, romantic, badly spelled descriptions of how much they missed each other, signed with half a page of "love's" on Bob's part, calmer, more domestic plans for the future written by Sue, with "Love ya" at the bottom. Sue and Bob weren't in all the same classes that year, so helpful friends — proud to be caught up in the drama — delivered notes from one room to the other, using their student council or office helper status to get them through the halls and claiming, always, to have a message for Sue from the nurse, or a note for Bob from the principal. A couple of the teachers knew what was up, but they must have thought it was cute (the way kids playing grown-up always are) because they never interfered. In the process of delivery the contents of the notes tended to lose a certain privacy, to spill all over the place, in fact. Sue and Bob's correspondence abounded with passionate confidences and arrows pointing to blank spaces with captions that read "This is where I kissed the envelope." And there were other enviably soppy exchanges, which Bob, at his receiving end, would stuff into his pants pocket while Sue put hers into that pregnant purse which hung from her shoulder or on the back of her chair during classes. (We stole it sometimes, just to scare her.)

Aside from the note passing, though, their relationship seemed tame. They were the old married couple of the eighth grade, more like chaperones at dances than like kids. They kissed sometimes while dancing, but mostly they just held hands, as if they had already explored each other so well that nothing else was needed. Sue often resembled a tired, not-tonight-honey housewife with Bob, already dreaming, as they held hands in the corner while the newer, younger couples danced, of a ring and a house and a kitchen and a baby. All the romantics of the junior high were positive they would get married. (We shivered at how close that put us to being grown up, trying out Mrs. with our names, and matching them with different boys' last names. "Just think" we'd whisper to each other, "nine months from now I could be a *mother*.") That notion scared and thrilled us, and it must have terrified the boys. In the middle of some make-out party embrace, drunk with Sue's hooks and fasteners, Bob must have agreed to anything she said, but sometimes, in the brighter hours, he looked a little wistful as he passed the boys out on the playground playing soccer and leaning into the engines of the older kids' cars, while he was surely headed for a station wagon.

He strayed once, with someone's visiting cousin, and Sue heard about it. Like the wife of an adulterous husband, she talked it over with her friends and decided at last to forgive him, but Bob had discovered he didn't want to be forgiven so, at the end of junior high, the first real romance of our class broke up. The ring went back, the bracelet disappeared, Bob was a bachelor again, and almost giddy with his freedom, while Sue moved through the halls like a divorcée. No one would make her mistakes again. Couples would take themselves seriously, but only because love was a necessary delusion, no longer quite so sacred. It was a word from a dozen songs, the rhyme to "dove" and "above," and changing as fashions and the week's top ten. We entered high school believing in it less, and ready for the soap opera to begin.

□

For about three weeks of my freshman year at college I had two roommates instead of one — the girl in the bottom bunk and her friend, who made our quarters especially cramped because, in addition to being six feet tall with lots of luggage, he was male. We slept in shifts — they together, until I came back to the room at night, then he outside in the living room on the couch, until she got up, then he in her bed and I in mine, or I in hers and he in mine, because it was easier for me to get out from the bottom without waking him, and he needed his sleep.... We never made it a threesome, but the awkwardness was always there (those squeaking bedsprings...), as it was for many girls I knew, and many boys. Coming back to the room and announcing my presence loudly with a well-directed, well-projected cough or a casual murmur, "Hmmm — I think I'll go to my room now," it occurred to me that it wasn't my roommate but I — the one who slept alone, the one whose only pills were vitamins and aspirin — I was the embarrassed one. How has it happened, what have we come to, that the scarlet letter these days isn't *A*, but *V*?

In the beginning, of course, everyone's a virgin. You start on equal footing with everyone else (sex is something comic and dirty — the subject of jokes and slumber-party gossip), but pretty soon the divisions form. (Sex is still dirty, but less unthinkable, sort of thrilling.) There's the girl with the older boy friend (he's in ninth grade); the girl who went away to summer camp and fell in love; the girl who kisses boys right out there on the dance floor for all the junior high to see. (That's the point, of course. If she wanted it to be a secret, she'd have gone out to the Coke machine with him, the way the other couples do.) But everybody's still a virgin. The question isn't even asked.

The first to go is usually a secretarial student, the one who started wearing bras in fourth grade, the one who pierced her ears in sixth, the one who wears purple eyeshadow to school. She doesn't talk about it, but she doesn't make a big thing of keeping it quiet either, so word gets around, and all the *good* girls whisper about her — they knew it all the time, what can you expect? She's probably older anyway, she must have stayed back a couple of years....

Then, maybe in tenth grade, or eleventh (if you live in a city, make that ninth), it's a good girl, one of your crowd. (You know because she called her best friend up the next day and — promise not to tell — told her.) At first you think it was a mistake: he took advantage of her, she didn't know what was happening — and you feel terribly, terribly sorry for her and wonder how she'll ever face him again. But she does; in fact, she's with him all the time now — *doing it again* most likely. You stare at her in the halls ("she doesn't *look* any different") and, though she's still your friend — you still pass notes in math class — there's a distance between you now. Woman of the world and little girl — hot ticket and (for the first time, the word sounds slightly unpleasant) *virgin.*

After that, the pattern becomes more common. The girl, when she breaks up with that first boy, can hardly hold out on his successor. And her ex-boy friend's new girl friend, naturally, has an expectation to satisfy if she wants a date to the prom. More and more girls are, in the words of those who aren't, *going all the way.* As for the ones who still baby-sit on Friday nights, or the ones whose dates are still getting up the courage to kiss them good night, they spend their time speculating — "does she or doesn't she?" (It's always the *girl* who does; not a combined act at all so much as an individual one.) The group of shocked guessers gets smaller and smaller until they — you, if you're still one of them — realize that the ones to be whispered about, stared at, shocked by, aren't the others now but themselves. It's hard to say at what point the moment occurs, but suddenly virginity isn't fun anymore. The days when it was taken for granted are long gone; so are the days when it was half and half (The Virgins vs. the Nons). The ones who *aren't* now take that for granted, and as for the ones who are, well — they don't talk about it much. Virginity has become not a flower or a jewel, a precious treasure for Prince Charming or a lively, prized and guarded gift, but a dusty relic — an anachronism. Most of all, it's an embarrassment.

So here we have this baffled, frightened virgin (she's third person now; I can't help wanting to disassociate myself from her category and all it seems to represent). She may not really be a prude or an iceberg (maybe nobody's ever tried . . .) but that's how the world views her. She's on the same team with Sensible Orthopedic Shoes and Billy Graham and Lawrence Welk and the Republican party. Old ladies — her grandmother's friends — love her (she can get a date with their favorite nephews any time) and wonder sadly why there aren't more girls around like that. A certain kind of man (boy) is very fond of her, too. He's the timid type — just as glad, really, not to feel that he's expected to perform. (He's an embarrassed virgin too, and the last thing these two need is each other, perpetuating the breed — as their nonvirginal contemporaries, in love-making, perpetuate the race — by nonperformance.) The sexual revolution is on, but the virgin isn't part of it.

The sexual revolution. It's a cliché, but it exists all right, and its pressures are everywhere. All the old excuses ("I might get pregnant," "I'm not that kind of girl") are gone. Safe and increasingly available contraceptives (for anyone brave and premeditative enough to get them) make premarital sex possible; changing moral standards, an increased naturalness, make it commonplace; elegant models of sexual freedom — Julie Christie, Catherine Deneuve — have made it fashionable. Consider a virgin in the movies. Is there a single pretty young heroine who doesn't hop unself-consciously into bed? (Who is there left for her to identify with — Doris Day?) Then there are magazines, filled with discussions of intricate sexual problems (the timing of orgasms . . . do I get one? do I give one?) while the virgin remains on a whole other level — her fears compounded. (Our old, junior high notion of sex was that it got done to you; the girl with the purple eyeshadow just let it happen. Today all kinds of problems in technique make the issue much more complicated for an inexperienced, media-blitzed girl: not just *will I* but *can I*.) The people who've been making nice, simple love for years now, while the virgin became more and more unique, have, quite understandably, gone on to other things. There is foreplay and afterplay and the 999 positions of the *Kamasutra.* . . . The train has left the station before the virgin's bought her ticket or even, maybe, packed her bags.

There are other pressures too, less remote than the images on a screen or the words on a page. Though individuality is officially admired, "Peer-group pressure" (a fifties concept) is very real when it comes to sex. Other girls assume a friend's sexual experience. So, more importantly, do the men she goes out with. The death of the formal date (with dinner and the theater, high heels and a good-night kiss afterward) has put a new ambiguity on male-female relationships. Just sitting around, talking and listening to music, while it may be lots more real and honest and all those other good 1973-type adjectives, is also lots more difficult for a virgin to cope with. If this is someone she likes — but doesn't love — there isn't any way for her to demonstrate simple fondness. The kiss that once said "I like you" now seems a promise of something more to come. And if, perhaps, she's decided that yes, this is someone she would sleep with, she may discover (final irony) that he isn't eager, when he finds out she's a virgin, to be the first. The situation seems unresolvable: virginity is a self-perpetuating condition. (Like the unskilled, unemployed worker, the virgin hears — time and again — "Come back when you've got some experience.") The only way out seems to be the crudest, most loveless and mechanical way possible: almost a reverse prostitution. It happens — as once young boys would be initiated in a brothel — because the idea now, for the late-bloomer, the high school baby-sitter — the idea is to get it over with as quickly, painlessly and forgettably as possible.

If it hasn't happened before, the pressure is really on at college. I'm looking back now to the beginning of my freshman year. What I should remember is my first glimpse of the college campus, freshman assembly, buying notepads and textbooks and writing my name and my dorm on the covers. Instead, my memory of September blurs into a single word: sex. Not that Yale was the scene of one continuous orgy. But we surely were preoccupied. Ask a friend how things were going and he'd tell you whether or not he'd found a girl. Go to a freshman women's tea or a Women's Liberation meeting and talk would turn, inevitably, to contraceptives and abortions. Liberated from the restrictions imposed by parents and curfews and car seats (those tiny Volkswagens), we found ourselves suddenly sharing a world not with the junior high and the ninth grade, but with college seniors and graduate students — men and women in their twenties. Very quickly, we took on their values, imitated their behavior and, often, swallowed their pills.

September was a kind of catching-up period for all the people who hadn't cut loose before. All that first week, girls trooped up the stairs at 3 and 4 A.M., and sometimes not at all. Fall, for the freshmen, at least, was a frantic rush of pairing off, with boys running for the girls and, strangely enough (there were so few of us, so many boys to go around) the girls rushing for the boys and the couples, finally, rushing for the beds as if this were musical chairs and if you didn't hurry you'd be left standing up. It was maybe the last chance to be clumsy and amateurish and virginal. After that, you entered the professional league where, if you weren't a pro, you had a problem.

I don't mean to reinforce the embarrassment, to confirm the hopelessness of the virgin's situation — "yes, things are pretty bad, aren't they?" — or to frighten anyone about to embark upon the brave new world of college or job-and-apartment. Because as a matter of fact there shouldn't be anything scary, or hopeless or embarrassing about virginity any more than there should be anything scary, hopeless or embarrassing about the loss of it. I'm not *for* virginity or *against* premarital sex, and I'm certainly not defending virginity for its own sake — the I'm-saving-it-for-my-husband line. Whether or not you're a virgin isn't the point; the question is what *kind* of a virgin or a nonvirgin you are, and whether you are what you are by choice or by submission to outside pressures. (Plenty of "freely consenting" adults are really victims of a cultural, everybody's-doing-it type of forced consent.) Some women can easily and naturally love a man or want to be close to him, maybe even without love. I have a friend like that — a girl I used to think of as promiscuous and hypocritical when she said of each new boy friend (and sometimes two at once), "I love him." I see now this was quite genuine. She has a giving and sharing nature and she loves very easily. She isn't racking up points in her sexual relationships; she truly wants to know as many people as she can. Not everyone can be that way; knowing someone means being known, giving up privacy in a manner that's difficult for many people. These days one's privacy is no longer one's own. Even the act of refusing to give it up is intruded upon.

It's no longer just the nonvirgin who subjects herself to intense scrutiny; now it's the virgin whose very refusal is scrutinized, maybe even more closely than her surrender would be. People don't talk much about who's on the pill or who's sleeping together, but there's endless speculation about who isn't. "What's the matter with her?" they ask. Is she frigid? Lesbian? Big-brother types offer helpful advice, reasoning that if she isn't interested in them except as a friend, something must indeed be wrong with her. Her abstinence, in short, is fair game for everyone.

Privacy — and freedom — can be maintained only by disregarding the outside pressures. Freedom is choosing, and sometimes that may mean choosing not to be "free." For the embarrassed virgin, unsure now whether her mind is her own ("Do I really want to go to bed with him, or do I simply want to be like everybody else?") — for her, there's a built-in test. If she really wants to, on her own, she won't have to ask herself or be embarrassed. Her inexperience and clumsiness will have, for him, a kind of coltish grace. Our grandparents, after all, never read the *Kamasutra*, and here we are today, proof that they managed fine without it.

□

Girls of my generation (I should call them women, I know, but old, pre-liberation habits linger on) are often asked for their opinions on Women's Lib (the abbreviation is, in itself, the beginning of a diminution of the cause), and one predictable answer, read off with a seemly giggle, is that every girl likes to have doors opened for her on dates. Or she can launch into a Rights of Women talk about the prostitution of marriage and the chauvinism of the media.

Most likely, though, she'll nervously, cautiously seat herself on the fence, legs crossed demurely at the ankle, chin out to show she is no southern belle, and torn between the desire to save her cake and the desire to eat it now, she'll say that yes, she's all for equal rights and equal pay, and day care centers are fine for some people, and TV commercials — though they certainly don't influence *her* — are a disgrace, but she doesn't care for the movement's *style* — those women are too loud and coarse, they come on too strong, they have no sense of humor, they intimidate and antagonize the very people they're trying to convert — other women. She doesn't like the bitterness she sees so often among feminists.

(Why is it that, like nuns, they're often so plain? Sour grapes, she'll say.) She *likes* men. She *wants* to get married and have children — she's for (the old cliché) *human* liberation.

It's an easy out, that line — incontestable. Is anyone in favor of un-equal jobs and unequal pay? Feminists would regard the fence sitter as a sellout and a traitor, and I guess they'd see me that way too. Because, while I'm conscious of the cliché, that is — to a great extent — how I feel. I do not feel inferior or unliberated, and while I recognize that there are women who do, women (for whom the movement does a great service) whose image of themselves needs to be changed, and that even those of us who *feel* equal to men may not get equal treatment, the truth is that the methods of the feminist movement turn me off. Sexist that, in some ways, I might be called, I think first of looks, and am aware of what it is about Germaine Greer and Gloria Steinem that appeals to me. Almost certainly they would reject the idea that their function is to give to the movement glamour, but much of their importance to the movement comes, unquestionably, from the slim, stylish, graceful-moving image they project. (Gloria Steinem can liberate as only someone on the other side of prison bars can unlock a door.) Women who are attracted to her use the same set of standards I use, when I find myself unattracted to them — they like her looks as I dislike theirs; they want to be asso-ciated with her style and poise as I want to disassociate myself from their stylelessness — from women too old to go blue-jeaned and braless, from the tousled haired and the tensely scrawny and the ones whose eyes bear the look of frustration and anger that have more than memories of un-fair pay behind them. Women with "Vaginal Politics" buttons pinned to the zippers on their jeans; women who call me *sister*, who speak, in locker-room, army-barracks lingo of being "fucked over by the crappy shit" men hand them. I feel my privacy intruded upon with orgasm and sex-object talk.

The actions of large groups, when they assemble, frighten me a bit. United we stand, divided we fall — I know that. But the effects crowds have on the people in them are often dangerous and deceptive. When individuals join in affection and good feeling (as at a folk music concert) the atmosphere of warmth (while it may be illusory and deceptive) seems healthy. But people in crowds stir each other up to a point where good sense is suspended by too much strong feeling in too-close quarters, too much chanting and foot-stomping and hand-clapping. I think of the foot-ball game I went to once, where the wild, touchdown-crazed crowds made the wooden stands we sat on creak and then crumble. Films of Hitler in action, of the Rolling Stones at Altamont — the analogies I make are rash and perhaps unfair to a movement that unquestionably does good. But it is, nonetheless, a movement held together by shared negative feeling, a sisterhood of bitterness and sometimes hate.

I grew up wanting to have babies. I reject what would be the feminist attitude that TV and baby dolls and the male-dominated American cul-ture brainwashed me. I *did* play with baby dolls and watch TV (and am appalled now, watching old reruns, to see the notions of A Woman's Place they uniformly presented), but it wasn't those things that gave me my dreams of motherhood, and what sexist notions they exposed me to I think I rejected. (Desi's tyranny over Lucy, and her sly wheedling always seemed — more than anything else — dumb.) I wanted to have children (and, if I'd been a boy, I'd have felt the same way) not because I had a low opinion of myself and considered myself good for nothing else or because my own mother presented an oppressed housewife image in our family (which she never did) but just because I like kids.

But something new seems to be happening. Friends of mine announce now that they don't intend to marry or that, if they do, they won't have children. Often they are children of divorced parents or parents who, they tell me casually, don't like each other much. It all seems strange and sad and unromantic, this lack of faith in families and permanence, the short-attention-span notion of finding lifelong companionship a bore and any kind of ties and restrictions a slur on that sixties ideal we grew up with, that what mattered more than anything else was *freedom*. It was a time when discipline and even simple regimen seemed unfashionable. When we wrote at school, we were encouraged to forget about grammar and concern ourselves with free self-expression — maybe not to write at all, but instead to nonverbally communicate.

At home we were not spanked or given heavy chores, most of us. And by some obscure route I think all that has brought us around to doubts about families and order in general. We are suspicious of anything that seems too rigid, anything that seems to endanger the carefree, don't-think-ahead life. It has been said, and it's true, that the future seems too uncertain for us to make plans, that the specter of The Bomb and ecological disaster hangs over us. The feeling many of us have about marriage and children comes from a kind of Peter Pan feeling about Youth — a stage of life so glamorized in our time that we no longer eagerly anticipate being grown-ups (as teen-agers used to, when growing up meant escaping the strict rule of parents). Now it is Youth, not adults, who wield the power. Getting married and having children means that, if you are not old, at least you are no longer young.

□

The words *ambitious, up-and-coming, go-getting* used to be the highest compliment awarded to a bright young man just starting out on his career. Back in those days, the label *businessman* held no unfortunate connotations, no ring of war-mongering or conservatism or pollution. The future may have been uncertain, but it was certainly considered, anyway, and the goals were clear: a good marriage, a good job, a good income — that was a good life.

My generation's definition of The Good Life is harder to arrive at. Our plans for the future are vague, because so many of us don't believe in planning, because we don't quite believe in the future. Perhaps we make too much of growing up with tension, from as far back as the Cuban Missile Crisis, but the fact is that the tension of the sixties put us in a kind of suspension. There were always fallout shelter signs, always secret servicemen and always, when the words "we interrupt this program to bring you..." flashed on the screen, the possibility of an assassination. When a plane flies low I wonder (just for a second) — is it the Russians? The Chinese?

So we don't plan. We make a thing of spontaneity and informality. (Parties just *happen;* couples hang around together — no more going on dates.) Looking ahead to the future, planning, and pushing are seen as uncool ("take it easy . . . no sweat"), aggressive.

It's impossible not to wonder where the young hip kids of today will be twenty years from now. Their parents say they'll settle down ("We were wild in our day too...") and some of them will — some will later join their parents' establishment world just as, for now, they've joined a group that is itself a kind of establishment. But there's another group, involved in much more than a fad, and their futures are less easy to predict. They've passed beyond faddishness, beyond the extreme activism of the late sixties and arrived at a calm isolationist position — free not just from the old establishment ambitions and the corporate tycoon style, but from the aggressiveness of the radical tycoon. The best thing to be, for them, isn't go-getting or up-and-coming, but cool. Broad social conscience has been replaced by personal responsibility, and if they plan at all, their plans will be to get away. The new movement is away from the old group forms of moratorium crowds and huge rock concerts and communes. Young doctors who once joined the Peace Corps are turning more and more to small-town private practices, Harvard scholars are dropping out to study auto mechanics or farming. Everybody wants to buy land in Oregon and Vermont. If we have any ambition at all now, it is not so much the drive to get ahead as it is the drive to get away.

When my friends and I were little, we had big plans. I would be a famous actress and singer, dancing on the side. I would paint my own sets and compose my own music, writing the script and the lyrics and reviewing the performance for the *New York Times.* I would marry and have three children (they don't allow us dreams like that any more) and we would live, rich and famous (donating lots to charity, of course, and periodically adopting orphans), in a house we designed ourselves. When I was older I had visions of good works. I saw myself in South American rain forests and African deserts, feeding the hungry and healing the sick with an obsessive selflessness, I see now, that was as selfish, in the end, as my first plans for stardom.

Now my goal is simpler. I want to be happy. And I want comfort — nice clothes, a nice house, good music and good food, and the feeling that I'm doing some little thing that matters. I'll vote and I'll give to charity, but I won't give myself. I feel a sudden desire to buy land — not a lot, not as a business investment, but just a small plot of earth so that whatever they do to the country I'll have a place where I can go — a kind of fallout shelter, I guess. As some people prepare for their old age, so I prepare for my twenties. A little house, a comfortable chair, peace and quiet — retirement sounds tempting.

I'm almost twenty now — two decades gone. I know now that I will never be a ballerina. That's not because of any conscious choice, because of anything I've done, but because of what's been neglected. It isn't that I ever longed to be one, but the knowledge scares me, that I can't — there's nothing, absolutely nothing I can do about it. I am too old to be a violin prodigy, or to learn championship chess; I'm closer to Ophelia now than Juliet. The word *woman* embarrasses me a little. (Why is that? Some leftover scrap of unliberation, that *boys* are *men*, while I remain, and will till I am fifty, always a *girl*.)

Once, I guess, youth was a handicap and coming of age an exciting, horizon-broadening time for long pants and freedom. For us, today, youth — while it lasts — is a time we greedily hold onto, a fashionable, glorified age when, if we don't quite *swing*, at least we're told that's what we do, that these are the best years of our lives — it's all downhill from here.

*E*stablishing a coherent identity, dealing with sexuality, and preparing for adult roles and responsibilities are three major themes associated with adolescent development. But social expectations about how young people should proceed with those tasks, as well as what those in their teens have valued in themselves, have differed significantly for males and females.

Teenage males have traditionally been encouraged to develop qualities and skills that would enable them to function as economically self-sufficient and psychologically autonomous adults. Although class, racial, and ethnic background have certainly played a central role in limiting or broadening opportunity for adolescent males, the majority have enjoyed a wider range of choices for exploring their interests and testing their talents than has been available to females, and vocational identity has been primary in the creation of a stable sense of self for young men.

For females, domestic skills have traditionally symbolized adulthood, and marriage has defined their place in the social and economic hierarchy. The ideology of domesticity that emerged in the nineteenth century urged women to consider their roles as wives and mothers to be primary. In nurturing and rewarding the qualities of submissiveness and loyalty in young women, society has thereby encouraged females to construct a sense of identity and worth around serving the needs of others.

The importance of class, race, and ethnicity in explaining variations in experiences among adolescent females is obvious from the selections in this chapter. For Harriet Jacobs, a black and a slave living in the South in the mid-nineteenth century, life was a daily struggle for psychological and physical survival. Under the ownership of her master Harriet was not free to make any important decisions in her life, including the choice of whether or not to marry. Acting on any aspirations for adulthood first required an escape from her oppressive circumstances.

The issue of sexuality was especially complicated for Harriet. The continual sexual harassment from her master and the jealous scrutiny by her mistress were demeaning and humiliating. The fact that Harriet persevered and succeeded in escaping attests to her exceptional determination and strength of character.

The social and economic realities of Anzia Yezierska's life directly account for the paramount importance of vocational identity for her. Through advanced education and a teaching career, Anzia hoped to free herself from poverty and become a middle-class American citizen. In bearing complete responsibility at the age of seventeen for all of her necessities of life and paying for her own education, Anzia had little time for the social activity and enjoyment usually associated with adolescence. As a poor Jewish immigrant, without the support of her family and alienated from her native-born age peers, Anzia had a lonely and difficult adolescence. Like Harriet Jacobs, she believed strongly in a vision of a better future, and she possessed an extraordinary determination to construct a meaningful life for herself in the face of tremendous odds.

Although Eliza Southgate Bowne, Maud Rittenhouse, and Joyce Maynard each grew up in different centuries, they shared some common concerns and expectations. From white, upper- and upper-middle-class, Protestant backgrounds, they all enjoyed special material and emotional comforts, leisure time for social activities, and access to advanced schooling.

All three indicated that they expected to marry and raise children, although Eliza and Joyce were more introspective about the subject than Maud was. In weighing alternatives to marriage, Eliza contemplated the stigma attached to being an "old maid" and the lack of opportunity for eighteenth-century women to explore interests outside the home. By contrast, Joyce resented what she felt was a stigma attached to the roles of wife and mother in contemporary society and defended her plans for marriage and motherhood as her own deliberate choice. Interestingly, Eliza thought that the arguments in defense of women's equal rights delineated by the noted eighteenth-century feminist Mary Wollstonecraft were too extreme, while Joyce criticized some of the means and ends of the current women's movement. Maud, too, expected that she would marry and described the qualities she sought in a spouse. She does not appear, however, to have considered the possibility of staying single by choice. It was Maud's mother who urged her to develop her artistic talents and continue her education beyond high school before she married.

Just how profoundly moral standards have changed is clear when attitudes and experiences concerning sex are compared among these three young women. Eliza Southgate Bowne and Maud Rittenhouse expected to remain virgins until they married. Although rules and roles in courtship and dating seem to have been more relaxed for Maud in the nineteenth-century frontier atmosphere of the Midwest, she worried, as Eliza had, about being too flirtatious and assertive in her relationships with young men. For Joyce Maynard and her female peers, premarital sex was no longer considered taboo, and they expected young males and females to express their interest in sexuality in equal and open ways.

From the eighteenth to the twentieth centuries the amount of time each young woman spent in educational institutions progressively increased. Differences in their respective experiences reflect regional variations in patterns of secondary-school development as well as changes in the quality and availability of educational opportunities for women in different historical eras.

Eliza's training in social and domestic arts at a private female academy in Boston represents virtually the only type of advanced schooling available to a very small number of young women in the eighteenth century. As a high-school student in a coeducational, Midwestern, public institution almost one hundred years later, Maud, too, was among a very select group of teenage males and females. Although her curriculum was more rigorous than that which Eliza studied, there is no sense that Maud or her female classmates were pursuing an education with any career ambitions in mind. High school and college for Maud provided a pleasant way of filling time before marriage.

That Joyce would pursue an academic course of study at a prestigious and formerly all-male college seems to have been taken for granted and not surprising in light of the fact that both her father and mother had professional careers. Even though Joyce expressed no explicit career aspiration, she made it clear that she believed that the choice would be hers to make.

The lives of all the young women studied in this chapter have illustrated the variety of ways society has directed the course of development for females in their teen years in the family, in school, and in the community and how for many young women, restrictions imposed on the basis of sex have been compounded by discrimination because of race, ethnic, and class background.

In recent decades there have been indications of increasing efforts to promote the development of those qualities in adolescent females that will enable them to imagine and create a diversity of meaningful lives as adults. The serious attempts to equalize access to educational and vocational opportunities so that young people of both sexes, and all classes and races, can express their talents and explore their interests to the fullest extent are hopeful signs that in the future young women will be free to choose to combine work and marriage, remain single and work, or choose marriage alone — with no stigma attached to any of those roles.

Bibliography

Bakan, David. "Adolescence in America: From Idea to Social Fact." *Daedalus* 100 (Fall 1971): 979–995.

Blos, Peter. *On Adolescence: A Psychoanalytical Interpretation.* New York: Free Press of Glencoe, 1962.

Brooks-Gunn, Jeanne and Matthews, Wendy Schempp. *He & She: How Children Develop Their Sex-Role Identity.* Englewood Cliffs, N.J.: Prentice-Hall, 1979.

Coleman, James S. *The Adolescent Society*. New York: Free Press of Glencoe, 1961.

Coleman, James S., ed. *Youth: Transition to Adulthood*. Chicago: University of Chicago Press, 1974.

Cott, Nancy F. "Young Women in the Second Great Awakening in New England." *Feminist Studies* 3 (1975): 15–29.

Demos, John, and Demos, Virginia. "Adolescence in Historical Perspective." *Journal of Marriage and the Family* 31 (1969): 632–638.

Douvan, Elizabeth, and Adelson, Joseph. *The Adolescent Experience*. New York: John Wiley, 1966.

Erikson, Erik H. *Identity: Youth and Crisis*. New York: W. W. Norton, 1968.

Erikson, Erik H., ed. *Youth: Change and Challenge*. New York: Basic Books, 1963.

Fass, Paula S. *The Damned and the Beautiful: American Youth in the 1920's*. New York: Oxford University Press, 1977.

Friedenberg, Edgar Z. *The Vanishing Adolescent*. Boston: Beacon Press, 1959.

Goethals, George W., and Klos, Dennis S. *Experiencing Youth: First-Person Accounts*. Boston: Little, Brown, 1970.

Hall, G. Stanley. *Adolescence: Its Psychology and Its Relations to Physiology, Anthropology, Sociology, Sex, Crime, Religion, and Education*. 2 Vols. New York: D. Appleton, 1904.

Handlin, Oscar, and Handlin, Mary F. *Facing Life: Youth and the Family in American History*. Boston: Little, Brown, 1971.

Havighurst, Robert J. and Dreyer, Philip H., eds. *Youth: The Seventy-fourth Yearbook of the National Society for the Study of Education*. Chicago: The University of Chicago Press, 1975.

Hiner, N. Ray. "Adolescence in Eighteenth-Century America." *History of Childhood Quarterly* 3 (Fall 1975): 253–280.

Keniston, Kenneth. "Youth: A 'New' Stage of Life." *The American Scholar* 39 (1970): 631–654.

Kett, Joseph F. *Rites of Passage: Adolescence in America, 1790 to the Present*. New York: Basic Books, 1977.

Konopka, Gisela. *Young Girls: A Portrait of Adolescence*. Englewood Cliffs, N.J.: Prentice-Hall, 1976.

Tanner, J. M. "Sequence, Tempo, and Individual Variation in the Growth and Development of Boys and Girls Aged Twelve to Sixteen." *Daedalus* 100 (Fall 1971): 907–930.

Welter, Barbara. "Coming of Age in America: The American Girl in the Nineteenth Century." In *Dimity Convictions: The American Woman in the Nineteenth Century*, by Barbara Welter. Athens: Ohio University Press, 1976, pp. 3–20.

Yankelovich, Daniel. *The New Morality: A Profile of American Youth in the 1970s*. New York: McGraw-Hill, 1974.

THREE

Young Adulthood

Childhood, adolescence, middle age, and old age are all familiar concepts in our everyday vocabulary. Young adulthood is not. This term, and its counterpart, early adulthood, have not achieved wide currency despite the fact that they are employed by specialists in the field of human development. Most people are unaccustomed to thinking of the years between ages twenty and forty as a distinctive life stage; therefore the labels affixed to this segment of the life span by scholars are not frequently used. Explaining why the terminology of experts has not been incorporated into popular discourse is not enough, however. The fundamental question remains: why are these particular years not ordinarily conceived of as a well-defined period of life? The answer is twofold.

The first reason is the amorphous nature of young adulthood. Because the decades of the twenties and thirties encompass such a variety of experiences, all central to articulating a person's life pattern, there has been a tendency to treat these years as synonymous with the whole of adult life. Reducing so diffuse and so pivotal a period to manageable proportions has proven to be a herculean task. In short, young adulthood is hard to get a handle on.

The failure to recognize young adulthood as a unified, cohesive life stage stems from other circumstances as well. Since this life stage includes so many critical experiences, researchers have preferred to examine its constituent parts independently, apart from the larger context of a person's life. For example, there have been intensive studies of marriage, parenthood, and the work career, each in isolation. As a result, much has been learned about particular turning points in the lives of young adults, but far less has been discovered about the overall course of continuity and change in their lives.

One of the unassailable conclusions of research so far (most of it focused on males) is that significant differences exist in the male and female

159

experiences of young adulthood. Gender is a crucial factor in determining how a person defines a satisfying adulthood. Although contemporary shifts in social mores have produced some unmistakable modifications in long-standing patterns, it is still accurate to contrast the primacy of work in the lives and identities of young men with the primacy of family concerns in the lives and identities of young women. While men in their twenties and thirties concentrate their energies on proving themselves in their chosen occupation, women of a comparable age are preoccupied with bearing and raising children, as well as supporting their husbands' careers.

Chronological age provides only a rough indicator of the parameters of young adulthood. To use the age of twenty or twenty-one to denote the time when most people assume adult responsibilities is to be suggestive rather than definitive. Similarly, the choice of the age of forty to mark the onset of middle age is a convenience, not a statement of fact.

Biological events do not fully define the boundaries of female young adulthood either, although they constitute an essential aspect of this life stage. This is the period when females are most active sexually and the time when they conceive and bear most of their children. Consequently, physiological alterations in the bodies of women, as well as their psychological concomitants, must be investigated before any complete understanding of this phase of the female life cycle is possible.

At puberty females become biologically capable of bearing children. When or if their potential becomes an actuality, however, depends on social, not biological, factors. Until recently the loss of virginity and the commencement of regular sexual relations were closely tied to the event of marriage. Pregnancy usually followed within a few years. Nowadays, however, sexual initiation often precedes marriage, and, as a result, many girls in their teens become pregnant. Whether they keep their babies, put them up for adoption, or decide on abortions, these adolescent girls have already experienced one of the critical events of female young adulthood.

Notwithstanding the current upsurge of teen-age pregnancies, childbearing is primarily associated with young adulthood in contemporary America. Although voluntary childlessness has now become a legitimate option for couples (there have always been some childless couples because of infertility problems), the vast majority of American women have at least one baby between ages twenty and forty. In other words, having a baby is still one of the most predictable experiences of female young adulthood.

Over the centuries, the frequency of childbearing as well as the conditions of childbirth have changed markedly. Today, reproduction is far less central to the experience of young women than it was in former generations. The frequency of childbearing has decreased significantly as has the span of time devoted to it. As a rule, contemporary American women have fewer children in a shorter space of years than their forebears.

The conditions of childbirth have also altered. Midwives and female relatives and friends have been replaced by doctors and nurses at deliveries. The setting for childbirth has become the hospital instead of the home. And the risks of childbirth to the mother, as well as the infant, have declined dramatically, especially in the last fifty years. These alterations are undoubtedly responsible for shifts in the psychological responses of women to pregnancy and childbirth. Apprehension and anxiety have to a large extent been replaced by joyous anticipation.

The widespread use of effective means of contraception today has also brought critical changes in the lives of young women. The fact that a woman's schedule of childbearing is not dictated by her biology, but is instead the result of deliberate planning, enables her to incorporate other activities in her life, such as education or work. Far less vulnerable to unwanted pregnancies, a young married woman can pursue a career on the same basis as her male peers. Another positive by-product of the regular use of birth control is the greater opportunity for sexual pleasure on the part of women. Fear of pregnancy inhibited the enjoyment of sexual relations for countless women in the past. Consequently, the removal of this anxiety constitutes a major change. The desire and ability of contemporary women to control their fertility has had a profound impact on the experience of female young adulthood. Female biology is far less determinative in shaping young women's lives than it formerly was.

The roles and responsibilities assigned by society also play a crucial part in structuring young adulthood for females. Equally significant are the meanings and feelings attached to those roles and responsibilities by women themselves. While no one experience marks the transition from adolescence to adulthood, certain social events have been used to indicate the commencement of young adulthood. Customarily, the ability to support oneself financially has signaled the onset of adulthood for males. Although in contemporary America girls are considered adults when they complete their education, embark on a job, or move away from the family home, traditionally the decisive event has been marriage. The social meaning of marriage itself has differed for men and for women. For women, getting married has been seen as an achievement — finding a means of providing material well-being and security. For men, marriage has meant increased economic responsibilities.

Young women in America have always been expected to marry, and the vast majority of them have done so. The timing of marriage varies, of course, but demographic studies show that the range of variation is not great. On the average, American women have married between the ages of twenty and twenty-three, except during the seventeenth century when they were likely to marry earlier.

Assuming the role of wife presages a major change in the life of a woman. The external conditions of her life are altered as well as her inner feelings. To temper the shock of this change, a sequence of microevents provides a gradual initiation into the role of wife. Courtship, engagement, the wedding, and the honeymoon are all elements in the process whereby a young girl is prepared for her new social identity as wife. The specific content of each of these ritualized stages, as well as their relative importance, has varied in different historical eras. But the persistence of such customs testifies to the magnitude of the transition from girl to wife.

Once married, a young woman undergoes a significant transformation in behavior as well as attitudes. Her change of surname and title from Miss to Mrs. (a change evoking little criticism until recently) symbolizes not only the shift in legal status, but a much more profound shift in orientation. Her primary loyalty is now to her husband, rather than her family of origin. New ties are forged with her husband's family as she assumes the role of daughter-in-law. Developing a viable relationship with her new husband is the essential task of the period immediately following marriage. Mutually acceptable patterns regarding household responsibilities, leisure, work, and sexual activity must be established. The underlying question in these decisions concerns the degree of independence to be possessed by the wife.

For a woman, the psychological ramifications of becoming a wife depend on whether she plays a subordinate role and the husband a dominant role, or whether a more egalitarian pattern is instituted. A number of factors are relevant here, including the age, temperament, and personality of individual partners; social class, educational, ethnic, religious, and racial background; and historical period. For some women breaking away from the family and entering marriage has brought feelings of more autonomy and independence. For others, perhaps the majority, the opposite has been true. Becoming a wife has meant submerging one's own identity in that of one's husband; living vicariously through him; and accepting his goals, interests, and needs as her own. Such self-sacrifice has been built into the traditional marital relationship.

Motherhood no longer inevitably follows marriage today, but before the systematic use of birth control, a young bride could anticipate conceiving a child within the first few years of marriage. Sexual activity within the context of marriage was bound to result in pregnancy, barring biological incapacity. The birth of the first child is a major life-changing event for most women. A new identity emerges — that of mother — and with it usually comes a heightened sense of importance, accomplishment, and self-esteem. Traditionally motherhood has been the only avenue available for women to gain such recognition.

Most women see motherhood as the most important role to be assumed in young adulthood. A host of new responsibilities begins. Whether or not she nurses the child, the mother pays an extraordinary amount of attention to the infant during the early months of its life. As the child matures and other children are born, the mother's role expands. The extent of the father's participation in child rearing has varied according to historical era. But in general, women have been socialized to see themselves as having major, if not total, responsibility for rearing their children.

How encompassing the mother role is depends in part on the number of children in the family. In large families, mothers are deluged with the tasks of child care and can find little time for their husbands or themselves. Theoretically, mothers of fewer children are free to devote some of their energies to activities other than child care, but ironically, the demanding ideal of child care that emerged in the era of small families (which began in the nineteenth century) makes greater claims on the mother to commit herself to her child's physical and psychological well-being. The stress on the quality of child rearing makes the mother exert as much effort, if not more, as when her problem was sheer numbers of children.

Bearing and raising children can trigger a wide range of psychological responses among women. While for many a sense of competence and accomplishment is enhanced, for others the experience brings feelings of being tied down and of having to sacrifice too much of one's self. Reactions change throughout young adulthood, again varying according to individual personality and life circumstances.

With or without children, a married woman is invariably also a housewife. Marrying as a rule involves setting up an independent household with one's husband and assuming a whole new series of duties and commitments. Again, what the role of housewife entails and how women have evaluated it has changed over time, depending on individual circumstances and the social value placed on domestic skills.

At a minimum today the role of housewife involves food preparation, cleaning, laundering, and shopping for food and other household essentials. The fact that men have been reluctant to share the tedious tasks necessary for running a home, coupled with the fact that generations of American women have been subjected to constant social pressure to excel at housekeeping because the home is a woman's special preserve, makes it extremely difficult for women to evade these chores. Improved technology has not altered this prescription. Although theoretically the role of housewife is invested with considerable importance, in reality the work that women perform routinely in the home has consistently been regarded as less valuable than that performed by men in the marketplace.

Traditionally, the events that have announced the transition from adolescence to young adulthood for American females have been centered in the family. From being a dutiful daughter in her parents' home, a young girl moved into the role of wife and housewife almost simultaneously, and soon thereafter assumed the even more taxing role of mother. The passage of years in a young woman's life was calibrated to the origin and development of a new family.

Increasingly, this is not the only pathway to maturity for young girls. Whether or not they eventually marry (and have children), contemporary young women are traversing other avenues from adolescence to young adulthood, the chief one being the commitment to a job or career. Establishing an identity as a working person is a means of achieving independence as well as proving one's ability to function in the world of adults. Whatever the nature of her job, the satisfaction derived from its performance, as well as the remuneration, give a young woman the sense that she has indeed crossed the threshold to adulthood.

Young women who remain single by choice are found in increasing numbers today. Their ranks are swelled by the multitude of divorced young women in today's society. To be female, unmarried, and in pursuit of a career is no longer considered deviant. Self-supporting single women will be a social group to be reckoned with in the decades ahead.

More and more married women are now working outside of the home for personal reasons as well. In the past, married women sought employment in the marketplace primarily out of necessity. While economic concerns are still the primary motivation — whether out of need or to improve the family's standard of living — many married women take jobs to escape the frustrations, isolation, and boredom of home life and the constant company of children. In seeking and finding fulfillment outside the home, these women gain a sense of achievement, self-worth, and independence.

Both the character and scope of the changes in contemporary young women's lives have been dramatic. An overview of the history of this life stage for women will put those changes in even bolder relief.

In the seventeenth and eighteenth centuries, there existed one socially sanctioned model for female young adulthood: women married, became mothers, and concurrently played an integral part in the ongoing work of their households. The years from ages twenty to forty were filled with successive pregnancies, endless rounds of household chores, and a sprinkling of community activities, such as attending church and visiting with neighbors. Wealthy or poor, the vast majority of young white women in colonial America conducted their lives according to this scheme. Although disruptions of this pattern by the death of a spouse were common, young widows frequently remarried and resumed their customary family roles. If they did not remarry, they usually assumed control of the family enterprise, be it farm or shop, and ran it until their sons reached maturity.

The organization of economic production facilitated the development of an easy and familiar relationship in newly married couples, because most husbands labored at or near the home, usually in conjunction with their wives. Regular and close contact with her husband in the course of performing routine household tasks enabled a young bride to adjust to the role of wife with a minimum of stress. Mutuality in work activities prepared the way for intimacy on all levels. Although colonial women were customarily instructed to regard their husbands as their superiors, the conditions of everyday life in the seventeenth and eighteenth centuries tended to negate the impact of this dictum.

The spread of commercial capitalism in the eighteenth century foreshadowed the breakdown of this unitary pattern of female young adulthood. By the early nineteenth century, in the urbanizing Northeast, the direction of change was apparent. The household economy was being supplanted by an industrial mode of production, which required that the workplace be a discrete entity. The placement of work at some distance from the home prevented young mothers from participating as they had in the productive process since they were needed at home to tend the children. The household tasks of young wives and mothers contracted further as more and more goods were manufactured outside the home and became available for purchase. Women, initially those among the white, middle and upper classes, spent a greater amount of time as consumer than ever before.

The emergent ideology of domesticity supplied young wives and mothers in the midnineteenth century with a rationale for their confinement to the home and their exclusion from the workplace. The lesson that women were naturally suited for domestic duties, and particularly the care of children, was conveyed by depicting those domestic responsibilities with exaggerated reverence. A woman who wished to leave that sacred domain was portrayed as a threat to divine as well as earthly order.

This influential corpus of ideas, centered around domesticity and motherhood, deterred young women before the Civil War from exploring alternative life paths. Yet circumstances arose that forced some young women to seek work outside the home to provide their families with income, even though this contravened the newly defined norms of female behavior.

In the cash economy that had become established by the early nineteenth century, a family was expected to live off the wages of the husband, supplemented by the essential but unpaid household labor of the wife. Not all families were able to sustain themselves under this arrangement. Households without a male breadwinner, or in which the male breadwinner was unemployed or underemployed, had no choice but to subject their female members, whether wives, daughters, or sisters, to the forces of the marketplace. At times women could earn money by contracting to do work at home, but often there was no alternative to taking a job outside the home, whether as a domestic servant, a factory laborer, or a seamstress.

The majority of female workers during the antebellum period were working-class immigrants or free blacks. Although, ideally, the young women of these groups preferred to stop working when they married, the precarious economic situations of their families often drove them back into the labor force after marriage. As a result, such women might spend a considerable portion of their young adulthood in the role of worker.

In contrast to this pattern, whatever work experience young native-born, middle-class women had was clearly temporary, as when they worked as teachers for a short time before marriage. Marriage removed these women from the labor force permanently, unless family fortunes deteriorated drastically. Spinsters and widows, of course, constituted another exception to this pattern. But it was economic necessity that propelled young women into the labor force.

Young women who worked in the early nineteenth century, whether native- or foreign-born, did so with the clear understanding that a woman's primary role in life was that of wife-mother-housewife. Although not all young women were successful in arranging their lives to conform to the dominant pattern, there was a near-unanimous consensus on the desirability of the expected role. Nevertheless, the seeds of another pattern were being sown by the second half of the nineteenth century.

A small but articulate group of middle-class young women had come to view work as more than a temporary diversion before marriage or an expedient during a family crisis. They conceived of an occupation as a vehicle for personal growth, a means by which to demonstrate their intelligence and maintain their independence. These bold women pioneered the idea that women as well as men were entitled to careers. Diverging from the mainstream by choice rather than circumstance, these women encountered a wall of resistance. Americans in the nineteenth century had become conditioned to thinking of young women solely as dutiful wives, devoted mothers, and efficient housewives. Any woman who challenged these notions faced an uphill fight.

In the face of seemingly insuperable obstacles, a small number of persevering women forged new paths for females in the last decades of the nineteenth century. Struggles to open advanced education to women had been successful by this time, so a primary rationale for disqualifying females from rewarding careers had been eliminated. These young women, armed with an advanced education and dissatisfied with the lack of options for women in an era of proliferating opportunities for men, were not content to emulate their mothers' lives. They entered previously all-male professions, such as law and medicine, and carved out new specializations for themselves, such as social work.

In addition to being pioneers in the occupational world, these women also broke ground in their private lives. The majority of late-nineteenth- and early-twentieth-century professional women remained single by choice. If they did marry, they frequently did so late in life and often remained childless. Their deliberate decision to dedicate their lives to a career marked this small group of women as exceptional at the time. As innovators, they had redesigned the map of young adulthood for females, plotting paths that had never before been charted. Not surprisingly then, the life experiences of these women differed significantly from those of their predecessors.

They were not, however, the only members of their generation to change their lives. By the final decades of the nineteenth century the contours of young adulthood had been remolded even for those native-born, middle-class women who adhered to the traditional path of marriage and motherhood. The scope of women's activities enlarged dramatically in the second half of the nineteenth century as numerous and diverse female organizations were established. Women's talents and energies were brought to bear on a wide range of endeavors on the pretext of finding new outlets for their altruistic tendencies. As a result, women enjoyed a latitude in the public sphere previously denied them.

The expansion of women's activities was in part made possible by the decline in the birth rate among native-born, white women that began in the late eighteenth century. The average number of children born to an American woman in 1800 was 7.4; in 1820 it was 6.73; in 1850 it was 5.42, and in 1890, it was 3.87. To achieve this reduction, various forms of contraception were employed, including abstinence and abortion, but not the modern forms of birth control. Such methods were not uniformly successful, but women had fewer children overall. In contrast to a system of family planning based on reliable means of contraception in which births are concentrated during the early years of marriage, this system produced a pattern of births spread over a woman's entire fertile period. However, the total number of births was lower than if no type of control had been used.

The implications of this altered birth rate for young women's lives were profound. Since women had fewer children, they could devote more time and energy to the upbringing of each child, as advocated in the prescriptive literature, with its emphasis on the maternal role. At the same time, however, young women were able to set aside some time for themselves, if only a few hours a week. Since a paid job was both impracticable and inappropriate for such middle-class mothers, they turned to the multiplicity of volunteer organizations for amusement as well as purposeful activity. Women's clubs, the temperance or suffrage movement, as well as customary social obligations filled the days of these turn-of-the-century young wives and mothers of the middle class.

During the first four decades of the twentieth century, the overall shape of female young adulthood remained essentially intact. Marriage and motherhood endured as the cornerstones of this life stage. A brief interlude on the job between the completion of education, high school or college, and the date of marriage had become acceptable for young women of all social classes. But there was still general agreement that marriage (and certainly motherhood) should mark the end of employment. A woman's twenties and thirties would be taken up with childbearing and child rearing, housekeeping, and volunteer and social activities.

The image of woman as wife and mother was deeply ingrained in American girls and relatively few considered an alternative path through young adulthood. Those who did choose careers usually remained single, and for those who married, it was still extremely difficult to combine marriage and career successfully. Yet, there remained young women who had to work during their twenties and thirties, continuously or intermittently, out of necessity. Such women were primarily immigrants and blacks, although during the depression of the 1930s, native-born women also fell into this category. For young women from impoverished families, all of whom worked when single, marriage, and even motherhood, did not close the door on the world of work. Deteriorating economic conditions forced these young women to rejoin the labor force.

While the configuration of roles of female young adulthood did not change during the first forty years of the twentieth century, the content of those roles did alter substantially. The experience of being a wife, a mother, and a housewife was quite different in 1940 from what it had been at the turn of the century, especially for middle-class women.

Nineteenth-century women, locked into a self-contained female sphere, had little in common with their husbands besides their family. Husbands and wives shared few activities or companions, communicated few ideas or emotions. A young woman's closest confidants were her female friends. Since sexual activity was highly controlled, physical contact probably produced tense moments rather than relaxed enjoyment. A pattern of formal, if not distant, relationships replaced the easy intimacy of former generations.

Since women were strongly discouraged from competing with men in the public arena, they became more dependent on their husbands for information as well as support. It is no wonder, then, that wives tended to inflate their husbands' importance. No longer close at hand during the work day, husbands, when actually present in the house, received special treatment. Wives catered to their needs and wants, preparing meals and clothing, cleaning the house, and entertaining guests. Instead of responding to their husbands in an informal, almost automatic way, wives became more self-conscious about their contacts with their spouses.

The early twentieth century inaugurated a less rigid compartmentalization of male and female worlds and consequently a greater degree of sharing between husbands and wives. The loosening of sexual mores enabled young women to achieve greater levels of intimacy with their husbands. Influenced by Freudian psychology, the movies, and the advertising industry, the post–World War I generation of young couples felt more at ease with each other. Middle-class brides were now likely to have spent a short stint in the labor force, probably in white-collar jobs, and were thus familiar with the routines of the business world. A husband could expect his wife to comprehend his career problems and offer him counsel. As a result, husband and wife were drawn closer together.

Motherhood also changed in character during the early decades of the twentieth century. As the birth rate continued to decline, reaching its nadir for this period during the depression, young women's lives became less constricted by the burdens of child rearing. A woman's maternal duties became more specialized. She could be more indulgent toward her children and treat them as individuals. As the role of mother became less time consuming than in former generations, a young wife could pay more attention to herself. Her involvement in activities beyond the home, both recreational and civic, continued to expand.

The movement of young women beyond the domestic realm depended in part on improvements in household technology. Labor-saving devices, such as the washing machine, the electric stove, and the vacuum cleaner, undoubtedly made the tasks of housekeeping less onerous. But in many cases the net effect of such technological advances was to transfer the responsibility for household drudgery from a domestic servant to the mistress of the household. Ironically, a "modern" housewife in 1940 might have been busier than her 1900 counterpart who had supervised a servant. At any rate, the nature of housework had altered considerably by the 1930s. In addition, the increasing availability of ready-made products had magnified the importance of the housewife's role as consumer, a role which also brought her out of the house.

Notwithstanding these important changes in female young adulthood, on the eve of the Second World War, the great majority of American women in their twenties and thirties were following directly in the paths of their mothers. Their obligations as wives and mothers defined their lives, and paid work was regarded as a temporary or conditional activity. A woman's identity remained predicated on her family roles regardless of her abilities or educational achievements. It took the shock of World War II to begin to modify the shape of female young adulthood, and even then women in their twenties and thirties experienced only limited change.

Combining marriage, motherhood, and work became a real possibility and necessity as a result of the wartime emergency. Women could get better jobs with better pay. Nevertheless, because of inadequate provision for child care, the mothers of infants and young children were less able to take advantage of these improved employment opportunities than the mothers of older children or childless women. Public opinion remained highly critical of working mothers with small children even during the war. Therefore, a considerable segment of the female population was prevented from capitalizing on the new opportunities.

After the war, the lives of young women reverted to the prewar pattern, and, in fact, came to resemble those of an even earlier era. The domestic ideology made a striking comeback during the 1950s despite compelling evidence from labor statistics that women no longer wished to be cloistered in their homes. Young women were inundated with messages urging them to dedicate their lives to their family's well-being and bury forever any chimerical notions of realizing their personal aspirations. Images of happy families living in suburban bliss surrounded by mounting piles of material possessions were instrumental in restraining young wives and mothers from branching out. The number of women pursuing professional careers plummeted while births skyrocketed, reversing a century-and-a-half-old trend.

The coercive power of the postwar version of the domestic ideology continued into the 1960s. Yet the murmurs of discontent were becoming louder. Young women, many of them college educated, were increasingly frustrated with the narrow future prospect that awaited them. While a brief taste of work experience whetted their appetite, they were to be forced to surrender their own ambitions at marriage to further the careers of their husbands. It was not until the late 1960s and the 1970s that a genuine change in the experience of female young adulthood occurred for many women. Growing numbers of female college graduates began to strike out in directions that their mothers and grandmothers had only dreamed about. Improved employment opportunities were generated during the 1960s and 1970s by legislative and judicial victories. Greater access to professional or advanced education coupled with expanding career openings enabled young women to move along paths that had been traversed only infrequently by their predecessors.

In the last fifteen years an altered social climate, the dramatic resurgence of feminism, and the cumulative effect of women's participation in the labor force have combined to influence young women to think of themselves in new ways. Many young women acquired the courage to believe that they were capable of the same things as their male counterparts. This refreshingly positive self-image was held by young women planning careers in fields such as law, medicine, and business. Furthermore, women have made significant inroads into the skilled trades. Working-class young women also have stopped thinking of themselves in traditional ways and have opted for careers in previously all-male occupations.

But ambitious young women are still confronting the same dilemma that faced their adventurous female forebears, namely, how to combine career and family. The solutions to this problem adopted by the current generation of young females are not entirely satisfactory, although they have proven viable in many instances. The first strategy is a familiar one — remaining single by choice, which was virtually the only permissible route for career women of past generations. While it has constituted an attractive option for numerous women, the majority of young career women appear unwilling to forego marriage. Many of these women have dealt with this troublesome question by postponing marriage until they were well established in their careers. Childbearing has also frequently been delayed by young career women, whether or not they have put off marriage. The success of such arrangements depends on the cooperation and support of the husband. Sharing of responsibilities for child care and household chores has been advocated as the liberated solution, but not much progress has been made in getting the husband to divide responsibility for these duties on a fifty-fifty basis with the wife. Consequently, most contemporary career women who are also wives and mothers must possess almost superhuman energy, drive, and determination, because, as their past counterparts, they must fill all these roles.

Many young women are no longer willing to remain in marriages that deny them the possibility for personal growth. Women's rebellion against the narrow confines of the domestic role is manifested in the rising divorce rate of the 1960s and 1970s. Single, divorced, or married, young women today are experiencing a freedom of choice known by no previous generation. Best of all, marriage and motherhood no longer foreclose all other options for young women.

A young girl growing up in colonial America faced little uncertainty about her future life course. Assuming that she survived to a marriageable age, roughly seventeen to twenty-five, she would almost always follow the predictable path and marry. Reaching adulthood meant moving into the role of wife. Those few women who remained single during the seventeenth and eighteenth centuries rarely did so by choice, since females of this era lacked any viable alternatives to marriage and motherhood. Therefore, if a woman did forego marriage, it was probably because of circumstances beyond her control such as illness, incapacitation, or unusual family obligations. The rising proportion of unmarried young women in some eastern seaboard towns in the late eighteenth century is traceable to the westward migration of eligible young men. Nevertheless, the great majority of females in early America did wed.

The fact that marriage was, in essence, foreordained for young women in the seventeenth and eighteenth centuries did not in itself make the period of courtship any easier. A young girl awaiting matrimony could be under enormous pressure to fulfill the expectations of her family, her friends, and the community at large. The longer she put off marriage, the greater the strain on her. The older she got, the more anomalous her position in society became. Clearly, it was virtually impossible to resist the demands of a culture that envisioned all adult women as wives and mothers.

By their late teens, then, getting married formed the major preoccupation of early American young women. The following excerpt from the diary of Jemima Condict, the daughter of an Essex County, New Jersey farmer, begins on her twentieth birthday in 1774. Her diary entries during the next few months reveal the extent to which the issue of marriage dominated her life. Her parents, friends, and neighbors all reminded her that she had reached the appropriate age for marriage. In the midst of an extended discussion on the merits of a particular suitor, Jemima's mother informed her that her father was buying a chest for her, and then asked more directly: "Don't you never intend to marry?" Although Jemima was acutely aware of her obligation to marry, she seemed reluctant to take the step. She balked at the thought a number of times, making disparaging remarks about herself and her fitness for marriage. In part, at least, her ambivalence regarding marriage stemmed from her unwillingness to abandon the comfortable role of daughter in a family where she was treated with kindness and respect. Yet, there are also hints that Jemima acknowledged tendencies in herself, such as her passion for writing, that portended difficulty in adjusting to the role of dutiful wife and helpmate.

Like many young girls in late eighteenth-century America, Jemima possessed considerable latitude in the selection of a potential mate. The chief responsibility for finding a husband rested with her, although presumably the displeasure of her parents at her decision would have prompted her to reconsider. By the era of the American Revolution Jemima's experience was typical, but during the seventeenth century parents had exercised the dominant influence in arranging the unions of their offspring. Although granting young men and women a larger role in the selection of their spouses is usually interpreted as a sign of progress, it is debatable whether a young girl's life was simplified or complicated by her greater freedom in choosing a husband in the late eighteenth century. One gets the impression from Jemima's lengthy account of her conversation with her mother about her possible union with her cousin that she would have welcomed a direct intercession by her parents. As it was, she resigned herself to leave the final decision in the hands of the Almighty.

Jemima Condict's entire existence was indelibly colored by her religious world view. Faithful attendance at the local Presbyterian church was only the most visible manifestation of her piety. The fact that she quoted the biblical texts of sermons in her diary offers more compelling evidence of the strength of her belief. But the most convincing testimony that religious values permeated her being emerges from her accounts of important episodes in her life. In retrospect, Jemima subjected her behavior to intense and rigorous scrutiny, using religious precepts as her guideposts. She reflected at length on her shortcomings and invariably concluded that she had failed to conduct herself as a devout young woman should. Consequently, she felt that she was undeserving of the blessings she enjoyed. She expressed her gratitude for her easy and protected family life, but she thought herself unworthy of such kind parents and such a privileged existence. Not all young women in eighteenth-century America were as hard on themselves as Jemima Condict was, but her outlook on life was indeed representative of that of countless young women raised in the Puritan tradition.

Jemima's frequent references to illness and death strike the modern-day reader as excessively morbid, but such observations must be viewed in the context of her times. Her sensibilities were molded not only by her religious upbringing but by her well-founded perception of the fragility of life. Jemima's comment that she might die before her aged grandfather was rooted in a firm grasp of the demographic realities of her society: "For old

172 □ *Young Adulthood*

must Die yet I may Die before him for ought I know." And, in fact, Jemima Condict died at the age of twenty-four, by which time she had married and borne a child, who also died.

—— 11 ——
Jemima Condict

WEDNESDAY AUGUST 24 1774. this Day I am entering another year I hope I may Live & spend It Better than I Did the Last or any that is Past. there Seams to Be a Great Alteration among the young People this year Some that was Before Bad anuf is now I hope become New Creatures. What & am I Still going on In Sin growing worse In Stead of better. What reason have I to be a Shamed!

SATURDAY OCTOBER FIRST 1774. It seams we have troublesome times a Coming for there is great Disturbance a Broad in the earth & they say it is tea that caused it. So then if they will Quarel about such a trifling thing as that What must we expect But war & I think or at least fear it will be so.

SUNDAY OCTOBER 2 Went to meeting & Mr. Chapman Preacht from Malcha the 3 Chapter and 7 verse.

This Day is tuesday & I mopeing all Day I suppose youl Say I am Lazy But Let that Be as it will I have jest Now Received a Letter & Who Should it Be from But my Old friend R W from Shemoken. I hear Some of our old Neibours is a Coming Down Ah Good! Lack a Day! Here they Come and I was Glad to see them. I Went out to meet them But I was so glad to see them that I felt all fool. I knew Not What to Say. they Say they Left our Cousins all well which Is very good news. But I hope to hear more about them for they will tary three weeks before they go Back. So I will Quit and lay my Pen a Side for to Night.

SUNDAY OCTOBER 9TH I went to meeting & Mr. Chapman Preacht from these Words, *for we must all apear before the Judgment Seat of Christ.* Corint 5 Chapter & 10 verse.

MONDAY, or training, I went to C C & workd Perdigus [prodigiously] hard all Day for they had roast meat & Bakt Podins But We got But Little of it! but however I Come of & got home about Sunset & took to my Bed & was Glad when I got there for upon my word Which you may Believe at this Present Junkture I was tired anuf But Stop Ive said enough.

SOURCE: *Jemima Condict Her Book; Being a Transcript of the Diary of an Essex County Maid during the Revolutionary War* (Newark, New Jersey: The Carteret Book Club, 1930). By permission of the owners of the original manuscript, The New Jersey Historical Society.

TUESDAY. Well how is it with you my friends? I think I feel Some What stiff in the joints But I hope to have Some Respet for to Day there Is a going to Be a Meeting at our house. Well the meeting is over & these was the words of the Text, *ye Believe In God Believe also In me.*

Oh I think this is a troublesome World for I a Poor Miserable Wicked Creature find But little Comfort but tis because my mind is taken up in Vanity & I am a discontented Mortal I am So Indeed.

FRIDAY OCTOBER 14 Went to See my Cousin J. W. She being not well & I Dont think ever will Be. O What a fine thing is health!

SUNDAY was Sacrament & there was Numbers took in to the full Comunion Mostly young People. Mr. Chapman Preacht on that Day from these, *then Said Jesus to them yet a little While am I with you then I go unto him that Sent me.* John the 7 Chapter & 33 verse.

SUNDAY NIGHT. Jest Now Received a letter and haveing Perused it found it Came from my Cousin W. C. I wrote a answer & then retired to Bed Biding myself Goodnight.

MONDAY is Come & the Lord In his Goodness has Spared me to See it.

I Being all the first Part of this Week very much toxacated in my mind about that afare for I Dont Know What to do.

> But Boast Not Mistaken Swain of thy art
> To please my Partial Eyes
> The Charms that have Subdued my heart
> Another May Dispise.

THURSDAY. Spent the Whole afternoon with my friends that Came from the West Branch & I heard them tel So much about It that I long to See it. they Bin at me to go up With them and Stay there this winter. I told them if it was But a Days Journey I would Go But I Could Not Bear the thoughts of Going So far from my fathers house. They told me there was young men Plenty there for me But I thought I was In no hurry for a husband at Present. And if I was I thought it was too far to go upon uncertaintys. So I Concluded to Stay where I was & I Believe I shant Repent it. A Husband or Not, for I am best of in this spot. But they are going I must now take my Leave of them & I Dont know but for the Last time So I wisht them Well. But they said that want anuf I must write to them. I Promist I would & after haveing taken our leaves of each other we parted. But I Believe they felt pretty heavy hearted. But they are gone So we will Leave them.

THURSDAY I had some Discourse with Mr. Chandler. he asked me why I Did not marry I told him I want in no hurry. Well Said he I wish I was married to you. I told him he would Soon wish himself on maried

agin. Why So? Because says I you will find that I am a crose ill contrived Pese of Stuf I told him that I would advise all the men to remain
as they was for the women was Bad & the men so much worse that It
was a wonder if they agreed. So I scard the poor fellow & he is gone.

SUNDAY Mr. Chapman Preacht from these words, Timothy the first Chapter & 12 verse. I Spent this evening in Writeing But the Worst of it is
What I write is Noncense. if I Did But Write that would Be instructive
or that would Do me any good or any one else twould be some Sence
in Spending Time & Paper. But No wonder I Can write Nothing thats
good for I Dont Do anything thats good. I hope I may Live to Spend my
time better And have Beter Imployment for my Pen for I must be Scrab-
ling when Leasure time tho I find But very Little time Now. Sometimes
after our people is gone to Bed I get my Pen for I Dont know how to
Content myself without writeing Something.

SUNDAY Did Mr. Chapman Preach from these words, *the exspectation of
the wicked shall Perish.*

TUESDAY went up to Swinefeild, a Number of us to get eat for I Cant
say But a hundred Men all Plast in the Wilderness Which was Something of a Pleaseing sight to Behold went down the Same Night to wach
with my Poor old Grandfather & So by that means Got Sight at my What
Shall I say freind mather. I went to Singing the Next night & Rid home
with Mr. maturaty & I Spent the week & its gone I cant recall it for
all the World.

NEW YEARS DAY Went to meeting & Mr. Chapman Preacht from Romans
14 Chapter & 8 verse; we Come Home tho Not without Some Difaculty
for it was very Bad going & we'd a young horse. When I got home found
Mr. M. W. the talor There at work & the Next Day I had to Work with
him; We had a Deal of Discourse about old times & Concluded our Chat
with wishing each other well. He is a Nice young man worthy of good
wishes; He said he hopt I wood be Suited but he never Should be; but
I think his fortunes good & I will tell you a reason why Because he want
to have such a Creature as I.

A friday & Saterday felt very malancholy To think What Life I had
livd.

SUNDAY Mr. Chapman from the 100 19 Psalm & 4 verse *I am thine Save
me.*

WENSDAY JANUARY 11, 1775, My dear father went to town & Came home
at Night & gave me a fine Present; it was a Long Cloak a Present indeed
Such a one as I did not Deserve; But you cant think how I felt When
he gave it to me I was Both glad & sorry. I was glad of the Present yet
I was Sorry I had not bin more Deserving & that I had Not Bin more

thankfull & behaved myself better in the Servis of So Kind a father; & I wanted my sister to have one.

MONDAY FEBRUARY 5, 1775, Was my Cousins Knockulated I am apt to think they will repent there Undertaking before they Done with it for I am Shure tis a great venter. But Sence they are gone I wish them Sucses And I think they have Had good luck So far for they have all Got home Alive But I fear Cousin N Dod Wont get over it well.

WENSDAY. Being full of thoughts about What to Do as I have this year Past. Sometimes I think I will Serting Bid him farewell forever But I thought I would talk to my mother & see if I could be Convinst one way or tother for I want to Hear the ground of What they have to say. So one Day my mother Says to me your father is going to get you a Chest I told her I should be Glad of one But Would not have her think twas because I thought to Marry. Why Says she Dont you never intend to marry? I told her People Said I was agoing to have Mr. ———. But they tell me they dont think it is a right thing; and it is forbid &c. But Cant none of them as I Can find out tell me where tis forbid So Says I, what Do you think of it mother; She said She did Not think it was Right except I thought It was myself. I askt her if she thought my thinking it was right would make it so. She said my thinking so would cause A Contented easy mind.

Well Says I, But that ant telling What you think about it She Said she had heard his mother talk about it & she was against his Coming here. She said Moreover that she was apt to think I would Live a dogs Life amongst them. this made me to think I would not have him. But I Still incisted upon hearing what she had to Say. at Last she told me that She had thought a great Deal about It & for her part Could Not see but that It was right & as for its being forbid She did not think there wos such a Place In the Bible. She Said Likewise that she Did Not See what Ministers Should marry them for if twas forbid. So after this and much more being said I turned it off with a Laugh & Said What a fool am I, I talk as if I was going to marry a Cousin In good earnest but Did not know as I had one that would have me but If I hold my toungue & Say Nothing others will have all the talk. they talk to me but Convince they Dont. I Could wish with all my heart I New the Right way & Could be made To Chuse it; but if it be rong Then What a fool was I While yong to Place my mind on such a one as a Cousin, its very true. Its o poor me what shall I Due! Due? Why I tell you What a conclusion I made & I hope I may hold to it & that Is to Trust in him Who knows all things for he knows What is best for me & What I ought to Do & What I ought not to Do. And will, I hope order things in mercy for me.

Look around the habitable World, how few Know their own Good; or knowing it persue. How void of reason are our hopes & fears. What In the Conduct of our Life apears Against our Pease we arm our Will Amidst our Plenty Something Still.

TEUESDAY went up to my Sister Ogdens and there was a house full of people & we had a great Sing indeed for the horse neck kites & the newarkites were Both assembled Together & there was the new maried Couple L. W. Juner & you may be Shure they cut a fine figer for She is a Bounser Joan And he a little Cross Snipper Snapper snipe. they tell me he Cryd When he was maried at which I Dont a bit Wonder for I think twas anuf to make the poor fellow bellow if he had his wits about him, for I am shure She Can Beat him. I Dont know tho But He is like Shon Roast Poark more Strengthinin; His Wife Said that Shonna Was Leser as She was, But then He was more Strengthenin, so I will Leave them to Make the Best of their Bargin. I Dont know as anyone has lost for She had a Doleful Long nose & he a Conceivd Chin Like myself.

MONDAY morning Resolved if Possible to have my toth out So Down I went to Dr. C. and he got his Cold iron ready. my toth was easy & I told him I Dast not venter. I new hed hurt but I Could Not make him Promis he would Not; tho I thought he began to Pety me a Little & that was what I Did it for; for its true I believe I want so fraid as I pretended to be. I was In hopes he'd Draw it eaFer for it & I Dont know but he Did for he was mighty Carefull, but when he Put his Contrivance in my mouth I puld them out agin. at Last they fell a lafing at me & Said if I dast not have A tooth Drawd I Never would be fit to marry. I told them I never Recond to be if twas as Bad as to have a toth Drawd. at which they all fell a lauging for I was fooll for them; but it want Long before I could put my Toth in my pocket & laugh with the Best of them. So I Come home but I got such a Cold in my face that it akt all the rest of the week, but When I got home I went to Bed for I hed slep but little for Some time before; I had Not bin there Long before I was Surprised with an Unuseal Pounding at the Door. at Last they opened the Door and in Come an old Woman Drest In Rags an obgect of Pity to behold & a little Dog following after. O She told a sorrowful Story anuf, if twas true & I Cant Say but It was, But it Lookt a Little Strange To me how She Would travil So far In A Day as she Said She had.

But she Had her Dog for a bed fellow & in the morning We Got Breakfast & Dont you think She took as good Care of her Dog as She Did of herself, I warrent ye. I Could Not But Laugh to See her, for She would Chew the victuals & then he must eat it out of her hand. What a Nasty Peace of Stuf She is Shure a nuf. But She is going & I Cant help But Pity her. What reason have I to give thanks unto the Lord that I am thus Provided for When I Dont Deserve the breath I Draw.

Yesterday Mr. ——— Come a Gin & wanted me to go with him to elisabeth town; I made Several excuses for I was resolvd Not go. But he would hear to none of them at Last I told him mother would not Let me go. So I winkt to her to Say No for She was Present. So She told him It would Not Due. then he fell to Coaxing her But She Said No I wont Let her go. So he Went of Gentleman like but I thought when he Got upon his little Nag that he Did not want a Button behind him for he almost Covered him himself. But he has gone of & I Believe hes Mad With all, but I Cant help it Now.

SUNDAY Mr. Chapman Preacht from Romans 6 Chapter & 23 Verse.

I Staid at my uncles that Night & on monday My Cousin J h & I went to See our old Grand Father. I found that old Saying to be true, Once a man & twice a Child for he is very Childish & tho he is the highness of a man yet he Is a Child. we staid there a Spell & then went Back agin, But i was a little Put to it to get away from poor old Gnd father.

I Pited him for I thought he would think he was old & Dispisd. he Says to me you are tird a Staying with me a ready. I made Some excuse So that I got away & Dont expect ever to Spend so much time with him agin for old must Die yet I may Die before him for ought I know.

MONDAY At Night I Did not know how to Contrive It to get a way without they knowing. how at last I Schemd it, for I had told them all Day that if J. H. was down I would go up with him. So it answered very well for they Knew No bettor. But I got Safe home & Glad on it too for I Like home the Best & tis a great mercy that I have Such a home to go to. The old saying is home is home, Let it be ever So homely & I think So, tho I Count Not my fathers a homely Home Nither I would I have you think so my friends.

*I*n nineteenth-century America work took men away from the home, and left wives in charge of household affairs. While the relegation of women to the domestic sphere impeded the ease of interaction between wives and husbands, it fostered the development of female friendships. Barred from the male world of work and politics, young wives sought each other out, both to celebrate and to commiserate. Forced to endure the frustrations of being fixed in a passive role in a society of actors and doers, wives created their own networks in which the interests of women took first place. In the nineteenth century women were often closer to their female friends than to their husbands.

Sarah Hill Fletcher was a new bride in the 1820s, just when the new order of family life was taking root. She had married Calvin Fletcher, a teacher and law student, in May 1821 in her hometown of Urbana, Ohio. Shortly thereafter, the couple moved to the brand-new settlement of Indianapolis, where Calvin embarked on his legal career. At the time of their marriage Sarah was either seventeen or nineteen (there is uncertainty about her birth date) and Calvin was twenty-three. Even though bride and groom were both quite young, the foundation for an unequal relationship had already been established. Sarah had been a pupil of Calvin's in Ohio, and after their marriage he continued to think of his wife as his inferior. At his instigation, Sarah commenced a journal, which she kept for the first three years of her marriage. Although designed as a pedagogical device to improve her writing skills, the diary of Sarah Fletcher, a section of which follows, reads as much more than an exercise in composition. It is an illuminating record of the experiences of a young woman who oscillated between feelings of accomplishment and worthlessness as she adapted to the role of wife in early-nineteenth-century America.

Given her former status of student, it is not surprising that Sarah treated her new husband with deference. In her eyes Calvin was clearly a more important person than she was. She admired him for his intellect, his industriousness, and his social poise. She was particularly sensitive about her educational deficiencies, and she applied herself diligently to those subjects that Calvin advised — reading, writing, arithmetic, and singing. In spite of her dutiful efforts to measure up to her husband's standards, Sarah Fletcher still felt inadequate in social situations, fearing that she would embarrass Calvin by her ignorance and awkwardness. Her off-hand comment on a new arrival in town supplies poignant testimony of her low self-esteem.

> At a distanc She looked very flashy & carried a very high head. I did not have the pleasure of geting acquainted with her. Perhaps if I had I would of found the lady as empty as myself.

Despite her misgivings about her lack of polish, the young Mrs. Fletcher plunged into the social life of pioneer Indianapolis. Most of her time was spent in visiting and hosting neighbors and friends. Teas, dinners, and formal parties, as well as quiltings, weddings, and other miscellaneous entertainments filled her days. Attendance at religious services was also a notable feature of her life. While it was not uncommon for Mr. Fletcher to accompany his wife on these occasions, particularly to dinners or parties, the social pattern disclosed in Mrs. Fletcher's diary is one in which men's concerns were sharply differentiated from those of women. As a lawyer, Calvin Fletcher was usually away from home on business, and when he rode the circuit he was absent for weeks at a time. Wives such as Sarah kept each other company when their husbands were gone, occupying themselves with sewing and other female pursuits. Sarah Fletcher soon built up a circle of female friends in town with whom she shared not only her time but her feelings.

Wives and husbands moved in separate orbits in Indianapolis in the 1820s. Men like Calvin Fletcher transacted business and engaged in politics while women like Sarah Fletcher were largely confined to the domestic sphere. Husbands played only a minimal role in household affairs. Although Calvin helped with the butchering, Sarah performed the bulk of household work, sometimes aided by a hired girl. Her tasks resembled those of a colonial housewife. She was responsible for producing and preparing the family's food. She kept a garden where she grew much of what appeared on the dinner table. She cooked and baked. She aided in butchering and was responsible for preserving the meats. She also manufactured essential household goods such as soap and candles. Mrs. Fletcher made clothing from scratch, including spinning the wool, in addition to mending all sorts of wearing apparel. One of her major duties, and undoubtedly her most burdensome one, was the washing. And, of course, she had to keep the fire, clean the house, and serve visitors and boarders. The Fletchers did not live in a self-sufficient household; they regularly bought a number of commodities. In her diary, Sarah mentioned going shopping a few times, but the only purchases specified were cotton, a comb, and possibly shoes.

Sarah Fletcher's household routine did not vary in any fundamental way from the traditional practices of her forebears, but there was evidence of change in another important facet of her life. In April 1823, Sarah noted matter-of-factly the birth of her first child, a son. Her list of those present at the delivery reveals an important alteration in childbirth practice. During the colonial era, women gave birth in their homes assisted by a midwife and a group of female kin and neighbors. Sarah Fletcher did have her baby at home in the presence of female friends, but a male physician and a nurse were also in attendance. For Sarah, childbirth was still a predominantly female event, but the intrusion of a male doctor on the scene foreshadowed the modern mode of childbirth in which professional physicians, usually males, deliver babies in hospitals.

Although her passage into motherhood reflected the influence of modern medical practice, Sarah Fletcher's childbearing history bore the imprint of the past rather than the future. While some native-born Americans were attempting to limit the size of their families during this period, the Fletchers adhered to the traditional pattern of uncontrolled fertility. Over the next twenty-three years, Sarah Fletcher bore ten more children, one approximately every two years.

—— 12 ——

Sarah Hill Fletcher

TUESDAY OCTOBER 23, 1821. I commensed Arithmetic.

FRYDAY OCT. 26. I commited the multiplication table.

SATURDAY [OCT. 27]. I red a few pages in the elements of Gesture &c. &c. and wrote a verse which was the last of essay on Man. This day is very pleasant and reather smokey. It appears a little like indian summer. We have had but very little rain in the place for about three weakes back and has been very favorable for those who has mooved in and are building.

SOURCE: Gayle Thornbrough, ed., *The Diary of Calvin Fletcher*, Volume 1, 1817–1838, *Including Letters of Calvin Fletcher and Diaries and Letters of His Wife Sarah Hill Fletcher*. Copyright © 1972 by the Indiana Historical Society. Reprinted by permission.

Sarah Hill Fletcher

THURSDAY NOV. THE FIRST. I was spining wool at Mr. Mcvains.

FRYDAY [NOV. 2]. Was cool and cleare.

SATURDAY [NOV. 3]. Was cold and cloudy & I had but little fire. Mr. F. went up the river about two milds.

MUNDAY NOV. THE 5 1821. I have been washing all day and Mr. F. has been helpin Mr. B. husk corne.

FRYDAY NOV. THE 9TH. It snowed very fast. The ground froze at night.

SATURDAY [NOV. 10]. Was windy and freezeing and Mr. F. went to Mr. R. [?] to take breckfast.

WEDNESDAY NOV. 14TH. I finished Reading the Vicar of Wakefield which was wrote by Goldsmith and returned it home. Then I borowed a singing Book from Mr. B.

THURSDAY [NOV. 15]. A very pretty day & Mr. F. calculates on finishing what he engaged to do for Mr. B. I commence the life of Washington again and I entend to read it through as soon as posible.

FRYDAY NOV. 16TH 1821. I was spining at Mr. Noldins.

SAT. [NOV. 17]. I was bakeing Pumpkin pys.

SUNDAY [NOV. 18]. I attended prayre meating at Mr. Stephens.

MUNDAY NOV. 19TH 1821. This day I was shoping. I onely bought half a pound of cotten.

THURSDAY NOV. 22D 1821. I spun some candlewick.

FRYDAY [NOV. 23]. I washed.

SATURDAY [NOV. 24]. Mrs. Noldin was makeing a bonnet. She came to me to know whether I could make it. I did not undertake it but I gave her all the instruction I posible could.

SUNDAY [NOV.] 25. I attended at Mr. Hockinses whareas I heard a verry good sermind delivered by an Newlight minister. ["New Light" ministers of the Presbyterian Church preached less orthodox views on doctrines such as predestination and salvation than did strict Calvinists.] The text was thus see then that ye walk circumspectly not as fools but as wise Redeeming the time because the days are evle.

FRYDAY NOV. 30 1821. Dr. M. took Bckfast at our house.

SATURDAY DEC. THE 1ST 1821. Mrs. N[owland] & Mrs. Buckner cawled to see me. I was made acquainted with Mrs. B. and she solicited me to pay her a visit.

MONDAY [DEC.] THE 3D. Mr. Royalston & Dr. M. to Coriden.

FRYDAY DEC. 7 1821. We killed a Beef Mr. Paxton & Mr. Blake healped to butcher & Mr. B. took tea with us. Saturday I was very much ingaged in trying out my tallow.

SUNDAY DEC. 9TH. I attended prayer meating at Mr. S[t]ephens's.

THURSDAY DECR. 13 1821. I wrote a letter to Mrs. Comer which was the 5 letter I wrote since I came here & never have recieved an answer.

FRYDAY [DEC. 14]. I diped candles & washed.

SATURDAY [DEC. 15]. Mr. Glover came.

SUNDAY [DEC. 16]. I recieved a letter from Miss Mariah Briton & a pattern with it. The Idea of geting a letter was very pleasing but when I red it I began to reflect to think how much more esteem an acquaintance expressed by writing to me & not one of my relatives evin sent a complement.

WEDDENSDAY DECR. THE 19 1821. I spent the evening very agreeable at Mr. Stephens's for they treated upon nothing but what was commendable.

SATURDAY DECR. THE 22 1821. I recieved a letter from Sister Louisa F. & Mr. F. recieved 7 which give us both great Satisfaction in peruseing them.

SUNDAY [DEC. 23]. I stayed at home all day & red my letter again & some nosepapers.

MONDAY [DEC. 24]. I did not dwo anything hard.

TUESDAY [DEC. 25] CHRISTMAS. Mrs. Bradly came to spend the day with me & Mrs. Paxton. She dined with us then we both went to Mr. P[axton] & took tea & set a while then I came home and went in to Mr. N[owland's]. I then came home again & red a chapter in the Bible &c.

WEDDENSDAY [DEC. 26]. I went to singing school & suffered very much with the cold. Thursday I washed & did not get done till late. I was setting by the fire nursing my hands for they ware very raw & inflamed by washing & Mr. F. was reading the History of America when nose came that Mr. R. had arived from Corydon. Mr. F. has gone to see him & wen I write a few more lines Ill go my self all though I feel very much fatieuged for it has been so long since I have heard the fiddle plaid that I think it would sound very malodious & I am jest going to s[t]art to hear it.

SUNDAY DECR. THE 30 1821. I herd a sermon delivered by an newlight Minister which I did not think commendable but we must alowe for it has not been but about three months since he began to speak in public.

MUNDAY [DEC. 31]. I did not doo much of anything.

TUESDAY JANUARY THE 1ST. 1822. I attended a party at Mr. Wiants. I enjoyed my self very well.

WEDENSDAY [JAN. 2]. Wm. Vance took tea with us & I visited Mrs. N[owland] & Mr. Russel plaid a few toons on the fidd[le] & we danced a few reels.

THURSDAY THE 3 OF JAN. I felt sore & sleepy.

FRYDAY [JAN. 4]. Was very cold. I think the coldes day we have had this winter.

SATURDAY JAN. THE 4 [5] 1822. At night. I now seat myself to commit a few things to paper that past through the day. This day has been remarkable cold & windy & Mr. and Mrs. Paxton came home from the Bluffs which they visited about a week. Mr. F. is absen at this time & I have a sever headache & bad cold. This day I mended a pare of overalls for Mr. Foot & a great coat for Mr. F.

SUNDAY [JAN. 6]. I staided at home all day with the same affliction I have hereto fore mention. Mr. & Mrs. Cu—— called as they were going to prayr meeting. They said perhaps they woud call on theyr return. I preparde for them they did not stop. I had my tea ready to set upon the table when Mr. Foot & Mr. C. both of them Atternys at Law came in. They drank tea with us & set till near sondown.

MONDAY JAN. 6 [7]. I cut out a Shirt for Mr. F. In the evening I visited Mrs. N[owland] where I got some little idea of playing Dominos.

TUSEDAY [JAN. 8]. I visited Mrs. B[radley]. Mrs. N. accompaned me. I spent the evening not so pleasant as I would wish for. She did not converse much upon any thing much. Mr. F. & Mr. N. came in after darke to escorte us home.

FRYDAY THE 11 OF JAN. 1822. In the Morn I washed. Mrs. N. came in jest as I commenced & Obsurved that Mr. [Dr.] Scudder would take us both to Mr. Woods about 2 M. east of this place & when we about ready the Dr. was called off.

SAT. [JAN.] 12. I did not doo much of anything.

SUN. [JAN.] 13. I stayed at home all day and read a few pages in Earl of Chesterfields Letters to his Son.

MOND. [JAN.] 14. I took Tea at Mr. N. where I had an introduction to Miss W. & Miss H.

WED. THE 16 OF JAN. I & Mrs. N. spent the Eve at Mr. Carters where we had plenty of cyder to drink.

TUSE. JAN. THE 22 1822. Mr. Gates was wedded to Miss Patsy Chinn both of Indianapolis. I attended the wedding. It was a very disagreeable day but not with standing there was a great concourse of people.

WED. [JAN.] THE 23. I attened at Mr. Ragans who gave them an infare whare we danced till a bout 1 o clock then we returned home.

THURS. [JAN. 24]. I had an invitation to a quilting which I did not attenend. The reason was I had company & did not think it proper for me to go when I had been up 2 nights & felt very much fatigued.

FRYDAY [JAN.] THE 25. Very cold & disagreea[b]le I did not do much of any thing.

SAT. THE 26 OF JAN. I did not do much in the morning. I calculated on washing but Mr. F. was called off to attend a trial before the Esq. whereas he gained the soot for his client. The same night Mrs. Bradley came & stayed with me till a bout 11 o clock & Mr. B. & Mr. F. was gone to a debateing school.

SUN. [JAN.] THE 27. Mr. F. went a bout 5 ms. West of this place a cross the River. After he started I went to Mr. N[owland's]. I set a few minuts. I began to feel very sick. I came home and went to bed.

MONDAY [JAN.] THE 28. I got better.

TUSEDAY [JAN.] THE 29. I attened a quilting at Mrs. Buc[kner's]. There were several ladys who were formaly from Kentucky & I think in there descorse a mong the Females they use a gradeal of vulgarity.

WED. [JAN.] THE 30. This day is very muddy & disag[r]eeable & I have this day maid some candle wick for Mr. Foot. Mr. Morris has wrote a pamphlet & had it put in print & Mr. F. is now gone to writ an answer to it & I am all a lone.

SAT. THE 2D OF FEBUARY. Mrs. Buckner dined with us. Mr. Osborn stayed hear the same night.

SUNDAY THE 3 OF FEBRUARY 1822. The hand bills come out in oposition to one which Mr. Morris wrote.

MONDAY [FEB.] THE 4TH. Mr. Luse arived at this place. He could not tell any thing of any account a bout Urbana.

TUSEDAY NIGHT [FEB. 5]. Mrs. Paxton & her Brother visited us & set till 11 o clock.

FRYDAY THE 8TH OF FEBR. I went to Mrs. B & assisted her with her quilt. We finished.

SAT. [FEB. 9]. I went to singing school & very much against my will.

SUNDAY [FEB. 10]. I went to the Printing Office.

MONDAY [FEB.] THE 11TH. In the P.M. noon I took Tea at Mr. Stevens'.

TUESDAY [FEB.] THE 12. Mr. S. mooved out to the Country 2 mi. from Indianapolis. The same day I had very pressing invitations to go a visiting with Mrs. N. & Mrs. B. to Mr. Yandes's but I did not feel disposed to go.

WED. [FEB.] THE 13TH. In the Evening Mr. & Mrs. P[axton] took Tea at my table. Then Mr. P. & Mr. F. went out a hunting & stayed till a bout 11 o clock.

THURSDAY THE 14TH OF FEBR. 1822. I was solicited to attend a party at

Mrs. Ragans. I had no anxiety to go therefore I staid at home. Mr. F. I suppose by this time is there but whether he will enjoy himself or not I cannot tell tho he appeard to antisipate a grateal of pleasure. I am all alone at this time & injoy myself very well. I use to think that I should be very lonesome when Mr. F. was abscent but it is quite to the revers if he dose not stay out till a late hour, for as soon as he starts & I get my domestic afares in order I then get my penn ink & paper & feel quiet Happy. I will this night endeavour to file Mr. F. scraps of writing while he is abscent. I have put the papers all in good order & Mr. F. has not come yet. I think that I have the easiest times since I have been maried of any girl that has entered in to the state of Matrimony with in a year. But I am afraid that I have spent my time so trifling (I may say) at the end of a few Year perhaps I may say if I had the same time to live over a gain I would Spende it quiet different tho I am confident that I have done my duty this night. I will now read a Chapter & go to repose for I know that I have satisfied Mr. F. request that he maid mention of when he started. I have wrote as much tonight as I have wrote with in 2 weaks & I hope he will not be displeased with my Composition.

FRYDAY THE 15 OF FEBR. 1822. Mr. M. Morris's second hand bill came out. That day I washed & went to bed very early. Mr. F. was writeing an answer to the hand bill & did not go to bed that night.

SAT. [FEB. 16]. He wrote till [he] got very sleepy. He then layed down & took but a short nap & then was oblieged to attend a trial at Mc[Il]vains.

SUNDAY [FEB. 17]. I spent the day at Mr. Ys. Mr. F. went to bed in the P.M. noon & Slept till after 8 o clock in the Evening. I awakend him & we both went to the Printing Office & Stayd till 2 o clock in the morning.

MONDAY THE 18TH OF FEBR. 1822. In the morning the hand bill came out & great was the mistery to know who the Legal voter alluded to where he mentions Col. Puff Back Capt. Swellback & myself.

TUSEDAY THE 19TH OF FEBR. I helped Mrs. Paxton make a pair of overalls.

WEDENSDAY [FEB.] THE 20TH. Very rainy.

THURSDAY THE 21ST OF FEBR. 1822. Mr. Paxton started to Urbana & cont[in]ues muddy & rainy.

SAT. [FEB.] 23. At night Mr. F. went to the Debaiting Scool.

SUNDAY [FEB.] THE 24. I went up to Mr. Buckners lot[?].

MON. THE 25 OF FEBR. Warm & pleasant. I washed & Irond.

TUSEDAY [FEB. 26]. Continude warm and clear. I suffered more pain that day than ever I did before except one time with a felon [a deep inflammation on the finger or toe].

WEDNESDAY NIGHT THE 27TH OF FEBR. Mr. Osborn came here & set till 11 o clock.

THURSDAY THE 28TH OF FEBR. 1822. He come back & set till after 12 o clock & Mr. F. wrote a peas upon Slander.

FRIDAY THE 1ST OF MRCH. Mr. Fletcher Started on the circuit. It is a very muddy & disagreeable day and I fear he will be very sick of his trip. Mrs. P[axton] stayed with me four nights then Mr. P. returned from Ohio. He brought 5 noose papers and three letters. I came home and broke the letters open & red 2 one from my Father & the other from Dr. Banes & one from Mr. Cooley which I could not read. I had very peculiar feelings. It seemed as if I was forsaken & Mrs. P. overjoyed. I did not envey her her happiness — for I know how I would of felt had it been Mr. F. returned.

TUSEDAY THE 5 OF MARCH. The same day that Mr. P. came I visited Mrs. Wick. I did not find evry [thing] in such print as I expected neither did I find such a polished Lady.

WED. THE 5 [6] OF MARCH. I began to make soap.

FRIDAY [MARCH] 8TH. I washed & recieved 2 letters one from Ingram & one from Britten.

SAT. [MARCH 9]. I could not keepe any fire & I spent the fore part of the day with Mrs. Paxton & the after noon with Mrs. N[owland].

SUN. 9TH [10TH] OF MARCH. I visited Mr. S.

MON. [MARCH] 10TH [11TH]. I began makeing shugar.

FRIDAY [MARCH] 15TH. Mr. Fletcher came home.

SUN. [MARCH] 17TH. In the Evening I walked up to Judg Wicks. I returned with Mr. Fletcher & we both went to the River and called in to Mr. McGeorge's.

TUSEDAY 19TH OF MARCH 1822. I washed with Mrs. Paxton. We got done & went to the Shoe makers shop.

WEDENSDAY [MARCH] 20TH. Mrs. Hendison was delivered of a Son.

THURSDAY [MARCH] 21ST. Mr. Mc[Il]Vain raised a house. Mr. Mc-Doogle called to see Mr. F. but he was not at home.

FRIDAY 22D OF MARCH. Mr. Gluver mooved.

SAT. [MARCH] 23D. Mr. Johnstone came to this place with the intension of staying all Summer to improve his Farm.

SUNDAY 24TH OF MARCH. Mr. F. started to Morgan County. After he started I went about one mild to a sugar camp. I returned & attended a Funeral & a burial. I did not see a single tear shed in the whole congegation except Mrs. Nowland when she shewd me w[h]ere her Child was buried.

MONDAY [MARCH 25]. I dined at Mr. Paxtons.

TUESDAY [MARCH 26]. Mr. Fletcher came home.

WEDNESDAY [MARCH 27]. It rained.

THURSDAY THE 28TH OF MARCH. Was very win[d]y. Mr. Brown started from here the same day & I felt a little concerned about him traveling through the woods.

SAT. 30TH OF MARCH 1822. I spent the day with Mrs. Bates & found her a very an agreeable Woman.

SUNDAY [MARCH] THE 31ST. I spent the day very idol for there were so many Candidates coming in that I could neither read wright nor do anything else.

MONDAY [APRIL 1]. The Election was held that was on the first of Aprile.

WEDNESDAY THE 3D OF APRILE 1822. Mrs. Wick Mrs. Paxton Miss C. & myself spente the P.M. noon at Mr. Nowlans.

SUNDAY 7TH OF APRILE 1822. It raind very hard & haild. Monday night & Tuesday morning continued raining.

APRILE 10TH 1822. This day Mr. F. & Mr. B[lake] entered in to an agreement about a house & lot which we are to take posession of as soon as it is finished.

FRIDAY 12TH OF APRILE. Mrs. P[axton] & Sally Ann Nowland & myself spent the P.M. noon at Mr. Buckners where I got the sight of a young Lady Jest from Kentucky. At a distanc She looked very flashy & carried a very high head. I did not have the pleasure of geting acquainted with her. Perhaps if I had I would of found the lady as empty as myself.

SAT. [APR. 13]. Mrs. P. & I set out some roots & made a begining at gardening. The waters are very high at this time & has been for a Week back.

APRIL 13TH 1822. Mr. Levington and Some other Men has been 10 ms. up the River on the Public Land cuting saw logs for several weeks. They made a contract with Mr. Yanders to delive[r] him two Thousan at one dollar per piece[?] & since rain they have come down by water.

SUNDAY 14TH OF APRILE 1822. This day is very windy cold & snows a little & the people are runing continually to see the River. I have a g[r]eat curiosity to see it my self but it is such a disagreeable day that I shall not go.

MONDAY [APR.] 15TH. This day is cool & beautiful Sun. The woods are very green at this time & furthermore I think that the Springs here are forwarder than what they are in the State of Ohio.

TUESDAY 16TH OF APRILE. This day I dined with Mrs. Smith.

WEDNESDAY [APR.] [1]7TH. I went to Givens's Store & bought one comb & on my return home I stoped to see Mrs. Wick likewise Mrs. Mitchel. I then came home & went to was[h]ing. Before I finished I was taken very sick. I did not stop till I got done then I was not able to set up but necessity compelled me to doo it.

THURSDAY [APR.] 18TH. I continued sick but did not go to bed for Mr. Curry was laboring with Mr. F. & in the P.M. noon Mrs. Buckner & Miss Hockings came and spent with me.

FRIDAY [APR.] 19TH. I was very bad & oblige[d] to go to bed.

SAT. 20TH OF APRILE 1822. Mr. Robertson from Columbus stoped to see us in the morning as he was passing through. Mrs. McGeorge & her sister called to see me & in the P.M. noon I walked down to the River where I saw a g[r]eat many people crossing. It is now nine o clock at night & Mr. F. is not at home.

SUNDAY 21ST OF APRILE 1822. Mrs. Wick Miss Carter & myself went to the River & had the pleasure of rideing up to the mouth of Fall Creek & back a gain to the forde in the flat.

MONDAY [APR.] 22D. Johnson mooved upon Market Street.

TUESDAY [APR.] 23D. I commenced makeing garden at Mr. B[lake's] house.

WEDNESD. [APR.] 24TH. I was at the same business.

THURSDAY [APR.] 25. I finished makeing garden except some few seeds in case there should bee frost. All three of the days that we were makeing garden were warm & dry.

FRIDAY [APR.] 26TH. Mrs. N[owland] Mrs. Bradly & myself spent the P.M. noon with Mrs. Yanders.

SAT. 27TH OF APRLE. Very cloudy cool & rainy.

SUNDAY [APR.] 28TH. Very pleasant & Mr. Glover & Mr. Smith returned from Jefferson[ville] the same evening. Judg Wick & his Lady spent about two hours very agreeablely with us.

MONDAY 29TH OF APRILE. I washed.

TUESDAY 30TH OF APRIL 1822. Mr. Osborn & Mr. Conner brecfasted with us.

WEDNESDAY 1ST OF MAY 1822. Was extremely warm. The woods are very beautiful at [this] time — And it appears that nature has been industrious. We have gentle showers evry day. The same day George Martin started to the State of Ohio near Fathers and about 9 o clock in the evening Mr. F. & I walked to Judg Wicks where we spent 1 hour. While we were there a whipperwill began to holow which reminded me of Urbana.

THURSDAY [MAY] 2D. This morning I planted some beanes. I was ingaged the balance of the day in Sowing.

FRIDAY 3D OF MAY. Very wrm and close not much air stiring. This day I had intro[d]uction to Mr. Homes who formerly lived in & about Dayton.

SUNDAY 5TH OF MAY. Mrs. N[owland] I & several others dined at Mr. Buckners. They had a variety and an excellant dinner.

MONDAY [MAY] 6TH. Mrs. Bradly & I took Tea at Mrs. Nowland's. Mrs. B. had been sick for a Week back and came out in order to gain her strength.

TUESDAY 7TH OF MAY. Very cloudy & rainy but not withstanding all that Mrs. N[owland] & I started to Spend the P.M. with Mrs. Scudder. Unfortunately she was not at home.

WEDNESDAY [MAY] 8TH. She Scent for us to go and take Tea with her. We did so. That night Mr. F. & I went to Mr. Paxtones and staid till 11 o clock. Mr. F. was writing for Mr. P.

THURSDAY [MAY] 9TH. I finished a pair of panteloons for Mr. Hall. Mr. F. was out all day appraising Lots.

FRIDAY [MAY] 10TH. This morning I went to my garden planted some corn & beans. Tomorrow the Election is; which the people are to elect a magistrate.

SAT. [MAY] 11. I did not doo much of anything.

SUNDAY 12TH OF MAY 1822. I attened Preaching at the Governer's Circle; it was the first Sermon that ever was delivered at that place. He took his texts in the 3d Chapter of Proverbs 17th Verse & left the words upon record her ways are ways of pleasantness; & all her paths are peace. In the P.M. he delivered an other Sermon. He took his texts in the XV

Chapter Luke 7th verse I say unto you, that likewise joy shall be in heaven over one Sinner that repenteth. He is a Presbyterian and a very good Orator. He will speak again on Tuesday in the P.M.

MONDAY [MAY] 13TH. This day it rained all day, and it has continued now for about 24 hours.

TUESDAY [MAY] 14TH. In the A.M. it rained & in the P.M. it was clear but mudy & Mr. F. & [I] attened Preaching at the School hous. The Sermon was delivered by Mr. Proctor. He took his text in the forty second Psalm 1st verse As the heart panteth after the waterbrooks; so panteth my Soul after thee, O God.

WEDNESDAY [MAY] 15TH. Clear & very warm, in the A.M. I was at work in my garden & in the P.M. I took Tea at Mr. N[owland's] with Mrs. Buckner. The Commissioners have set for 3 or 4 days & Mr. F. has been with them the most of the time. I suppose it is a greate advantage for him to doo so if not I know in reason he would not devote so much of his time from his study (not that I am accuesing him of being unstudious) to be with them & others for he is a man among an hundred that is one who knows his business as well.

FRIDAY 16TH [17TH] OF MAY 1822. In the A.M. I washed & read about 7 pages in Chester Fields letters to his Son which compleeted the Book; And in the P.M. I attended Preaching.

SAT. [MAY] THE 17TH [18TH]. I ironed and piddled about.

SUNDAY [MAY] 18TH [19TH]. I staid at home all day & Mr. F. attened two Sermonds. The same Evening Mr. F. & I walked up to Judg Wick's and set till about 9 o clock.

MONDAY THE 20TH OF MAY 1822. Rainy and disagreeable, & Mr. Proctor, Dr. Cow, Mr. Linton, Mr. Fletcher, & myself, we all dined at Mr. Nowland's.

TUESDAY THE 21ST. I rode out to the Country about two miles to Mr. Brinton's with Mrs. N[owland] & Mrs. P[axton].

WEDNESDAY [MAY] 22D. In the A.M. I transplanted Some Beets & Parsnip's And in the P.M. I took Tea at Mr. Ralston's.

THURSDAY FRIDAY & SATURDAY [MAY 23, 24, 25]. I was makeing soap and in ill health all the time.

SUNDAY 26TH OF MAY 1822. This day Mr. Fletcher calculated to starte to Morgan County for the purpose of attending the sale of Lots but he was disapointed; it commensed raining early in the morning & continued on all day; I still remain sick.

MONDAY [MAY] 27TH. I get no better but notwithstanding all that; I went to scrubing Mr. Blake's house in order that we might moove on Tuesday. I had several very pressing invitations to attend a Tea drinking at Mr. Nowlands but when I was done cleaning my hous I was not able to attend.

TUESDAY 28TH OF MAY 1822. We come in to Mr. Blake's hous & took possession for one Year.

WEDNESDAY [MAY] 29TH. I was ingagued in fixing my house & Mr. F. was helping Mr. Paxton to build fence.

THURSDAY [MAY] 30TH. I washed & scrubed & done the greatest that ever I have done Since I have been here.

FRIDAY [MAY] 31ST. This day Mr. F. started on the circuit. This morning we got up very Early & it was quiet pleasing to hear the birds how cheerfully they Sung; their notes so mingled that a person could not distinguish one bird's note from another. This day Mr. Wrice a Presbyterian Preacher & Dr. Cow dined with Mr. B[lake] & myself. It is very growing weather at this time; this day we had a gentle shower & evrything in our garden appears to grow & flourish.

SAT. JUNE THE 1ST. I visited Mrs. Wick.

SUNDAY [JUNE] 2D. I Staid at home all day & Mr. B[lake] attended Preaching. In the P.M. a number of Ladys & Gentlemen Called on me. Mrs. W[ick] & Mrs. Buckner took Cofee with us; after sundown Mr. B. went with me to Judg Wick's & I staid with the Madam all night & got up early Monday Morn 3d & came home waken'd Mr. B. got breakfast & dinner & Set Mr. B. to geathe[r]ing bean Sticks & I visited Mrs. Wilson. Got some eggs to set a hen.

TUESDAY [JUNE] 4TH. Mrs. Scudder spent the P.M. with me.

WEDNESDAY [JUNE] 5TH. Mrs. S. & myself Spent the P.M. with Mrs. Bates.

THURSDAY [JUNE] 6TH. I was[h]ed and scrubed in the Evening. Mrs. Wick came in and took Tea then I went home with her & Staid all night.

FRIDAY [JUNE] 7TH. I irond & mended. The same day Mr. B[lake] bought a cow & calf from Mr. Johnstone & give 10 dollar's.

SAT. [JUNE] 8TH. I Spent the P.M. with Mrs. Wick.

SUNDAY [JUNE] 9TH. Mrs. Wick & I attended methodist Preaching; in the P.M. it rained & continued on all night without much intermission.

MONDAY [JUNE] 10TH. We had a very hard rain. It laid the corne & Potatoes flat to the ground, thundered before the rain.

TUESDAY [JUNE] 11TH. I was altering a dress.

WEDNESDAY 20TH [12TH] OF JUNE 1822. I took dinner with Mrs. Wick; she had her table spread with the fruits of her industry; such as beans & beets. I then came home & intended to Spend the P.M. at Mr. Nowland's; while I was makeing preparations to starte I received a Letter from Mr. F. which States he would not be at home until Friday or Saturday; but notwithstanding all that I looked for him all the P.M. on Thursday neither was I disapointed.

FRIDAY & SATURDAY WHICH MADE THE 15TH OF JUNE I was washing.

SUNDAY [JUNE] 16TH. In the morning I feel quiet unwell; Mr. Blake & Mr. F. dressed themselves. Mr. B. went to Sabbath School & Mr. F. went to Mr. Ray's office, & left me all alone in which time I composed these few lines. In the Evening Mr. F. & I went to our lot.

MONDAY [JUNE] 17TH. I irond.

TUESDAY [JUNE] 18TH. I finished a pair of pantaloons for Mr. B[lake].

WEDNESDAY [JUNE] 19TH. In the A.M. it rained very hard. I hemed two hankerchief's for Mr. B. In the Eve I went to see Mrs. Wick.

THURSDAY [JUNE] 20TH. I went to Mr. Paxton's in order to get Mrs. P. to assist me in Sewing.

FRIDAY [JUNE] 21ST. I washed & scrubed, there has been a greatdeal of talk about celebrating the fourth of July all this week.

SAT. [JUNE] 22D. I irond & finished another pair of pantaloons.

SUNDAY [JUNE] 23D. Mr. B[lake] rode to the country & Mr. F. & I staid at home all day.

MONDAY [JUNE] 24TH. I commensed a roundabout for Mr. B. but did not finish it till Wednesday on the account of being sick; it is very dry at this time, but our gardens flourish & grow.

FRIDAY [JUNE] 28. Mrs. Bates spent the P.M. with me like wise Mrs. Drake.

SAT. [JUNE] 29TH. It rained.

SUNDAY [JUNE] 30TH. Mr. Cutler & his Son with us.

MONDAY JULY 1ST 1822. I washed.

TUESDAY [JULY] 2D. Very Wet.

WEDNESDAY [JULY] 3D. This day Mr. F. is ingagued in writing toasts for the forth of July.

THURSDAY THE FORTH OF JULY. This day there apered to be a great stir & livelaness among the people. The men had a barbacu & dined inder the green sugar trees at the West end of Washington St. The Evening of the same day Mr. Crumbaugh had a large party held at his dwelling.

FRIDAY [JULY] 5TH. Mr. B[lake] Started up Fallcreek.

TUESDAY [JULY] 9TH. I getherd a large mess of young Corn & Mr. Foot dined with us. In the P.M. Mr. F. & I visited Mr. Johnson's a mild & a half in the Country. I was highly pleased with accommodation we met with.

WEDNESDAY [JULY] 11TH [10TH]. In the P.M. we had a ver[y] hard rain & Mr. McCarty staid all night with us.

FRIDAY EVE [JULY 12]. I went down to Mr. P[axton's] & Set till 8 o clock.

SAT. [JULY] 13TH. Mr. F. set off about 1 o clock for Columbus & I Staid all nigt with Mrs. Wick.

SUNDAY 12TH [14TH] OF JULY 1822. This day Mr. Jones departed his life about 8 o clock in the Morn. I have not the least doubt in my mind but what he was prepared to depart from this world of sin & folly. I fear it will be very sickly t[h]is Summer, it appears so at this time. This day I attended baptist Preaching at the School hous. Mr. Jones is to be buried this P.M. I think we have had as hard a rain this day as ever I saw & very high wind; I am all alone & very uneasy fearing that Mr. F. & the Judg are caught in the storm & perhaps crippled.

MONDAY [JULY] 15TH. Last nigt Mrs. Wick staid with me & this morning Mr. Wick came & took Breakfast with us. Monday night I staied with Mrs. W. & we were both very much frighened.

THURSDAY [JULY] 18TH. I spent the day with Mrs. N[owland] & Mrs. P[axton] & that night went to Mrs. Wickes. About 9 o clock Mr. F. returned from court & we staid with the madam all night.

THURSDAY [JULY] 25. I Spent the Eve with Mrs. Bates & after Sundown Mr. F. & I called on Mrs. Walpole and the Eve f[o]llowing we took Tea with her.

SAT. [JULY] 27TH. Mr. F. started to Winchester. That day we had hard thunder & rain; Mr. F. was in it all.

SUND. [AUG.] 11TH. I visited the Sick.

WEDNESDAY [AUG.] 13 [14TH]. Mrs. P. spent the day with me. About 9 o clock in the Eve Mr. F. had a chill purhaps an hour then the fever continued till 10 o clock the nexte day at which time I left him alone & rode out to Mr. Wood's but I left him with great r[e]luctanc[e] on the account of his illness.

THURSDAY 15TH OF AUGUST. Mr. F. still remains unwell.

TUESDAY 27TH AUGUST 1822. Mr. F. has just raised out of a very severe attact of the fever & I fear he will expos himself so much that he will be sick again. This day is cloudy & wet & Mr. F. has ventured out.

SUNDAY 1ST OF SEPT. Very cludy & rainy. This day I wrote a letter to Father & Mother. The people are generaly healthy at this time.

THURSDAY THE 5TH OF SEPT. 1822. The three Miss Walpoles called on me for the first time.

(It has been considerable sickly this season)

THURSDAY [SEPT.] 12. They all took tea with me.

WEDNESDAY 18TH OF SEPT. I commensed drying grapes. Campmeating commensed the 13th of Sept. and held four days. Court commensed at this plaice Sept. 26th 1822 for the first [time]. Several strange lawyers attended it.

SAT. THE 28TH. The three miss Walpols give me a call.

SUNDAY 29TH. Mr. F. and I walked a half a mild towards Mr. Lintons mill.

OCT. THE 10TH 1822. I resume once more to note down a few things, to wit, within one week Mr. F. has been at the expense of purchasing 6 yards of shirting and two pare of shoes. We have not had but 3 hard frosts this fall, people are still sickly.

WEDNESDAY 16TH OF OCT. 1822. Mr. F. and I went a grapeing.

OCT. 20TH 1822. I commensed reading Schultz's Travels.

SAT. THE 2D NOVE. 1822. Mr. F. and I geathered our Beets carrots and Potatoes. In the Eve butchered a pig.

MONDAY [NOV.] THE 4TH. I was spining wool.

TUESDAY [NOV.] 5. In the morning Mr. F. & I bilt A corn crib. In the P.M. and all next day I was ingaged stewing pumping [pumpkin] out of dors. It rained all the P.M.

FRIDAY [NOV.] 8TH. Mr. F. started to Winchester.

SATURDAY [NOV. 9]. I went down to Mr. P[axton's] and called at Mr. N[owland's].

SUNDAY [NOV. 10]. I staid at Mr. Col. [?] I finished my book.

MONDAY [NOV. 11]. We had high winds from the South so much so that I could not keep any fire. About two oclock in the P.M. Mr. Nowland departed this life it was said very happy. He said he had maid his peace with God and was willing to go.

TUESDAY [NOV. 12]. Mr. Proctor delivered a very pathetick Seirmon, on the occation. His Text red thus It is better to go to the hous of mo[u]rning than the hous feasting.

THURSDAY [NOV.] THE 14TH. Mr. F. returned from Winchester.

SUNDAY [NOV.] 17TH. Mr. F. started to Martinsvill. I spent the day very idol, for my hous smoket so bad I could neither read write or doo anything els. In the night it rained very hard, next morning there was snow to be seen. It was cold and disagreeable and I had to pick up all my wood.

WEDNESDAY [NOV.] 20TH. Mr. F. returned home.

THURSDAY [NOV.] THE 21ST. We moved back into our hous —

FRIDAY [NOV. 22]. I washed and fatiegued myself I believe more than ever I did before.

SAT. & SUNDAY [NOV. 23 AND 24]. I spent very idle thou[g]h Sun. I commensed reading Thompson's treating upon Spring Summer Autumn & Winter.

MONDAY [NOV. 25]. I began sewing & have been ingagued evry day this week except this day Saturday and it has snowed all day.

SUNDAY [NOV.] 24TH. The snow was about 3 or 4 inches deep. Mr. F. did not return till in the night, He had suffered very much with the cold. Monday I washed & [did not] doo anything more of any consequence. The balance of the week I was sick.

TUESDAY 17TH OF DECR. 1822. We butchered a beef.

SAT. [DEC.] 28TH. Mr. F. has this day spent about 6 dollars for my sake. In the Evening we went to Mr. B. [?] and spent till 10 o clock.

MONDAY [DEC.] 30TH. We butchered our hogs and I was in gagued in preserveing my lard and sausage's and worst every day till Fri. That day I diped candle's.

SAT. [JAN.] THE 4TH 1823. Very wet and thawing. I assisted in puting up an ash hopper and exposed myself very much.

SUNDAY [JAN. 5]. Cold and feezing.

MONDAY [JAN.] 6TH. Sarah ann Nowland helped me to wash.

TUESDAY [JAN.] 7TH. I spent the day with Mrs. N[owland] and made a dress.

WEDNESDAY [JAN.] 8TH. I visited Mrs. Wick and made a shimmee.

THURSDAY EVE [JAN. 9]. Mrs. N. spent with me.

FRIDAY [JAN. 10]. Mrs. Wick.

SUNDAY 12TH OF JANUARY 1823. Mr. Johnson dined with us.

WEDNESDAY [JAN.] 15TH. Mr. Brackenridg began bording with us.

THURSDAY [JAN. 16]. Mrs. Buckner & Mrs. Linton spent the P.M. with me.

MONDAY JANUARY 20TH 1823. Very muddy and snowing. I road to Mrs. P[axton's] and staid till the next day.

FEBRUARY THE 1ST 1823. Mr. F. was taken with the agu fever again. For one Weeak we have had as cold weather as I ever felt.

SUNDAY 9TH OF FEBR. We can descover a little alteration, and I think the Winter will soon brake.

WEDNESDAY [FEB.] 12TH. I was sewing at Mrs. N[owland']s.

THURSDAY [FEB. 13]. I visited Mrs. Wilson.

TUESDAY [FEB.] 18TH. I was shopping & purchased the amount of five dollars.

THURSDAY 6TH OF MARCH 1823. I was solicited to attend a Tea party at Mr. Walpole's. I did not attend on account of ill health.

WEDNESDAY [MARCH] 12. I commensed reading the horrors of Oakendale Abby a romance and finished Friday 14th 1823.

SAT. [MARCH] 15. Mr. F. & I visited Col. Paxton.

WEDNESDAY [MARCH] 19TH. I boiled my last pumking.

TUESDAY 25TH OF MARCH 1823. Miss Mc Doogle spent the P.M. with me. I thought her a very inteligent girl.

APRILE 4TH 1823. Mr. F. started to Morgan county.

SAT. [APR. 5]. I visited Mrs. P.

SUN. [APR. 6]. Our school commensed which I hope will be of greate benefit to the children of our Town.

MON. [APR. 7]. Cloudy and rainy and Mr. B[lake] and Dr. D[unlap] fixed my bed stid.

TUES. [APR.] THE 8. I had a number of Lady's called upon me.

THURSDAY [APR. 10]. Mrs. Dayly washed.

FRIDAY [APR. 11]. I fixt up a stand of curtans.

SATURDAY [APR.] 12TH. Mr. F. returned home from M[a]rtins Ville.

SUN. EVE [APR. 13]. Walked down to Col. P.

MON. [APR. 14]. I was quiet unwell. Made some gardin.

TUES. [APR.] 15TH. I was delvered of a son. Dr. Mitchel was with me the rest of the copany was Mrs. Nowland Mrs. Mitchel Mrs. Bradly Mrs. Colup and Mrs. Paxton. Betsy Huggins staid with me 2 weekes then done my worke one weeke. Betsy Vanblaricum staid 2 days. Margret Hyet came on Wednesday the 7th day of May and staid two weekes. Scalded her foot on Thursday. Staid till Saturday the 24th.

FRI. 30TH OF MAY. I fraimed a quilt.

SUN. THE 8TH OF JUNE 1823. Mr. F. & myself wal[k]ed to the River.

TUESDAY THE 8TH OF JULY 1823. Miss Eliza Linton came to stay with us.

SAT. [JULY] 12TH. My finger began to get sore.

TUES. [JULY] 15TH. I took a quilt out of the fraim.

SUN. 17TH OF AUGUST 1823. We got a Girl by the name of Polly Crawford.

FRIDAY 12TH SEPT. 1823. Mr. F. started to Columbus.

WEDNESDAY 22D [24TH] OF SEPT. I recieved a letter from him which gave me great satisfaction. I had just come from Mrs. Wick's who was very sick with the fever and felt very much distressed for her situation, (asking myself whether I could bare things with as much fortitude or not. She certainly displais a g[r]eat [d]eal of philosophy). The letter relieved me.

MONDAY 29TH OF SEPT. 1823. I visited Dr. Cow's Daughter's. I found them plain and neat but unsociable.

OCT. 3D. I recieved another letter from Mr. F. he was then at Burlington Green County.

SUNDAY 12TH OF OCT. 1823. I rode about two miles in to the country.

SUNDAY THE 19TH. I spent the P.M. at Mr. Willson's.

TUES. THE 25TH OF NOVE. 1823. Mr. Paxton started to coriden [Corydon, Indiana]. I staid with Mrs. P. all night.

FRI. 5TH DECR. Mrs. Nowland had a quilting where I heard some talk of a party which is to take place at Washington hall on the 25th. I had an interdu[c]tion to Brown and think her a very ag[r]eeable and inteligen Girl.

FRI. 12TH INST. I spent the Eve with B. F. Moris Lady. I found her a very sociable woman though I did not injoy myself in the least altho I might appea[r]ed to do so. Mr. F. was present a great part of the Eve which rendered me quiet unhappy & imbarast thinking he was mortified at my actions. I made no convercesion and trembleing fearing there mite be some question asked that would expose my ignernce. He's taken a greateal of pains with me. It seames as if my eyes are just opened and I view evry thing in its darkest dyes and some times make myself miserable again. I reflect I know it is my duty to be cheerful and make evrything appear in the best light.

SUN. DECE. 14TH 1823. Cold and all nature is robed in a mantle of snow.

WEDNESDAY 24TH OF DECR. 1823. Mr. F. and I attended a ball at Washington hall.

THURSDAY & FRIDAY [DEC. 25 AND 26]. I did not do much of anything.

The nineteenth-century ideology of domesticity promised women life-long protection and security. Yet for large numbers of American women over the years, this promise of perpetual immunity from the problems of the real world has proven illusory. Anticipating that they would like "happily ever after," they have had their expectations rudely shattered, often within a brief span of time. Marriages have frequently been broken during the period of young adulthood. Whereas today the primary reason for marital disruption among people in their twenties and thirties is divorce, prior to the twentieth century, the most common cause of broken marriages was the death of a spouse. In either case, many young wives and mothers have been thrust involuntarily into a role for which they were not prepared by society — head of the family. Accustomed to defer to their husbands, they were now suddenly placed in the position of authority in their families, responsible for making decisions and providing sustenance. Whether widowed, divorced, separated, or deserted, they had no choice but to overstep the limitations of the feminine role and assume control of their own lives. Thus, often in spite of themselves, many young women have learned to function independently and in so doing have developed a more positive self-image. One such woman was Mary Ann Owen Sims of Dallas County, Arkansas, who was widowed in 1855 on the eve of her twenty-fifth birthday.

Born in Tennessee in 1830, Mary Ann moved to Arkansas with her family in 1838. Her father became a prosperous farmer and held a number of important public offices in the state before his death in 1846. She was very attached to her family, particularly her mother, and she attended a boarding school with her sister near their home. Thus, Mary Ann grew up in polite southern society and internalized the definition of femininity prevalent in the midnineteenth century. When she was a month shy of seventeen, she married Dr. John D. Sims, who was ten years her elder. Dr. Sims, a physician, soon settled his new family on a small plantation which he managed in addition to his medical practice. Judging from Mary Ann's recollections, the Sims's marital relationship was both happy and loving, even though Mary Ann's youth and inexperience as a housekeeper made her excessively dependent on her husband. Before Dr. Sims's death in June 1855, Mary Ann had borne three children, a son, William Harvey (Willie), and two daughters, Josephine Castera (Jo) and Mary Louella (Lu).

Widowed before she was twenty-five, Mary Ann Sims was confronted by a crisis of unprecedented magnitude. Not only was she grief stricken at the loss of her beloved husband, but she was also left with three little children, aged two, five, and six. Her emotional anguish was compounded by practical problems she had never encountered previously. First and foremost, she faced the burden of supporting her family. Most urgently, however, she had to contend with her father-in-law, who attempted to wrest her husband's estate from her and her children. During her bereavement she sought solace through religious meditation, a recourse typical of women of her era, but her sorrow was unquenchable in her initial stage of mourning. Another way she attempted to deal with her grief was by composing a retrospective account of her late husband's life and then commencing a journal of her own.

This selection from Mary Ann Sims's diary begins in January 1856, almost six months after her husband's death. Although still very much caught up in her grief, the young widow had, by this time, started to take constructive steps toward reordering her life. She realized that she would have to fill both her expected role of mother and the unfamiliar masculine role of provider. Of necessity she assumed responsibility for the material welfare of her family. Managing the family's small cotton plantation with its complement of slave laborers constituted her central task. While expressing dismay at the intricacies of financial affairs, Mrs. Sims nevertheless was able to cope with the matters that required her attention, and had formerly been handled by her husband. It is essential to note that Mary Ann Sims, like virtually all upper-class southern women of her era, could rely on her staff of enslaved domestics to perform the onerous chores of running a nineteenth-century household. In this respect, she possessed a clear advantage over her less-privileged counterparts. Although her financial situation appears to have been precarious, the fact that the majority of her wealth was concentrated in slaves enabled her to enjoy a life of ease.

Making business decisions, as well as supervising the daily operations of the household, still left Mrs. Sims with plenty of time for what she considered her primary role, that of mother. In light of the emphasis placed on maternal nurture in the prescriptive literature of the antebellum era, Mrs. Sims's commitment to her child-rearing duties is not at all surprising. Yet her personal plight reinforced her dedication to her children's well-being. As a single parent, the sole burden of raising the children fell upon her. Indoctrinated with the idea that the quality of care received by children was critical for their development, Mrs. Sims spent an inordinate amount of time worrying about her youngsters. Her solicitude for them was manifested in her concern for their educational progress and, even more importantly, their spiritual progress. In addition to teaching them the basics of reading, writing, and arithmetic, she felt it incumbent on her to inculcate in them the proper religious values. And, of course, she fretted continually about their physical health as well.

Because Mary Ann Sims lived such an isolated existence, her young children played an especially large part in her life. After Dr. Sims's death, the children became the center of her universe. They were her daily companions as well as a ready source of affection and consolation. Without them, Mrs. Sims might not have been able to surmount her personal tragedy. Even so, the young widow persistently noted her loneliness and boredom. Mary Ann Sims thought of herself as an educated woman with refined sensibilities. She yearned for stimulating companionship and bemoaned the fact that her neighbors did not share her intellectual interests. But, with the exception of churchgoing and occasional visits to and from family members and friends, Mrs. Sims was deprived of the social intercourse she craved. Most of her free time was spent reading, and her comments on the books she read form a valuable measure of her intellectual development. In addition, literary quotations punctuate her diary, revealing her affinity with the life of the mind. Left to rely on her own resources, Mary Ann Sims gradually discovered her individual identity.

Misfortune was the catalyst to personal growth for twenty-five-year-old Mary Ann Owen Sims. Forced to stand on her own for the first time in her life, she found the inner strength to deal with her problems in a concrete way. The untimely death of her husband also prompted her to reexamine the presuppositions that undergirded her life. Her journal was not only a refuge where she could unburden herself of her deepest feelings, but also a means of gaining a new perspective on herself. As her grief receded, self-pity was replaced by a determination to meet the challenges of her new situation directly and openly. Chastened by the experience of widowhood, Mary Ann Sims reassembled the pieces of her life and moved into the future with confidence.

—— 13 ——
Mary Ann Owen Sims
1856

JANUARY 1 Welcom[e] new year—prehaps it will help to bind up the the wounds that has been inflicted in the past year that is now receeding from one view and and [*sic*] will soon mingle with the blue on memories horizon deal gently with me 56 for I have been soarly tried—but I have now learned not to expect much and am easily satisfide—I left Mothers this year for my own home where I will try and live this year—it was very cold and we had a very uncomfatable drive Willie complained a greateal of his head and had to be carried in the servent's arms part of the way—I have emploied a Mr Edmanson to oversee for me and shall keep all the servents at home but realy I hardly see how I am to keep house every thing brings back the rememberance of the one who was the light and life of my "Forest Home" realy my little home looks as darke to me as the world would appear if the Sun himself were bloted out—for surely he was my sun I have been so buisy to day I have had no time for reflection

[JANUARY] 2D WEDNESDAY I have been very buisy to day in arra[ng]ing my house hold Willie complains very much of his head and often says "if my Papa was here he would cure me" alas poor child he will often mis[s] and wish for a farther how I mis[s] him myself how loanly and cheerless my little home appears—when at night the children are all asleep I find myself sometimes listning for his foot steps (for he was want to come home frequently at night when he had been absent sevrel days Practising Physic) but the reality will soon come back that we have met our last time on earth then Faith and hope points to that land where those who have loved here will meet again oh I will think of thee Love though thou are gone fo[r]ever I can near forget love no *never never*

but we will meet again love to part no more fo[r]ever

where the Angels dwell love we will live f[or]ever

[JANUARY] 6 SUNDAY we have apretty day to day Willie appears better Bro William came over alittle while this morning I spent the rest of the day in instructing Jo and reading Heavenly father draw me closter still to the[e]

[JANUARY] 8 TUESDAY very cold to day Willie appears no better I am fearfull some of the nerves of his head is [i]njured he complains a greateal of his head how loanly I am no one to speek to save my little ones

[JANUARY] 10 THURSDAY cold and clouday Willie appeard better this

SOURCE: Clifford Dale Whitman, ed., "Private Journal of Mary Ann Owen Sims," Part II, *The Arkansas Historical Quarterly* vol. 35, Autumn 1976. Reprinted by permission.

morning but the pain in his head returned as sevier as ever this evening I sent to P[rinceton] this morning for some medicine for him I hope it may do him good he suffers so much the day cloased in with a sleet every things looks so dreary

[JANUARY] 13 SUNDAY the holy Sabath morning how I wish it was in my pow[er] to spend it as I ought Willie appears better it is pleasent to day — Mrs garrett came over and spent the day with me she is a poor widow who live a 1/4 mile from here she has allways been very kind in visiting me when my family has been afflicted

[JANUARY] 14 MONDAY I have been busy all day casting up accounts and attending to business i had no idie that it was as much trouble to superentend and take care of a family as it is I feel tried sometimes — and how do I mis[s] him who was always so attintive to my wants but it is selfish to wish [for] thee on my account when I see our little ones in their insocent prattle and play say and do things that gives evedence of future intelect then do I wish for thee that thou might be made glad but what avails tears sighs or prayers thou are gone forever yes forever

[JANUARY] 17 THURSDAY we have a beautiful day to day Luellar was quite unwel[l] last night — Ben came over and spent the day — the Misses Bithel came over lait in the evening and staid all night they are dear kind girls an[d] visit me often (their Father is a is a [*sic*] Physi[ci]an and lives about amile from here I may as well say here they have long since moved away the el[d]est and youngest have marr[i]ed in the last two years I hope they are doing well)

[JANUARY] 18 FRIDAY the young ladies left this morning I accompanied them as fare as Mrs garretts — staid only a few hours — when [I] return[ed] home [I] felt mo[re] loanly than ever — but I will strive on and try to do my duty to my children and look faraward to the time when I will flee away and be at rest

[JANUARY] 19 SATERDAY cold an[d] snowing spent the day in attending to my household and instructing my children

[JANUARY] 20 SUNDAY it is too cold to go to church Dr Smith came down and spent the day with me in the evening Bro Ryland came and staid till late

[JANUARY] 21 It is exceedingly cold to day and Willie quite sick Lord sustain me in this trial

[JANUARY] 24 comparitively warm to day spent the day in sewing reading and instructing the children which is now my cheef delight to watch their little minds unfolding themselves as it wer[e] so me little pittle opens wider evry day displaying the germ of interlect that lies enfolded there in — but still nothing can wean my feelings and thoughts from him who is with me no more

[JANUARY] 25 it rained all night and an[d] continued without interm[is]sion all day I do not think I ever saw a more constant rain I have spent the day princapaly in attending my children and reading "a leagend of Montrose" the subject and the Auther is enough to vouch for its beeing interesting — but when night spreads her darke mantle over the earth and we all are gatherd within doors it is then my heart misses it[s] kindred tie and pines for the[e] dear love

[JANUARY] 26 it has been raining all day except a few moments the sun shone out as if to assure us that it was not a deluge again the day has been very drea[r]y and only eclipsed by my own sad reflections I have spent it in instructing the children sewing and reading but there is an "acheing void this world can never fill"

[JANUARY] 27 SUNDAY it is cirtainly the coaldest weather I ever felt I spent the day in learning the children and reading what a pleasent dream I had last night thought I was with him but the s[w]eet vision soon passed

[JANUARY] 28 the sun shone bright to day for the first in sevril I spent the day as yesterday

[JANUARY] 29 quite pleasent I spent the day in attending to my family I once thought I could not live without my Husband but he who tempers the wind to the shorn lamb has given me strength sufficient for my need X X

[JANUARY] 30 this is the most pleasent day we have had for some time Mr Gibson and Bro William were here all day on buisness how glad I will be when I get my buisness more settled allway[s] beeing accostom to have someone to depende on it is quite new to attend to buisness transactions and it pesters me no little — Mary Williams Anna and Nelly Ruck[s] came over and spent the night they are young girls in their teens and full of fun and frollic happy youth they were not much company for me who if not soberd by years I am by trouble

2D FEBUARY it was very pleasent this morning but the day closed in with snow such is the fait of life in the morning all is b[r]ight but we advance the[n] recied as the mir[a]ge and at the close the brightness has all disap[p]ear[e]d X X

[FEBRUARY] 11 MONDAY I spent all the past week at Mothers save two days I went to Princeton one day and one day attended a dinner party at Mrs. Walshes given in honor of the marraige of her [son] Mr William Walsh to Miss H[enrietta] Holmes the bride looked lovely and the groom happy and all "went merry as a marriage bell"

[FEBRUARY] 12 it is a lovely day to day it came like sunshine mid clouds after [we] had so much bad weather I have been quite buisy to day I have just finished killing my meat for the year and evry farmers wife knows I have had a buisy day

[FEBRUARY] 14 we have a real spring day to day — I have spent it in attending to my house hold and instructing the children they appear twice as dear to me as when their father was with me

[FEBRUARY] 16 it is very pleasent to day I have read a goodeal in Heroditus Ancient history What a great source of enjoyment is reading I can hardly see how any one can live without it it is a perfect relief to the mind to forget its own griefs in the pleasuers and sorrows of others who has gone before us — oh how I pine for association [of] some kindred mind all of my neighbours are good honest kind people but they seem to have no idie beyond their little s[p]here of action they do not appear to have a feeling nor aspiration higher than the things of this life satisfying their physical wants — this is the last day of the week oh that I may throw aside all earthly consideration and spent to morrow in the servise of the Lord

[FEBRUARY] 17 SUNDAY we have a beautiful day after hearing the childrens morning lessons I attended church (leaving the children at home fo[r] fear they would ketch the mumps) listened to a discourse from Bro Salley I did not like it very much I thought it rather leaned towards materialism — dined at Bro Rylands — returned home in the evening bring[ing] their little daughter home with me

[FEBRUARY] 18 MONDAY it is as pleasent as yesterday I comenced gardning to day in the evening Cousin V[irginia] Toney and sevrel other laidies came to spend the night with me I was glad of their company I allways feel so loanly — and then they were old friend[s] who lived some way off and scarsely ever visited me

[FEBRUARY] 19 TUESDAY misting rain this morning notwithstanding the unfavourablnes of the morning my guest[s] took their leave and and [sic] I spent the day as usual learning the children and attending to my family

[FEBRUARY] 22 warm and misting rain for the last two days but cleard this evening and to night the moon shines most beautiful save now and then a cloud passes over its face but soon disapears leaveing it more bright than before from contrast so like the star of faith it may bee dim[m]ed for a while by trials and troubles but anon it will shine out in all its lusture I stay at home a greadeal and devote my time princaply to my children I scarsely ever see company indeed it is wearisom to me I had rather be aloan for I feel aloan no one appears to care for me and oh the future looks so darke

[FEBRUARY] 24 SUNDAY we have a clouday sabath — I staid at home to day the horses has all been so buisy during the week I thought it too hard to ride them to church I heard the chilldrens morning [lessons] read some in the Scriptures and some seliction of Poetry made by my dear Husban and preserved in a scrap book how nearly every line bring[s] to my mind some thought or sentiment of his oh how I do mis[s] thee espesially on this day when circumstances prevented us attending worship it was our want to read the *word* together to converse together and strengenther each other in the way of Ri[gh]tiousness alass I am aloan — but oh I put my trust in him who doeth all things well and try and be submissive to his will what a simple thing it is to say "Thy will be done" but oh how hard it is to say and feel it from the heart Lord grant I may continue in the right way what ever thou seest fit to afflict me with and oh that I may raise my little ones up in the fear and admonitions of the Lord and live to see them gatherd in to the fold of the good shepperd then suerly will I feel my task here is accomplish[ed]

[FEBRUARY] MONDAY 2[5] we have a most lovely day I spent the morning in sowing some garden seeds and hearing the childrens morning lessons in the evening I went to call on Mrs. Jackson they are now living at the place Dr Bethel formaly occupied I found Mr[s] J[ackson] a very nice lady talkative and agreeable our neighbourgood is changing very much our old neighbours are mooving off and new ones coming in and my dear husban will scarsely ever be thought of save by me

[FEBRUARY] TUESDAY 27 it was raining this morning when I first awoke and has been ever since no kind of out door worke can be done spent the day in reading and attending to my family how I do mis[s] my Husband it takes all my fortidude to live without him

[FEBRUARY] 28 we have a most lovely day it makes me allmost forget the burden of my grief and rejoice I derive great consolation from the society of my children it has been my greatest endevour since the loss of my Husban to teach them to trust in the Lord at all times and how delightful it is to me to see the confiding faith they have even when older h[e]arts are bowed down even our little babe will say dont cry mama papa aint dead he's in the Good Mans house — and even once soon after Dr['s] death (she was near 3 years old) she was quite sick and waked me up and put her little arms which was hot with feever around my neck saying mama is the good man in the ground I could not immagin why she asked and I answerd no he is in the clouds well she exclaimed what made them put Pa in the ground I tried to explain that her father was not there then she said ["]mama when I die can I see Pa can I see you and Willie an[d] Bunk and Aunty" I answered in the affirmative ["]oh mamma["] she cryed ["]I do want to see Pa mighty bad but I dont want to die now" and once when Jo was near six years old I was at Mas and she was very anxious to go to see her aunt Martha who lived about a mile from Ma's I toled her there was no one to go with her she would have to go by herself she read[i]ly consented to that If I would let her go at last I consented not think[ing] she would go far before before [sic] she would get alarmed and turn back When I found she had gone I sent after her and when I questio[ned] her if she did not ged alarmed "Yes Marm once at a black log so I said my prayers and I knew the good man would'nt let any thing harm me then so I went on" I mearly mention thees circumstance[s] to show it is even good for a child to have a confiding faith in God it makes even them strong in trials but oh the blessing it is to [a] matured mind X X X

MARCH 2 we have a pleasent [day] I attended worship at Mt Pleasent taking Willie an[d] Lu with me we spint the evenin[g] at Bro Rylands returned home in the evening thus have I been trying to do my duty to my creator but how short I have come but God who Judges the h[e]art knows mine how I do mis[s] my Husband in the congregation — When I consider my situation rightly I have no cause to complain but much to be thankfull for I have had kind Parient and affectionate Husband a few Friend[s] in the little sphere I move in Withall a contented mind and a heart that loved to lean upon its creator — and now that the loved ones are passed and passing aw[ay] why no[t] say thy will be done shuredly he who has bestowed so many blessings has a right to give trials too

[MARCH] 9 SUNDAY I[t] was pleasent this morning but clouded up in the evening Lu had a chill yesterday and I could not leave her to attend church to day Brothers William and Benj[amin] came over and spent the day it recall[ed] the happy seens of childhood for us to meet around the same hearth but she the best beloved of the band was not with us I think of Sister very often but she has a home of affection of her own and is the hap[p]iest of us all, thoug[h] deprived of the society of a Mother Brothers and sister but distance can never sever the tie that binds us Willie went home with his uncle Ben very much a gainst my wish but there was no refusing them I dislike to be deprived of the society of my children if only for a few days

13 MARCH very cold and clouday this morning it snowed a little we cirtainly have the most backward spring I ever noticed it is near the Midle of March and not a sign of vegitation yet I have spent the day princaply in making a pot of soap and reading the Presidents message rather a new idie reading the Presidents message over a pot of soape but every thing must have its cource from the Pallace to the cottage although I have many things to take my attention still my heart remembers its bereavement and pines for him that is gone

[MARCH] 30 I have been so very buisy for the past two weeks that I have hardly had time to reflect — I have just returned this evening [from] ma[']s where I have been spending a few days she had a very sevier attact of the Rhumatism of the heart but appeard to be intierly relieved when I left her — Ann appears to be quite sick this evening — thus another week has commenced but who shall tell it[s] ending many will have looked their last on this earth and be called hence to give an account of the deeds done in the boddy oh Lord prepare me to give a strict account

31 MARCH I have been uncan buisy to day Ann the cook is sick and it takes I & Phillis boath to do her worke but I shall not complain I have such good health and my children keep so well this is the last of Marche 56 what change in my existence since March 55 but as the old addage has it tide and time waits for no man I presume the best we can do is to make our thoughts ageree with the diferent sittuations that each wave on the tide of time brings us th[r]ough it is is [sic] a sevier struglle sometimes I hope with the star of Faith and hope for my guide [I] may atlast pass over the sea of time and cast anchor safe in the Haven of of [sic] a happy Eternity how I long for companionship I look forward with much anxiety to the time when my children can understand me

APRIL 2 MONDAY it rained last night and all nature look[ed] refreshed this morning I have felt quite unwell to day but I have learn[ed] to suffer mentally an[d] Phisicaly without complaining Mother sent my papers and a couple of letters from Sister to day dear Sister I want so much to see her — the papers are full of Politics as this is the year for the Presidental election the American Party has just nominate[d] Filmore and A I Donelson of course I take sides as every one does so I espouse the cause of Filmore history will show you the result

[APRIL] 6 SUNDAY —
> Frequent the day of God returns
> XXXX XXXX XX
> But oh how slow devotion burns
> How langued are its flames

I attended worship at Mt Pleasent — listened to a short discourse from Father Wade found Mother at Home when I returned I was very glad to see her so much better than she has been for seven or eight months

[APRIL] 7 Mother spent the day and went home this evening

[APRIL] 9 Old Father Wade came down and spent a couple of days with me

[APRIL] 10 I took the children and went over and spent the day with old Mrs Garrett thus does my life pass of[f] in dull monotony

[APRIL 13] SUNDAY attended service at Mt Pleasent return[ed] home accompanied by Father Wade he has been quite an intelegent man but he is now very old and childish he remained with me till tuesday 15

[APRIL] 16 WEDNSDAY we are all well to day for which I feel very thankfull W[e] had a very sevier storm last night which blew down a goodeal of timber it will be a great inconvenience in the farm for we are nearly done planting Cotton

[APRIL] 18 FRIDAY I was confined to my bed nearly all day yesterday with the head ache and this morning Josephine was taken with a sevier attact of the croup I hardly thought she could live an hour I sent for Mrs garrett and Dr galispe a Physi[ci]an who has laitly come in the neighbourhood he soon relieved her but oh how cold did his attention seem to me — Lu was taken to night with an attact of the same kind but not so sevier

[APRIL] 19 Jo is better but Luell still continues quite sick but I hope it is more the effect of the medicin I gave her last night Bro Salley Sister Ryland came and spent the night with me

[APRIL] 27 SUNDAY so another Sabath has passed away it rained last night and the day has been so cloudy that I was affraid to take the children out owing to their recent illness I was fearfull they might relaps consequently I could not attind worship but remained at home all day aloane

THURSDAY MAY FIRST we have a most lovely day appearing more so prehaps from contrast beeing the first fair day we have been blessed with for the last two week I have been very buisy in gardning to day Dr Hughes came to buy some sheep this morning I try to manage my buisness to the best advantage of my little ones but still I do not loose sight of the last promice I made their Father to raise them up in the fear of the Lord time s[t]ill moves on — it has been nearly a year since my dear Husband di[e]d still the memory of him of him [sic] is still green in my soul it is a bright arseas [probably "oasis"] in a dreary waste.

MAY 3 I have been very busy to day having my sheep sheard every little incedent brings bak the contrast between this and last year oh that I could be more resigned to my fait and be content to live aloan when ever I think of the Redeemer and what he sufferd for our salvation I feel perfectly resign[ed] but when I recall the passt I can not help feeling a spirret of rebelion for nature will claim his own affliction XXXX XX X

JUNE 26 I arrived home this morning after an absence of nearly seven weeks on a visit to my sister who resides in a pleasent little village about sixty miles from here I did not make many acquaintences while I was absent owing to the illness of Sister we did not see much company but the society of my only Sister I never tire of — and here I am all alone to night this the first aniversary of my Husbands death well can I understand the Poet when he says "there is a cloud rolling across my soul streaked with fire" yea burns and burns and never consumes how my poor heart suffers god a loan can tell and I have learned the heard lesson at last to suffer and be still some times I think it more than I can beare but I trust in the Holy one and he gives relief

JUNE 28 I have been very buisy in "putting my household to rites" and instructing my children I have concluded to teach them half the day — it is very confineing and often tries my patience but [if] the[y] learn to makile [probably "make"] intelegent good women and a noble man I will feel fully compensated how forsably I feel the responsability of a Mother and utirly do I feel my incapibilty of doing my duty at all time[s] having so much to think of as I have

[JUNE] 29 we have [a] beautiful morning but as the sun begins to ascend the zeneith it becomes warm and at the Miridian the heat is almost intolrable — I attended church to day for the first time in sevrel weeks how it made my heart rejoice to meet my christian friends once more — oh Maker keep me in the rite way and Save me from all temp[t]ations to do evil for it is to Thee and thee only that I look for strength

3 JULY it is a clear bright day — I went to Mothers this evening found Anna Rucks and Brother and Mr Steverson a Baptist Minist[er] I should have spent a pleasent social evening but my head ached so I had to go to bed

[JULY] 4 we all rose this morning in high spirits as we were going to atend a barbacue and speaking in the vacinity of Princeton so accordingly after breakfast we (save Ma Willie & Lu) all don[n]ed our best attire and set out I had to stop a while at Bro Williams for Sister Martha who was to ride with me when we arrived at our distination which was in the woods (near a shady riverlit) where a tempora[r]y stand had been erected for the orators and seats for the audiance — we found quite a motly Group of carriages buggys wagons and cartes — men women children and servents — after a while we made out to obtain as comfor[t]able seats as the place afforded the seremonis of the day commenced after music Miss Lou Holmes with two other young Ladies (Miss[es] Taylor and Fenwick) was conducted upon the platform Miss Holmes presented the gentlemen with a beautiful flag she accompanied the pr[e]sentation with a very appropriate address well deliverd it was recieved by R Dedman Esqr at the same time delivering a a [sic] very embarrissing reply afterwards Mr B Fuller read the decrelation of Independence. Dr Write delivered an oration it was nothing extra but I rec[k]on he did his best he was followed by Mr. Cameron his was just an address as might have been expect[ed] f[r]om a young graduate just from collage afater that we all had music and formed in pro[ce]ssion and went to dinner where evry thing done credit to the managers of the table afterwards the croud dispersed very orde[r]ly considering it was so amnivirous — I return[ed] to Mothers warm and tired

[JULY] 5 I was samoned home this morning in great has[t]e on account of the illness of one of the servents — but she is now doing very well havin given birth to a fine girl X X

11 JULY we are well to day Luellar had a chill yesterday in the evening old Mr Sims came to see me I did not think he would have ever come to see me again after haveing treated me so badly in takeing away the servent he gave Dr but he is his Father and I must treat him kindly

[JULY] 12 quite pleasent for the time of year Mr S[ims] complains of feeling sick and has been lying down nearly all day — Lu had a chill and was quite sick for a while but in the evening she is up again

[JULY] 13 another day of rest gave Lu some medicine Mr Sims did not get up till after breakfast he complains of feeling very unwell it is wearesom to talk to him he is so deaf — I have spent a nother Lords day a loan with my own thoughts which is not very pleasent sometimes but I hope I may be enable[d] to do my duty in all things and at all times

[JULY] 14 Monday it is exceedingly warm to day Lu had a chill at ten oclock and the feever makes her very sick it has abated a little this evening she is now in a sound sleep — this evening Mr Sims went visiting — I feel more loanly this evening than I have for months I am perfectly wearied out living such a loansom life without any one to speak to save my children and servents but I s[t]ill look forward to the time when my child[r]en will be large enough to enter into my thoughts and feelings Lord grant I may live to see it

[JULY] 19 we are needing rain very much we have not had any for 3 weeks Luel has been quite sick to day I feel very uneasy about her she is so frail and delicate but I trust in the Lord he doeth all things well and I hope if it is his will he will spare my little ones to me to be a stay and comfort in age

[JULY] 28 MONDAY we need rain very much evry thing looks as if it had been seared with an iron — Lu is recovering slowly the rest of us are we[ll] for which I feel thankful I have been very buisy in put[t]ing things to rites as I spent the last week at Mas I would not have left home with Lu but Mr Sims got in to a mighty tantrum some of my negroes had stole[n] his pocket book so I sent for my Brothers and went to Mas and left them to settle it as best the[y] might he could not find it and went away very mad and I have not heard of him since X X X

24 SEPTEMBER it has been near two months since I have writen aline here my time is very much occupide and I feel very unsettled it is a mingling of thoughts as it were a state between sleeping and waking — I feel myself gradually recovering from the keen anguish of my great

grief and coming back again to the a waking up as it were I begin again
to take some intrust in what is takeing place around me and not living
so much in the past but looking in the future and forming plans of life

*A*ttending college was a new experience for middle- and upper-class
young women at the end of the nineteenth century, which required
a special kind of determination and strength. Negative popular and
professional opinion about women's higher education held that females in-
tent on developing their intellectual skills did so at the cost of their femininity. Physicians and psychologists reported the dangerous effects of
studying on the female reproductive system and psyche, which rendered
young women unfit to assume their responsibilities as wives and mothers.

During an era when the roles of homemaker and mother were considered the essence of female adulthood, those women enrolling in college
with the idea of pursuing a career after graduation were asserting themselves dramatically. The majority were forced to choose between marriage
and a career. Most who opted for a career set out consciously to create an
alternative to marriage and motherhood, imbued with the belief that
women as well as men were entitled to jobs outside the home and that
work provided an important means for personal growth and development.

The resistance against women who aspired to male-controlled professions took many forms, ranging from blatant hostility and discriminatory
hiring practices to more subtle forms of harassment and ridicule on the
job. Such obstacles are graphically described in the account that follows.

The author, Florence Finch Kelly, was born in a small rural community
in Illinois in 1858, the youngest in a family of eight children. When she was
eleven her parents moved to Kansas where they continued to farm.

In her autobiography Florence recalled that at a young age she planned
to become a novelist, but she was reluctant to discuss her desire or hopes
to attend high school and college because she "well knew how fantastic
and silly and impossible such dreams would seem to [her] family and
friends." Her father at first refused her request for financial assistance to
enroll in the county high school, explaining that she had all of the education she needed, that she would no doubt soon be marrying some nice
young farmer, and that the more she learned in school the unhappier she
would become.

Through the intercession of an older brother and her mother, Florence's
father finally consented to help. After earning a teaching certificate, she
taught for two years in a district school in Kansas. The experience confirmed that this traditional career, virtually the only career choice for
single women throughout the nineteenth century, was not what she was
seeking. In 1877, Florence Kelly, then age twenty, and her brother pooled
their savings and enrolled at the University of Kansas, a newly established
land-grant college.

Her ambition to become a novelist remained strong, although Florence realized that she would have to find a way of supporting herself while writing fiction. "Economic necessity," she stated in her autobiography, led her to think about a career in journalism. In 1881 after a summer job with a Topeka newspaper, she left for Chicago and then Boston to find employment.

Beginning in the midnineteenth century, women were hired by newspapers as editors of women's pages or writers of gossip columns. But their efforts to break into news and investigative reporting were continually thwarted. Florence Kelly ably documents the discrimination on the basis of sex that women encountered in their attempt to become active and equal participants in the male work world.

Unlike many among the pioneering first generation of female college graduates, Florence tried to balance a career with marriage. "I had always expected and intended to marry, sometime, and had never envisaged my future without the accompaniment of marriage and motherhood," she wrote. "Nor had I ever, as did all the young and even the older women I knew in my youth and middle age, resented my sex and wished I had been born a man. On the contrary, I had, and have, always been glad and proud of it, and of the privilege it gave me of bearing children."

In 1885 she entered a business partnership, and soon after a marriage partnership, with Allen Kelly, whom she had met while working in Boston. After her marriage and the birth of her first child a year later, Florence's career assumed lessened importance. Her husband's jobs took them to New York, California, New Mexico, Pennsylvania, New Zealand, and Australia.

When Allen Kelly died in 1905 Florence moved to New York and joined the staff of *The New York Times*. For the next thirty years she wrote book reviews and feature articles, and she published novels, short stories, and poetry of her own. Her autobiography, *Flowing Stream*, appeared in 1939 when she was eighty-one.

—— 14 ——

Florence Finch Kelly

Account of my assets showed that I had arrived in Boston with twenty-five dollars and two letters of introduction, a little more than doubling the capital on which I had invaded Chicago. But I had learned much in that city and had now a better understanding of what to do and how to do it, and a clearer realization of what I would have to contend with. I still had very little conception, however, of what a stone wall I would have to batter my head against before I could make a breach in it big enough to crawl through.

SOURCE: From *Flowing Stream: The Story of Fifty-Six Years in American Newspaper Life* by Florence Finch Kelly. Copyright, 1939, by E. P. Dutton & Co., Inc. Renewal, 1967, by Sherwin F. Kelly. Reprinted by permission of the publisher, E. P. Dutton.

One of my letters of introduction, sent to me by my Lawrence friend, Annie Diggs, was to a woman who had an office position on a small magazine that was the organ of a liberal religious movement, and to her I went at once. She gave me cordial welcome and told me of a quiet and pleasant street within easy walking distance of the heart of the city where she thought I could find an inexpensive furnished room, and we had a friendly talk that was warming and cheering to my heart. But she knew next to nothing of general journalistic conditions except that there was a woman doing work of one sort or another on almost every daily or weekly paper in Boston. I soon found a pleasant furnished room in the locality of which she told me, had my trunk sent from the station, bought a few things in cans out of which I intended to get my meals until I should find a job and have an income. Then, ready for whatever might come, I went to present Mrs. Starrett's letter to Miss Lilian Whiting, who was on the staff of the *Boston Traveler*, writing for it art and literary criticism and feature articles, chiefly about the interests and activities of women, and attending to any other matters put into her hands. She also sent a weekly letter on literary, artistic, social and general matters to a Cincinnati newspaper of importance.

I found her to be a young woman of about my own age, very eager about many of the things that interested me, and we became good friends. She received me cordially and gave me much information that I greatly needed about journalistic conditions in Boston, especially about the attitude of the newspapers toward women. Every newspaper in Boston, she told me, had realized that it needed a woman on its staff to deal with the many important activities of women — their clubs, organizations, meetings, movements of various kinds — which gave them many women readers who wanted these matters reported promptly and adequately. But, she added, on every paper of standing, every one on which I would want to work, the position was already filled. Therefore she advised me to submit articles to the editors of various papers, and whenever I landed anything to follow it up with something else as soon as possible, and thus perhaps I could work my way, after a while, into something permanent. And, of course, the woman already on some paper might get ill, or die, or go away, and then I could apply at once for her position, and would have this published work to show what I could do.

The advice seemed good and I hurried home to set to work on it. The information I had collected in Chicago — by-product of my work for the David Cook establishment — on legislation during the previous year by the several states on temperance and measures connected with the feminist movement seemed promising, and I classified it by states and worked it up into two articles, one on each subject. I took them to the *Boston Herald*, where an assistant editor read them while I waited and said he would take the one on temperance legislation but did not want the other. They would publish it soon, he assured me, and would pay me ten dollars for it after publication. Much elated, I went home, my mind brimming with ideas and plans, and a few days later took to the same editor a short piece I had written about what Boston meant to young people who came to the historic city, eager for all it could give them and hopeful of opportunity for work they longed to do. He read and accepted it at once, and it appeared a few days later; for that I was paid two dollars and fifty cents. The money seemed too precious to be spent — my first triumph in the city of my dreams! — but my necessities were too urgent for indulgence in sentiment and it went the way of all money. My long article, however, did not appear, and after two or three weeks I went to the *Herald* and made inquiry concerning it. The editor who had accepted it seemed rather blank about the matter and inclined to deny having ever seen it. But I stood my ground and reminded him of several little incidents connected with his reading and acceptance of the manuscript, and finally he recalled the transaction and asked me to wait while he looked for the article. After a long time he told me he could not find it, and that evidently it had been misplaced and lost.

"In that case," I said, "of course you will pay me for it." "Certainly not," he replied decisively. "Why should we? It's of no use to us and we will not pay for it." We had a little argument about the matter, but I would not accept his contention that they were absolved from payment because it had been lost, telling him that he had accepted it, had kept it, promised to publish it very soon, made it their property, and if they had lost it I was not to blame and the money was due me just as surely as if they had printed it. Finally he conceded payment at half price, but no more. I accepted the compromise because I seriously needed the money and feared that if I refused to take half I would get nothing. I went home with the five dollars in my pocket and a heart flaming with indignation over the injustice, and over the loss of the much needed money and of whatever credit the published article might have brought me. It was my first, but far from my last, experience of the ruthless injustice to which my sex would submit me in the newspaper world. For I did not believe that he would have tried this crooked game upon me if I had been a man....

I tried again and again, one paper after another, and then tried them all over again, to find a position to do any kind of regular work, to suggest possible things I might do, or articles I might write, racking my brains and exhausting my ingenuity as day after day I tried desperately to break the deadlock into which my efforts seemed to have fallen. Every effort I made met a blank, flint-faced stone wall in which there was neither door nor hole nor crack through which I could thrust so much as a finger.

In office after office I was met by the stereotyped statement, "We don't believe in women in journalism," uttered with an air of finality that evidently was intended to destroy all hope in any skirted applicant. Sometimes an editor, possessed of the authority to make the statement weighty, would say, "I don't believe," etc., thereby seeming to make the situation still further beyond hope, or a milder-minded one would throw responsibility upon his superiors and quote publisher or managing editor as being utterly opposed to women in newspaper offices, the implication being that such was their position and that therefore any further effort on my part was entirely useless. Sometimes I tried to discover what mental processes had led to their conclusion. I was told that the men in a newspaper office didn't want women around, and that a woman was practically useless in journalism anyway because there was so little she could do. If I asked for specifications of some of the things she couldn't do I always received the same reply, that you couldn't send a woman to a fire, that she would be quite useless if sent on such an assignment and, since there were times when a city editor had to concentrate all his staff on such an event a woman would just be in the way.

Another stone wall against which I was forever butting my head was the conviction universally held by managing editors that a woman did not have the physical strength to withstand the steady, hard pull of newspaper work; that she would be made ill by it so much of the time that she would be of little use to the paper. If I countered by telling the editor that my health was good and that during the four years of my college work I had never missed a day, he would reply with grim and conclusive emphasis that no woman could stand up under the steady grind of a newspaper office, that women did not have the mental ability to be of more than limited value on a newspaper and that it was useless to bother with them when there were plenty of men who were more competent.

But the newspaper editors of that time must not be judged by the very different mental attitudes of half a century later. They were representatives of the ideas then almost universally held, the voices of their own time; and if the desires and ambitions of any young woman led her to challenge those ideas and to try to do battle with them in their strongest entrenchments, inevitably she would have a hard road to travel. . . .

It was not only a hard and perilous road, but also it could end in only one or the other of two possibilities. Either, I knew, I must accept defeat and retreat from the siege I was making of the stone walls of entrenched conservatism, or I must keep on butting my head against those walls in the hope of finally cracking the surface or of wakening from the other side some welcoming response. The thought of accepting defeat and retreating never once entered my mind as I kept up my efforts all through that lovely late summer and early autumn of 1881, diligently making new assaults and renewing old ones against the stone walls. But all that time, also, I was enjoying to the depths of my heart the possibilities I found in Boston. I loved its crooked old streets with all their memories of events and days of high historic moment, and I could not see enough of the Common, with its lawns and elm trees so serene and stately, and the beautiful Public Garden beside it. Thrilling to every memory, I explored Faneuil Hall, Bunker Hill, and the Old North Church and its tower, looking from its windows and imagining Paul Revere pacing the opposite shore and watching them with anxious eyes. In its ancient cemetery I found enough quaint and curious relics of past days to fill many an hour.

...In October my good friend, Mrs. Annie Diggs, came from Lawrence to spend the winter in Boston. She had very little money, and she proposed that we find a large room that we could share, with the privilege of a little cooking in the kitchen, where she would prepare our meals, and we could divide the expense. I told her that I was at the end of my resources, my income inadequate and precarious and my prospects not at all good, and that until I could earn my share of such an arrangement I would not undertake the plan lest I add to her financial burden. But she so encouraged me by her cheerful and complete confidence that I would soon be on my feet, and so warmly insisted that in the meantime I must let her share with me what she had, that her faith in me won my consent. We found a large and pleasant room adequately furnished for our needs, whose landlady was willing for us to do what cooking was necessary in her big basement kitchen; and there we lived happily and comfortably through the winter until Mrs. Diggs returned to Lawrence in the spring. Soon after we made this arrangement, my father unexpectedly sent me a small sum of money — not much, but enough to tide us over immediate difficulties. I had not asked him for help and my family did not know what straits I was in, so I suspected that my mother, anxious about me, with a mother's brooding care, had persuaded him to relax by so much his determination to withhold all aid and comfort for what he considered my wild-goose chasing. I deeply and warmly appreciated his help in a time of need far greater than he knew; but for the loyal and generous friendship of my friend, Mrs. Diggs, I felt that I owed lifelong gratitude, and such gratitude still flames brightly in my heart for the steady and continued helping hand in a hard place. For I had come to the point where, if I ate, even meagerly, I could not pay for a roof over my head; and if I kept the roof in place I could not eat. But her generous offer made it possible for me to go on trying, with the surety behind me of home and food, understanding, encouragement, and a friendship firmly based on mutual liking, regard and a wide and varied circle of intellectual interests.

In mid-November Lilian Whiting told me she had heard that the *Globe* had decided to have a woman on its staff, and advised me to apply at once for the position if I thought I would care to work on that paper. I cannot now recall whether or not I had previously tried to open the door of the *Globe*, but it is possible I had not because of the attitude toward it of all the people I had met. Miss Whiting, for whose opinion I held high respect because she had won success, had counseled me against it, telling me it would be useless and that the reputation of the paper was such that for me to work on it or do anything for it would injure any chance I might have in other newspaper offices, while everyone I knew always spoke of the paper slightingly, as if it were beneath the notice of any reputable person. If I had not thus paid attention to the judgment of others it is possible that I might have secured the position before I did.

The managing editor prefaced his interview with me with the plain and emphatic statement that Colonel Taylor — owner and publisher of the *Globe* — did not believe in women in journalism, that he had always been opposed, and was still, to having a woman in the office. But he had decided that a woman was needed in order to carry out his ideas as he wanted them treated and therefore they were going to hire a woman for the first time since the paper had come under his ownership. Especially, he emphasized, they wanted a woman to do millinery openings. They had tried all the men on the staff, one after another, and not one of them could handle the work acceptably. Did I think I could do it as it should be done? I told him I was sure I could, and he went on to say that they had decided to pay more attention to the interests of women and would want me to prepare a woman's column every week for the Sunday issue. Could I do that? Again I assured him that I could, and that this would be directly in my line because I was much interested in women's activities. I would also be expected, he told me, to do some reporting of various kinds. Had I done anything of that sort? I told him briefly of my rather varied but limited experience as a reporter, and by that time his impression of me — for he had been observing me keenly all through the interview — seemed to decide him to launch another question, which evidently he had been holding back until he could find out something about me. "We also need," he went on impressively, "an art critic. We have no one on the paper who knows anything about art, and we can't get the advertising of the art galleries unless we pay attention to art matters. Can you do art criticism? Do you know anything about art?"

While I was in Chicago a few paintings by an artist well known at that time had been exhibited in a jewelry store — as far as I know, there were then no art galleries in that city — and I had spent an absorbed and deeply interested hour studying them. But they were the only oil paintings I had ever seen until after my arrival in Boston. My heart went down with a dull thump into my boots. But I had to have that job. It was the first possibility that had opened before me during all my three months in Boston and there was not likely to be another. It was this job or nothing, and I had to have it. So I swallowed hard, looked at him composedly and said, yes, I knew something about art and was sure I could handle the work.

And so I went out of the office with the bargain concluded and the instruction to report for work the next Monday morning. I remained on the *Globe* for three years and left it then for reasons of my own which will appear in due place in this narrative. I could have stayed there indefinitely had I so wished. My salary was to be ten dollars a week. Nowadays that seems an impossibly trifling sum for a newspaper to offer as weekly salary. But money was then worth in buying power two or three times its present-day value and it was not, I think, an unusual sum to be given as a beginning salary to a new and untried reporter. At any rate, to me just then the prospect of ten sure dollars every week was like having the key to a treasure house. I could and did live on it pleasantly and comfortably, although very economically and narrowly, until I was able to add a little now and then from other sources.

At first my work included some reporting, inconsequent little happenings worth no more than ten or a dozen lines each, mere matters of trivial routine upon which I was being tried out. At once I planned and started the weekly column of special interest to women, which I discovered, much to my surprise, Colonel Taylor wanted to make a distinctive feature. I was to learn, a little later, that he had decided on imparting to the *Globe* a strong general appeal to women readers and that this column for women was to be a special point of the drive. It dawned on me then that he had decided to have a woman on the staff because he had discovered that he would have to do so to make such an appeal successful, and that the absurd excuse given me by the managing editor, that they wanted a woman to do millinery openings, was merely a face-saving gesture. Colonel Taylor would not retire from his position of not believing in women in journalism, and therefore it was desirable that the woman he was adding to his staff should not be encouraged to think that she was of any real consequence to the paper. But the millinery openings continued to be a regular part of my duties until, more than a year later, another woman was added to the staff to release me from these and other matters for more important work. And I recall that from the start I made a special effort with the openings, dressed them up a bit in unusual descriptions and tried to make them readable. My method seemed to be liked, and I learned long afterward that it was that kind of thing that Colonel Taylor was searching for, a fresh and unusual presentation of everyday things, so that readers would turn to his paper for sprightly and entertaining style in its account of ordinary happenings....

I chose as the standing title of my woman's column, "The Woman's Hour," a phrase I had taken bodily from an incisive sentence, "The woman's hour has struck," in a recent speech by a member of the state legislature which had attracted much attention and been widely discussed. An introductory half column or more was always somewhat editorial in character, discussing some question, happening or personality that was timely and of consequence to women, while following this were clippings, condensations, paragraphs, brevities, the whole filling a column and a half or more. My aim was always to diversify the column and give it a great variety of interests. It made an instant hit among the readers it was meant to reach. The wife of the legislator who had made the speech from which the title was taken came to the office to see me and tell me how much she and her husband appreciated the compliment to him and his speech in my title and introductory article, and cordially wished me every success. As she was a prominent feminist, I was pleased and found stimulus and encouragement in the long talk we had together. Of more immediate consequence was the fact that the managing editor liked the title and layout of my woman's column and approved the method of treatment — which meant, of course, that "the colonel" was, at least, not displeased. I kept up this feature during the entire time of my work on the *Globe*, never missing a Sunday and always preparing copy for one week or more in advance if I were away for a week or two. For the powers above me were insistent that it should never be allowed to drop out, even for one issue.

After the first few months I did not do much reporting, and after the first two or three weeks the character of the assignments given me became more important....

[T]he work of most importance and value that I did for the *Globe* was, I think, my editorial writing. I made my way into it very easily and very soon. Although it had been so difficult to make an opening there, and the sentiment of both publisher and staff had been so strong against taking a woman into the office, I found that, after I did get inside, any door that I wanted to open yielded readily to my touch. One of the small jobs to which I was at once assigned was to prepare every Saturday for use in the Sunday issue two or three columns of social news composed of short paragraphs clipped or condensed or rewritten from items in city and suburban papers or turned in by members of the staff concerning social personalities or happenings, along with any sort of flotsam and jetsam I might collect that would give variety and interest to the page. The second week I was there I ventured, just as an experiment, to write several editorial paragraphs and scatter them through the copy. Sunday morning I looked eagerly to see what had happened to them and my heart sank when I could not find even one anywhere in the social columns. Sadly disappointed and much discouraged by the conviction that they had been tossed into the wastebasket, I went on reading the paper. Presently, when I turned to the editorial page, there I saw my paragraphs, all of them, honorably disposed in that exalted company!

My heart sang for joy all the rest of the day, and on Monday morning I hastened to ask the managing editor if he would like me to write more editorial paragraphs. He said he would be glad to see anything I wanted to turn in. After that the path was straight and broad and I trod it diligently, at first with paragraphs and then with editorial articles, both short and long. Within six months I was relieved of the social page duties and of all reportorial work, with the exception of occasional special matters which it was considered desirable for me to take care of, and was working regularly and chiefly, save for the attention devoted to art and feminist matters, on the editorial page.

My paragraphs were especially liked and I was never able to furnish as many of them as the managing editor wanted. In my youth I had a sense of humor and I was also inclined to be mildly irreverent toward many things which those mid-Victorian days stodgily accepted, and when these two were combined in a brief paragraph of a sentence or two the result was likely to be the kind of thing Colonel Taylor wanted — although I did not then know this was his policy — to give pungency and piquancy to his editorial page and to make people chuckle and say to one another, "Did you see so-and-so in the *Globe* this morning?" I never could convince my superiors that paragraphs, like poets, are born, not made, and that, as Balzac makes one of his characters say about love, "like a belief in the immaculate conception, it comes or it doesn't come." If it came it leaped from my pen, all complete and finished, like Minerva from the head of Jove; and if it didn't come, to sit and rack my brains and try to coax one out was useless....

I was deeply earnest and very ambitious about the editorial part of my work, for it was the kind of newspaper writing which I believed I could do best and which I most enjoyed doing, and I wanted to advance in it to a responsible, important, well-paid position. So I gave all the study I could to such matters as they came up, especially those that were controversial, as most of them were, trying to inform myself as to the merits of their different aspects, their history, background, significance, in order to be able to write about them with understanding and authority....

After my first year the chief editorial writer was Allen Kelly, who had been on the editorial staff for two years or more before I joined it, and had been advanced to that position when the chief writer left the paper. Consequently, I became his principal and, most of the time, only assistant. Between us for almost two years, until he left the paper, we wrote most of the two to three columns of editorial matter that the paper ran every day. If one of us was away for a day or two or longer, the other took up the responsibility and struggled with the added work as best he could, although the managing editor usually called in some other member of the staff to help out on such occasions. But it was still rather grilling work and demanded long hours and steady attention. Nevertheless, I was always quite willing to accept the responsibility and the increased work, and I rejoiced in them because they meant to me perfect surety that my work was wholly competent and acceptable, and I hoped that before long this would be recognized by increased and adequate salary and that acknowledgment of my competence which would have been given to a man in my position. As the *Globe* appeared every morning and as its editorials had to be fresh and up-to-date with news developments, we two editorial writers both worked seven days a week until, after a few months, I suggested that we alternate on Sunday duty at the office. With a little forethought and extra work we could have enough good and timely stuff left over on the galleys to enable the one on duty to take care of the page for Monday easily and without having to stay all day. For many months, therefore, I had full charge on alternate Sundays of the editorial page for the next day. Usually the managing editor was not there, although he sometimes came in for a little while Sunday afternoon or evening. That was why I happened to be alone in the office on a Sunday in the spring of 1884 when General Benjamin F. Butler announced a sensational decision that was of national consequence, of first-class interest to the people of Massachusetts and of very great importance to the *Boston Globe*. And thereby hangs a tale, a tale which makes it necessary to explain, to a generation that barely knows his name, the significance of General Butler to that period.

In the time of which I write he had struggled and fought for a dozen years to be governor of Massachusetts. In the meantime he had spent several terms in Congress, where he had kept himself rather constantly and always turbulently in the public eye. He was a man of very real ability and a capable administrator, while his endowment of mental alertness and keenness, energy, resourcefulness and audacity was very high. He had also a witty and a ruthless tongue. As a criminal lawyer for forty years, he had won both fame and fortune and had schooled his naturally unprincipled mind in all the devious and complicated ways of the criminal law. During the Civil War he had accomplished some important things and had filled capably some difficult positions, all of it to the accompaniment of such controversies, angry recriminations and scandals as still makes malodorous whatever memories are left of him. After it was over his desire for public office was strong and determined, and he hoped to open a path that would lead to the presidency.

Elected in 1882 on the Democratic ticket to the highest office in the great state of Massachusetts, he began at once to put himself prominently, actively and spectacularly in the public eye. To that end he set about overhauling the public charitable institutions of the state and endeavoring to show that they were being run unscrupulously, dishonestly and to the accompaniment of atrociously evil practices. Some of the details his investigations brought forth belonged in the class "not fit to print" and a few papers indignantly refused to print them, but most of the Boston papers did publish them, although only a few did so in full. How much credence they deserved nobody ever knew. His followers asserted they were entirely true and his opponents declared there was no truth in them. The clamor rose high and shrill and General Butler disported himself actively in his beloved spotlight. All Massachusetts except the Butler following, which was hilarious, groaned in horror, dismay and furious humiliation. Harvard University, whose gracious custom it was to give the final touch of honor to the governor of the state by bestowing upon him, with all the accompaniment of high ceremonial dignity, its most important honorary degree, announced that it would that year withhold the award. And Governor Butler, informed of the decision, was instant with his famous retort: "Harvard University? Ah, yes! We hung one of their professors not long ago!"

His reference was to the trial and execution, thirty years before but famous to this day in criminal annals and their popular accounts, of Professor Webster who in a moment of savage anger killed Dr. Parkman and concealed his body in a vat of chemicals. No one supposed for a moment, and the authorities of Harvard least of all, that after this slight the governor would attend Commencement. But the situation was very much to Ben Butler's liking. With full military escort in all the gold lace and brass buttons, pomp and display that could be mustered, he rode in stately dignity across the Charles River to Cambridge and the commencement exercises, and was the center of curiosity and observation throughout the function. He did not receive the accustomed honor, but he "stole the show" of Commencement Day, and his exploit dominated the newspaper accounts of the affair.

Although he was not re-elected for a second term as governor, his one term was filled with excitement and bitter controversy induced by his investigations of the state's charitable institutions, especially that of the Tewksbury Almshouse, which produced particularly noisome results. My own personal conviction about the matter was that probably the institutions needed an overhauling, for apparently they had been run for a long time in a rather irresponsible way. But Ben Butler had a crooked mind, trained in crookedness; and if there was a crooked, disreputable way of reaching a worthy objective he would take it in preference to one that was straight and justifiable.

The *Globe* had been supporting General Butler for some time before his election as governor and continued its support afterward, although with moderation and a measure of independence sufficient to warrant its leaving him at any time it might wish to do so. It was a Democratic paper and the governor had been elected as the head of the Democratic state ticket, and therefore Colonel Taylor was keeping his paper in line with the state organization of his party. He had also other reasons of his own for upholding General Butler to an extent that was always a little uncertain, since thus he was carrying out his policy of attracting attention to his paper and setting people to talking about it. For he had found that to defend Butler, even mildly, was a sure way to reach this end.

In the early spring of 1884 General Butler announced his willingness to become the candidate for the presidency of the new Anti-Monopoly and Greenback party. The announcement appeared in the Sunday morning papers of a Sunday that found me in charge of the editorial page of the *Globe*. The managing editor had told us that he was not coming in that day, and Colonel Taylor, I chanced to know, was out of the city for the day. The only person on the editorial staff who was in the building was the news editor. I knew we ought to have an editorial on Butler's announcement because it was far and away the biggest piece of news, both nationally and for Massachusetts, that had happened in many a day. For there were such rumblings of discontent all over the country as might well presage the rising of a politico-economic storm, and in that case Butler might be able to ride it into the White House. The development, I knew, would have to be treated with the greatest caution; Butler's announcement must be taken seriously and with friendliness, but without in the least committing the paper to his support. There was no one to consult, and so I wrote for the next morning's leader an article that seemed to me to take a wise and careful view of the matter, asked the news editor what he thought about it and, when he said that as far as he could tell it sounded all right, sent it to the composing room and went home.

Apparently my editorial simply went into the hopper along with my other copy, and so, thinking it must have been all right since no one had been displeased by it, I dropped it from my mind and went on with my daily work. But some weeks later I learned what had been its aftermath. A friendly acquaintance in the business office told me that when Colonel Taylor arrived on Monday morning his usually stern, immobile face was beaming with gratification and he wanted to know at once who wrote the Butler editorial. While someone went to get the information, he said that he had been anxious about the matter after he saw the Sunday papers but this editorial had dealt with it in exactly the right way, and he wanted to know who had made such a good job of it. My informant said that when he was told that "Miss Finch wrote it," his countenance fell instantly into stony lines, his mouth snapped shut and he turned on his heel and walked into his private office without another word. Colonel Taylor could not forget that he "didn't believe in women in journalism."

I have told this incident at some length partly because it is vividly illustrative of the spirit of the times, which not only was vigorously opposed to any attempt by women to do unusual things, but even more violently objected to their success when they did; but I have related it especially because it helped me to a decision that made a turning point in my career. For it let me know that I had gone as far as I could on the *Globe*. For more than a year I had worked without increase of my initial salary of ten dollars a week; then it had been raised to fifteen dollars. I had also developed several small sources of outside income — a connection as Boston correspondent of an art journal in New York City, a weekly bit of work for *The Woman's Journal* and an occasional chance piece of writing that came my way — and these brought to my scanty purse enough to enable me to live more comfortably than at first, but not yet enough to enable me to save anything or even to utilize as I ought the advantages Boston offered.

The injustice of my situation stung me to the quick. Viewing my work objectively and with all modesty, I knew that it was quite as good and as important as that of my men colleagues, and that it was more varied and more difficult than that of most of them. But there was not one of them but was paid twice, or more than twice, as much as I. Recently I had asked for an increase which had been refused, although the *Globe* by that time was firmly on its financial feet and its circulation and prosperity were rapidly increasing. So now I knew, with this new proof of Colonel Taylor's immutable prejudice, that there was no possibility of greater reward or further advancement on the *Globe*. As the work was all anonymous, what I did there would add nothing to my journalistic reputation.

My thoughts began to turn toward New York City as perhaps holding better possibilities than Boston, where I was familiar enough with the newspaper field to know that it offered nothing better than I already had. I decided that I must make a change of some sort, for to continue the work I was doing at such niggardly, inadequate and unjust payment was most unwise. The stone walls had been penetrated far enough that the work I wanted to do was permitted and accepted, but not far enough that it was acknowledged and given its just financial reward. But it seemed the [better] part of wisdom to keep my purpose to myself for the present, to look into the situation in New York and to try to save some money against the venture. . . .

When I began work on the *Globe*, the few Boston people I knew all turned compassionate eyes upon me. When I told them how happy I was to have got a job at last they were sympathetic and rejoiced with me, but, they would add, how unfortunate it couldn't have been on the *Transcript!* For the *Globe* was then in strong disfavor with "the better classes" of Boston who considered it a rowdy, disreputable sort of paper, and connection with it a discredit to anyone, especially a woman. This was largely due to its politics. For it was a Democratic organ, though it was never hidebound in its allegiance and was inclined, more or less, toward independence and liberalism. And the "better classes" of that day in Boston being, almost to the last man, convinced of the deep-dyed iniquity of anything bearing the Democratic label, a Democratic newspaper was something that no respectable person ought to read, or touch, or have anything to do with. The few friends and acquaintances I had made were sure that I would have to associate with a low, rowdyish, disreputable lot of men in the *Globe* office, and they made me feel very apprehensive as to the surroundings I would have on my new job, overjoyed though I was to have it and determined to succeed in it; and I was grateful to find that they did not allow their contempt of the paper to interfere with the friendliness and interest they had so kindly accorded to me personally.

But I soon found that my office associates were as pleasant, wellbred and agreeable a lot of young and slightly older men as one would be likely to meet in newspaper or business offices anywhere. Among them were many recent college graduates, mainly from Harvard and Yale, and to these were added a few more every year. Apparently this was a part of Colonel Taylor's carefully planned scheme of building up his paper, feeding into it steadily young blood with the wider horizons and the better trained minds of college youth, and endeavoring to identify them, if they made good in the work, with its interests and possibilities. It was an astute policy, for most of those I knew stayed with the *Globe* all their working years and rose to the highest positions on its staff. During my time the whole fourth floor, both editorial and news staffs, was ebullient with the blithe, high spirits of youth. But that did not interfere in the least with the very considerable quantities of work, most of it of excellent quality, which everyone turned out. Toward me, not once did any of my associates ever show anything but respect, regard and good fellowship, and never once, not even at first, did anyone ever intimate to me that I was unwelcome. Nevertheless, I knew that I was unwelcome at the start, from what the managing editor had told me when I applied for the position and from what some of them admitted to me afterward. But among them I was to find some of the best friends of my whole life, and also my marriage mate, whose mother gleefully told me, when we became engaged, that he had been one of the most bitterly opposed of the whole staff to my advent.

A very few times it happened that one or another of the reporters, among whom were a good many who did belong to the ruder sort, forgot his good manners when he did not know that I was within hearing or did not realize that I could not avoid knowledge of his actions. But invariably afterwards, when he realized that I might have been made uncomfortable by his misbehavior, he was abjectly miserable in his contrition and made or sent to me profuse apologies. I recall an afternoon when I was working late and was alone in the editorial offices except for two men at the news desk in the middle room. I heard them greet someone coming in and was conscious of their voices in low conversation. Presently I was aware of someone coming into my own room and, looking up, I saw a tall young man from the city staff with whom I had a pleasant but casual acquaintance. He was blushing a bright red to his ear tips and at once began a painfully embarrassed, fumbling apology — hoped I hadn't heard what he said in the news room yesterday — didn't know I was there — was awfully sorry when he learned I was, and so on, looking more abject and miserable with every word. I cast down my eyes for a moment while my thoughts went flashing around the situation, trying to think what I could say to him. For I had heard him, and his language had been, to put it very mildly, extremely unprintable. But I could not let him know that I had heard. Scarcely knowing what I was going to say and desperately hoping inspiration would come, I looked up at him blankly and innocently and asked, with what I hoped would pass for guileless curiosity, and with emphasis on the "did," "What did you say?" He gasped and his face went several shades redder, and then a look of relief came over it and his embarrassment left him as my question made him feel sure that I had not heard a word of his talk. Shaking my head in response to his gulped, "You didn't hear?" I promptly seized the moment and with a casual, "Oh, by the way," began to ask him about some matter he had recently reported in which I was interested. We chatted about it for a few minutes and he went away relieved and happy, and never again did he repeat his misstep.

I had never been accustomed to tobacco smoke at home or anywhere else, and when I entered the *Globe* office it was rather unpleasant to me. But I decided at once that no one was to know this, and that, since I was going as a sort of interloper into a domain men considered especially their own, I would do nothing and say nothing that would interfere with their usual habits and customs. To those of my friends and acquaintances who told me, as most of them did — for that was the mid-Victorian age and they were merely voicing one of its dearest tenets — that I ought to insist on the respect due a lady, I replied, "If I can not by merely being myself win their respect and courtesy, I shall deserve what I get." So I ignored tobacco smoke, and within a day or two every man in the office had asked me courteously, "Does this smoke annoy you, Miss Finch?" and I had replied smilingly, "No, not at all! Please go right on and smoke all you want to, for I don't mind in the least." I noted with inner amusement that the oftener I gave this assurance the more pressing was their desire to know if I was quite sure I didn't care, some of them even venturing to say they wouldn't smoke if it was unpleasant to me. But that did not impress me, for I was sure they were merely betting on what they believed to be a sure thing. And wild horses could not have drawn from me the admission that tobacco smoke did, at first, make me a bit dizzy, nauseated and headachey, although I soon grew accustomed to it and really did not mind it at all.

One of the men in our little editorial room who wrote a daily column of short, snappy paragraphs titled, "Slings and Arrows," smoked a pipe that must surely have served Noah in the Ark and had never been cleaned since the flood. He was the constant subject of gibes and protests from the other men in the room because of the vile odor of his ancient pipe, and they accused him of smoking in it old rubbers, boot heels and decayed onions, though they could win from him nothing but smiling retorts. Sometimes, when they were unusually scathing in their comments, he would ask me if I found his pipe disagreeable and offer to get a new one if I did. Secretly I quite agreed with the other men about his malodorous pipe and tobacco, but I kept to the rule I had made at the beginning and always told him that I didn't mind his pipe at all and anyway my desk was right beside the window and the wind blew all the smoke the other way.

As soon as my first summer on the *Globe* began to heat the atmosphere of Boston I thought it advisable to deal with the matter of coats in the office, as I had already done with that of feet on desks. I said to them that a newspaper office was not a drawing room but a place where people had to work hard and needed to be as comfortable as possible, and that I had no objection at all to coats off on hot days, or any other time, or to feet on their desks when they were tired.

During the latter part of my stay on the *Globe* I was away for a month's vacation, visiting my family in Kansas, and I told a young woman who had been added to the city staff that if she liked she could occupy my desk during my absence. When I returned I found several signs in large letters, "Smoking Not Allowed," pasted over the sides of my desk and asked one of my colleagues what had happened. With many chuckles he told me that the young woman had promptly taken a firm stand on smoking, announcing at once that it must be stopped. But, he said, they had not been impressed, and then she had had the composing room print these signs and she had pasted them on the desk in very plain sight. The result, he went on, was that the moment she came into the room, even as soon as they heard her coming, every man there lighted up pipe or cigar, even if he didn't want to smoke at the moment, and puffed away for dear life, until the air was blue. Similarly, he added, she had at the start banned coats off and feet off the floor, and so they had made it a point of honor to take off their coats when she was in the room, whether or not they were too warm, and to put their feet on their desks whenever their work permitted.

In the spring of 1884 our Mr. Soames ... left the *Globe* and went to the *Morning Telegram* of Troy, New York, to be managing editor. He told me he had intended to ask me to go with him as editorial writer, to take full charge of the editorial page, but that he had had to give up the plan because the publisher and owner of the paper, State Senator Charles A. MacArthur, was violently opposed to permitting a woman in the office and had said point blank that he wouldn't have it. He added that he had especially wanted me because of the paragraphs and "unique" editorials I wrote, but was taking Allen Kelly for the position, and that he wrote so well, so vigorously and so interestingly that he hoped "the old man" would be satisfied with his work and he would stay a long time. But "the old man," he put in a bit doubtfully, was cantankerous and very few people could get along with him.

As the days passed that spring and summer I grew more and more dissatisfied with my position on the *Globe*, which showed no prospect of improving economically or in recognition of the value of my work. When Allen Kelly left I applied for the position he had held as chief editorial writer, stressing the fact that for many months I had had charge of the editorial page on alternate Sundays and citing some of the many important leading editorials I had written. I took it for granted that an advance in position would automatically carry an advance in salary. My request was courteously but very definitely turned down, but with the assurance that in recognition of my services the *Globe* would be glad to do for me anything it could. Promptly I asked for an increase of salary and was told that this was at present impossible. At once I decided that I would leave the paper as soon as I could make it possible. My thoughts and desires at once turned to New York City as a desirable change of field. I knew that in Boston there was little likelihood of an opening that would in any way better my position, while in New York not only would the newspaper field be larger and probably less bound in prejudice, but also there would be much better opportunity for free lance work. And as a cultural center the city by the Hudson already gave signs that it would soon outstrip Boston in the race for preeminence. It did not take me long to decide that to New York City I would go as soon as I could add a little more to the small sum of money I had saved during recent months.

With late summer, when I began to consider the wisdom of handing in my resignation within a few weeks, Allen Kelly returned and took up again his old position on the *Globe*, having had enough of Troy, the *Telegram* and Senator MacArthur, and glowing with interest in a plan he was working on for establishing a weekly paper of his own in some town not far from Boston. On a hot and sultry afternoon after his return he said to me that he thought we had the editorial page well provided for and didn't I think it would be pleasanter canoeing up the Charles River than working in the office. I had nothing on hand that had to be attended to that day, so I said I could easily take the rest of the afternoon off and we soon were paddling up the Charles in the shade of the fine trees that lined its banks.

A summer shower darkened the sky and we drew up beside a thick clump of trees and found shelter from the pelting rain under their branches. We talked of his scheme for a newspaper of his own and of my intention to leave the *Globe* very soon, and he suggested that I join him as a partner in his project. I laughed at the idea and said I would prefer to make my newspaper experiments in a city. Suddenly becoming gravely serious he wanted to know if, anyway, we couldn't make it a partnership for life. After due consideration, lasting several days, I said I thought we could — sometime — but not yet — there was much I wanted to do first.

A little later Mr. Soames came over from Troy to find another editorial writer to fill the vacancy and when I told him I intended to leave the *Globe* very soon and go to New York City, he offered to me the place on the *Telegram*. I asked what about Senator MacArthur and his embattled front against a woman in the office, and he laughed and assured me he had made it all right with the Senator and the way was clear if I really intended to quit the *Globe*. But, he added, he would have to make the offer a tentative one and engage me for two weeks on trial, the situation to be permanent if I gave satisfaction. The proviso annoyed me, because I knew that had I been a man, my work on the *Globe*, with which Mr. Soames was thoroughly familiar, would have been amply sufficient to warrant my unconditional engagement. He agreed with me but said it was the best bargain he could make because of the Senator's prejudice against women, and I consented to think about it and let him know the next day. I did not feel sure about Mr. Mac-Arthur's conversion and neither did Allen Kelly when I talked the matter over with him. Accordingly, he wired to Arthur MacArthur, the Senator's son, associated with him in the ownership and management of the paper, who replied that he had authorized Mr. Soames to make the offer.

I had no misgivings about being able to make good and win through to the permanent position, but the condition nettled me and I had to argue the matter with myself, reminding myself that the prejudice against women was still so strong that we must take things as they were, prove our fitness, make ourselves welcome under existing conditions, be realists and accept our handicaps and not grumble about them, or we would get nothing. And there would be a considerable increase — ten dollars a week — over the salary I was getting on the *Globe*, or was likely to get there for a long time, and would be the same — twenty-five dollars a week — that would be offered to any man. There was keen satisfaction in knowing that it would give me economic equality and I realized that there would be professional prestige in the position, since I was to have full charge of the editorial page, which would probably be of some advantage to me when I should, later on, try my luck in New York City. For thither I still intended to go, at some later date. So I told Mr. Soames I would go as soon as I could arrange for my departure from the *Globe*, and handed in my resignation. Nor did I omit to remind the managing editor of his insistences when I applied for the position that newspaper work was too hard for women, who would be of little use in an office because they would be ill so much of the time, and to call his attention to the fact that in three years I had not missed a day because of illness, while there wasn't a man on the staff who, during the same time, had not been kept away from the office by sickness anywhere from several days to several weeks.

It was saddening to leave the large circle of acquaintances and friends I had made in Boston whose cordial interest in me I so warmly appreciated and valued. I had come to Boston alone, friendless, almost moneyless, shabbily clothed, a crude young woman from the Western prairie, and yet had been received by everyone I met with friendliness, and if I had not been so busy I might have multiplied by many times the very considerable number of good friends I was leaving behind me.

...Long ago the conviction came to me, and has grown with every year, that a required study by all young people, both young men and young women, somewhere in high school or college, ought to be the detailed story of the long struggle for the freedom of women, because it is of the very highest consequence in the history of civilization; it illuminates as nothing else does the innate intolerance of human nature and how unhuman and evil are its works — which it is good for one's soul to realize; it shows vividly and dramatically how much we owe to those who went before us, something that is very, very good for youth always.

*D*espite the social pressures against women working outside of the home, many millions have been forced to do so for economic survival. For these women, the work options have been few and the obstacles many. In the early decades of the twentieth century, employment choices for the working class were limited to unskilled factory or farm labor, some form of domestic service, or, for the most desperate or rebellious, prostitution. In the industrialized work world both unions and employers refused to train females for skilled, better-paying jobs. For poor black women, further discrimination on the basis of race barred them from even unskilled factory jobs.

The majority of women forced to work were employed in domestic services. An estimated 1.2 million held jobs in this category, which included not only housekeepers, but maids, hotel chambermaids, and cooks, according to the 1890 census. At least 50 percent of female domestic workers were immigrants or daughters of immigrants.

Domestic service was regarded as the lowest of jobs in terms of status, pay, and skills required. In interviews with working women at the turn of the century, an overwhelming majority expressed a preference for factory work, as grueling and exploitative as it was, over domestic employment. Household servants generally worked almost twice as long per week as did women in the factories. Hours on the job were not clearly defined, and domestic servants were expected to be on call from early morning until late evening, every day of the week. Domestic workers complained that they had no time to themselves or for social activities, there was no letup from the rounds of tedious chores, and the pay was meager. In addition, many described the emotional loneliness of living in another household without being a part of the family and the sense of isolation from other workers.

These themes are poignantly illustrated in the following letters written in 1911 and 1912. The author, Aleksandra Rembieńska, immigrated to America from Poland, borrowing the money for her journey from her Aunt and Uncle Karolska in Poland. After paying the loan back to them, Aleksandra hoped to save enough from her earnings as a domestic servant to bring her brothers and sisters to America. The only relatives living in the United States at the time she wrote these letters to her family were another aunt and uncle. Although they lived nearby in Brooklyn, New York, Aleksandra lamented that she did not see them very often because of her heavy work load.

Her letters describe the drudgery and monotony of her daily routine as well as her feelings of isolation and loneliness. On one occasion she wrote, "I am in America and I do not even know whether it is America, only it seems to me as if there were only a single house in the whole world and nothing more, only walls and very few people." However depressing in its nature, her job allowed Aleksandra to be economically independent and it sustained her hope that she would be able to bring her brothers and sisters to America.

Aleksandra felt no sense of urgency about marrying. Although she described a serious suitor in America to her parents and made an effort to reassure them about the young man's character and reputation, at the same time she expressed ambivalent feelings about marriage per se. Her observation that young male immigrants had a harder time finding employment than did young female immigrants suggests that her reluctance to wed may have stemmed, in part, from a sense that such a step would complicate rather than ameliorate her economic situation.

Between 1890 and 1915 millions of immigrants settled in America, the majority from eastern and southern Europe. Their struggle for survival in the United States was especially complicated by the burdens of adjusting to a new culture and learning a new language. Absorbing new values, customs, and language proved an exhausting process, both physically and emotionally.

Cut off from her family, her culture, and her past, Aleksandra Rembieńska struggled virtually alone in the new world. As a young woman and as an immigrant she endured special hardships with her new freedom.

—— 16 ——
Aleksandra Rembieńska

BROOKLYN, N.Y., OCTOBER 14 [1911]

My Dear Family:

In the first words "Praised be Jesus Christus."...

And now, dear parents, I inform you that I am in good health, thanks to God, which I wish you also with my truest heart. And now I am on duty [a maidservant] and I do well, I have fine food, only I must work from 6 o'clock in the morning to 10 o'clock at night and I have $13 a month. And now, dear parents, I implore you don't grieve about me, thinking that I am without money. When I read those letters — because there came four letters in a single week, 2 from Auntie Karolska, 2 from you dear parents, on the same day — so when I read those letters I became very sad, that there in our country is trouble between you, my parents, and the Karolskis. Why do you mind what I say to her? She urged me to send money to her, and not to you and so I sent it to her, but not my last money, only that which I sent. I had still some 10 or 20 roubles, but I wrote intentionally to auntie [that the money I sent was my last]. And you thought, dear parents that I sent my last money away. But you know yourselves that I cannot remain without a cent, because I am in the world [among strangers]. I almost laughed about your sorrow. As it is I have spent more than 50 roubles on myself for the coming winter, and nevertheless I am not so beautifully dressed as all the others. Only I regret to spend money, I prefer to put it away rather than to buy luxurious dresses, like Olcia Kubaczówna who buys herself a new dress every week and doesn't look at money and doesn't think what can happen. She thinks only how to dress and says she does not need to think about anything more. But I am not of the same opinion; I think about my home. I have brothers and sisters and I intend to help them all to come to America. First I will take Stasia, let her hope to come in the early spring, about Easter, and let her be patient and wait. I would take her now, but in winter there is no such work as in spring. And now, dear parents, you may hope that I will send you for Christmas 10 roubles. I would not send them but, thanks to God, I have some, and I have work, so every month money comes to me. I only ask our Lord Jesus for health, and then no bad fortune will overtake me. I go dressed like a lady only I am sad, because I must remain at home and cannot go outside at all.

SOURCE: Letters of Aleksandra Rembieńska, in *The Polish Peasant in Europe and America,* by William I. Thomas and Florian Znaniecki (Reprint ed., New York: Dover Publications, 1918).

I am not far away from Uncle and Auntie Kubacz, but I cannot see them more than twice a month. Olcia is in service like me and also can see nobody more than twice a month; but she is far away, she must come on the street-car. When we meet together a young man comes directly to us. Now, dear parents, for girls there is work in America, but not for men. Mańka wrote to me a letter also and she wrote to —— that they had sent him a ship-ticket. But I once heard Mańka say [perhaps jestingly] that Aunt Julka is in the habit of having a good time with other men, and so maybe Mańka is a mischief-maker.

Now, dear parents, I write to you, that you may give nobody my address. When you receive my letter, hide it, in order that nobody may catch the address. And I request you, tell auntie not to give my address to anybody. [Why she made this request is not clear. It is possible that she did not want a former suitor in Poland to know about the marriage proposal she describes below.]

Dear parents, I am very sorry; are you indeed angry with Aunt Karolska? What is the trouble? Tell me, do you visit them? Now I beg you, there is no reason for you to be angry; you can call on them, and I will be more than glad to hear that you are not angry.

And now, dear parents, I will write you that I have an opportunity to be married. I have a fine boy, because uncle and auntie have known him for 3 years. He is good, not a drunkard, he does not swear, as others often do. From him I have not yet heard a single bad word or oath; he has not this habit. I don't know whether I shall marry this year or not — just as you advise me, my parents. He wishes that it may be now, and he begs uncle and auntie because he is boarding with them. I don't like in him that he is as small as Antek Łada. He is pretty, that is true. Wait a little; for Christmas we will send you a photograph; then you will see him. As to what I wrote about your photograph, you need not send it, because it will be very expensive. And now, dear parents, I beg you so very much, let nobody learn that I am going to be married and that I have a young man. Let only my family [yourselves] know everything, no other people, neither brothers nor sisters. I beg you, let nobody know what I wrote in this letter. Say only "She wrote nothing; all's well," and let that be all. Don't say anything about this matter. And when I send the photograph, hide it also, please, so that nobody may see it.

And now I have nothing more to write, and I bow to you, dear family, and I wish you every good. May God grant that this letter finds you in good health, and I ask you for a quick answer....

Aleksandra Rembieńska

And I request you, dear parents, send letters with stamps, because I have great difficulties. A letter with a stamp arrives sooner.

O Dear Family [Parents],

I write this letter to you on November 20, and I got your letter on November 20, and I begin this letter with the words [usual greeting].

And now, dear family, I inform you that I am in good health, thanks to our Lord God, and I wish to you also happiness, health, and good success. And now, dear family, I let you know that in October I did not work for two weeks because I did not like to work for nothing, and I left this place because they wouldn't pay me more than $12. And now I am in another place, only far away from uncle, for it is necessary to travel an hour to uncle; but uncle comes to meet me every second Sunday. I am well enough, I receive now $16 for this month. I don't feel lonesome, because there are two of us girls in this household. The master and mistress are Polish. We are near a church and they send us every Sunday at 6 o'clock in the morning to the mass. We have every day 18 rooms to clean, and to cook and to wash linen. It is myself who wash every week about 300 pieces of linen, and iron it. But I have easy washing because I don't wash with my hands; the machine washes alone, I only cover the linen with soap and put 5 pieces into the machine at once. After 15 minutes I take them out and put in new ones, and so by noon I wash all the 300 pieces. I iron 4 days, from 6 [A.M.] to 8 P.M. I do nothing but iron for those 4 days. Dear parents, you admonish me so severely to be on my guard. But I cannot and do not walk about the city. I cannot even go out before the house for a while. I am in America and I do not even know whether it is America, only it seems to me as if there were only a single house in the whole world and nothing more, only walls and very few people. Now you ask about this young man about whom I wrote, whether he is a Catholic. Well, he has been boarding with the Felikses for probably 2 years, and when I was with them I have seen. He says his prayer and wears a cross on his breast. I hope I am not yet so stupid as not to know with whom I have to speak. He is even from a country not far away from ours, government and district of Łomża. And now, dear [sister] Stasia, don't think that I will hurry and have the wedding the soonest possible; perhaps there will be no wedding at all. Don't forget to get ready and come. It will be more lively when we are both together. You ask for my photograph. I have none ready. I will send you one in December. I will go soon to a photographer. And now, dear parents, don't think that I am with nobody to care about me. I have a good uncle and auntie; I did not expect they would be so good. They care about me as about their own child; they will allow nobody to do me any wrong. When I go to them I am as bold and grateful, as in my own parental home, but still more so. If you don't believe me, then, dear family, please ask uncle and auntie. They will tell you that it is true.

And now, dear family, I have nothing more to write, but only I send you low bows and wish you every good.

I have received the photograph, for which I thank you very heartily, and I will send you soon an American one, with this young man. And now I have nothing to write, only I greet you, parents, and brothers and sisters, and I wish you all health and happiness. I greet also Aunt Karolska and ask and beg her pardon. Let her not be angry with me, but I had no time to write another letter particularly to auntie. Be so good, auntie, and accept from my parents this same letter, because I should write to you the same as to my parents. I have nothing more to write, only I ask you, auntie, for a speedy answer, and I beg you once more, auntie, let nobody know from these letters about the young man. I request you, dear parents, give this whole letter to auntie to read.

[Aleksandra Rembieńska]

YEAR 1912

O Dear Auntie:

I received your letter on February 20 and I write you on February 25. Dear auntie, you wrote 3 letters and I know nothing about them; I received only this one. O dear auntie, you write to me that I either don't wish to write or that I have forgotten [you]. O dear auntie, I will not forget until my death. I write letters, one to auntie and the other to my parents. Perhaps somebody has intercepted those letters at the post-office and does not give them to you. Now, dear auntie, I inform you that I am in good health, thanks to our Lord God, which I wish also to you, dear auntie. May God help you the best; may I always hear that you are doing well; I shall be very glad then. And now dear auntie, I inform you that I am in the same place in service with an English[-speaking] master and mistress who don't know a word of Polish, and I don't know English; so we communicate with gestures and I know what to do, that's all. I know the work and therefore I don't mind much about the language. But, dear auntie, I went intentionally into an English household in order that I may learn to speak English, because it is necessary, in America, as the English language reigns. I am in good health, only I am a little ill with my feet, I don't know what it is, whether rheumatism or something else. I walk very much, because from 6 o'clock in the morning till 10 o'clock in the evening I have work and I receive $22 a month, and I have 7 persons, and 16 rooms to clean, and I cook; everything is on my head. And now, dear auntie, you wrote to me about Staś Filinak that he wished to know my address; you can give it to him. You wrote to me that he said that our Lord God punished him because he did not take me. It is not true. He did not do me any wrong. I pity him very much. You ask me whether my address is the same. It is the same and it will never change, and secondly, the Kubaczs have lived already 10 years at the same place and the address is the same. And now, dear auntie, please don't be angry with me for not answering directly, for I have no time, neither in the day nor the evening. I am always busy. And now, dear auntie, I thank you very much for the news, for now I know everything. You ask about that young man, what happened. Nothing happened, only it is so that I did not wish to marry him, because I don't wish to marry at all; I will live alone through this my life to the end. He is a good fellow, nothing can be said, his name is Tomasz Zylowski. He wants it to be in summer, after Easter, but I don't think about marrying, I will suffer alone to the end in this world. O dear auntie, I write you that I have nothing to write, only I ask you for a quick answer. And now I beg you, auntie, write me what happened with [two illegible names of boy and girl]. I wish you a merry holiday of Easter time. O dear God, why cannot I be with auntie and divide the egg together with parents and brothers and sisters! When I recall all this, I would not be sorry if I had to die right now. Dear auntie, Mańka wrote to me a letter; Jablońska with [illegible masculine name] will come to the Kubaczs.

[Aleksandra Rembieńska]

W orld War II dramatically transformed women's economic status in American society. The crisis brought more than six million women into the labor force, an increase in female workers of over 50 percent, while the number of married women working doubled. When the war ended, many millions of women continued working, and by 1950, for the first time in the country's history, married women constituted a 52 percent majority of the roughly ten million females employed. Despite those statistics, the question of women's proper social and economic location came under reconsideration during the 1950s. Traditional ideas reemerged, and popular opinion among both sexes held that women would find fulfillment and happiness only as wives and mothers.

The belief was affirmed in such autobiographical accounts as *Call Me Mother*, which was first published in 1950, and reprinted in 1955 and 1956. Typical of a genre of popular women's writing, the book details the daily, exhausting tasks of housekeeping and motherhood with self-conscious exuberance. Whatever the sacrifices or frustrations faced in their domestic environments, the protagonists always seem able to see the lighter side of life, never doubting that cheerful self-sacrifice for spouse and children would bring ultimate happiness for women. Reviewers, usually male, described these popular autobiographies as "rib-splitting," "uproariously funny," "screamingly funny," and "hilarious."

Perhaps the uncritical glorification of women's place at home was a case of the authors protesting too much. Whatever the final assessment, these writings affirmed prevailing norms concerning women's aspirations and responsibilities at the time they were published.

In the selections from *Call Me Mother* that follow, author Virginia Taylor Klose describes the importance of her mother as a role model and source of values about womanly behavior. While she expressed an awareness that a "new woman" was emerging in American society, one trying to free herself from male social and economic domination, she found the model unappealing. Throughout the book Mrs. Klose minimized the importance of work in her own life, emphasizing that she never desired a career.

In proposing marriage, Virginia's future spouse stated emphatically: "A woman's place is in the home. There'll be one career in this family. Mine!"

After twenty years of marriage and six children, she wrote, "I can't help but agree with him. A career is a fine thing for a woman. But a man is better." Although when she took a job and noticed that her children viewed her "with the same gleam of interest they formerly reserved for their father," she was not pleased. "A primitive instinct began to assert itself," and Mrs. Klose decided that her children needed their mother. The choice is perceived to be career versus marriage and motherhood. The "lady experts" in the broadcasting field of whom she writes are portrayed as stereotypes, inept in domestic matters and without homes of their own.

Virginia's discussion of pregnancy and childbirth strikingly illustrates a radical change in procedures and attitudes over the centuries — and between the 1950s and the present. She rhapsodized about modern methods of delivery in a "gleaming, antiseptic, kleig-lighted chamber, full of instruments, chromium and masked men." Her negative feelings toward natural childbirth advocates are explicit. Placing full confidence in her professional physician, she purposely avoided sharing her concerns and feelings about her pregnancy with other women.

Born in 1911 in St. Louis, Missouri, Virginia Klose attended private Catholic schools and college. Her father was a newspaper editor. This autobiography was written when she was thirty-nine.

—— 17 ——

Virginia Taylor Klose

If I had it to do all over again I think I'd just take a correspondence course in obstetrics and dispense with any other formal education, since most of my adult life has been spent in the delivery room, a place much easier to get into than college. . . .

A career is a fine thing for a woman. But a man is better. With this primitive feeling, which I've never shaken off and never wanted to, I went to Maryville College in 1928 to pursue a bachelor of arts degree. That it was a woman's college made it easier to pursue the arts than the bachelors, but somehow we managed both, adding zest to the chase.

I had absolutely no designs on earning a living and it hardly seems possible that I could have been so feckless in the midst of so much dedicated female purpose. In that generation of awakening feminine drives, what was I after? Outside of a man I hadn't the foggiest notion.

All I wanted, being a simple, uncomplicated schizophrenic, was a degree and, eventually, a husband. I didn't want to be president of U.S. Steel or Secretary of Labor or live dangerously in the unexplored world opening up to women, even though all around me were fine examples of the NEW WOMAN who had just about finished the job of unshackling

SOURCE: Reprinted by permission of Curtis Brown, Ltd. Copyright 1950, 1955 by Virginia Taylor Klose; © 1956 by Virginia Taylor Klose.

herself socially and economically (though biologically and emotionally she's still working on it) from male domination.

My generation finally pulled off the miracle which enabled us to compete with men for jobs, tabs and income tax blanks. But somehow this subdivided female who went about with one head concentrating on business, the other on what happened to the laundry, didn't appeal to me. I had no desire to compete with any man, except companionably, swapping jokes at the breakfast table, laughing louder at my own and being supported while I did.

Also it seemed to me that for every girl who had real talent and a bona fide career there were hundreds drearily holding down routine jobs, washing their stockings at night and hoping to God some man would phone, take them out to dinner and not let them pay their own check.

Of course I was a willing victim of my background. The women in our family were all parasites expecting support in exchange not only for the best but also for the worst years of their lives, and I was brought up in this tradition.

No woman in her right mind would ever joust with a male for this role in the household, Mother said. Furthermore, a man should not only sign the chits, but should, at all times, wear the pants. (She could hardly have foreseen a world of Bermuda shorts marked "HIS" and "HERS.")

In such a hothouse atmosphere the male ego was bound to flourish and pay off, suffering none of the damage which currently fills the psychiatrists' couches with gentlemen whose psyches have been defeated by ladies.

While Mother delicately refrained, in these girl talks, from mentioning the more robust aspects of marriage, she had the enthusiasm of a Soviet propagandist for its psychological facets, the burden of her party line being "a man must be handled."

In accordance with this theory she never met my father in the evening and announced flatly that the cook had quit, she'd smashed a fender or was overdrawn at the bank. She softened him up first. That my father exploded just as loudly as a time bomb when he heard the bad news never dampened her enthusiasm for this theory for one minute. She kept right on "handling" him for twenty-eight years, firm in the belief that the kid glove and the wedding ring were inseparable.

The increasing economic independence of women left her cold. "They'll regret it," she predicted, though she voted, smoked and bobbed her hair. But that's as far as she went. From her point of view college for the female was for strictly cultural purposes and had to be handled with great care lest it backfire and defeat the destiny for which the female had obviously been created — marriage.

Naturally I lapped this up and with a mind thoroughly poisoned against gainful employment I was able to enjoy four years of Greek, Latin, French, literature and history which made me as unfunctional as a hoop skirt.

At the end of freshman year I announced I was on the dean's list and Mother said very tactfully, "That's lovely. But I wouldn't mention it to Roger tonight if I were you. Remember, men still like the feminine type, in spite of careers, colleges and the twentieth century. And they *don't* like women who pit themselves against them and talk all the time."

She had me there and we both knew it. I chewed that one over as I dressed for Roger, my date of the evening. He was a Yale sophomore taking me out because I knew Milton's "Sonnet on His Blindness" — an embarrassing reason having nothing to do with sex.

What made it a feature story was that Roger was not only a fancier of the Muse, but the heir to a spectacular fortune. A chorus girl with an eye to a well-turned wallet couldn't have schemed herself into a happier setup than I had stumbled into, led by the blind poet.

"Now, remember. Don't talk too much," Mother warned just before this bonanza appeared, as she surveyed me for wrinkles, showing slips and twisted seams.

"Don't worry, Mother. Roger likes me because we have the same taste in poetry. That's why he's taking me out."

Mother looked at me incredulously and said flatly, "He's still a man. Just remember that."

My prize appeared and escorted me into his custom-built Chrysler with the top down. It was a soft summer evening, moist in the tropical fashion of St. Louis in June. The stars were out. A great night for Milton.

"What would you like to do?" Roger opened the meeting, shifting smoothly into second as we purred off.

"Oh, anything you'd like to do," I volunteered, remembering Mother's advice and trying the feminine, fluffy "I'll-go-where-you-go" routine.

"Fine," he said happily. And without another word about Milton or anybody else, he drove straight to Forest Park, up to Art Hill, slammed on the brakes and made a heroic pass at me.

His technique was as skilled as a professional shopper's in a supermarket and I felt more like a national brand than an English major. I could see instantly it wasn't going to be a fit night out for sonnets.

No quotations came to mind at the moment and the only printed words I could think of were on menus. Virtuously disengaging myself as much as possible (since we looked like a pair trying out for their Red Cross senior lifesaving badge) I suggested we tackle some barbecued beef instead. This robust announcement, coming on the heels of a tactical defeat, turned Roger's lust into the kind of thrifty rage only a man with fifteen million dollars can afford.

"If that's the way you feel about it, I'll take you home," he said economically, through clenched teeth. And he did.

"What on earth happened?" Mother cried as I walked in from my brief flyer into letting the male call the shots.

"Nothing. That's the point," I said, leaning against the piano as I recounted the triumph of beef over passion.

Father listened attentively and when I finished he looked up from the book he was reading and said, rather reflectively, that while he felt the sonnet form was permanently established in English poetry, he had to agree with Roger that it would never take the place of a girl — especially on a warm summer night — with the top down.

Mother felt that my request for barbecued beef had injected a note of gluttony rather than poetry into the affair. And she returned to her original thesis that while one might have a general average of ninety-two in college, one might have a batting average of zero with men.

By the time commencement rolled around and in spite of a début at the Veiled Prophet Ball, the traditional trap which had been set in my junior year, I still had nothing in sight but my degree.

Since it would no more have occurred to me to get a job than to set fire to City Hall, my problem was simplified. Obviously there would have to be a short-standing wait for My Life's Work, wherever he was. Casting about for a romantic spot for the vigil I chose Paris, where I decided to do some graduate work at the Sorbonne.

"Well, you can't make a career out of that," predicted a farsighted classmate.

"I can try," I answered hopefully, thinking shrewdly of all those moonlight nights on deck going over. There were bound to be men lurking somewhere. Behind the potted palms at the afternoon *thé dansant*. Or hiding under a steamer rug. And who knows? With any luck at all one of them might persuade me not to waste the best time of my life in the dusty amphitheaters of the Sorbonne.

As it turned out this was highly wishful thinking and I came home a year later undedicated to anything expect the proposition that a woman is meant to get married. Unfortunately even after a second trip abroad, this time with my hopeful parents, and searching diligently through Europe's museums, graveyards, public buildings, restaurants, shops, theaters and ruins, I still had no visible means of support to introduce to them. When we got back to St. Louis even Mother asked, "What are you going to do now?" in the tone fellow surgeons use over a patient beyond the scalpel.

"I guess I'll get a job," I answered desperately, throwing in the towel and facing up to the twentieth century.

My father, in a that's-more-like-it voice, said, "Why don't you go into radio?"

"What would I do?" I wondered, immediately regretting my rashness.

"Talk! What else?" he replied.

Armed with a letter of introduction from him to use as a door opener, I made the rounds of the St. Louis radio stations. The letter opened all the doors. But unfortunately they shut almost immediately. Finally I got around to a brand new station run by two young men reported to be open to suggestion.

The program director, a blue-eyed blond chap in white linens, who looked a lot like the Prince of Wales, read my father's admission of paternity while I watched his face for signs of immediate employment.

As he outlined to me the station's need for a woman newscaster, his secretary, a dark, intense little girl, knelt at his feet and wiped off his buckskin shoes with some whitener. The performance was so oriental that I began to suspect this was no program director, but a maharajah with a whole raft of women kept in purdah, probably in the control room.

Discreetly I began backing toward the door when he startled me by offering me, not the shoeshine concession which I'd been expecting, but a job.

"How much will you pay me?" I asked, remembering suddenly I was supposed to get paid.

"Forty dollars a month," he replied magnificently, holding out his hand.

I shook it and departed in a daze. Obviously I could be had cheap. But it was comforting to know that I was had.

Five days after my début as a radio newscaster they could hardly pry me from the microphone long enough to close the station. I soon found that everyone on the staff of a small local station doubles in brass. In a pinch the program director might fill in for a missing vocalist or the organist emcee the Kiddie Show, if he had a rubber hose and no other job in sight. Most of the schedule was recordings and there was very little live talent. Or even talent.

The local merchants who bought the one-minute commercial spots all insisted on being billed as "jolly" or "friendly" or "good old." These jolly, friendly, good old characters evidently sat glued to their seats and when their spots came on, if the announcer so much as breathed heavily while delivering them, they rushed down to the station, stomped into the manager's office and threatened to smash the transmitter.

The station ran from six A.M. till midnight, opening with the Farm to Market News and Weather and closing when its theme, Grieg's "Last Spring," poured its haunting melody into the night. In addition to the tasty fare dished up in the mother tongue, there were a number of foreign language broadcasts as well as a good supply of religious ones.

One of the merriest souls around the studio was a gentleman who made his living singing hymns and quoting the Bible and whose off-the-air vocabulary could have won him the championship on any waterfront in the world.

It was the program director's constant nightmare that this dispenser of The Word would some day forget he was quoting from Matthew or Mark and lapse into the newest one about the farmer's daughter, an eventuality which would undoubtedly cause the FCC to pocket the station's license.

A permanent feature of the program log was the "Kiddie Show," which was then in its heyday on every local station in the nation. On these shows an assortment of unfortunate children were wont to display their doubtful talents from ten to eleven every Saturday morning.

When the kiddies came in, the staff became the center of a milling throng of pawing, yelping small fry and, I suspect, some child impersonators. There is something exceedingly sad about a child all slicked up, reciting "The Shooting of Dan McGrew," then segueing into a tap routine while a doting mother, aunt or grandmother stands by hissing, "Smile like I said, Grover."

The hour a week set aside for this questionable entertainment was dreaded by everybody on the station staff. The secretaries and clerks used to stand in a group in their big, glassed-in office and look out at the little Mickey Rooneys and Shirley Temples as they congregated with their curls, their banjos, accordions, tap shoes and harmonicas, and swear this made them firm believers in birth control.

I leaned more toward matricide, feeling always that these children were victims. We used to argue the ethics and philosophy of the situation until the bookkeeping came to a standstill, the typing schedule fell behind and all the continuity was late for mimeograph.

Frequently on these occasions the station manager came in and wondered if the staff had suddenly gone on strike. Then he'd look out on the mezzanine and see the prodigies and their relatives and say, with relief: "Oh, it's only the damned little kiddies!"

Not long after beginning my newscasts I began to get a daily card from a fan expressing an opinion of me which could only have been shared by my mother. It was always signed "An Ardent Admirer."

This adulation went to my head with such winey effect that several weeks later I walked into the program director to let him know that I was not being wasted on the desert air. That I had, in fact, a devoted and very articulate following.

"Really?" he inquired with mild enthusiasm. "Tell me about it."

I did.

"Some nut," he remarked. "Happens all the time."

Six weeks later the program director and I became engaged and the next morning I found a note on my desk to see him after my broadcast.

"You wanted to see me, Boss?" I asked, tossing him a last bone.

"Yes, I do. Friday morning will be your final broadcast. You're fired." He grinned broadly.

I was stunned. "But... but my program is very necessary. What about my 'Ardent Admirer'? That card each day?"

"I've been sending those cards to you," he said happily. "I'm getting a replacement for you. I think a woman's place is in the home. There'll be one career in this family. Mine!"

Now, after two decades of rearing our six children, I can't help but agree with him. A career is a fine thing for a woman. But a man is better.

□

There's nothing like a dame, according to Rodgers and Hammerstein. But they'll never know what a dame who's also an expert is really like until they do a homemaking musical. An event which would probably advance the sales of baking powder, but dispel any illusions these gentlemen may still entertain toward the cooking sex.

Some years ago, due to my husband, who turned out to be not only my best friend but my agent, I hired out as a celebrity interviewer on a radio show swarming with lady homemaking experts. They could do everything I could do, but they could do it better. And I went into their presence in the proper spirit of reverence, short of breath, my knees knocking together.

Since these programs are set up by the advertising agency as delicately as the State Department prepares for a love feast at the summit, I met first with the account executive responsible for the show and his assistant, an efficient lady named Miss Evans, who purportedly knew more about women than women do.

We spent a very clinical morning discussing the American housewife and it came over me — as it always does when I'm with agency people — what an impressive thing she is. Not in her majestic role of woman, wife or mother, but as consumer. It's a tremendous experience to meet with whole groups of well-paid people worrying themselves into ulcers and early strokes over woman's buying power.

The realization that I might become involved personally in the great crusade to guard the American woman against crumbling cakes, gray wash or husbands who look elsewhere for their fun because the floors aren't properly waxed made me cold all over.

When Miss Evans finished the Starch Reports on the reading habits of the female — a much more telling index than anything Dr. Kinsey ever dreamed of — she said crisply, "Now Mrs. Klose, how would you approach the woman listener?"

On my hands and knees and wagging my tail, I thought, shuddering at the monster which the statistics had just conjured up. I felt trapped.

"Well," I began safely, hoping the blankness of my face would be mistaken for a glaze of feverish intellectual activity, "I've been a woman for a long time . . ."

"Have you done any writing lately?" she broke in with a no-nonsense voice.

"Yes. I've been collaborating with my husband on some nighttime comedy shows for the last few years."

"Comedy?" Miss Evans looked alarmed. As well she might. (I have had the same reaction whenever I've read over any of the old scripts.)

"Sponsored?" the account man asked sharply.

"Yes. Soap," I answered.

"Mmmmmm," he murmured. "Let's go out and kick this around at lunch."

At midnight my husband picked me up at the Waldorf, where we'd been kicking it around over lunch, cocktails, dinner and floor show, since noon.

"How did you do?" Woody asked eagerly with a mixture of husband-agent enthusiasm.

"Fine. I'm elected," I said.

"Good. You're going to like this job," he prophesied, calling a cab.

"That's an understatement. I'm going to love it," I promised, remembering the considered opinion of an agency vice-president we know. "Next to inherited money, there's no pleasanter way to make a living."

The following Monday morning, a snowy February day, I caught the 7:32 from the country for the two-and-a-half-hour run to New York and presented myself at the agency for the first official program meeting. The conference room was crawling with brass, client and staff, assembled for the kickoff.

The lady food expert who headed the project, and who was a terrific item in the budget, was charming the client while her assistants, the white-robed vestals from the experimental kitchens, hovered in the background, mentally beating their yolks and whipping their whites.

Several other writers and a chatty little guest-getter stood in the corner with the star of the show, a young lady with high cheekbones, freckles, and hair parted in the middle and braided around her head.

Completing the group involved in these mysteries were the director, a gentleman with a pencilled-in mustache, a beautiful young man hired to deliver guests on time at the studio and a poor wretch with the Indian sign on him who was to be liaison between the numerous females on the show and the agency.

Suddenly the milling around stopped and we were invited to sit down at the long blond conference table. The agency president, a distinguished looking gentleman, sat at one end, the client at the other. It was the latter who intoned the services: "As of this moment, you are all on the payroll." Hallelujah. The meeting began.

Miss Evans, who had written a five thousand word presentation with lantern slides which had sold the client lock, stock and cereal on the program, now proceeded to read at some length from her dissertation while we sat in stunned silence.

It seemed the show was to be primarily a cooking demonstration, not only because of the sponsor's product, but because the foundation of the American home was said to rest incontrovertibly on the American stomach.

(Miss Evans, perpetually dieting to keep herself at skeletal proportions, not only had no stomach, but no home. She lived alone in a tiny apartment with a housecoat, black coffee and a typewriter.)

Also included in the new program would be interviews with celebrities. However, it was the expressed belief of the food expert (who broke in here with great enthusiasm) that none of them would have a chance against a thirteen-egg angel food cake. Naturally this observation set the sponsor purring like a cat with a casserole of creamed shrimp.

Other features of this bonanza to the little homemaker would be tips on decorating, gardening, table setting, beauty, charm and how to cope with children, a home product of whom many of the ladies on the staff had heard, but with whom most of them, so far, had had no truck.

Though it was conceded there was already a plethora of cooking and charm shows on the air, the sponsor was assured this one was going to be different. He was also informed that it would immediately have a higher rating than all the daytime shows on the air. I was surprised nobody suggested short-waving it to our armed forces overseas.

The agency brass sat, polished and beaming, delicately refraining from pointing out the one other outstanding feature of the show. It had a budget big enough to keep a full tank division in the field for a year.

Prayer meeting concluded, Miss Evans said crisply:

"Girls, let's go out to lunch and develop a format."

Whereupon we repaired to the Algonquin. On the way visions of sponsored martinis and London Broil swam through my head, only to be shattered, as soon as we arrived at the hotel, by Miss Evans, who wore her hat and ate at her desk every day unless she was dragged bodily from the office by a client or a vice-president and who now announced that we must have a room.

"We'll have lunch sent up," she said, calling room service as soon as we got into the old high-ceilinged chamber where we were to caucus in the proper spirit of dedication to the American Woman.

"Send up four chicken sandwiches and four pots of coffee. You don't want a drink, do you, girls?" she asked, turning away from the mouthpiece and right back to it without waiting for an answer. Then she phoned the housekeeper for a card table and three chairs, and the drug store for a carton of cigarettes.

"Now, Ethel," she said, turning to the Food Expert (a lady who liked to be called "Chief"), "tell us what you have in mind."

"Well, honey," said Ethel, tossing her long beige veil away from her face and over her shoulder and smiling infectiously at us, "this is the way I look at our show. We've got to find out what that little woman at home — that nice, friendly little neighbor on the back street with a husband, children and a little house with its spotless kitchen and its ruffled curtains at the window — really wants."

She paused for breath at the end of this lyric outburst, took a pencil in her well-manicured hands and, her collection of heavy gold bracelets tinkling an accompaniment, wrote down a series of subject headings. COOKING — MARKETING — BEAUTY — CHARM — SHOPPING — FLOWER ARRANGEMENTS — SELF-IMPROVEMENT — BUDGETING OF TIME — CHILDREN.

"That's a fine beginning," said Miss Evans. "Now have any of you writers got any ideas? Just for a starter." One of our group, fresh from magazines and new to the magic world of radio looked up sharply and said, "Why does the sponsor have to have three minutes of commercial time on this program? I think that's far too much."

Two hours later, in a haze thicker than an all-night poker session, the girls were still arguing about the sponsor's right to three minutes of his own program time — a privilege granted him not only in the Constitution, but also by the FCC. The friendly little neighbor on the back street had disappeared, ruffled curtains and all, into the fog.

Only one major decision was made that afternoon and it proved to be a Pyrrhic victory for the magazine writer. She was set on going south in March and had managed to come out of the hassle about commercial time with an assignment for a special feature on Florida.

Miss Evans, looking a little dubious, asked for a fuller explanation of what to expect from this side trip.

"Oh," said the writer, vaguely waving her hands as writers do, "I'll just jot down everything I see as the train rolls south. The sunsets, the sky, the lush tropical landscape, all the funny things I hear, the dishes I like best, the people I meet."

"But how will you work it out for the show?" demanded Miss Evans suspiciously.

"Honey, don't worry about her," said Chief. "This girl's a writer. She knows what to do."

Which turned out to be a slanderous underestimate. The writer in question went south on a nice healthy expense account and sent back dispatches that could best be described as "A Rainy Day In The Attic," type of high school composition that flourished around the beginning of the century in select girls' schools.

Since nobody could figure out how to use this expensive foolscap it was filed in the wastebasket. We never saw our southern correspondent again because the management chose this excuse to sever commercial relations with her. But I heard around town that she was sporting a wonderful tan and enjoying some terrific memories.

Instead of writing three days a week in the country, I found that I was required to be in the studio in New York Monday through Friday, and life suddenly became very demanding. For the first time in my experience I got a dose of being a real working mother — a creature who deserves a place in history, if not next to the Lone Ranger, certainly in the vicinity of Tonto.

I soon found that my relationship with my four young sons became simply a week-end thing, because I tiptoed out in the morning while they were sleeping and got home at night just in time to see the older three, if they still happened to be awake, in their beds. The youngest, two-year-old Christy, was always sound asleep. The children began to look at me with the same gleam of interest they formerly reserved for their father. And while I had told myself for years that this could be wonderful, it wasn't.

A primitive instinct began to assert itself and I became increasingly conscious of the fact that children need more than hired help, even though it may be excellent — as it was in my case — to care for them while a mother is gone. They need that familiar old beast of burden, Mommie, when they get up in the morning, come home from school, go to bed at night, have a small problem or a big triumph.

This relationship was now impossible for me because in my new double life my work day began at six when I dressed, drove twenty-five miles to Poughkeepsie with my husband and caught the 7:32 to New York.

At nine-thirty I was in the studio checking my script for the run through. The master of ceremonies, the star, the director, Miss Evans, Chief and the high priestesses who did the actual cooking and the beautiful young man who escorted the guests were already there.

Outside was the studio audience, composed chiefly of middle-aged women with nothing else to do. They stood patiently in line until the ushers opened the heavy doors, at which time they jostled and rushed for the front rows where they might be picked by the emcee for the morning quiz with its substantial prizes.

Many of them were pros who never missed a day and came equipped with paper bags which they rattled all during the broadcast. These they filled afterwards with samples of the sponsor's products which were tossed out prodigally by the beautiful young man, who looked equally at home guiding an ambassador or staggering along under a pyramid of cereal boxes.

About airtime there would invariably be a frantic last minute conference between the writer, the director and Chief, because the script had only one "golden," "crunchy" or "fluffy" describing the sponsor's product and he was on the teletype from Chicago raising merry hell. Hastily we'd add "crunchy" three more times and wait for the arrival of the celebrity who'd been interviewed a week or two before.

The star of our clambake had simply to go through the motions of the cooking demonstration that was set up for her by the experts in the model kitchens. And since the interviews with the celebrities were written for her, practically all she had to do was be able to read and tell time by the big studio clock so the show would get off the air on schedule.

The young lady in question had been a vocalist with a small town band and, recently arrived in New York, had won the part of cooking goddess on the show over two hundred other actresses at the audition. The reason given for the choice, though no television was involved, was that she resembled the picture on the box of one of the sponsor's products.

This seemed to be her chief qualification for the job, with the result that if the script didn't spell out "Good morning, Ambassador Whiffletree, it's a great pleasure to have you with us this morning," she'd sit stolidly across the microphone from Ambassador Whiffletree and clam up. When that happened the great radio audience, waiting at home for a little statecraft with their "How to Make a Jelly Roll That Really Rolls," wondered if the program had gone off the air.

After the show we all retired to an audition room to run through the next day's effort and the director held a post-mortem on the just-finished classic. Our star would come in, yawn loudly, kick her shoes across the room, sprawl on the sofa with her legs wide apart like a cello player minus her instrument, and complain bitterly that the script didn't say "Good morning" and how was she to know she should say that to the Ambassador?

For my part I always found it difficult, after interviewing someone like General Carlos Romulo, who was, at the time, president of the U.N., to ask him if he'd mind if we tied in a little apple pandowdy with the question of recognition of Red China.

However, the guests went gallantly along with this gimmick, because they were all selling a cause, a book or a show. But it never failed to make me cringe, watching them go through the alimentary canal to do it.

When Mother's Day came around I, being the only one on the staff with children, was asked to do a script for the occasion. So, having just read a very interesting newspaper story about a woman with thirteen children who cooked, sewed, washed and mended for her tribe and had survived beautifully, I came into our daily brain-trust meeting with the clippings and an idea for the show. When we had finished checking our program for the next day — "Popovers That Really Pop" and a sewing tip on how to make your husband a new shirt out of an old sheet — I presented my memo.

"What is this for?" asked Miss Evans with an incredulous look on her face.

"Why, it's my idea for the Mother's Day show. I think we should have this woman on as a guest. She has thirteen children and look at all the things she does! I think she's spectacular."

"Well, I don't. I think she's disgusting! Thirteen children. Ugh! Sounds like a litter," said Chief, lifting her nostrils daintily and looking sympathetically at Miss Evans.

So we had as guest on the Mother's Day show an anemic little woman who was full of beautiful, professional sentiments about mothers in general and her own in particular, a lady of eighty-two, who some of us privately agreed after the show, should never have gone near a delivery room.

Working with lady experts calls for a great deal of fortitude and the men in the agency who had to deal with our particular program called it "The Mare's Nest." They'd find any excuse possible to get out of coming to what were euphemistically called our "conferences."

One of the vice presidents who always pulled S.R.O. when he showed had particular grounds for mayhem. Chief unfailingly gave him not only the V.I.P. treatment but the full benefit of her ante bellum charm. For some odd reason his advent always prompted her to order a basket of fruit for the conference room table. When the going got exceptionally coy, Chief would playfully toss this gentleman a peach or a tangerine, which he usually belted right back with a restraint which I admired. It was pretty apparent that he'd much rather have made a fresh fruit salad on her Lily Daché.

On the lower levels of our operation where the grubbing was done — dictation, typing, research and schedules — our public relations weren't so buddy-buddy. Every morning when I got to the office from the studio I could count on finding one of the secretaries missing. She was the crying type who always spent her morning coffee break in the ladies' room weeping over the daily pushing around she took from her boss, our expert with TEMPERAMENT.

Poor Millie's eyes were perpetually red and the lids so puffed she looked like she had an allergy of the conventional kind. She would sob and sniffle out her heartbreak, leaning against the paper towel machine, while I attempted to buck her up with motherly advice, along two widely divergent lines.

"Millie, why don't you either quit or strangle her? There's no middle road."

This would cause a fresh outburst from Millie which always sent me back to the office without completing my mission.

The other secretaries were made of sterner stuff and they just dared anybody to give them a line of dictation after five o'clock or criticize the spelling of cummerbund with a K.

Some months after I became engaged in these questionable efforts to help the little housewife with her life's work, I walked in to Chief's office and announced I was pregnant.

If I'd announced I was Benedict Arnold I would have had a warmer reception. Looking furtively around her office Chief said, in horror, "Don't tell anybody."

"I won't have to. Wait and see," I said expectantly.

"Never mind. I don't want to replace you until I simply must. Don't tell a soul," she warned me as I went off with my happy secret to interview Abbott and Costello, who were doing two weeks at the Roxy.

Late that summer the movie "Life with Father" had its world premiere at Skowhegan, Maine and I was sent up with our entire cast and staff to do our shows from there and to interview the stars, Dorothy Stickney and Howard Lindsay.

As I boarded the midnight Boston and Maine in a dreadful maternity number with butcher boy jacket and portholed skirt, my husband kissed me good-bye fondly and said, "Darling, I think this time the celebrities are going to be more interested in you than you are in them."

That did it. On my return I resigned and invited the entire staff to the farm for an end-of-summer picnic.

Having alerted my housekeeper, the neighbors and friends for miles around that the experts were coming, I made feverish preparations to see that the whole place would pass at least half of their rigid requirements for the American Woman.

Cobwebs that had lived comfortably unmolested in corners for months were vigorously brushed off. Linoleum was scrubbed within an inch of its life and brass that had been lacklustre for years suddenly found itself putting your eye out. The place was so sanitary it wasn't fit to live in.

Since none of the experts would trust me with the dessert, a confection they felt I was much too simpleminded to pull off, they promised to bring it. This was to be the *pièce de résistance*, the clincher that would cause the sponsor to pick up the next thirteen weeks option as soon as he sank his teeth into it. This gentleman, who was nothing if not generous, had not only chartered a bus to bring the staff to the farm, but even came along for the fun.

Jolly as this seemed, it caused everybody to walk softly because clients on outings, even though footing the bills, are about as welcome as deadly nightshade in a sheep corral.

Right on schedule the bus rolled into the barnyard and children, dogs, Woody and I went out to greet the happy homemakers. As soon as the door opened and Chief got out I knew something was wrong.

"Jinny! Jinny!" she said in a frantic whisper, "something terrible has happened. Is there a room near your kitchen we could close off?" she asked, looking wildly around and motioning to her high priestesses who were carrying large pans covered with towels.

"The breakfast room," I said. "But what in the world's wrong?"

"Never mind! Hurry! Take us there!" she pleaded. I got them all in the house, into the breakfast room, closed all the doors as fast as I could.

"I'll never know how it happened. I'll never know how it happened," Chief kept moaning as the vestals unveiled their bakery goods, which turned out to be uncertain looking devil's food cakes of a type I was long familiar with, having baked more than my quota. They would not come out of the pans and kept falling spiritlessly to pieces every time any attempt was made to cut them. No gumption at all.

"We can't let the client see this!" Chief wailed, wringing her hands.

My housekeeper, who had been standing by ready to burn vigil lights in front of the experts, quietly went and got a spatula, a silver knife and some boiling water and brought them in. "Would you mind if I tried to cut the cakes?" she asked.

"That would be wonderful, Bergie," I answered, knowing her skill and horse sense in the kitchen.

As she worked reconstructing the crumbling ruins the ladies who were getting paid for producing these miracles watched her with increasing relief.

When she had the last piece cut and sufficiently camouflaged to look normal, she said crisply, "Musta put too much baking powder in them," and went back to the kitchen.

That evening as the bus left for New York Bergie stood with me watching it pull out. Then she turned, wiped her hands on her apron and said with some asperity, "Them experts!"

□

One day I was walking down the main street of our town when I came face to face with the wife of one of the village barbers, whom I hadn't seen for quite a while. She surveyed my burgeoning midriff with alarm and, instead of saying hello, or complaining about the weather — our surefire conversation piece — she said with disgust and some asperity, "Virginia! What'd you go and do that for? You had a nice family." There was so much accusation in her voice that I almost found myself apologizing for my forthcoming sixth child and overlooking the very intimate implications of her remark.

Reproduction of more than two or at most three children is a topic of conversation more loaded than the Bomb. Yet nothing in the world seems more natural to me and my husband than that we should have children — as many as we want — and without being singled out as curiosities.

The inordinate interest in our birth rate began in 1936, the day after our engagement was announced in the St. Louis papers, while the nuptial couch was still unreserved in the honeymoon hotel and the only tiny garments on my mind were monogrammed and trimmed with lace.

I remember the occasion well, because that was the evening my father came home enraged after keeping a luncheon date with an elderly relative who toasted us with his cocktail, put his glass down firmly and said, "Of course Virginia and Woody won't have any children. Certainly not for years." Whereupon my father gave him a fine indoctrination in privacy and walked out without touching the blue plate special.

But this was only the beginning, as we were to discover several weeks before the wedding, when an aunt I rarely saw made it her business to hop a train and descend on us. Ostensibly she came to see the trousseau and the groom, but actually on a secret mission of her own.

Born in the nineties, she was titillated by the twentieth century's birth control, planned parenthood and the twin bed, which she considered the greatest invention since the wheel. Nobody could figure out why she left her own household of husband and three growing children to sit around our houseful of bridal confusion until one evening when she came quietly into my room as I was dressing for a party. She shut the door very gently and with the furtive look of an agent about to unload a cache of heroin tiptoed over to me and whispered, "Virginia, has your mother told you? There's something you should know. Sit down."

I was fascinated, thinking there was some undisclosed family skeleton about to dance out of the closet and rattle its bones for my benefit. I sat down. She cleared her throat and flushed and said, "Do you know about...about...limiting your family? You know you don't have to have children, Virginia." Then she stopped and waited.

I thanked her for her interest in my welfare and future, misplaced though it was, and said that my *fiancé* and I had a rather normal notion that children were a part of marriage. I didn't have the heart to tell her that we also thought it was nobody else's business but ours.

She left next day without referring again to our future and I have often laughed when I've sent her an announcement of each succeeding child's arrival and wondered what she thought about them.

When our first son was born the day after our first anniversary — during his earlier years he often caused a whole rash of raised eyebrows in the various cities in which we lived by announcing happily, "I was born the day after Mommie and Daddy were married" — we got the customary felicitations on his appearance and everybody seemed quite pleased. We seemed to be following the "Mollie and me and baby makes three" routine, so favored by a happily defunct generation of song writers.

Nobody asked us any terribly personal questions at this time because people just took it for granted that we were living according to all the statistics of the insurance companies, the savings banks, the budget boys (you never hear of them anymore) and the planned parents. Actually nothing could have been farther from the truth because we've always ad libbed and never followed a script.

When Nicky, our second son, arrived eighteen months after the first, we discovered we were out of order on two counts. First, there is supposed to be a space minimum of two years between children. Several starchy matrons informed me that "everybody knows that." Secondly, in addition to our second child's not waiting the prescribed two years, he was a boy instead of a girl, thus violating the then unwritten law of the typical American family.

I believe the ideal unit pictured in vacation, cereal and automobile ads in those days was a father, a mother, one boy and one girl. All smiling happily over Wheaties, the Rockies or a new Chevrolet. And here we were with a repeater! Quite a few people dropped into my hospital room and, instead of sharing my enthusiasm, leaned over my bed and said, "Isn't it too bad? Another boy! I hope you're not too disappointed." I couldn't believe anybody seriously meant that kind of remark, but I found out after a while that quite a few people felt very sorry for us having two males on our hands.

Some of them said, with an air of finality, "Well, anyway you have a nice family now and the two boys will be company for each other as they grow up." A few added thoughtfully, "But you'll find you'll be lonely when they get married because girls stick to their mothers but boys always go with their wives." I don't know which made me madder, the tacit conclusion that this was the end of our family or the picture of a child sticking to me the rest of its life.

We bagged the legal limit when Kevin arrived in Toronto in 1940. Fortunately for my blood pressure we were across the border and didn't have any old friends to drop in and commiserate with me. And though I had plenty of encounters with people like customs and registration men and some Canadian friends, everybody seemed admirably restrained and reticent on the subject of our rising birth rate.

The first next-door-neighbor we had simply bowed stiffly to us but never uttered a word from Christmas Eve when we moved in to our house until two weeks before the baby's arrival in August. Then she leaned over the garden fence as I was bending with some difficulty to pick some sweet William and said, "Will it be soon?" I said it would be in two weeks. Whereupon she smiled, went in the house and we didn't have another word until the following November.

After Kevin was born we found that whenever we were presented to strangers by someone who knew us our friend would unfailingly say, "I do want you to meet Virginia and Woody Klose. They have three boys! Three! Think of it! And all boys!"

Our fourth son, Christy, really put us in the big league. Questions about our income, our nervous systems and our monthly meat bills became routine. By 1947 when I joined the staff of the radio homemaking show my trademark was Motherhood just as Heinz's is 57 Varieties.

I remember with particular glee a morning meeting on that show when Chief took out her ever-present memo pad and said,

"Now girls, I want you to remember that the three things that women are most interested in are food, dogs..." Her voice trailed off and she searched vainly for number three. Everyone sat mouse quiet and when the silence got thick as cheese, I ventured, "Children?"

"Why, Jinny! Of course, Honey! That's exactly right!" I was made.

When our fifth child, Debbie, was born our fate was sealed. We knew we were asking for it and the only thing to do was to be sporting and answer all comers. And, too, after years of preparation we found it easier to face the cross examination.

With the arrival of our sixth child, Victoria, we became real pros. There's hardly a personal question we haven't had tossed our way. No matter how intimate and from what source we are never floored. But when anyone gives me the real show stopper, "Six children! *Now* are you going to stop?" I like to look him in the eye and say, "What! You've only got one? Only two? When are you going to start?"

When I was about to have my sixth child there was a perfect rash of articles and a deluge of pictures in all kinds of periodicals showing a growing cult of Nature Girls in the throes of what is called "natural" childbirth. Several starry-eyed missionary friends of mine who were also pregnant at the time asked me if I wouldn't like to indulge in this form of torture. But I said, "No." My basic reaction to it all is a simple "Ouch!"

Having completed six tours of duty in the delivery room I would like to bring in a minority report from those of us who believe in unnatural childbirth and take our analgesic straight.

Just after Edward the Eighth renounced all for Wallis and about the time Neville Chamberlain was getting his umbrella mended to take to Munich, I became *enceinte* for the first time. And although this last event hadn't the world shaking repercussions of the first two, I still remember it vividly.

My initial visit to the obstetrician's office was something I didn't toss off lightly. The self-conscious women sitting around the room in various stages of pregnancy, the way they eyed each newcomer to see if she bulged more than they, the fixed smile and dreadful gaiety of the nurse as she popped in, slim and remote, beckoning each patient to the waiting table, the piles of magazines entirely devoted to diapers, "toidies" and nursing bras, for one awful moment made me want to yell, "Gee, I was only kidding," and flee.

When I finally got into the inner sanctum, stripped down to the bare and enveloped myself in the large white tent, open down the front, which is the ceremonial garment of the obstetrical ritual, rigor mortis had practically set in. Meanwhile the nurse stuck me for a Wasserman, took my blood pressure and weighed me in with the cool detachment of a cattle dealer appraising a heifer at an auction. This accomplished, she told me to climb on the table, lie down and put my feet in the stirrups. All of which I did, completely mesmerized, waiting for some kind soul to put a lily on my chest. Instead, there came the obstetrician, closing in for the kill.

According to the "natural" theory mine was the wrong reaction. I should have grinned, hopped on the table, filled with a great surge of reproductive pride and said to the doctor with a smile of happy anticipation, "This is going to hurt a lot, isn't it?" Instead I practically got him to sign an affidavit that the forth-coming birth would be as painless as modern medicine could make it.

Thus began my first nine months of waiting for a bundle from heaven. Armed with a small empty bottle, a diet list whose futility I soon realized and instructions to get plenty of sleep and exercise and keep in a happy frame of mind, I made my escape from the incubator and met my husband.

We had a good stiff drink, which was not what the doctor ordered, and began arguing about names. As the months wore on and I looked more and more like a Japanese wrestler, I began to part company with a whole school of old wives' tales. First to go was the one about the radiance of the expectant mother. That look in her eye. That look in her middle was what they meant and it was far from fetching.

All this time I dreamed of a nice, healthy baby but search as I might, I could find none of those exalted sentiments in my soul which are supposed to lurk there during the period of gestation. The sublime feeling of creation. The overwhelming mother instinct which makes you run up to strange children on street corners and pat their tousled heads. All I wished was that I could bend over and tie my shoe or get in a bus without having old ladies spring up and offer me their seats.

Now if I'd been preparing for a "natural" birth during this and all the other nine month periods I've spent incubating, I would have been attending classes and learning how to crouch around the house like a leopard, stretching my pelvis.

I could have spent many a fine afternoon in any one of a dozen uncomfortable positions, such as sitting tailor fashion on a radiator cover figuring out next week's menus, or doing a little pelvic rocking on the living room floor, while reading helpful articles on the strange and wondrous biological changes taking place in my interior. That seems a little to me like locking the old barn door after the horse has been stolen, but perhaps I'm too unnatural to grasp the significance of the new theory.

Also my husband could have become a vital part of the performance, poor thing. Instead of just having to watch me expand, hear about my indigestion and lie manfully about the chic of my new maternity model, he could have gone to night school with me and learned about the birds and the bees. This is supposed to give the prospective mother a great sense of security. Probably because she knows if she's got him on the front row at an obstetrical lecture he can't be out ogling some shapely blonde.

But my six pregnancies have been much more restful and relaxing. Instead of worrying about my pelvic muscles I have taken a very objective view of that portion of my anatomy, thus leaving myself free to sit down a lot and catch up on a great deal of back reading. In place of attending lectures at which I could learn to breathe properly through my chest and abdomen, I took frequent naps, lying on my left side. With my mouth open, my husband tells me.

I purposely avoided groups of pregnants, so I was spared the details of hearing about mongoloids, cretins and children born with a caul, which seem to hold an abnormal prenatal fascination for certain types of females. I didn't, on my maiden voyage to the maternity ward, drop by the hospital well in advance of the stork to take a gander at the facilities which would be at my disposal in the delivery room.

Nor did I gallop off with my husband to consult a psychiatrist and a pediatrician about the coming offspring's behavior and needs. I figured its behavior would range from that of brat to angel and that if anybody needed a psychiatrist in the near future it would be me. As to the infant's needs, both physical and spiritual, my husband and I were pretty sure they'd be basically the same as ours. This ignorant attitude paid off with a peace of mind which far outweighs, I'm sure, the awful knowledge being acquired by the Nature Girls in training for their finest hour.

It takes an elephant twenty-two months to reproduce, if I remember correctly. And it takes me almost as long. So my first trip to the delivery room came after a series of false alarms which had just about convinced my husband and kin that my condition was not one of delicacy, but obesity.

My deliverer too was beginning to take a dim view of my performance. So he said he thought he'd better blast for junior. This he did with enough Pituitrin to blow up the Coulee Dam. Thus I started on my unnatural path to the delivery room.

I didn't play cards at five o'clock in the morning with a group of nurses, doctors and my husband. In fact I was very anti-social and just lay there squirming and wishing my husband, at the foot of my bed, cool and immaculate in blue gabardine, would drop dead for looking so well groomed. As the nurses and interns paraded in and out with their set smiles and peptalks and questions about my contractions, I kept asking the sixty-four dollar one, "When do I get knocked out?"

They kept evading me but leading me to believe I'd get a snootful of something when the time came. As far as I was concerned the time had come and gone, but when I mentioned this all I got was a pitying look, as though my I. Q. and a worm's were on the same level.

After a while the curtain-raiser was over and we progressed to the final act. Nurses flew in and out, bells rang, lights flashed, "Calling Dr. Kildare" sounded all over the P. A. system and the banana cart came rumbling down the hall and into my room with the speed of light. I was invited to hoist myself on for the ride and, with the help of my husband and two nurses, managed the superhuman feat. Off I rolled to my delivery room début.

In that gleaming, antiseptic, kleig-lighted chamber, full of instruments, chromium and masked men, all I looked for was the gas pump. There is where any resemblance between me and a mother in "natural" childbirth becomes purely fictional. I have read that she goes happily into the delivery room, an eager beaver who has wrung from her obstetrician the promise of a mirror strategically placed so she can watch the proceedings.

I go in excited at the thought that after two whiffs of gas I'll be out like a light. The natural childbirth laborer, I understand, tosses aside the nitrous oxide mask placed on the pillow for her relief and rises up with a wide smile on her face, much as though she were watching television.

I'm the strictly unnatural type who grabs the mask out of the anaesthetist's hands and starts gulping the gas myself if there's a split second between a pain and a whiff. When the two-way stretch between the obstetrician at the foot of the table and the knockout boy at the head starts, I may be in the middle, but not for long. Then's when I bargain. They say "Push." I say "Gas." No gas, no push.

This system has worked very well with the three obstetricians I've used up in the U.S. and Canada. And every time I have awakened from my deep, unnatural slumber to find a new Klose has appeared on the planet while I was out to lunch, I have never had any inclination to complain. Deliver me!

A variety of patterns combining domestic life and work activities has emerged among young adult women in recent decades. Great numbers of women are choosing to live with a partner without getting married. (The number of unmarried men and women living together increased by 800 percent in the 1960s.) Those deciding to marry appear to be doing so at later ages, while others are rejecting marriage altogether and demanding the right to make their own sexual choices without being criticized for choosing nontraditional roles.

In past centuries single women have been regarded as social deviants. Where marriage offered women the only legitimate and respectable path to economic and emotional security, those remaining single were viewed variously as physically unattractive, full of unresolved psychological or sexual conflicts, or incapable of making emotional commitments. Although such attitudes have not disappeared, the single state is increasingly being accepted as a viable choice for women to make. And, more appear to be making that choice. The proportion of single women between the ages of twenty and twenty-four has increased by one-third since 1960.

One example is Sandy, a twenty-four-year-old retail department manager for a large corporation, whose interview is reprinted here. Sandy contrasted her own freedom and independence as a young adult with the situation her mother and aunts faced at a comparable age. Despite the pressures to get married that she felt from her mother and peers, Sandy was rejecting the idea. She feared boredom and confinement as a housewife, was concerned about having to conform to sex-typed roles, and was uncertain about how she would integrate marriage with a career. Remaining single was her conscious choice.

Despite a growing acceptance of women's rights to decide to remain single, many problems and tensions remain. One that Sandy addressed is that of fitting into a social group and finding acceptance among both family and friends. With the emergence of what psychologists and sociologists are defining as a *singles identity*, the feeling that one is part of a larger group in society with a legitimate style of living, the sense of being an outsider that Sandy expressed may be alleviated. As single women become more visible, recognition based on individual character and accomplishment will, one hopes, replace that which rests primarily on marital status.

In the descriptions of her educational and work experiences, Sandy clarified the subtle and obvious ways institutions force women to conform to traditional, stereotypic behavior. The resentments and harassment Sandy faced at school and on the job are reminiscent of attitudes that Florence Kelly described in an earlier selection. But like Sandy, many young women today are experiencing more freedom and flexibility in determining their own futures.

—— 18 ——
Sandy

All my aunts and uncles and cousins and parents are in Springfield. They all grew up in Springfield. They all got married, and they all stayed in Springfield. And in our generation, we all just got up and moved out. I've got a cousin in Canada — another in New York, my sister in Colorado, and I'm up here. All this happened within maybe the past two or three years. The whole family is kind of flabbergasted. Where did they go? Why? None of the older generation of women ever even had their own apartments. They got out of school and they got married.

They all think I'm more liberated than I am really. My mother

SOURCE: Interview with Sandy, in Lucia H. Bequaert, *Single Women Alone & Together.* Copyright © 1976 by Lucia Bequaert. Reprinted by permission.

worked all the time she was married, but she worked as a teacher, which is sort of a traditional thing. And she was a nurse for a while. My other aunts don't work at all. They were housewives, and raised their kids, the whole bit. And here I am with the crazy hours, working nights, going to meetings with men, business administration major — kind of far out for them.

My mother worries about me, I'm sure. She tries not to say anything because she knows it irritates me. We don't get to talk that often these days, so we'd rather not argue when we do get a chance to get together. She thinks I like my job, and that I'm going to be a success at it. I think she's proud of me. But it's things like, "Aren't you dating?" and "Barbie's pregnant again." And, I know she'd like some grandchildren....

...I get very aggravated with the pressures from everybody. I don't think I want to get married. I don't think I have the personality for it. I get impatient, and irritable. Maybe if I were married and still working, it would be better. But I've seen so many of my friends get married right away, to young guys who have about the same kind of job that I do, and they're sitting at home with nothing to do. I go crazy with two days off from work in a row; I'm climbing the walls of my apartment!

We went through the weddings right after graduation, and now the baby showers are starting. One girl is a part-time teacher. Only one girl I know has a career — my college roommate. She and her husband are both in the service. Right now, he's stationed in Europe, and she's here in the States, both going their own way. For most of them, that's not what they wanted to do. They wanted to get married and be housewives, and they love it. But I'm the only person I know who's doing what I'm doing; I don't have any idea why I'm different from those girls.

□

I went to a really big high school, over a thousand kids just in my graduating class. But I was with the same small group in the advanced program from seventh grade on. I was in lots of activities in high school, and I worked, too, because we went to school on split shifts, so I had an afternoon job. The guidance counselor recommended that I go to River City College because it's small, and for a private college, quite inexpensive; it receives a lot of support from the Presbyterian Church. And it was far enough away so that I was living in the dorm, but still close enough to home.

I might have been happier at a bigger school. River City is a very conservative college. Like that show on TV, it stopped sometime around the 1950s. The women had dorms on one side of the campus and the men had dorms on the other side. We had required chapel, and the big issue my senior year was, could we actually have coed meals? Sunday afternoons our senior year, we could visit, but during the week the men weren't allowed beyond the lobby. The men could be in the library until eleven, but the women had to be back in dorms by ten. Men could live off campus, women couldn't. Men could have cars their freshman year, women couldn't. And a funny thing happened there recently. Someone instigated a suit, claiming discrimination against women, so they set up hours for men, and men could not live off campus anymore. Instead of letting up on the women, they have clamped down on the men to keep it equal.

I was the only girl in the entire department of business administration. About two years previously, another girl tried, and the department chairman gave her such a hard time that she finally changed to secretarial science. As it was, he recommended that I go into retailing, stay out of manufacturing, stay out of the industrial end of it. It turned out he was right. It *is* easier for a woman to get into retailing — and I like it. I started out as a secretarial major, and did typing on the side for the whole four years I was in college. But I had to take some administration courses to meet requirements, and I got interested. All of a sudden, there I was, just a few credits away from completing a major in business, so I kind of hustled, taking nothing but administration courses, and I graduated. I think I kind of snuck it in on them. They didn't know what I was doing until it was too late! . . .

. . . I really didn't have any concrete plans when I got out of school, just some foggy notion of making a big success, conquering the world; but it hasn't happened like that.

I started out in this training program which was kind of crazy. There were twenty-one of us, six women and the rest men. Most of the guys didn't expect to see women in the training program at all. One fellow, who started the same day with me, said he thought it was so nice that the store manager included the secretaries in the opening-day meeting with the trainees! And he was very embarrassed when I told him I was a trainee too. He thought it was to be all men. Well, we ended up going out a few times.

The training program was very thorough, and you get responsibility early. The whole idea of the program was to get you early into high-level jobs. When you make that jump, there's a difference in pay, in status, in the hours you work. Right now, I'm overdue for that promotion, and I'm getting a little edgy. You see, they started the training program when the economy was brewing. They got real enthusiastic and hired too many trainees; now they're left with all these talented people sitting there. The government's been all over them to implement affirmative action, so they have to promote women, and I'm the only woman left from my group. All the rest got married, and they're all pregnant. Yet the economy's so slow, and they're not opening new branches, so that there is a backlog of people before me who haven't been promoted either. They just can't promote me. But I feel that I can't stay where I am too much longer, either.

It's a touchy situation in another way, too. I have a lot of responsibility for my age. There are two kinds of people at work — the young kids in their twenties who are getting started, and the middle-aged men in the store, family men of forty or fifty, who have made being a division manager the peak of their career. And there's resentment. I wouldn't have a department as large as I do if it wasn't for affirmative action. They had the opening, and they had to fill it, and I was the only woman there.

The resentment is really obvious at meetings. The men sit on one side of the room, and the new ones sit on the other, and we look at each other. And at a party, one guy said, after a couple of drinks, "Look at her, she's just a kid. Why, I have a daughter her age, and she's married." It made me feel kind of funny. Not that they can really affect my career or my promotion, but it's awkward. I'm doing a good job. I got my job mainly because I'm a woman, but it's worked out well. I'm running a sound operation, and everything's all right, knock on wood! But there is no one at work that I can really ask for an honest appraisal because my boss isn't about to tell me why I'm not being promoted. It's a very delicate situation. And with the economy the way it is, and two million experienced people with families to support, looking for jobs, I just can't get up the nerve to risk pushing the issue or looking around somewhere else. My big problem is, I don't dislike the job. There are frustrations, and sometimes I get really fed up, but I don't hate it enough to walk out on it. I have to get a little more emotional, either good and angry so I'll really look for a new deal, or else I'll really have to get going and push someone to get that promotion. . . .

. . . This job, and the first move, was really a big shock, especially to some of the other women in the training program who had never been away from home before. You know, all of a sudden, the first apartment, the first car, just handling the finances. I was sure that first year that I was going to be flat broke at the end of every month, and not be able to pay the rent. I'd never had any of that before. I think I was afraid, and I didn't have to be, because it all worked out. I've never missed a rent payment or a car payment, and I've never had to call home for money. But at the time, I was terrified. I'd never signed a lease before, or bought insurance; but Daddy wasn't there to go to, so I did it. And I had no trouble getting housing, as a single woman.

In a big apartment complex, it was all kind of impersonal. If you didn't look like you were going to destroy the place, the agent couldn't have cared less whether you were single or not. And I felt perfectly safe, until last week when my apartment was broken into. I came home and everything was dumped out all over the place. That really upset me, the shock of knowing that some guy was going through all my things.

. . . [On her social life] I don't do too much. I'm tired, and I like to go home. On Sunday, I do the laundry, and clean the place up. And I make myself a big breakfast, and sit around and relax. Besides, I work crazy hours, especially at Christmas. By the time you lock up and come home some nights, you're exhausted. My day off keeps changing, so I can't really sign up for a course or anything. I'm too tired for hobbies . . . usually I see a lot of the people I work with, because their hours are crazy, too, and it's easier to be in touch with them. They're mostly older than I am, some married, some single.

I used to be very self-conscious about going to a married friend's home by myself, but now that they don't try to get a date for me, we're very relaxed about it. If I want to go for a drink or for dinner, I'll go by myself, or I'll go with a group of girls. I don't make a habit of going to a bar by myself, because you get stared at, and people try to pick you up. And that's not what I was looking for. I know the student hang-outs don't mind if you're alone, but I'm kind of out of the bluejean stage now. I want something just a little more sophisticated, and an older crowd.

But the whole thing of social life is kind of crazy. There are no rules. You never know how to handle it. When I was first in the training program, I dated some of the guys. We'd go out for dinner, and I'd know that he couldn't afford to pay for me, because we made exactly the same pay. But it was always very touchy, you could never suggest paying your own way, because he would be offended, or he'd think I was try-ing to be a libber, and you can't let them call you that! Even with mar-ried friends, the husband always has to buy me a drink.

Y oung adulthood is the stage of life when women finally confront the realities of the female role. Although girls are taught what is ex-pected, permissible, discouraged, and forbidden for women during childhood and adolescence, these lessons are apt to be partial, distorted, and, most important, second-hand. Girls must await young adulthood for a complete initiation into the female role. Between the ages of twenty and forty, then, they learn what it means to be a woman in concrete and per-sonal terms. They select a mate, they marry, they bear children and care for them, and they run a household. Frequently they hold a job in addition to everything else. In doing all this they come to appreciate the distance be-tween the male and female worlds.

Men in their twenties and thirties are concerned with mastering a trade and establishing themselves in it. Their careers are at the forefront of their lives, with family matters almost taken for granted. In most cases parenting is a peripheral activity for young men, who continue to believe that their wives should assume primary responsibility for child rearing. The experi-ence of women in the same age category is almost the reverse. Family events dominate young women's lives, and the duties of motherhood re-main uppermost in their minds. The proliferation of young women in the labor force in recent years, many of them mothers of small children, has been interpreted as foreshadowing a breakdown of the traditional dichot-omous pattern of young adulthood. Yet, women still play the major role in housekeeping and child care, their jobs as a rule taking second place to family needs. The versions of female young adulthood presented in this chapter illuminate the ways women from different backgrounds have dealt with these perennial issues.

The seven women encountered in this chapter represent varied backgrounds and life situations. Mary Ann Owen Sims and Virginia Taylor Klose came from the upper levels of the social structure; Sandy, Jemima Condict, Florence Finch Kelly, and Sarah Hill Fletcher from the middle; and Aleksandra Rembieńska from the lower level. During the period of their lives reviewed here they resided in different sections of the country — Jemima Condict in New Jersey, Sarah Fletcher in Indiana, Mary Ann Sims in Arkansas, Florence Kelly in Massachusetts, and Aleksandra Rembieńska and Virginia Klose in New York. It is not clear where Sandy lived. Jemima, Mary Ann, and Virginia lived in rural areas, while Florence, Aleksandra, and probably Sandy lived in urban areas. Sarah lived in a small, newly established town. All of these young women were American-born except Aleksandra, who was a Polish immigrant. Two were Catholic — Aleksandra and Virginia. Sandy's religious background is not specified. The rest were Protestant. With respect to education, this group of women included three college graduates — Florence, Virginia, and Sandy. Mary Ann had a good education for her era, and Jemima apparently did also. Sarah received instruction in a number of subjects from her future husband.

In terms of marital status this was a diverse group, consisting of women who were single, married, and widowed. Sarah Fletcher and Virginia Klose were married, and Mary Ann Sims was a widow. All three were mothers. Of the four single women, all expected to marry except Sandy. We know that Jemima Condict and Florence Kelly did marry. Although this group of seven women constitutes quite a broad sample of young American women, investigation of the experiences of young black, Hispanic, and Jewish women would fill out our picture even further. Nevertheless, these seven young women provide us with ample evidence for delineating the core issues of female young adulthood.

Without a doubt, marriage and family are of central importance in the lives of young women. Except Sandy, all these women considered the roles of wife and mother to be essential components of their identity. This is self-evident in the cases of Sarah Fletcher, Mary Ann Sims, and Virginia Klose. Jemima Condict and Aleksandra Rembieńska, while single, were concerned with choosing a potential husband. As for Florence Kelly, it is clear that she was unwilling to forego marriage even though she was determined to pursue a career as a writer. Only Sandy expressed no desire to marry, preferring to concentrate her energies on her work.

Once married and caught up in the routine of housekeeping, young women begin to realize that their idealistic vision of the role of wife must be tempered. The birth of children further chastens them, as they come to grips with the day-to-day burdens of motherhood. Still, the degree of disillusionment with the traditional female role varies considerably. Virginia Klose conformed to the realities of married life with relatively little discomfiture. She thought highly of her husband and was not reluctant to assume the subordinate role in the marital relationship. Sarah Fletcher, while also filling the expected role of submissive wife without complaint, was clearly intimidated by her husband and may not have enjoyed being married as much as she insisted. Mary Ann Sims was especially lavish in praise of her deceased husband, but memory undoubtedly colored her recollections.

Being a mother is regarded as a positive experience by most young women. The women in this chapter are no exceptions. Although Sarah Fletcher's initiation to motherhood was too recent for her to comment on in her journal, both Mary Ann Sims and Virginia Klose expressed satisfaction with the maternal role. Mary Ann was effusive in her descriptions of her little children and Virginia clearly cared about her children's welfare. No doubt these women occasionally were frustrated by the responsibilities of motherhood, but they preferred to emphasize its benefits.

Since the latter part of the nineteenth century, the standard timetable for female lives has included a few years spent in paid employment prior to marriage. Until recently, young women's employment was expected to cease when they married or certainly when they became mothers, unless financial conditions dictated otherwise. Thus, most young women have tended to regard work as a temporary activity rather than a lifelong commitment. They value the independence a job gives them, but they do not view success in the workplace as the primary measure of their identity. The minority of women who aspire to careers are often compelled to choose between marriage and work. The experiences of the women studied here illustrate the possible meanings of work in the lives of young women.

Florence Kelly took her work as an editorial writer seriously and projected a career for herself. Nevertheless, her career was interrupted by her marriage and was not resumed fully until her widowhood. Aleksandra Rembieńska, the domestic servant, was pleased with the remuneration she received, but she did not find any intrinsic value in her work. Sandy, the young business executive, was much closer to Florence Kelly in her outlook on work. To her, marriage was an unlikely event, given her disposition, and she determined to focus her life on her career. While Florence was reluctant to remain single, Sandy apparently savored the prospect. Virginia Klose's work experience falls into another category. Married and the mother of four children, she resumed her career in radio at her husband's instigation, but she decided that she could not continue it when she became pregnant again. In short, she considered her primary role to be mother, not career woman.

Although young women today enjoy the widest variety of employment options ever, they still face the issue that has perplexed young women since the nineteenth century — how to reconcile a career with marriage and motherhood.

Bibliography

Adams, Margaret. *Single Blessedness: Observations on the Single Status in Married Society.* New York: Basic Books, 1976.

Bane, Mary Jo. *Here to Stay: American Families in the Twentieth Century.* New York: Basic Books, 1976.

Bequaert, Lucia H. *Single Women, Alone & Together.* Boston: Beacon Press, 1976.

Bernard, Jessie. *The Future of Motherhood.* New York: Dial Press, 1974.

Bernard, Jessie. *Women, Wives, Mothers: Values and Options.* Chicago: Aldine, 1975.

Blood, Robert O., Jr., and Wolfe, Donald M. *Husbands and Wives: The Dynamics of Married Living.* Glencoe, Illinois: Free Press, 1960.

Carter, Hugh, and Glick, Paul C. *Marriage and Divorce: A Social and Economic Study.* Rev. ed. Cambridge, Massachusetts: Harvard University Press, 1976.

Cowan, Ruth Schwartz. "The 'Industrial Revolution' in the Home: Household Technology and Social Change in the 20th Century." *Technology and Culture* 17 (1976): 1–23.

Degler, Carl N. "What Ought to Be and What Was: Women's Sexuality in the Nineteenth Century." *American Historical Review* 79 (1974): 1468–1491.

Giele, Janet Zollinger. *Women and the Future: Changing Sex Roles in Modern America.* New York: Free Press, 1978.

Goode, William J. *Women in Divorce.* 1946. Reprint. New York: Free Press, 1956.

Hoffman, Lois Wladis, and Nye, F. Ivan. *Working Mothers: An Evaluative Review of the Consequences for Wife, Husband, and Child.* San Francisco: Jossey-Bass, 1974.

Komarovsky, Mirra. *Blue-Collar Marriage.* New York: Vintage Books, 1967.

Kreps, Juanita M. *Sex in the Marketplace: American Women at Work.* Baltimore: Johns Hopkins University Press, 1971.

Laws, Judith Long, and Schwartz, Pepper. *Sexual Scripts: The Social Construction of Female Sexuality.* Hinsdale, Illinois: Dryden Press, 1977.

Lopata, Helena Znaniecki. *Occupation: Housewife.* New York: Oxford University Press, 1971.

Rossi, Alice S. "Transition to Parenthood." *Journal of Marriage and the Family* 30 (1968): 26–39.

Rubin, Lillian Breslow. *Worlds of Pain: Life in the Working-Class Family.* New York: Basic Books, 1976.

Scholten, Catherine M. " 'On the Importance of the Obstetrick Art': Changing Customs of Childbirth in America, 1760 to 1825." *William and Mary Quarterly* 3rd ser., 34 (1977): 426–445.

Smuts, Robert W. *Women and Work in America.* 1959. Reprint. New York: Schocken Books, 1971.

Wertz, Richard W., and Wertz, Dorothy C. *Lying-In: A History of Childbirth in America.* New York: Free Press, 1977.

Westoff, Leslie Aldrige, and Westoff, Charles F. *From Now to Zero: Fertility, Contraception and Abortion in America*. Boston: Little, Brown, 1971.
Williams, Juanita H. *Psychology of Women: Behavior in a Biosocial Context*. New York: W. W. Norton, 1977.

FOUR

Middle Age

Middle age has acquired a new face of late, one that highlights its challenges and opportunities instead of its problems and pitfalls. A host of recent writings, both popular and scholarly, has focused on the potential for growth in this life stage rather than the inevitability of decline. Persons who formerly were counseled to make a sensible adjustment to their loss of power or function are now advised to search for their true self and formulate a revised life plan that incorporates their new understanding of themselves.

This vision of midlife as open-ended has been a liberating one for women educated to think of the years from ages forty to sixty-five as downward steps on the path to old age. Many older women have responded enthusiastically to the upbeat message in this altered conception of middle age, and some have remade their lives with newly defined goals. As a result, the substance of a middle-aged woman's life is no longer as predictable as it once was. Though she may still be a wife, a mother, a housewife, and a grandmother, a contemporary woman in her forties or fifties might also be a student, a worker, a divorcée, or a novice embarking on a career. The options that she now possesses were not available to her mother or grandmother. Nor are they all viable options for women of her own generation whose socioeconomic status, ethnic background, or previous life history preclude their exercise. Nevertheless, the fact that middle-aged women today are not faced with massive opposition when they choose to reassess their lives and reorder their priorities constitutes an alteration of major importance in women's life patterns. Placing the experiences of the present generation of middle-aged women in a broader framework will enable us to comprehend the magnitude of these changes as well as to evaluate their significance.

Historical and cultural variation in delineating the boundaries of middle age suggests that chronological measurements are of limited value in defining this stage of life. Although the years from age forty to sixty-five are currently spoken of as the middle years, it is reasonable to conjecture that middle age commenced earlier in the life span and encompassed fewer years when the life expectancy was lower than ours. In 1798, for example, Abigail Adams referred to a thirty-three-year-old man who had just died as "Quite a middle aged Man." [1] Before the twentieth century it was customary to regard adulthood as a relatively undifferentiated period of life; consequently, middle age was not as clearly demarcated a life stage as it is now.

Investigations of biological development have provided us with more exact indicators of middle age. Recognizable signs of aging such as graying hair, wrinkles, and slowing reaction time serve as useful guideposts for marking the advance of middle age. For women, however, one major physiological event occurs during middle age — the menopause. Nowadays, American women experience the menopause at about the age of fifty, but it is thought that in earlier centuries the average age at menopause was substantially lower. How the conceptualization of female middle age is related to the timing of menopause is still largely unexplored. While the cessation of the menses occurs at approximately the midpoint of middle age today, it is conceivable that menopause could have marked either the onset or the conclusion of middle age in the past. The relationship depends in large part on the meaning attached to the termination of a woman's reproductive capacity. If women are valued primarily for their ability to produce children, then menopause constitutes a decisive dividing line in their lives. Alternatively, if women fulfill other vital functions in society besides childbearing, then menopause looms as a less portentous event in their lives. In other words, the status of postmenopausal women is linked to the definition of women's role in society.

From the standpoint of a woman's biological development, menopause is best understood as the crucial turning point (the climacterium) on a continuum representing the aging process. Simply put, it is the time when women cease to menstruate and therefore can no longer become pregnant. The hormonal changes that accompany this process trigger certain symptoms, the most familiar being hot flashes. The fact that the body decreases its production of estrogen at this time leads to the most common long-term effect of menopause, the atrophy of vaginal tissues.

Other symptoms that are associated with menopause, such as emotional fluctuations and depression, are less directly traceable to physiological causes. Despite a voluminous literature purporting to demonstrate that a whole battery of psychological complaints is rooted in hormonal imbalances, there is good reason to believe that the cultural setting as well as the personal life history of an individual woman play a greater part in explaining these manifestations than female biology itself.

---

[1] "Abigail Adams to her Sister," Philadelphia, 9 July 1798, in *New Letters of Abigail Adams 1788–1801*, ed. Stewart Mitchell (Boston: Houghton Mifflin, 1947), p. 200.

Menopause does not interfere with a woman's ability to engage in or derive satisfaction from sexual relations. But her reaction to menopause may be colored by the removal of the fear of pregnancy. Greater sexual enjoyment may be possible for women once they are no longer able to conceive. On the other hand, in societies in which sex is restricted to the purpose of procreation, all sexual activity may cease at menopause.

Although biological development is of central importance to any discussion of female middle age, there is no justification for the all-too-common view that physiological changes offer a sufficient explanation of female behavior during the middle years. The issues that confront women at this time of life are far more complex and stem from alterations in social roles and self-perceptions.

Middle age augurs change in a woman's major social roles, those premised on her responsibilities in the family. Although a woman continues to function as a wife, a mother, and a housewife while she is in her forties and fifties, the content of these roles alters during the middle years, minimally for some women and drastically for others. Being a wife takes on a different meaning after twenty or thirty years of marriage. In some instances, the marital relationship may deteriorate over the years and in others it may improve. A number of factors contribute to the outcome — the presence or absence of children, the development of different interests by husband and wife, or the involvement of one or both partners with other persons. In recent decades, divorce has become more frequent in middle age as couples who have been married for a number of years, and whose children are grown, find it impossible to sustain the marital tie under new circumstances. Whether a women is voluntarily or involuntarily divorced in middle age, she experiences a severe shock when she finds herself no longer in the customary role of wife. In previous generations it was more common for a woman to be widowed than divorced in middle age. In either case, however, the loss of the role of wife constitutes a profound change in the pattern of a woman's life. Countless middle-aged women throughout American history have been compelled to adjust to the new role of widow or divorcée.

Modifications in the role of mother occur as a matter of course as women reach their forties and fifties. Since a majority of contemporary women complete their childbearing during their twenties, the typical middle-aged woman today is the mother of adolescents or young adults. Her concerns are sharply differentiated from those of a young mother, since she strives to meet the distinctive needs of older or grown children. In past generations, however, child rearing was far less specialized. A middle-aged mother was likely to have a houseful of youngsters ranging in age from toddlers to twenty-year-olds; consequently, she faced the whole gamut of child-care problems simultaneously. Motherhood in middle age largely resembled motherhood in young adulthood.

A similar continuity of experience was evident in the housewife role in earlier generations. Women with big families continued to perform their accustomed chores; the transition to middle age entailed little change in household routine. Nowadays, however, middle-aged mothers whose children have reached maturity are able to cut down on the time they devote to housekeeping. The role of housewife becomes less demanding when children are no longer regularly in the home. In brief, a woman's responsibilities to her immediate family diminish as her family goes through the normal stages of development.

Movement through the stages of the family cycle also leads to a new role for women in middle age, that of grandmother. As a woman's older children marry and begin to have children of their own, she inevitably becomes a grandmother. The exact content of this role varies, depending on time, place, ethnic background, and social class, but essentially it consists of an extension of maternal functions. In the era when large families were the rule, it was not unusual for a woman to have a grandchild of the same age as her youngest child.

The passage of time signals the appearance of a new generation on the family scene, but it also presages the disappearance of an older generation. One of the hallmarks of the middle years is the aging of one's parents. The role of daughter assumes greater salience in middle age as a woman's elderly mother and father require more care and attention. In most cases the role of daughter terminates in middle age as well. Since women are entrusted with responsibility for family matters in our society, middle-aged women are literally "middlemen" in their families, supporting enfeebled parents and at the same time bolstering the confidence of their own children on the brink of adulthood.

On balance, then, a contemporary woman undergoes significant change in her family roles during middle age. Typically, she gains a new role — grandmother, loses an old role — daughter, and completes the duties of child rearing expected of a mother. She may also lose her role as wife. The net result of these alterations is that today's middle-aged woman is left with a substantial amount of free time. Unless she has been holding a job all along, or been engaged in some other time-consuming activity, such as volunteer work, the chances are that the advent of middle age will pose a dilemma for her.

Notwithstanding the fact that modern American women are involved in all sorts of extrafamilial pursuits, there is ample evidence that large numbers of them are faced with problems of psychological adjustment at middle age. The loss of familiar roles, particularly the role of mother, leaves women who have been socialized to believe that motherhood was their all-consuming purpose in life at loose ends. In many instances, an emotional crisis develops during which a woman questions her self-worth and agonizes over her future prospects. For many women the solution to this problem, often referred to as "the empty nest syndrome," has been to reinvigorate their lives by taking a job or resuming their education. However, the assumption of new and unfamiliar roles can also produce stress. The decision to embrace a new role can itself cause anxiety, especially if the new role is not consonant with conventional expectations for middle-aged women. Adjustment to changing roles, therefore, is a prominent psychological issue for women in midlife.

Yet the psychological themes of middle age go well beyond adapting to altered roles. For one thing, the ways that people look at themselves tend to change in middle age, reflecting a heightened sensitivity to the passage of time. Contemporary theorists suggest that during this period of life people truly realize they are mortal. The perception that life is finite unleashes a torrent of thought and emotion directed toward determining how to make the most of one's remaining years. The introspective process may involve efforts to clarify one's identity and in so doing to set forth new goals for the future. Some contemporary women have used such reflection at middle age as a means of moving from a family-oriented self-concept to one premised on a much broader understanding of individual needs and potential.

From another perspective, middle age represents the peak period in the life span, the "prime of life." A feeling of competence or mastery suffuses a person during the middle years, the logical outcome of decades of learning and preparation. Pride in one's accomplishments, confidence in one's skills are the touchstones of middle age. But since American women today are normally judged on the basis of appearance and sexual attractiveness rather than intelligence or achievement, the waning of youth is cast in a far more negative light for females than for males. A middle-aged woman finds it difficult to convince herself that she is in the prime of life when she has lost her most valuable asset — her youth. As a result, she is limited in her ability to reap the rewards of her manifold accomplishments. The context in which a woman grows older, then, plays an important part in how successfully she will deal with the psychological issues of midlife. As is true for all other life stages, the trajectory of individual development in middle age is subject to cultural influences that either support or impede growth.

Generalizations about psychological, sociological, and even biological themes of middle age need to be tested for their historical validity. The necessity for a historical framework for studying middle age is indisputable. Yet the history of middle age in America has yet to be written. Some clues exist in demographic evidence and studies of attitudes toward aging, but in essence there is no agreed-upon outline of the history of this life stage. At best, then, we can offer some tentative suggestions concerning the experience of female middle age over the centuries.

Survival to middle age was not assured for either men or women in the seventeenth, eighteenth, or nineteenth centuries. That a great number of people did live through their forties and fifties should not blind us to the fact that death in the early stages of life was far more common than it is today. Moreover, women had a greater likelihood of dying before middle age than men because of the dangers of childbearing. High maternal mortality rates prior to the 1930s testify to the fact that the attainment of middle age was indeed a landmark for women caught in a continuous cycle of childbearing during their fertile years.

For those women who produced children throughout their fertile period, middle age represented, first and foremost, the stage in life when childbearing ceased. Otherwise, it constituted a period indistinguishable from young adulthood in most respects. Child rearing and housekeeping duties continued apace. Such women remained primarily occupied with their role as mother throughout the middle years, since their last child usually did not leave home until they were close to sixty. Although exceptions to this pattern existed, such as the single woman or the woman who was widowed at an early age and did not remarry, by far the majority of American women living in the era when no fertility limitation was practiced spent their middle years taking care of their children, their husbands, and their households.

The precondition for change in the substance of middle-aged women's lives was the reduction of family responsibilities, particularly child care. This could only occur if efforts were made to control fertility, so that women would not have to have children as long as they were biologically capable of doing so. The birth rate in America began to decline in the late eighteenth century and has continued to do so, with the exception of the "baby boom" period following World War II. The long-term trend was for women, on the average, to bear fewer and fewer children. In the nineteenth century, when birth control techniques were haphazard and unreliable, pregnancies might be spaced over the woman's entire fertile period, whereas more recently, family planning has led to a concentration of births in the early years of marriage. This compression of the family cycle has altered the shape of a woman's middle years; with her childbearing limited to her twenties, her forties and fifties are no longer completely taken up with child care.

The lightening of child-rearing responsibilities in middle age did not automatically transform the lives of white middle-class women. Those late nineteenth-century, native-born Protestant women who were the initial beneficiaries of the modern fertility pattern had learned the lessons of domesticity too thoroughly to challenge the dictum that woman's place was in the home. Consequently, they chose to spend their expanded discretionary time in ways that did not entail a fundamental redefinition of their social role. These women still thought of themselves primarily as wives and mothers, only now their sphere of action encompassed the entire community and not just their own household. They joined in activities ranging from social and literary clubs to associations designed to remedy the major ills of society. They had been told that they were morally superior to men, and they intended to bring their influence to bear on the problems men had created.

However hard a middle-class woman worked at volunteer causes, she was strongly discouraged from competing with men on their own ground. Thus, it was rare for a privileged woman in her middle years to be found in the work force during the first three decades of the twentieth century. On the other hand, objections were not raised when poor middle-aged women took jobs because of economic necessity, especially if they were black or foreign-born. This double standard regarding paid work for older married women broke down during the Second World War as a result of the pressing need for labor. Women of all ages and classes were encouraged to serve their country by accepting employment, and they did so willingly, if not eagerly.

In terms of female life patterns, the war years marked a turning point for middle-aged women who were not economically disadvantaged. Never again would a paid job be looked upon as inappropriate for women of this age group, whether married, divorced, widowed, or single. The demand for workers in the postwar economy, and the precedent of wartime employment, ensured that middle-aged women were in the labor force to stay. In 1950, 38 percent of women between the ages of forty-five and fifty-four were in the labor force; in 1960 the figure was 49.8 percent; and in 1970 it was 54.4 percent. The definition of legitimate female endeavors had been broadened in response to changing social and economic conditions. Yet, by and large, work did not provide a springboard to a new conception of life for middle-aged women. The tenacity of cultural norms in the 1950s and 1960s made it virtually impossible for married working women to conceive of themselves as anything but wives and mothers.

Since the vast majority of women workers in the 1950s and 1960s were clustered in routine jobs, poorly paid, and with minimal opportunity for advancement, this idea was not difficult to believe. The experience of working in itself did not fundamentally alter these women's self-concepts. The ways middle-aged women looked at themselves continued to reflect the century-old values of domesticity. Paid work was rationalized as an auxiliary activity of women, as one more way they could serve their families. That a job or career could be a means to self-fulfillment, a vehicle for personal growth, was inadmissible. If, as a by-product of her work experience, a middle-aged woman developed an enhanced sense of self-esteem, this was an unanticipated benefit from a generally unrewarding situation. No overt challenges to the reigning social ideal were raised, and the notion of the husband as breadwinner was preserved intact.

Those middle-aged women who elected to stay home divided their time among family duties, volunteer work, and recreational pursuits. No longer preoccupied with child care, these women frequently exhibited symptoms of "the empty nest syndrome." The label itself conjures up an image of a woman whose entire identity is subsumed under the heading "mother" and who therefore has no real purpose in life once her children have grown up and left home. Ironically, this unflattering depiction of middle-aged women went to the heart of the dilemma faced by the postwar generation of older women. Demographic forces had reshaped the contours of women's lives by the midtwentieth century. American women were living longer and spending a briefer portion of their life span in raising children. Yet they had a paucity of options for filling the postparental years. They could escape from the deadening routine of housework, shopping, and socializing only by taking a menial job or volunteering their services to a charitable cause. Whatever they chose to do, they had little opportunity to realize personal goals, since it was taken for granted that a woman's primary identity was rooted in her roles of wife and mother. Although the overall pattern of their lives had diverged notably from that of their counterparts a century earlier, middle-aged women were still being asked to think of themselves in the self-limiting ways that had thwarted so many nineteenth-century women.

The difficulty of coping with the emptiness of the middle years engendered negative reactions in numerous women — depression, alcoholism, drug dependence. Although medical authorities tended to explain these disorders by linking them to the physiological changes of the menopause, an alternative interpretation views them as covert modes of rebellion against the stultifying regimen of women's lives. However, the accumulating discontent of middle-aged women was not expressed solely in counterproductive ways. By the 1960s, the grievances of middle-aged women were being articulated openly. After feminism reemerged on the American scene in the late 1960s, middle-aged women from all walks of life were inspired to transform their identities.

Many middle-aged women were dissatisfied with family roles and yearned to assert themselves, and in the 1970s some were able to make constructive changes in their lives. Others, however, were handicapped by insufficient education or work experience, constrained by adherence to ethnic or religious traditions that defined the female role very narrowly, or lacked the psychological resources to move beyond the conventional script for middle age. Yet even if the majority of middle-aged women followed in the well-worn paths of their mothers and grandmothers, they were definitely aware of the altered landscape of female middle age. The pathbreaking women who had adopted new life-styles in their forties and fifties were at the forefront of their own generation, and they have provided future generations of American women with a new model for middle age.

M any women in colonial America did not live to see their children reach maturity, marry, and begin families of their own. Because this experience was denied to so many mothers, those women fortunate enough to survive to middle age in the seventeenth and eighteenth centuries must have felt a particular pleasure at witnessing their offspring launched on their adult lives. When the child who left home was a daughter, the mother, however powerful her feelings for her male children, strongly identified with the young woman about to be initiated into the roles of wife and mother. Here was the girl to whom she had taught her housewifely skills and in whom she had confided those special secrets passed only from mother to daughter. This was the person who, on one level, was an extension of her very self. It was natural, then, that a middle-aged mother would attempt to ease her daughter's way into womanhood by giving her material aid, practical advice, spiritual counsel, and, of course, affection.

Although there is little doubt that countless colonial mothers played an important part in aiding their daughters during the transition from girl to wife and mother, written evidence documenting this process is rare. The following series of letters from Elizabeth Ward Saltonstall (born 1647) to her daughter Elizabeth (born 1668) provides a tantalizing glimpse into the relationship between a middle-aged mother and her newly married daughter in late seventeenth-century Massachusetts. The first two letters date from the period shortly after the younger Elizabeth's marriage to the Reverend John Denison (c. July 1688). John Denison died in 1689, and the young widow married the Reverend Rowland Cotton on September 22, 1692. The third letter was written two years after Elizabeth's marriage to Rowland Cotton.

The Saltonstalls were a leading family of Haverhill, Massachusetts. In addition to their only daughter Elizabeth, Nathaniel and Elizabeth Ward Saltonstall were the parents of three surviving sons: Gurdon (born 1666), Richard (born 1672), and Nathaniel (born 1674). Although the Saltonstalls possessed greater resources than the majority of families in the Massachusetts colony, there is little reason to believe that Mrs. Saltonstall's experiences in middle age differed in kind from those of her less affluent counterparts in seventeenth-century New England.

As a wife, mother, and housewife, Mrs. Saltonstall's duties and activities were essentially the same in her forties as they had been in her twenties. Her children were older, of course, after two decades of marriage, but the family still remained at the center of her universe, and her time and energy were directed toward ensuring the welfare of its members. The marriage of her daughter did not alter Mrs. Saltonstall's life fundamentally; it only added to its complexity. The fledgling Denison household at Ipswich in a sense constituted a satellite of the extended family, a point well illustrated by the placement of the two younger Saltonstall boys, Richard and Nathaniel, with their newly married sister and her husband. To Reverend Denison was delegated the responsibility for educating his wife's brothers, a customary practice. Mrs. Saltonstall's solicitude for her daughter did not cease at marriage, it merely altered in response to the young woman's new circumstance. Since Elizabeth's primary loyalty was now to her husband instead of her parents, Mrs. Saltonstall assumed a more restrained attitude toward her daughter. Nevertheless, the reports of supplies sent to Elizabeth for her new household, as well as the lengthy instructions regarding housing, animals, food, clothing, and deportment, reveal the mother's genuine concern that her daughter set up housekeeping in a manner that would reflect favorably upon her own family. The voice is that of the experienced housewife speaking to the novice, excessively didactic perhaps because of the deep emotional bond between mother and daughter.

Elizabeth Saltonstall's concern for her daughter's well-being manifested itself not only in explicit recommendations on practical matters but, in keeping with her Puritan background, in advice on her spiritual condition. She enjoined her daughter to watch over the state of her soul constantly, for life was very fragile and death could come at any moment. It is possible that Mrs. Saltonstall's preoccupation with the theme of death in these letters, although common enough among seventeenth-century Puritans, was, at least in part, related to her perception of herself as aging. A mother always feels older when her first child marries. Sensing her own mortality, Mrs. Saltonstall may have believed it was her duty to remind young Elizabeth of her vulnerability, and the transitoriness of life, at a time when her daughter's mood surely was more one of celebration than sober reflection.

One of the most important ways middle-aged mothers supported their married daughters in colonial America was to assist them at childbirth. Elizabeth Saltonstall's 1694 letter to her daughter, then the wife of Rowland Cotton, reveals the elder woman's distress at not being able to be with her daughter at this critical time. Even though this was not Elizabeth's first pregnancy, the seriousness of the occasion warranted Mrs. Saltonstall's presence. Knowing that she could not be at her daughter's bedside, she hastened to assure Elizabeth that Madam Cotton (Rowland Cotton's mother) would be an invaluable attendant during delivery. Nevertheless, Elizabeth Saltonstall anticipated her daughter's disappointment and offered prayers and apologies as well.

One final insight into the world of middle-aged females in the seventeenth century can be gleaned from these letters. It is frequently observed that people in their forties and fifties represent the middle ground between the past and the future, that they form a bridge between their parents and their children. Although three-generation families were not as common in the colonial era as they are today, Elizabeth Saltonstall was conscious of her role as a mediator between the generations in her family. Her letters abound in references to family members of her parents' generation, and she makes a point of reminding her daughter to treat her new husband's grandmother with the respect due her because of her great age. Besides demonstrating the veneration for the elderly in seventeenth-century New England families, these comments suggest the pivotal role of the middle generation in cementing the bonds between the young and the old. Since men were occupied in public affairs, it fell to middle-aged women such as Elizabeth Saltonstall to sustain family continuity.

—— 19 ——
Elizabeth Ward Saltonstall

ELIZABETH AND NATHANIEL SALTONSTALL TO
ELIZABETH SALTONSTALL DENISON

DEC. 6, [16]88

Loving Daughter,

I have sent by Marten Ford your [bro]thers stockings. Pray lett them

SOURCE: Robert E. Moody, *The Saltonstall Papers, 1607–1815.* Selected and edited and with biographies of ten members of the Saltonstall family in six generations. 2 vols. (Boston: Massachusetts Historical Society, 1972). Copyright © 1972, Massachusetts Historical Society. Reprinted by permission.

be well dried before they wear them and do them that evidence that they have wore them a while to line them. I would have done it [but] I could not gett them dry time enough. I have sent lineing and yarn [wi]th the stockings. I have allso sent you sope when you want more [torn] yarn and we will indeavour to get it some for you though it was [not] without some trouble that we get this done. Your father was [forced?] to make two journeys to the hous before we could get it we have [received?]. Rich and Natt are gone to send theyr on arands. We want them for many things espetialy to read to Your Grand who is verry... for want of them but we are all willing for their sake to deny [ourselves?] hopeing God will give them hearts to improve their time ... to their best advantage in all respects not knowing how short... may be, call upon them to be constant in prayer reading [the?] [wo]rd of God learning their Catechisme keep them allways [emp]loyed when home mind them allso to be studious att their... when att schoole. Your Father, Grand and Myselfe [present?] hearty love to my Son with your selfe with humble and... for his great care and pains with the children... give them wisdome to improve such an oppertunity.

[Pray] present my Service to your good Grandmother with whome ... maintaine good corrispondence deny your selfe verry far to please her Consider her relation age goodnesse all call for honnour and respect from you her weaknesse of body and the infirmities of old age call for patience and pitty from you consider if you should live to be old you may stand in need of the same from others, it is certainly your [du]ty next to pleasing God and your husband to indeavour to plese.... The Lord give you grace and wisdome to do your duty in the... relations he hath set you in remember my love to your... brothers pray be carefull of them... respect... requires it the more give them [great?] charg they go out upon ...except verry firme lett me min[d y]ou again to see their stockings ...uly dry before they were them. Lett their shirts also be [dried?] before they put them on att any time; remember your... on and neglect not to write to him I shall add no more but... implore the blessing of God upon you all. Your affectionate mother,

Eliz. Saltonstall

ELIZABETH WARD SALTONSTALL TO
ELIZABETH SALTONSTALL DENISON

[HAVERHILL] APRIL 10 [16]89

Dear Daughter,

We have by Mr. Wainwrights bark sent all the things you desired when you were last att Haverhill as neer as I can remember. Your father will bring you a note of the particulars. He hopes to be att Ipswich tomorrow if nothing hinders. The beddin sent you must be responsible for when I call for them. Therefore procure flocks with what speed you can. You may sooner do it than we can. In the box of candles upward of 28 that you will, after you have taken off about 10 or 11 and find the rest larger candles ... into the cask of meat I put in as much brine as would ... whether enough to cover the meat I know not but if you have brine left of other meat that is good to fill it up it will do me. The meat is of the best we had and I am sure well preserved. Your father tells me when he was last att Ipswich you were —— ing of hireing cows which I am truly troubled att. You are inaquainted what it is to live upon hire. I wish you may never know the trouble of it by experience but I certainly think your hire cattle was verry needlesse. Had you had but 3 cows of your own they would have been more benefitiall to you then 5 or 6 upon hire and enough for your family at present. Had we known you had wanted sooner you should have had tow from hence and shall still have one if it may prevent your hireing, if it be not to late. Could you have hired only a house to have lived in without one foot of land I know not but it had been your best way but you have those neer you that are better able to advise then I am but you will certainly find great inconvenience to take much businesse upon your hand and forced to hire all your help. We may speak it by experience, therefore hire but for necessity and but one year at farthest and no cattle. If it be not done allready you may be sencible by your own experience how unsteady servants are ther fore little incouragement to keep a great dairy. I need not say much to perswade you to take the first oppertunity to purchase land to build upon, that so you may have a place of settlement of your own. I doubt not but are you sedulous about it and you will be advised to it by your best friends who are solicitous for your good. Your father gives me hopes of a peice of land neer the Church that it is probable may be purchased.

I write things as they come to mind though abruptly. Concerning summer cloathes for the children, I did intend that peice of blue and white cloath wove by to den ... should be for that use if it be not milled too thick. To lay out much in cloathing for them while they are growing will becom in a great measure lost but if that cloth will not serve, your father will procure more. Pray remember to send home the childrens old cloaths and stockings that are not useful for them. If either of the childrens old serge coats will or stockings will do you any pleasure for your boy you [were?] best keep them otherwise send that with the rest when Ric. or Nat comes. Pray be careful to call upon the children to ... use their time well not knowing how short it may be. Many young ones are taken away by death in this place and others ... here in about 5 or 6 weeks Aire son and daughter a girl of Ad Grely, Joseph Dow, John Maverick, Richard Currier. We have so many examples of sickness and mortality that I cannot but stand amazed to think of Gods great goodnesse to our family in continuing our lives and health in so great a measure. The Lord give every one of us hearts to improve His spareing mercy towards us. Present my service to your Honoured Granddam whom I would have you as Duty injoynes you highly to houner and respect and indeavor to please her to your verry utmost though you deny yourself for to do it. My hearty love and respects to your good husband with hearty and reall thanks for his great paines with my poor boys. I hope they will be so wise as to improve so choice an oppertunity to theire own advantage. I shall trouble you no farther at present. While I am writing Richd. and Nat are come home. The relation they give us concerning your removeall will divert your father's journey to Ipswich till you are a little settled. I hope you will receive the things sent by Mr. Wain[wright's] bark tomorrow or next day. We could get no wooden dishes made to send now. We have sent what wooden ware we could get with what we could spare from home. Your Father and Grandfather remember ther kind love to your good husband and self. I am dear daughter your loveing mother,

Eliz. Saltonstall

I have according to your desire sent the flax and hemp seed but I allmost wish I had not. It will but accation more [burden?] upon your land and you will find it difficult to hire any help in season.

Daughter — The small Cask I have sent is Apples for Ric. and Nat from their Grandfather.

NATHANIEL AND ELIZABETH SALTONSTALL TO
ROWLAND AND ELIZABETH COTTON

AUGUST 27TH [16]94,
FINISHED SEPTR. 3. [16]94

Dear Daughter,

We are extreamly refreshed with the good tideings your Father mett with att Boston by my Sons letter wherin we have an account that you are all alive and in health and as an addition to all that you have your good Mother Cotton with you whose indefatigable labour of love has been such as neither you nor we can be suffitiently thankfull for. God only is able to reward itt. It is certeinly a duty incumbent on us to observe all Gods providences so amongst others His wise disposall in working about those things which we are apt to looke on as our greatest disappointments for our best good. Had I according to my purpose and contrivance accomplished a journey to Sandwidge it might have proved to you the greatest inconvenience imaginable. In all probabilyty it would have occationed your being deprived of Maddam Cottons good company who by reason of her exquisite skill in difficulte cases, as she has formerly been so if the case should require may be under God the instrumentall means of preserving your life. We have all great reason to acknowledge with humble thankfullnesse her unexpressible love and kindnesse to your self and family we comfort our selves that the neext letter will give us an account of your safe delivery; it's our duty patiently to wait Gods time for the accomplishment of all His great workes; and to returne an answer before now but I beg that the [business?] and disturbances we are under by reason of ould Jersey [the family cow] being billeted in the house besides about 60 Garrison people [war refugees] and but little help may bespeak an excuse for me. Give allso my humble ... to Maddam Cotton if with you with unfeigned thanks for the very great kindnesses to you and in your self to us who [have?] a great concern for the welfare of you and yours both soul and body as for our owne: the necessities of the family inforces me to break off I can therefore add no more but humbaly leave you to the protection of the All suffitient God praying that He would please to lead you safely through all those troubles and dificulties you may meet with in this vale of tears and at last receive you to eternal Glory. I am dear daughter your verry loveing mother,

E. S.

*T*he childbearing histories of women in the years before family limitation was practiced on a wide scale guaranteed that the majority of women would still be occupied with child rearing during their forties and fifties. Since a woman's last child was not born until she was close to age forty, as was typical prior to the end of the nineteenth century, she would be almost sixty before this child reached maturity; her middle years, just as her younger years, would be taken up with caring for children. Even though she would no longer be hindered by pregnancy, her duties as a mother would remain central to her life.

The idealization of motherhood in the nineteenth century particularly affected middle-class women for whom the home had become the exclusive domain. From a very early age, females were inundated with teachings designed to persuade them that their supreme mission in life was shaping the characters of their children. By the time they had reached middle age, women were well aware of the pivotal nature of their position. Yet they also had become conscious of the personal cost of dedicating their lives to their children's welfare. Mandatory domesticity could be a potent source of frustration, if not bitterness, for women who had already shouldered the burdens of child care for two decades and who could look forward to more of the same for the next two decades. Their outward conformity to established social norms did not invariably mirror their inner state. The following selection from the 1856 diary entries of Ellen Birdseye Wheaton of Syracuse, New York, presents telling evidence of the conflicting emotions of a genteel housewife on the verge of middle age. The pious tone and stilted literary style tempt the present-day reader to discount the authenticity of the writer's feelings. But Mrs. Wheaton's mode of expression should serve as an additional reference point for analyzing her perspective on life.

On the surface, Ellen Wheaton appears to be an exemplary wife and mother. Born in Pompey, a village near Syracuse, in 1816, she was educated at schools in Cortland and Albany, where she received special training in music. At the age of eighteen, she married Charles Wheaton, a promising young merchant. By 1856 she had borne twelve children, one of whom had died in infancy. Members of Mrs. Wheaton's own family played a prominent part in her life, and during the period covered by these diary entries, her mother was recuperating from an illness in her home.

Although it is accurate to characterize the Wheatons as middle-class, it is important to note that prior to 1856, Charles Wheaton had suffered serious financial reverses that jeopardized his family's social position. This downturn in fortunes had unpleasant ramifications for the family's dealings with certain relatives and friends, a situation that caused Mrs. Wheaton much consternation.

The most conspicuous feature of Ellen Wheaton's life was her large brood of children. Acutely conscious of the responsibilities of motherhood, Mrs. Wheaton tried as best she could to meet the material and emotional needs of her eight daughters and three sons. She took pride in their accomplishments, anguished over their problems, and often sacrificed her own pleasure to advance their interests. The staggering dimensions of her task are vividly conveyed by the incongruous image of a woman preparing her adult daughter for a teaching position at the same time as she weaned her infant daughter. Even with household help it is a wonder that Mrs. Wheaton found any time for her own enjoyment. But remarkably, her schedule included reading, churchgoing, visiting with friends, an occasional lecture, and some travel.

Judging from external attributes, Ellen Wheaton's life epitomized the virtues of domesticity. But the record of her inner life preserved in her diary reveals the strain of molding one's existence to a model that denigrated women for affirming their own identity. Having internalized the precepts of domesticity, Ellen Wheaton did constant battle with herself over her failures to live up to these standards. Each glimmer of self-pity was promptly followed by a fresh vow of self-denial. Each expression of despair elicited a pledge to put on a brave front in the face of adversity. Repeatedly, Mrs. Wheaton attempted to convince herself of the rewards of her way of life. Yet the deliberateness of these efforts, coupled with the facts of her life, suggests that here was a woman who had seen through the façade of domesticity.

Ellen Wheaton was unable to confront her disillusionment with marriage and motherhood directly. Having invested so many years of her life in her husband and children, she could not overtly challenge the canons of domesticity. Instead she blamed her pessimistic frame of mind on her husband's financial misfortunes. But it is clear that a deeper malaise pervaded her being. When she reflected on her fortieth birthday that the prime of her life was almost over, the prospect that faced her was twenty more years of catering to the needs of her children and husband. She sensed that she had reached the limits of her mode of existence, that the future promised her nothing more. Ellen Birdseye Wheaton died in 1858 at the age of forty-two.

—— 20 ——
Ellen Birdseye Wheaton

TUESDAY, EVE. JAN. 15TH [1856] The family are in bed, and I ought to be there too, but I want to whisper a few words to my journal, ere I go. I am weary, and desponding, & want comfort somewhere. Mother has been more unwell than usual, today, and it makes me very sad and fearful for her. I know not, what is this strange disease she has upon her, but it is something serious, and alarming, and I feel very much the want of some friend and helper to lean upon, some one to advise and to comfort. Now, in the time of trial, I think oftener, than ever, of that dear Father, "who is not lost, but gone before,["] and of those tried and faithful ones, who departed in their prime. Then too, these family troubles, come thicker and faster, and the way looks dark on every side. My Husband is still, far away from home, and my heart grows weary, in longing for him. Oh, it is such a long and weary time, since he left us. Perhaps it may be given me to know in the words of the poet,

> How sublime a thing it is,
> To suffer and be strong —

Tho' I fear, not the latter clause — These trials make me feel how weak I am.

WEDNESDAY EVENING [JANUARY 16] Another day, is gone, another night is come, and finds me just as weary as ever. I expected E. & Emma from Utica in the P.M. train, but they did not come. Cornelia has gone out for the evening — Mrs. H. came in and spent an hour or so, in a sociable way, that I really enjoyed — She is one of the most prized, of my old friends, and I love to have her so near —

No news from Charles yet, and I suppose the mails are delayed by the great storm of last week, which reached very far South — I am afraid he will have a tedious journey home, for there is a large body of snow on the ground which must of course obstruct the travelling very much. There have already been some serious accidents, in consequence of the snow upon the railroads —

I looked into Longfellow last night for a little while, and was surprised to find (what indeed, I had noticed before, but forgotten), how aptly and truly he expresses my own thoughts, and many times the most delicate shades of feeling, of which I am conscious. I seem in reading some of his pieces, to have found an old & sympathizing friend, who knows &

SOURCE: *The Diary of Ellen Birdseye Wheaton*, notes by Donald Gordon (Boston: privately printed, 1923). Copyright 1923 by Louise Ayer Gordon. Reprinted by permission of Crawford Gordon.

Ellen Birdseye Wheaton

feels my sorrows, just as well as I do myself — How delightfully solemn & tender, are many of his expressions — such as these —

FOOTSTEPS OF ANGELS.
He the young and strong, who cherished
  Noble longings for the strife,
By the road side fell and perished,
  Weary with the march of life!

They the holy ones, and weakly
  Who the cross of suffering bore,
Folded their pale hands, so meekly,
  Spake with us, on earth, no more.

And the Psalm of Life from which I cannot extract a little where all is so perfect, and many others — There is some thing elevating, ennobling and yet soothing and comforting in his poetry, almost more than any other I know, and then he seemed to reach down to the deepest recesses of my thoughts — and give voice & utterance to what before, was only felt, not expressed — So I will say again, in his own words,

> Such songs have power to quiet,
>   The restless pulse of care,
> And come like the benediction
>   That follows after prayer. —
>
> Then read from the treasured volume,
>   The poem of thy choice,
> And lend to the rhyme of the poet,
>   The beauty of thy voice.
>
> And the night shall be filled with music,
>   And the cares, that infest the day,
> Shall fold their tents like the Arabs,
>   And as silently, steal away —

SATURDAY JAN. 18 [19]. Brother Lucien came up to see Mother and transact some business for her, which she is anxious to get off her mind. Aunt H. also came to-day, and was very glad to meet him. This A.M. a load came from Pompey, and it was as usual, a very trying and confused day — At night, they all went taking Lucia up to the Hill with them to stay a week or two.

SUNDAY A.M. [JANUARY 20] I went to hear Mr May, and found the weather intensely cold. C., Ed. & Henry went with me — In the evening Lute & H. came down from the Hill, and talked a good deal on business & other matters with Mother. It was late when we retired, and we had been asleep a little while, when Mother called us, saying she was much worse, and Ellen was already up with her — Lucien went after the Dr. about 2 o'clock, got some medicine for her, and she became more quiet towards morning. L. & H. left about 11. for the East, and I went out for a nurse, as it seemed evident that she must have one. I got on the track of one, was disappointed, and finally obtained another, who came in the evening. I also rode over to Salina with Frank, and saw the Misses Newell, about their sister's case. They were very kind and friendly and promised to come & see Mother soon. The new nurse proved to be an old acquaintance & does very well. —

TUESDAY, A.M. [JANUARY 22] Expect my husband to-day, & hope he will not disappoint us.

8 o'c. P.M. Charles has arrived looking very well, and in pretty good spirits — It was an occasion of great rejoicing to us all.

THURSDAY [JANUARY] 24TH. Mother seems better than she has been before in a fortnight, and I really feel much encouraged. Mrs Dr. Hopkins from

Skaneatles called to see her, this A.M. I went out this P.M. and did some errands — This evening we sent our excuses to the party by Edward, and about 1/2 a dozen children go to the hop —

WEDNESDAY, JAN. 30TH I have been trying to do something towards making Edward some shirts, in addition, to my other occupations, for the last few days, and it has confined me to the house very closely — I am troubled somewhat, with the Rheumatism in my right arm, and I don't think sewing helps it much — Yesterday Mr & Mrs Lawrence, came to call [on] us, and kindly brought us a bag of apples — This A.M. they came again, and Julia spent the forenoon with me. We had rather a painful conversation, on matters and things deeply concerning our welfare. — I have about come to the conclusion, that there is neither honor, nor truth, neither gratitude nor friendship in the world — I have been favored for a long period, with prosperity, but now that misfortunes have begun to come, they seem to roll on thicker and faster. — Perhaps we shall be made yet, to drink it to the dregs — May we be sustained under it all, and bear all, as knowing that "he doeth all things well."

Mr. Birdsall took tea with us, and sat a little while afterwards, before leaving for Binghamton. Ellen sang him, his two favorite songs. He seems in Miserable health. Cornelia has been helping her Aunt H. to nurse J. F. to-day, and to-night she & Emma, went to Society to Mr. Leonards. Edward has gone to Mr. Ulvons [?] to a party — But the baby wakes, and I must stop.

FRIDAY FEB. — 1ST. We have received an invitation to a party at Mr. Leavenworths, and Cornelia and Edward think they will go — Of course I cannot think of going — I think it right that they should go, for C. has not been out to a party this winter — tho' it is somewhat inconvenient — for me to prepare her — I have kept her in, very closely, as we seemed to be the subjects of so much censure, and I do not wish to give any occasion — But very likely it will make no difference for our relations are determined to hate and injure us, if possible. Heaven save me, from the tender mercies of blood relations —

We have heard of a situation as teacher, in the South which Cornelia thinks of taking, if she can get it — She has written, applying for it, and is now anxiously awaiting an answer — I think it is best, for her to try and help herself in some way, and this seems to be the most eligible at present — It will be a trial to part with her, and particularly to lose her music, and her help to Ellen, but we must give it all up — There are a great many sad changes, in this wearisome world of ours —

WEDNESDAY, FEB'Y, 6TH Well, they went to the party, and enjoyed it very well. Also last night at Cobleigh's. There are so many calls upon Cornelia, that she gets but little time, for anything like work —

SAT. FEB. 9.TH. For a wonder, I sat quite still nearly all day, and sewed, which is more than I have done, in a long time before. Cornelia and E. went to Mr. Woodruff's to spend the evening — Charlie is getting over a severe attack of croup, which has kept him pretty sick for a week — Mother is also improving considerably — and anticipates going home soon. —

SUNDAY, [FEBRUARY] 10TH. This P.M. I went to the Discussion meeting with Charles, — which is the first time in a year, I believe. I did not enjoy it much. To-night, we had a real old fashioned sing — just at twilight — How many more shall we have? Simon Reedy has called to see us to-night, and made us a very pleasant call. He is a genuine Irish wit — and humourist —

I feel sad and fearful, in view of the future, and dread to look forward — There is a dark cloud resting upon our prospects, and I cannot penetrate it. But time will unravel the mystery, and make it all clear — At any rate, I will try to be calm and cheerful, and to bear adversity, as I ought — God help me to feel right and to do right —

MONDAY, FEB. 11TH. I am quite sick with a cold and sore throat, with severe headache. Went into Mrs MCarthy's, an hour or so with my work, and had a pleasant chat — Mrs Hollister was there, a little while —

TUESDAY [FEBRUARY 12], I was miserable enough all day, and kept my bed part of the day. When Dr Cator came in to see Mother, I got some advice & medicine from him, he says I have an ulcerated sore throat.

WEDNESDAY [FEBRUARY 13] I am better to-day.

THURSDAY [FEBRUARY 14] Ellen Pomeroy, spent the day with C. and L. G. S—— came to tea. Had considerable conversation about the South, with her —

SATURDAY [FEBRUARY 16], Frank called on his way to Elbridge with J. B—— Charlotte and Frank came by the cars, but an accident detained them about two hours. — C. returned to E. in the P.M. and F. to Pompey — There was a little appearance of a thaw this morning, but by three o'c. it is growing cold and snowing fast. We are having a very hard winter. Since Christmas, there has been uninterrupted sleighing, and many very severe snowstorms — I have been in a sleigh twice this winter, and then only for a few minutes. I am really tired of this hard weather, it is so uncomfortable all around the house. All the water pipes are frozen up, the cisterns are nearly empty, and we are in great want of water.

This past week, I have read Grace Lee, a novel by Julia Kavanagh, and have been much interested in it — It is a fascinating but tiresome story. Not quite equal to "North & South" I think. I have also lately read, "King Henry 8th, and his Six Wives" —

Cornelia received a letter this evening from the gentleman, to whom she applied for a situation as teacher. He had written to a lady, at the head of a large school, for a teacher, but had received no answer, and could not tell what he should do, but will write again, in a few days. She feels very much disappointed, and thinks the thing is settled — However I tell her to go on, and get ready for some place all the same.

SATURDAY FEB. 23. Charles went to Binghampton on Thursday, — for two or three days. On Friday Eve. a letter came to Cornelia from Mr Davis, saying, that he had not procured a teacher, & would like her to come on immediately. So that she has her way clear before her.

Charles returned from B. this evening, and says he will go with her next week, as his route to S. C. lies, with hers, to within 36 miles of her destination. But he always has so many hindrances, about getting away, that I fear they will not go so soon, — and yet I dread their going, very much. But as he is circumstanced, I know that he is much more pleasantly situated there than he can be here, and so I am reconciled to his going, and to being left alone. C. takes pleasure in the thought that she shall be enabled to help herself, and relieve her Father somewhat, in this time of trial —

FEB. 24, SUNDAY. This morning, I went to the Market Hall, & heard a sermon. The old Congregational Church still continues to meet there, every Sunday A.M. and though they are few in numbers they have a stout heart. — The long contested suit between them and the Plymouth Church has at last been decided in their favor, — and now the question is, what to do next. — I know not, — but it looks hopeless, to try to do any thing — in the way of keeping up a Church. — Minnie & Lucia came from Pompey, on Friday — after an absence of six weeks. In the P.M. Frank took me up, to see Maria Brady, who seems to be very near death, with a fever. She lived with us almost two years, and I feel much interested in her. —

FEB. 27TH WEDNESDAY. Charles told us, this day at noon, that he had recd letters from the South, which make it important for him to be there as soon as possible. He wishes C. to be ready to go on tomorrow — So we have got to be busy —

THURSDAY, [FEBRUARY] 28TH Ellen A Pomeroy has been here, talking over the subject, and has finally decided on going South with Cornelia in pursuit of a situation as teacher. She had already given up, her Western plan. — I have been arranging Charles' clothes, for packing, and getting Cornelia's things together — Went out and got a variety of little items. —

This evening Charles, got away at 7 o'c. P.M. to go as far as Binghamton to-night, where he expects to be called as a witness in a suit to come off there. The girls go on in the morning. I was up late packing.

FRIDAY A.M. [FEBRUARY 29] Ellen finished packing the last trunk, and we had breakfast. — Then Cornelia ran over to Mr. H's and bade goodbye. The man came for the trunks and then for her. At the last moment, I decided to go to the cars with her. When we got there, there was quite a company assembled of friends from all sides. The girls kept up good courage, to the last and went off, apparently in good spirits — I came home feeling almost sick, with fatigue and excitement — I find I have another of those terrible sore throats.

MARCH 1 SATURDAY MORNING, This is the morning Mother had decided upon, to go home, and she and Julia got off, about the same time, that the others did — yesterday. She did not feel quite as well as usual for a day or two, but I think, it was nothing serious — She has been here, about 9 weeks — and is much improved, since she first came. After they left, it seemed very lonely and still — but there was enough to keep us busy putting the house to rights —

SUNDAY, A.M. [MARCH 2] Went to the Market Hall and had a little conference. A storm came on to-night, of a real wintry sort, snowing and blowing fiercely — and lasted all night. I have had a letter from Charles written from Binghamton. The girls had not yet reached there.

TUESDAY, A.M. [MARCH 4] brought me a letter from Charles written from N. Y., saying they should try to reach Washington for Sunday. The storm has come on again, and it is tremendous here.

WEDNESDAY [MARCH 5]. Another letter from Charles, from W. which they reached some time Saturday Night [March 1], very much fatigued. Sunday and Monday [March 2 and 3] they remained there, and I learn by a letter from Mrs. Cook to her daughter, that the girls attended a Congressional Ball at the National on Monday Eve. [March 3] — She and Mrs. Mason assisted them to dress and went with them. The next morning [Tuesday, March 4] at 6 they were on their way to Richmond.

FRIDAY [MARCH 7]. I had a message from Mrs. Ellis, that she would come and take tea with me this P.M. and I sent in, for Mary Hutchinson to meet her, but soon after dinner, word came, that Mr & Mrs Geddes were at Mr. E's and we were all to go over there — So we countermarched and went there and spent a sociable afternoon. Mr & Mrs Moses, came in, after tea. Mr. & Mrs Geddes left, about 8 o'c — Then there was a proposal to go to Mr. Morgan's, and see some table moving, but at last, the gentlemen decided to go, and return with a report for us, if there was any thing worth the trouble. We waited till ten and then, as they did not return, we put on our things, and came home. Have heard nothing more from the table-movings. Found a letter for me from Charles, dated Richmond Va. where they staid Tuesday night. They were expecting to get to Warrenton, Wednesday Evening. I hope now, in a few days, to get some account from the girls of their adventures — I feel very anxious to know how they got along. Charles complains of a dizziness, which troubles him somewhat, & which he attributes to the motion of the cars, and perhaps eating improperly. I hope it is nothing worse —

SATURDAY MARCH 8TH It is pleasant to-day, but very cold and windy. — Frances W. staid here all day. Eliza Wells called here to go home with Frank, on her return from Diana Dodge's funeral. I was obliged to go out this P.M. and I found the cold very piercing — I was thoroughly tired out, with such a confused and wearisome day.

SUNDAY, [MARCH] 9TH I think much of the absent ones, to-day, as I do not go to Church. The children are terribly restless to-day. I wish I could look in upon Cornelia for a little while this P.M. and see how she prospers, for, I suppose she has entered upon strange scenes. May she have wisdom, granted her to act wisely and prudently — But I must try to be patient, and courageous for her.

MARCH 12TH, WEDNESDAY, This A.M. Edward brought a letter from the P. O. with Charles writing upon it. I was very sure I should have one to-day, and of course was very glad to get it. He had got on safely, as far as Columbia, and was very well. Says the climate there is delightful, streets dry & dusty, and warm enough to do without fires, during the day. A most remarkable contrast to this ice-bound region, we inhabit. The girls parted from him, on Wednesday the 5th, on their route to Warrenton. I do hope to get some news from Cornelia this week. I had a very kind and pleasant letter from Louisa last night, which really was like balm to my wounded spirit — She is a dear, good woman. But I depend most upon Charles' letters. They are so kind, so frequent, and so just the thing, I don't know how I could get along without them. It has snowed very much here, since Sunday [March 9th], and to-day the wind has been high. I have never experienced so severe a winter, since my recollection. There having been now, eleven weeks of constant sleighing, without one really thawy day. I have been very industrious to-day, and am as tired, as a *"man, a mowing"*

Ellen has concluded to sing, at Mr Held's concert next week, and has commenced practising a little for it. Mrs. McE. came in to-night, and I settled with her, and paid her up. I hope I shall be enabled to get along, this Spring, without hiring so much help, as I have formerly done. Sometimes I fear, that I don't realize our position fully, and that I am indolent and forgetful of my duty. I dont mean to be so, and I do not wish to consult my own ease, if I know myself. — But I am willing to sacrifice ease, and leisure, to the welfare of my family, if I may thereby promote these ends —

MARCH 13, THURSDAY This day I am forty years old. Is it possible? I cannot realize it, and yet at times, I feel old and worn. When I look around and see this numerous flock of children, I can realize it, fully, and feel, that the prime of my life is, pretty far gone. But it seems only yesterday, since I was married. And so the years roll by, and if I am permitted to live, shall in a little time find myself, wrinkled, old and gray.

This morning brought me a delightful letter from Cornelia, and two from Charles, that did me good like a medicine. She is pleased with her position and the family of Mr. Davis, tho' she had not begun her duties, as yet. Ellen had not yet got a situation, but there were good prospects for her. I took the letter over to Mrs. Ellis, (who has had no letter yet from Ellen,) and read it to her, & Mrs. Morgan. I sat half an hour or so, and came home to find Sophronia here. She spent the P.M. and Ellen M. W. came about 4 o'c and staid also — Had a pleasant visit with them, and Jarvis called for them about 7. o'clock —

FRIDAY P.M. MARCH 14TH Went to the New Rooms to witness the exercises in the High School. There was a very full audience present, and the performances were very interesting. The rooms are very beautiful, and well arranged, and there is a fine piano in the school room. On my return from there, went into Harriets, and being warmly urged, staid to tea. G. B. W. returned from a fortnight's absence in the city while I was there. Came home in the evening and wrote Cornelia a long letter.

SATURDAY [MARCH 15]. Charlotte came from Elbridge today, & Frank came from Pompey, to take her home. She is a good deal worn out, with their weeks examination, and goes home for a weeks vacation. When she returns, she expects to have a new boarding place, and I trust will have some additional comforts. Mother continues to improve. About three o'clock, I had a call from Mr. A. Cobb, on a matter of business — It was rather a disagreeable affair, and I got along with it, indifferently well. Company to tea.

SUNDAY, [MARCH] 16TH. Last night there were several alarms of fire, and this A.M. I learn the Gymnasium Building was burnt down, and the Malcolm Building much injured. Work of Incendiaries. Went to Market Hall to Church, this morning & heard Mr Davis read a sermon. This P.M. it is snowing profusely. — A letter from Charles this A.M.

WEDNESDAY [MARCH 19]. This was a very drizzling snowy day, and Ellen, in preparation for the Concert, was obliged to travel about the streets altogether, too much, for her good. The concert was pretty well attended, for so bad a night. Ellen sang four times and was called out once. I have heard her sing better, tho' the audience seemed much pleased.

THURSDAY, P.M. [MARCH 20] Called at Mr. Hillis, an hour or two, and then went to Mrs. Walter's and took tea. No one there, but Mrs. Cook, who gave me a very pleasant account of her seeing the girls in Washington — She said they enjoyed their stay much. — Had some qualms, about going there, but guess it was for the best.

SATURDAY MARCH 22ND brought Sisters Emma and Charlotte, from Pompey, with Mr. Kendall and Frank all to dinner. Then the girls had company in the P.M. and so the day passed in bustle and confusion. It is uncertain whether C. returns to Elbridge, & E. will remain some days, on a visit. Edward having heard some obscure threats about the Sheldon Block being in danger from Incendiaries, has kept watch, for the best part of two nights, and I of course am somewhat disturbed, by his coming in about three o'clock in the morning, so that I dont rest very well. My baby is much out of tune lately, owing to teething, I fancy. I am desirous to wean her, next month, but I am much afraid it will be a critical thing for her.

SUNDAY, A.M. [MARCH 23] Went to a meeting at the Market Hall, & heard a sermon read by Mr. Davis. After meeting there was some talk of what had been done towards a settlement between our Church and the Plymouth folks. It looks about as likely to happen as ever, and I don't think they want any settlement, only to get hold of the Church property. I am sick of the whole thing. This P.M. went to the First Pres. Church with Sister E. After waiting a while in the porch, Mr. E. Bradley, invited us to sit with him. The Church was quite full, & [sic] listened to a discourse by Mr. Newell of Salina. Rev. Mr. Hall, was also in the pulpit. The best part of the service, was the music and the organ which was very finely played —
   To-night, after tea, to my surprise, had a call from Horace. While he was here, James and Lucy Ellis, came in and sat awhile. Lucy looks sad when she sees my children — poor woman! — 10 o'clock, P.M. Edward is sleeping on the lounge, preparatory to going out at midnight, to watch, & the babies are all in bed, so that I am really enjoying a very few minutes of quiet and leisure, the first I have had to-day. To make the most of it, I want to do, at least, half a dozen things, among which are several letters to be written. What shall I do first?

[SUNDAY] MARCH 30TH. Our Spring is advancing rapidly, and yet we have not had one pleasant, warm day, — not one real spring like day yet. However, it is rather bright to-day, — and the sky looks softer than usual. The past week, has been as usual, a busy one, for me, with very little relaxation, except what I find in a change of occupation. I had Miss V. O. the tailoress, here one day, and worked hard, with her, to get thro' — After it was over, went to tea at Mr. Hutchinsons and spent the evening. It is rare for me to go out to tea. Friday A.M. [March 28] brought me letters from Charles, and Cornelia. They were both well, & doing well. Cornelia, says she gets along well, in teaching, and finds the Family very kind & pleasant. Flora Fleming was there on a visit at the time of her writing — To-day I have been to meeting, as usual, and found nothing very edifying there. There was the usual singing & prayer, and a short sermon, and afterwards came the business meeting, in which the difficulties were again talked over, and resolutions passed. It seems to be settled, that there will be no amicable arrangement of the difficulties, and I hope the thing will be dropped now —

WEDNESDAY [APRIL 2]. The weather has been quite soft and spring like to-day, and fearing there would be a rain, by tomorrow, I concluded to walk up to the Hill and call on some of our friends there. Sister Emma accompanied me, and we called at Roberts' by the way. — Went to Clarissa's and saw the new baby, and had a very cordial reception. Afterwards stopped at Mrs. G.s, but she was too unwell to be seen. Afterwards went to J.'s, and being very kindly invited, remained to tea. When we were ready to start for home we found it raining quite hard, and borrowed umbrellas, and came home thro the mud, rather weary — Read stories to the children, part of the evening —

FRIDAY P.M. [APRIL 4] Had a short visit from Mrs Ellis, — but she did not stay to tea — Sister E. is almost sick with a cold, and is preparing to go home to-morrow, morning. This evening bro't me a letter from Charles, enclosing a Rail R. Bond for $1000, to be used in releasing my furniture from Sherriffs Sale. — After tea, went over to G. B. W's to see about it. Came home heartsick and weary.

SAT. A.M. [APRIL 5] Very early this morning, the house was astir, to see Emma off, in the cars, and as I did not sleep much thro' the night, in consequence of little Mabel's restlessness, I felt rather poorly today. —
Have had a very trying & exciting day, and have not at last, got matters arranged quite to my satisfaction — It has been quite a new experience for me, and an unpleasant one, but I hope, I am none the worse for it.

SUNDAY P.M. [APRIL 6] This forenoon wrote a letter to Charles, and afternoon went to Sec. Bap. Church. But did not find it specially interesting, and left before the close. E. M. W. was here to lunch and dinner. This evening the girls are gone to meeting. I think of the absent ones, when Sunday night comes, and feel lonely — Cornelia always said she enjoyed the Sunday P.M. dinner the best of any meal, in the week and when that time comes, I always think of her, and then this twilight reminds me of her music and her Fathers. Oh how much we miss the music. I don't hear as often from her as I should like — and yet I know, she has much to occupy her time, in her school, besides all her numerous correspondents, so I will try not to complain — I often picture her to myself surrounded by her pupils, and their attention fixed upon her, as she dispenses the knowledge to them. In all her letters she seems quite cheerful and contented. Oh! for patience to bear all these separations, and mortifications meekly, and rightly, and for wisdom to act rightly in these difficult passes of life — I, who have so long loved to lean upon those stronger than I, must now learn to rely upon myself in trials and emergencies, feeling that all human aid is vain, and help must come alone from above, Ah!

> Life is truly a strife,
> 'Tis a bubble, 'tis a dream.

and rudely indeed, are we tossed about upon its billowy surface. — How changed its aspect to me, in the last few years! So lately it seems, that I was so hopeful, so bright, when nothing had power to depress me long, but had always some bright anticipations to cheer me forward. Surrounded by friends, fortune smiled, and life seemed really worth living for. Now, when fortune frowns, friends frown too, or what is worse desert us, entirely. Clouds of care & anxiety, unknown before, settle down upon me, and I walk, from day to day, as in a maze — not seeing my way clearly towards any future object. Many times so weary and heart sick, that life seems utterly worthless — But this is not the right mood, for me to indulge in, and I will be up and doing:

> With a heart for any fate,
> Still achieving, still pursuing,
> Learn to labor and to wait —

SUNDAY, APRIL 13. Another week has gone its round and here am I, trying to say a few words, to make a slight record in my diary, that shall mark the flight of time, and the way in which it passed. Nothing of any note, I think has occurred the past week, that I remember. Brother Frank came down Tuesday, and remained till Wednesday — He was almost sick with a cold. I have been mantua [a loose-fitting gown] making, and trying to get [the] children fixed for Spring. Have begun a needed domestic reform in the water pipes of the house, but it is not yet fully completed. These waterworks are very expensive, at the best, and are almost always out of order. The weather is fine today, tho' cold, but Spring comes on apace. No one of the family, has been to Church, but Ellen, who went to hear Mr. May — She and I, and Florence, have been writing to Charles to-day — Last Thursday [April 10], brought us, a very interesting letter from Cornelia, and full of amusing incidents. — She writes very well, and we are always eager to read her letters —

SATURDAY, APRIL 19TH. During the past week, have been putting Charlie into jacket & trousers, and think him much improved by the change. He is delighted, with it, and it is amusing indeed to see the airs he puts on. Clara wrote a long account of the change to her Father, and sent it in the same enclosure with one of my own. To day, brought me letters from Charles and Cornelia and some commissions to execute for Cornelia, which I must go about next week, I suppose. Emma's school is closing this week with a great deal of bustle, and then she will be at liberty to stay at home for a while. Ellen is preparing to act a part in some private theatricals next week, also to sing in Mr. Held's concert. Julia has written to invite Ellen to come to Pompey and spend the summer, and I wish it were possible to let her go.

[FRIDAY] APRIL 25TH. Theatricals, & concert, have come and gone, and passed off very successfully. Ellen appeared well as Widow Pottle, and acted much better than I expected. The concert was well attended & she sang very well, tho' I think I have heard her sing better. Sarah Hull, & Mr. Kinnicott, came down from Utica, to attend it, and Sarah, staid here. Emma is suffering terribly from the tooth, ache — but will not have her tooth extracted.

SUNDAY A.M. APRIL 27TH. This A.M. Henry bro't me a letter from Charles, which I have answered to-day. Also learning that Florence could go to P. with D. W. and wife to-day, I wrote to Julia, to send it by them. Florence went, about 1/2 past three to stay a few weeks. All the morning, Lucia and Henry were talking about Pompey, and how much they wanted to go there. They wished I would let them walk up, they knew they could, &c. Of course I said no, emphatically, and treated it as a piece of arrant nonsense. But about 2 o'clock they were missing — Did not come home to supper, and when the sun went down, it bro't no children. Edward went out, in the evening and looked for them, but could hear nothing — At last, we decided they must have gone to P — as they were so anxious to do. I did not feel very, uneasy, for I felt sure they were safe. Well the next A.M. about 10 o'c. Sister Emma and Brother Frank arrived with the children safe and tolerably sound. They walked about 7 1/2 miles, when Dan, over-took them, and carried them on to Pompey. Lucia was somewhat footsore, but Henry never complained at all —

WEDNESDAY, APRIL 30TH. I am trying to wean my darling baby, and I find myself rather unstrung by it — I slept very little, last night. Tonight she is to sleep with Betsy, and I fear she will cry a great deal. April 30 — It is a trying thing to do. I wrote to Cornelia on Monday A.M. [April 28] — a good long letter, so also did Ellen. Last night, Ellen wrote to her Father, in answer to one from him recd in the morning. I added a few lines and sent a programme of the concert.

*I*n the late nineteenth century working for pay was off-limits to a proper middle-aged lady since it violated the precept that men were destined to be the breadwinners for their families. To members of the middle class, a working mother represented a direct challenge to the foundations of family life and social order. A similar conception of woman's place existed among working-class families of foreign birth. Old world customs forbade wives and mothers from becoming wage earners, regardless of how needy the family was. With few exceptions, the cultural traditions of immigrant groups at the turn of the century reinforced the ideology of domesticity on the crucial point of married women's work outside the home. So powerful were these converging cultural streams that in 1900 only 5 percent of married women in America held jobs outside the home.

In spite of these strictures, not all married women were able to avoid taking a job. If a man could not support his family, or he squandered his wages on drink or entertainment, the ideal division of labor between husband and wife was undermined. In such instances, wives and mothers, as well as widows, whatever their age, were forced to earn a living in addition to fulfilling their household and child-care responsibilities. Poor women were sometimes able to obtain remunerative work to be done at home such as sewing, laundry, or taking in boarders. This compromise enabled poor mothers to remain near their youngsters while still producing much-needed income for the family. Frequently, the labor of children was also necessary, as in the sweatshops in the garment industry.

Not all poor wives and mothers were fortunate enough to secure homework. Black women were particularly hard-pressed to find jobs. The persistence of discrimination after emancipation of the slaves made it extremely difficult for black males to fill the breadwinner role. Therefore, a disproportionate number of black women of all ages were forced to seek employment to assist their families financially. Middle-aged black women, whatever their marital status, were much more likely to be found in the labor force than middle-aged white women, since poor black women were expected to earn money throughout their adult lives. Among women aged forty-five to sixty-four in 1900, 11.5 percent of the native-born white women, 13.9 percent of the foreign-born white women, and 41.8 percent of the Negro women were employed.

Prior to the First World War the majority of black people in America resided in the South. For southern black women virtually the only employment was some form of domestic service, a job such as cook or nursemaid. The following document, published in 1912 in a national magazine interested in awakening public opinion on the problems of poor people, contains the reflections of an anonymous middle-aged Negro Nurse living in a Georgia city. Born in the decade after the Civil War, she grew up in a society that offered blacks few improvements over the conditions of slavery. Survival was the paramount goal for the vast number of southern blacks who lived at the margin of subsistence. As a result, children were called upon at an early age to aid in the support of their families. The Negro Nurse had commenced work as a servant at the age of ten and had continued to work in white households ever since. Married when she was twenty, she was the mother of three children before she was widowed at the age of twenty-five.

Thrust into the role of sole provider for her three children, she struggled to make ends meet on her meager wages. When she was forty her family's economic situation was just as precarious as it had always been.

In fact, both the Nurse's eighteen- and thirteen-year-old daughters were already supplementing the family income by holding jobs as a laundress and a nursemaid. Although as a rule a family expects to have a modicum of financial security by the time the parents are middle-aged, this was not a realistic hope for the families of poor female workers like the Negro Nurse. Middle age did not bring these women any respite from toil or worry.

The description of the Nurse's labors conveys a vivid impression of the arduous daily routine of a female domestic servant. Primarily responsible for the care of the mistress's four children, ranging in age from eleven months to nine years, the Nurse was also required to perform a variety of other household tasks during her spare time. Although inadequately recompensed for her diverse services, she had no recourse given the structure of the labor market in pre–World War I southern cities. In her own mind, being perpetually on call was the most odious feature of her job, for it forced her to neglect the welfare of her children, not to mention her personal interests. In essence, the demands of her job meant that her own family had to take second place to that of her employer. This situation was replete with irony, as her duties of child care elicited maternal impulses which, under normal circumstances, would have been channeled toward her own offspring. Every day she witnessed the advantages enjoyed by the children of her employer, all the while recollecting the impoverished home life of her own children. Her distress was compounded by the fact that she herself was denied time for relaxation or recreation.

The conditions of the Nurse's work were demeaning as well as demanding. In her view, she was treated little better than a slave, forced to acquiesce to the degrading rituals of a segregated society and continually expected to exhibit a submissive posture toward her white employer. That she was referred to in disrespectful terms constituted an additional grievance in her eyes. As a woman and as a mother of teenage daughters, she worried greatly about the ever-present potential for sexual exploitation of black women of any age in the South. Given the constraints of her job, the Negro Nurse fulfilled her family obligations as effectively as she could.

The parallels between the life of the Negro Nurse and the lives of her more privileged peers in 1912 are few. At the time when middle-aged women were beginning to enjoy greater opportunities for individual enrichment, this poor widow had no option other than unremitting toil. Although ultimately she hoped to overcome her dependency and experience freedom as a reality, her immediate concern remained what it had been for years — supporting her family. The attainment of middle age did not perceptibly alter her life. For poor women like her, mired in an unbroken cycle of work stretching from childhood to old age, the only meaningful break in their lives occurred when they were too old or too sick to work.

Anonymous Negro Nurse

I am a negro woman, and I was born and reared in the South. I am now past forty years of age and am the mother of three children. My husband died nearly fifteen years ago, after we had been married about five years. For more than thirty years — or since I was ten years old — I have been a servant in one capacity or another in white families in a thriving Southern city, which has at present a population of more than 50,000. In my early years I was at first what might be called a "house-girl," or, better, a "house-boy." I used to answer the doorbell, sweep the yard, go on errands and do odd jobs. Later on I became a chambermaid and performed the usual duties of such a servant in a home. Still later I was graduated into a cook, in which position I served at different times for nearly eight years in all. During the last ten years I have been a nurse. I have worked for only four different families during all these thirty years. But, belonging to the servant class, which is the majority class among my race at the South, and associating only with servants, I have been able to become intimately acquainted not only with the lives of hundreds of household servants, but also with the lives of their employers. I can, therefore, speak with authority on the so-called servant question; and what I say is said out of an experience which covers many years.

To begin with, then, I should say that more than two-thirds of the negroes of the town where I live are menial servants of one kind or another, and besides that more than two-thirds of the negro women here, whether married or single, are compelled to work for a living, as nurses, cooks, washerwomen, chambermaids, seamstresses, hucksters, janitresses, and the like. I will say, also, that the condition of this vast host of poor colored people is just as bad as, if not worse than, it was during the days of slavery. Tho today we are enjoying nominal freedom, we are literally slaves. And, not to generalize, I will give you a sketch of the work I have to do — and I'm only one of many.

I frequently work from fourteen to sixteen hours a day. I am compelled by my contract, which is oral only, to sleep in the house. I am allowed to go home to my own children, the oldest of whom is a girl of 18 years, only once in two weeks, every other Sunday afternoon — even then I'm not permitted to stay all night. I not only have to nurse a little white child, now eleven months old, but I have to act as playmate or "handy-andy," not to say governess, to three other children in the home, the oldest of whom is only nine years of age. I wash and dress the baby two or three times each day; I give it its meals, mainly from a bottle; I

SOURCE: A Negro Nurse, "More Slavery at the South," *The Independent* Vol. 72, 1912.

have to put it to bed each night; and, in addition, I have to get up and attend to its every call between midnight and morning. If the baby falls to sleep during the day, as it has been trained to do every day about eleven o'clock, I am not permitted to rest. It's "Mammy, do this," or "Mammy, do that," or "Mammy, do the other," from my mistress, all the time. So it is not strange to see "Mammy" watering the lawn in front with the garden hose, sweeping the sidewalk, mopping the porch and halls, dusting around the house, helping the cook, or darning stockings. Not only so, but I have to put the other three children to bed each night as well as the baby, and I have to wash them and dress them each morning. I don't know what it is to go to church; I don't know what it is to go to a lecture or entertainment or anything of the kind; I live a treadmill life; and I see my own children only when they happen to see me on the streets when I am out with the children, or when my children come to the "yard" to see me, which isn't often, because my white folks don't like to see their servants' children hanging around their premises. You might as well say that I'm on duty all the time — from sunrise to sunrise, every day in the week. I am the slave, body and soul, of this family. And what do I get for this work — this lifetime bondage? The pitiful sum of ten dollars a month! And what am I expected to do with these ten dollars? With this money I'm expected to pay my house rent, which is four dollars per month, for a little house of two rooms, just big enough to turn round in; and I'm expected, also, to feed and clothe myself and three children. For two years my oldest child, it is true, has helped a little toward our support by taking in a little washing at home. She does the washing and ironing of two white families, with a total of five persons; one of these families pays her $1.00 per week, and the other 75 cents per week, and my daughter has to furnish her own soap and starch and wood. For six months my youngest child, a girl about thirteen years old, has been nursing, and she receives $1.50 per week but has no night work. When I think of the low rate of wages we poor colored people receive, and when I hear so much said about our unreliability, our untrustworthiness, and even our vices, I recall the story of the private soldier in a certain army who, once upon a time, being upbraided by the commanding officer because the heels of his shoes were not polished, is said to have replied: "Captain, do you expect all the virtues for $13 per month?"

Of course, nothing is being done to increase our wages, and the way things are going at present it would seem that nothing could be done to cause an increase of wages. We have no labor unions or organizations of any kind that could demand for us a uniform scale of wages for cooks, washerwomen, nurses, and the like; and, for another thing, if some negroes did here and there refuse to work for seven and eight and ten dollars a month, there would be hundreds of other negroes right on the spot ready to take their places and do the same work, or more, for the low wages that had been refused. So that, the truth is, we have to work for little or nothing or become vagrants! And that, of course, in this State would mean that we would be arrested, tried, and despatched to the "State Farm," where we would surely have to work for nothing or be beaten with many stripes!

Nor does this low rate of pay tend to make us efficient servants. The most that can be said of us negro household servants in the South — and I speak as one of them — is that we are to the extent of our ability willing and faithful slaves. We do not cook according to scientific principles because we do not know anything about scientific principles. Most of our cooking is done by guesswork or by memory. We cook well when our "hand" is in, as we say, and when anything about the dinner goes wrong, we simply say, "I lost my hand today!" We don't know anything about scientific food for babies, nor anything about what science says must be done for infants at certain periods of their growth or when certain symptoms of disease appear; but somehow we "raise" more of the children than we kill, and, for the most part, they are lusty chaps — all of them. But the point is, we do not go to cooking-schools nor to nurse-training schools, and so it cannot be expected that we should make as efficient servants without such training as we should make were such training provided. And yet with our cooking and nursing, such as it is, the white folks seem to be satisfied — perfectly satisfied. I sometimes wonder if this satisfaction is the outgrowth of the knowledge that more highly trained servants would be able to demand better pay!

Perhaps some might say, if the poor pay is the only thing about which we have to complain, then the slavery in which we daily toil and struggle is not so bad after all. But the poor pay isn't all, not by any means! I remember very well the first and last place from which I was dismissed. I lost my place because I refused to let the madam's husband kiss me. He must have been accustomed to undue familiarity with his servants, or else he took it as a matter of course, because without any lovemaking at all, soon after I was installed as cook, he walked up to me, threw his arms around me, and was in the act of kissing me, when I demanded to know what he meant, and shoved him away. I was young then, and newly married, and didn't know then what has been a burden to my mind and heart ever since: that a colored woman's virtue in this part of the country has no protection. I at once went home, and told my husband about it. When my husband went to the man who had insulted me, the man cursed him, and slapped him, and — had him arrested! The police judge fined my husband $25. I was present at the hearing, and testified on oath to the insult offered me. The white man, of course, denied the charge. The old judge looked up and said: "This court will never take the word of a nigger against the word of a white man." Many and many a time since I have heard similar stories repeated again and again by my friends. I believe nearly all white men take, and expect to take, undue liberties with their colored female servants — not only the fathers, but in many cases the sons also. Those servants who rebel against such familiarity must either leave or expect a mighty hard time, if they stay. By comparison, those who tamely submit to these improper relations live in clover. They always have a little "spending change," wear better clothes, and are able to get off from work at least once a week — and sometimes oftener. This moral debasement is not at all times unknown to the white women in these homes. I know of more than one colored woman who was openly importuned by white women to become mistresses of their white husbands, on the ground that they, the white wives, were afraid that, if their husbands did not associate with colored women, they would certainly do so with outside white women, and the white wives, for reasons which ought to be perfectly obvious, preferred to have their husbands do wrong with colored women in order to keep their husbands *straight!* And again, I know at least fifty places in my small town where white men are positively raising two families — a white family in the "Big House" in front, and a colored family in a "Little House" in the backyard. In most cases, to be sure, the colored women involved are the cooks or chambermaids or seamstresses, but it cannot be true that their real connection with the white men of the families is unknown to the white women of the families. The results of this concubinage can be seen in all of our colored churches and in all of our colored public schools in the South, for in most of our churches and schools the majority of the young men and women and boys and girls are light skinned mulattoes. The real, Simon-pure, blue-gum, thick-lip, coal-black negro is passing away — certainly in the cities; and the fathers of the new generation of negroes are white men, while their mothers are unmarried colored women.

Another thing — it's a small indignity, it may be, but an indignity just the same. No white person, not even the little children just learning to talk, no white person at the South ever thinks of addressing any negro man or woman as *Mr.*, or *Mrs.*, or *Miss.* The women are called, "Cook," or "Nurse," or "Mammy," or "Mary Jane," or "Lou," or "Dilcey," as the case might be, and the men are called "Bob," or "Boy," or "Old Man," or "Uncle Bill," or "Pate." In many cases our white employers refer to us, and in our presence, too, as their "niggers." No matter what they call us — no matter what they teach their children to call us — we must tamely submit, and answer when we are called; we must enter no protest; if we did object, we should be driven out without the least ceremony, and, in applying for work at other places, we should find it very hard to procure another situation. In almost every case, when our intending employers would be looking up our record, the information would be given by telephone or otherwise that we were "impudent," "saucy," "dishonest," and "generally unreliable." In our town we have no such thing as an employment agency or intelligence bureau, and, therefore, when we want work, we have to get out on the street and go from place to place, always with hat in hand, hunting for it.

Another thing. Sometimes I have gone on the street cars or the railroad trains with the white children, and, so long as I was in charge of the children, I could sit anywhere I desired, front or back. If a white man happened to ask some other white man, "What is that nigger doing in here?" and was told, "Oh, she's the nurse of those white children in front of her!" immediately there was the hush of peace. Everything was all right, so long as I was in the white man's part of the street car or in the white man's coach as a servant — a slave — but as soon as I did not present myself as a menial, and the relationship of master and servant was abolished by my not having the white children with me, I would be forthwith assigned to the "nigger" seats or the "colored people's coach." Then, too, any day in my city, and I understand that it is so in every town in the South, you can see some "great big black burly" negro coachman or carriage driver huddled up beside some aristocratic Southern white woman, and nothing is said about it, nothing is done about it, nobody resents the familiar contact. But let that same colored man take off his brass buttons and his high hat, and put on the plain livery of an average American citizen, and drive one block down any thoroughfare in any town in the South with that same white woman, as her equal or companion or friend, and he'd be shot on the spot!

You hear a good deal nowadays about the "service pan." The "service pan" is the general term applied to "left-over" food, which in many a Southern home is freely placed at the disposal of the cook, or, whether so placed or not, it is usually disposed of by the cook. In my town, I know, and I guess in many other towns also, every night when the cook starts for her home she takes with her a pan or a plate or cold victuals. The same thing is true on Sunday afternoons after dinner — and most cooks have nearly every Sunday afternoon off. Well, I'll be frank with you, if it were not for the service pan, I don't know what the majority of our Southern colored families would do. The service pan is the mainstay in many a home. Good cooks in the South receive on an average $8 per month. Porters, butlers, coachmen, janitors, "office boys" and the like receive on an average $16 per month. Few and far between are the colored men in the South who receive $1 or more per day. Some mechanics do; as, for example, carpenters, brick masons, wheelwrights, blacksmiths, and the like. The vast majority of negroes in my town are serving in menial capacities in homes, stores and offices. Now taking it for granted, for the sake of illustration, that the husband receives, $16 per month and the wife $8. That would be $24 between the two. The chances are that they will have anywhere from five to thirteen children between them. Now, how far will $24 go toward housing and feeding and clothing ten or twelve persons for thirty days? And, I tell you, with all of us poor people the service pan is a great institution; it is a great help to us, as we wag along the weary way of life. And then most of the white folks expect their cooks to avail themselves of these perquisities; they allow it; they expect it. I do not deny that the cooks find opportunity to hide away at times, along with the cold "grub," a little sugar, a little flour, a little meal, or a little piece of soap; but I indignantly deny that we are thieves. We don't steal; we just "take" things — they are a part of the oral contract, exprest or implied. We understand it, and most of the white folks understand it. Others may denounce the service pan, and say that it is used only to support idle negroes, but many a time, when I was a cook, and had the responsibility of rearing my three children upon my lone shoulders, many a time I have had occasion to bless the Lord for the service pan!

I have already told you that my youngest girl was a nurse. With scores of other colored girls who are nurses, she can be seen almost any afternoon, when the weather is fair, rolling the baby carriage or lolling about on some one of the chief boulevards of our town. The very first week that she started out on her work she was insulted by a white man, and many times since has been improperly approached by other white men. It is a favorite practice of young white sports about town — and they are not always young either — to stop some colored nurse, inquire the name of the "sweet little baby," talk baby talk to the child, fondle it, kiss it, make love to it, etc., etc., and in nine of ten cases every such white man will wind up by making love to the colored nurse and seeking an appointment with her.

I confess that I believe it to be true that many of our colored girls are as eager as the white men are to encourage and maintain these improper relations; but where the girl is not willing, she has only herself to depend upon for protection. If their fathers, brothers or husbands seek to redress their wrongs, under our peculiar conditions, the guiltless negroes will be severely punished, if not killed, and the white blackleg will go scot-free!

Ah, we poor colored women wage-earners in the South are fighting a terrible battle, and because of our weakness, our ignorance, our poverty, and our temptations we deserve the sympathies of mankind. Perhaps a million of us are introduced daily to the privacy of a million chambers thruout the South, and hold in our arms a million white children, thousands of whom, as infants, are suckled at our breasts — during my lifetime I myself have served as "wet nurse" to more than a dozen white children. On the one hand, we are assailed by white men, and, on the other hand, we are assailed by black men, who should be our natural protectors; and, whether in the cook kitchen, at the washtub, over the sewing machine, behind the baby carriage, or at the ironing board, we are but little more than pack horses, beasts of burden, slaves! In the distant future, it may be, centuries and centuries hence, a monument of brass or stone will be erected to the Old Black Mammies of the South, but what we need is present help, present sympathy, better wages, better hours, more protection, and a chance to breathe for once while alive as free women. If none others will help us, it would seem that the Southern white women themselves might do so in their own defense, because we are rearing their children — we feed them, we bathe them, we teach them to speak the English language, and in numberless instances we sleep with them — and it is inevitable that the lives of their children will in some measure be pure or impure according as they are affected by contact with their colored nurses.

*T*he courage to criticize the time-honored formulation of woman's destiny was generated in the charged social climate of the late 1960s and the 1970s. Although feminist perspectives on women's situations originated and spread primarily among younger women, the impetus to reevaluate conventional assumptions touched numerous middle-aged women as well. Today, a growing number of women in their middle years are choosing to define themselves in ways that were inconceivable to their counterparts in previous generations. They have questioned the verities that have undergirded their existence from earliest childhood and decided that being wives and mothers is not enough. They have come to view themselves as independent persons and not as adjuncts to a husband or a child.

The middle-aged women who achieve a new understanding of themselves, their families, and their role in society traverse a variety of paths, none exactly alike, and none simple and straightforward. A shift in external circumstances, such as divorce, can precipitate a change in life-style that eventually leads to an inner transformation. The displaced homemaker is a familiar figure today as a result of the rising divorce rate. Such women have undergone divorce after lengthy marriages that shielded them from the necessity of earning a living, making important decisions, and, in general, dealing with the troublesome problems of contemporary life. Suddenly and irrevocably forced to assume control over their own lives, these women, given the altered social climate, are free to move in a new direction. Not all of them are able to capitalize on their situation and restructure their lives. Nevertheless, the opportunity afforded by an alteration in marital status during the middle years has provided the stimulus to change for many contemporary women.

Other middle-aged women find that the process of self-examination is set in motion gradually as incidents and insights coalesce to create a mounting dissatisfaction. Once under way, the process of self-discovery may accelerate through exposure to new ideas or sharing common grievances with other women. The journey toward personal liberation consists of an unpredictable sequence of emotional and intellectual experiences that culminates in a fresh perspective on one's self. The pieces of a woman's life are rearranged in a new mosaic, one that is more of her own creation. Changes in outer and inner lives are then interwoven in a complex and individualized fashion.

For Anne Lasoff, whose compelling account of her rebirth in middle age follows, the catalyst to change was the inexplicable rebellion of her teenage daughter. Caught in a family crisis she did not comprehend, Anne

Lasoff, a woman in her midforties, began to explore some of her unstated assumptions about her life. With the aid of a family therapist she came to visualize herself in an altogether different way, to acknowledge parts of herself that had been suppressed, and to develop ways of actualizing these aspects of herself. For her, the means of validating herself was writing. Expressing her emotions through writing enabled her to come to grips with the unresolved issues of her life, to articulate previously inchoate feelings and desires. But writing was not just a therapeutic device. After years of hard work, it became a professional pursuit, an activity deemed legitimate in the eyes of the world as well as in her own eyes.

However, the discovery of her hidden talents as a writer is not what gives Anne Lasoff's story its significance. Its value is in the typicality of her life history before she commenced her search for self-knowledge. Outwardly, this middle-aged housewife was a prototype of her generation. Married at an early age to an uncommunicative man, the mother of four children, Anne Lasoff never speculated that her own interests were distinct from those of her family. Her identity was rooted in her roles of wife and mother. Yet deep inside her the materials to construct a different identity lay dormant. The nature of her particular aptitude makes her example somewhat unusual, since the average woman does not possess the ability to become a creative artist. But the essential point, that underneath the surface of this very ordinary late-twentieth-century female life there existed layers of unrealized potential, makes the case of Anne Lasoff instructive as well as enlightening.

Representative of scores of women who had conformed their lives to the expected pattern of marriage and motherhood, Anne Lasoff grew to understand that there was more to her than she had been led to believe. When women like her emerge at middle age and struggle to forge new identities out of the remnants of past and present experience, they are often judged by people who fail to recognize the great distance they have traveled, the obstacles they have overcome, and the self-doubts they have suffered. The strength and commitment of these middle-aged women in the face of family and societal pressures suggest the depth of feeling involved in the process of liberation. Anne Lasoff's moving chronicle of her personal odyssey provides a revealing glimpse into the unfolding of a new female identity.

—— 22 ——
Anne Lasoff

My life's story is the story of two lives. The incubation for my second life began ten years ago, when I was forty-two. During the next five

SOURCE: From *Working It Out*, edited by Sara Ruddick and Pamela Daniels. Copyright © 1977 by Sara Ruddick and Pamela Daniels. Reprinted by permission of Pantheon Books, a Division of Random House, Inc.

Anne Lasoff

years I underwent a transformation triggered by family crisis. My daughter hovered toward drug addiction.

Attempts to cope with her problems made me aware that I needed to order *my* life in a new way. I discovered that writing not only brought order but filled me with a sense of accomplishment I had never before experienced.

The change this produced in every sphere of myself has made my earlier life seem formless and blurred. I recall important events or turning points as if they happened not fifteen or twenty or thirty years ago, but in another lifetime and to someone else. Yet I know that one cannot dismiss the past, for it is the foundation of the present and the future. It must be considered in the quest for self-knowledge.

□

I grew into timid maturity. I was an earnest, conscientious student; I still regret that I never had the courage to cut even one class in high school. I'd envy the flagrant girls who dared hang out on street corners or who went riding with boys or who smoked. I remember locking myself in the bathroom to practice how to use a cigarette. I was so clumsy at it I soon gave up and never tried again.

Though I excelled in English, I took a commercial course because I was afraid of the sciences. I realize now that I should have gone to college. Perhaps I would have begun writing earlier. Though I was always reading, no one seemed to connect my compulsive reading with higher education.

My mother would lend money to her brother, an impoverished rabbi with a large family. It was understood that his children had to have an education befitting a rabbi's offspring. A bricklayer's daughter could get by with just reading.

When it was time to marry, I married. I tell it casually because it happened that way. The year 1945, the war winding down. I was corresponding with a boy stationed in Belgium. Though he was from my neighborhood, we had never met. He was a friend of a friend. When he came back to the States, he came to see me. My letters had intrigued him. He never left my side again.

Two days before the war officially ended, Joe and I eloped to City Hall. I look back and wonder what was my hurry. It seemed the thing to do. Everyone was getting married.

Unlike the Vietnam veterans, the GI's of World War II were all heroes. If Joe appeared quiet, I attributed it to his war experiences. He was in the Battle of the Bulge. His truck was shelled. He was the only survivor.

I romanticized his shyness. I waited for the battle trauma to recede so we could really communicate. I knew he loved me. I thought I loved him.

Joe's formal education, like mine, ended with high school. His interest in words was mostly confined to the sports page. I was a romantic; I didn't think our intellectual differences would matter. When I was with Joe, I didn't read or discuss what I had read because I sensed he was not interested. If I persisted he would say, "That's all you have on your mind, you don't know anything about the real world."

But when I was alone, it was as if I had never married. I could still lose myself in a book.

Apartments were scarce. We moved in with my family. My mother could never break through Joe's shyness, but my father and he became good friends.

A year later our first child, Beverly, was born. Then we were able to get an apartment in my mother's building. This was the beginning of conflict with my mother which has continued over the years. We never openly quarreled, but I sensed her disappointment in how I managed my home and my family. My mother equated good housekeeping with virtue. She could not understand my negative attitude toward housekeeping. I did it because I had to. Unlike most of the other women I knew, I derived no pleasure or satisfaction from it.

My mother's theory was, "First finish all your household chores. Then read." But to me the task of cleaning was eternal. Whenever I finished, it would be time to begin all over again and so I interspersed my cleaning and cooking and laundry with my reading. Housework to me was like the mythological rock of Sisyphus. I would push it away, but it would only roll back again. Endlessly.

My mother felt it her duty to help me with my work. She would come into my house, see the dishes in the sink, and wash them before even taking her coat off. Before I was awake, she would knock at my door, eager to do my laundry or shop for me. I resented her help because it only served to delineate my shortcomings. But I could not hurt her feelings by telling her to let me manage alone.

If we had not lived so close, my mother's disapproval would not have mattered. But she was always on hand to point out my faults, always under the guise of "for your own good." Not until I began to write would I overcome the sense of inadequacy my mother instilled in me. I have even been able to develop a sense of humor about house-keeping, to poke fun at the ladies with the neat houses who seem to find an almost orgiastic pleasure in discussing housework.

When Beverly was two, I gave birth to Ellen. My father died soon afterward. I was so immersed in caring for my children I don't remember mourning for him then. The loss hit me a few months later. I felt I had lost a friend. I had always identified with him. We were both dreamers and impractical while my mother's head sat squarely on her shoulders. Now whenever I came across an interesting idea I would still say to myself, "I'll tell Papa about this," then realize he was gone, there was no one to tell.

The years passed quickly. I gave birth to a son, Steven. I do not remember being discontented or frustrated or feeling trapped in the role of mother and housewife. At that time having families was the "in" thing. The media played up family togetherness. The women's movement with its searching questions about motherhood was still to come.

The unknown creature slept soundly within. My life seemed to flow smoothly; there were no disturbing ripples. If Joe and I didn't have much to talk about besides the family and household affairs, it didn't matter. The children filled the empty spots. Joe's shyness and introversion extended to our daughters, but I was used to it by now. Our son was close to his father. He trailed him like a shadow, though Joe rarely showed him affection. I talked and gave affection for both of us. If something big was missing from our relationship, from my life, I didn't notice. Occasionally I would daydream about writing, but when I tried to write I had nothing to say.

These were my innocent years. I enjoyed caring for the children. I didn't learn the facts of life — that having children can be fraught with heartache — until they were teen-agers. During their childhood I rarely worried about their futures. I assumed that their lives would be like mine — school, work, marriage. They would just shift from one stage to another as the time came to do so.

This was the 1950s. There was no drug problem, at least not among middle-class kids. Drugs, we thought, were only used by the under-privileged. There was no student unrest, no burning of bras. The country was recuperating from the war. The civil rights movement was just beginning to stir. Vietnam was an obscure spot on the map.

Occasionally I would read about juvenile delinquency, but it had no meaning for me. If I thought about it at all, I blamed the parents for neglecting their children. I knew I was a good mother, my children would not cut out.

□

My first life ended and my second began when my oldest daughter entered high school. Until then Bev had never given us cause for serious concern. She had been a fair student, she had many friends. I assumed she was happy. She was rarely moody or sullen or rebellious. I took it for granted that to be a mother was pleasant and easy. Now I was to lose this grant.

Bev became restless; staying home was like being imprisoned. She cut classes, she lost interest in school. She dropped her old friends and found others who were as daring as she had become. Instead of going to school she would hang out on street corners. Bev did all the things I never dared to do as a teen-ager. She even looked like the girls I had envied — slim, pretty, and outgoing.

The drug culture, which was to envelop the middle class, was just beginning. Bev and her group experimented with drugs the way earlier generations experimented with tobacco and liquor. I did not know how to discipline her. I had never needed to before. I did what many parents did and do. I pretended that I didn't see what was going on. I told myself she was going through a difficult adolescence. She was becoming one of the delinquent children I used to see on the streets and mutter about self-righteously. I had been disdainful of parents who allowed their children to be so undisciplined. I had wondered where those kids' parents *were*. Now I knew. We were at home, hiding our heads like ostriches, hoping that if we didn't see what was happening, it would go away. Guilt set in. But what was I guilty of? Philosophers blame society, but mothers blame themselves.

In the midst of my concern about Bev I became pregnant again. At this time, 1964, abortions were still illegal. Although I could have had one for medical reasons and because of my age, Joe and I felt pregnancy was God's will. It never occurred to us even to consider an abortion.

This pregnancy was different from my others. I had no patience for the necessary contemplative preparation for another child. I was always depressed, torn between fretting about Bev and brooding about the future of the new baby. I was losing my confidence as a mother.

The first time Bev came home stoned I realized that she needed professional help. I could not turn my head away any longer. In my ninth month I took my unwilling daughter to a psychiatrist. He was a kind, elderly man who patted my hand and joked about my pregnancy. He said, "Don't worry so much about your daughter. She is suffering from a minor ailment called 'self-limiting immaturity'." It would take ten years of our lives before she outgrew this ailment.

I came home feeling relieved, but the next day the high school dean called me in for a conference. He suggested I sign Bev out of school, with the implied threat that he would expel her if she didn't leave voluntarily. She had lost all interest in her studies. He felt that she would only get into one scrape after another if she stayed.

Perhaps I should have protested, asked for guidance or for time to think, but I was exhausted with the weight of the baby. I kept seeing myself trudging along the halls of the school obviously pregnant, with my reluctant daughter in tow. I had had enough. I wearily signed the papers.

A few weeks later I gave birth to a healthy, husky boy, Corey. The new baby brought with him new luck. After struggling for many years, Joe and his partner finally became successful in business, operating several lucrative gas stations. We moved into a new home, a few miles away from my mother. In spite of my worries about Bev, I was able to relax a bit, away from my mother's critical eyes.

For the first time since my marriage, I did not have to worry about money. Joe encouraged me to buy things for myself, for the house. He insisted I have household help. When he decided to buy an expensive car, I was uneasy. I said, "It would be nice, but can we afford it? The children always need —"

He interrupted me. "Listen to me. I've worked hard all my life. Now I've reached a point where I can live well. All you ever worry about is the children, the children. We are also entitled to pleasures. It's time you learned how to live."

Telling everyone it was a present for me, he bought the car.

By now most of my friends were returning to the business world. Their children were maturing, becoming independent. The women resumed their careers as bookkeepers and secretaries. They were entering a new phase while I seemed to be standing still — even moving backward. I had to stay home to take care of the new baby. I was so preoccupied with Bev's problems I tended Corey automatically. My love for him was tinged with self-pity.

Intellectually I understood that I was not the only one who had a child involved with drugs. Emotionally, however, I only thought of myself as Bev's mother — as if Bev were an extremity of mine, another arm, another leg, which I couldn't control. When she hurt I hurt.

If I attempted to talk to Joe about how badly I felt, he would say, impatiently, "The more you talk, the worse you make it."

I could not understand his objective attitude, his detachment. I would say, "But aren't you frantic also? She's your child too."

"I am worried about her. She needs help, but I have to make a living for the family. If I carry on like you, we'll all starve. You've got to take hold of yourself."

I knew he was right. I was grateful that at least one of us was strong, but I could neither put aside nor push under the gnawing pain and fear.

Because Bev presented a veneer of stability she was able to find office work easily. The jobs never lasted. After a few weeks she would come in late or not at all. She would always be high, as if the pressure of responsibility were too much to handle without the prop of pills. Each time she found a new job I would be optimistic. Each time she lost it I would panic.

I knew Bev needed regular counseling, but she would never cooperate, never keep appointments. We were told that it was a waste of time and money unless she herself wanted help. Finally one psychologist suggested that perhaps the whole family needed guidance. I did not think much of the idea. There was nothing wrong with our family, I thought. But I was desperate. Reluctantly, I made an appointment with an agency specializing in family therapy.

Casually I had met and married Joe. Casually too I met Dr. H., the man who was to play such an important part in my becoming a writer. I was not impressed at our first meeting. How could this slim young man, younger than I was, know the pain I felt? Dr. H. spoke softly with a Midwestern accent. Evidently he was a WASP. I thought of myself as a typical Jewish mother whose existence is vindicated solely through her children.

Dr. H. appeared so unassuming, with his horn-rimmed glasses over solemn brown eyes, that for the first few visits I could not remember his name or even what he looked like. Yet he was able not only to relieve my pain but to give legitimacy to the creature within. We were to have a Svengali-Trilby relationship. He was to tell me to write and I wrote.

At our first session Dr. H. introduced himself and invited us to find seats in the comfortable, softly lit office. I sat alone on one side of the room, Joe and the children on the other side.

Immediately I began to tell the doctor about Bev. Far from commiserating with me, he didn't seem particularly moved.

"Tell me about yourself. What kind of family life do you have?"

I became impatient. I felt he was asking the wrong questions.

"You don't understand, the problem is Bev, not us. How can we help her?"

For the first time Dr. H. raised his voice. "*You* don't seem to understand. Bev is only part of what's happening in your family. Unless you learn to cope with your daughter you will destroy yourself and the rest of the family. Nothing is gained by your hysteria, your overreacting to whatever Bev does. She must lead her own life. You can't live for her. Now tell me about yourself, not about your daughter."

The therapy was actually a course in learning about ourselves. I saw myself through the eyes of my family. I was surprised and hurt, but in the end I discovered who I really was and what I could be.

I had pictured myself as softhearted, maternal, ineffective — an unappreciated martyr. But Joe said, "Anne should never have married. Her head is always somewheres else. She is apart from the family even though she is always home. If we sit in the living room, she sits in the kitchen by herself, reading. Even now she sits away from us."

I expected my children to defend me, but they agreed with Joe. I could not understand why they were picking on me. We were here because of Bev.

I talk as easily as I breathe. Now I had so much to say in my defense I could have talked the whole session — I felt I could speak for everyone — and would have. But Dr. H., losing patience, finally said, in a casual, almost teasing way, "Why don't you write about how you feel so the others will have a chance to talk?"

"Why don't you write..." A few simple words and my life changed.

My first letters were full of self-pity. "No one understands me. If my daughters loved me, they would clean their room. I devote my life to my family and get nothing but criticism in return."

Gradually the letters became more reflective. "Perhaps Joe is right. I do stay apart from my family at times. It isn't because I don't love them. It's because I must keep part of my life for myself. They aren't interested in what interests me. Though I am surrounded by people, I am beginning to realize how lonely I am. I feel as if I live in two houses. In one I am huddled together with my family. In the other I am all alone, looking for someone to talk to."

Every few weeks I would write a letter. Each time I finished, no matter how depressed I may have been, I felt more peaceful, less lonely. Previously, I had absorbed experience and trauma like a sponge. Now I discovered that writing not only brought a sort of order to my life but gave me a sense of accomplishment I had never felt before. My shortcomings as a housekeeper and as a mother became unimportant. Creativity replaced the sponge.

The letters were becoming a carefully written journal. I slowly developed my own style. I would not be content unless I found the exact word, the exact phrase, to express myself. I would rewrite many times.

Whatever happened in my family, no matter how emotionally involved I was, part of me coolly stood aside, making mental notes. I was both the participant and the audience in the drama of my life. In the midst of anger or hurt or aggravation, I would be thinking of how to write about it.

I became so involved with the writing I stopped panicking about Bev; she became more relaxed because I didn't pick on her so much. There was still tension between us. She still had her problems. She could not hold a job, she still took pills. She drifted. But I was able to cope with her. The pain was lessening. Bev's adventures became ink for my pen. She once remarked, "If it wasn't for me, you would never have had anything to write about." I grudgingly agreed with her.

We continued family therapy for about a year. Then Joe, with Dr. H.'s approval, decided it was time to stand by ourselves. I had always complained that Joe could not express his feelings. Yet in therapy he spoke freely. I realized for the first time how concerned he had been about me, even more than he was about Bev. I did not realize how "neurotic" I had become.

Dr. H. was like a magician. Deftly, quietly — yes, magically — he brought our family closer. All of us benefited from the therapy except Bev. Change in her would not come for several years, not until she was ready and independently willing to help herself. We could not do it for her. I finally understood that if I was to be able to help and support and accept my daughter, I had to help and support and accept myself first.

I continued to write to Dr. H. The following Christmas I received a card from him. Svengali writing to Trilby.

"I look forward to your letters. You are slowly finding yourself. You have a responsibility to develop your talents as a writer."

Me . . . a writer? I wrote back: "I only write to crystallize my life. I hoped you would find my letters worthwhile, but it didn't matter. Creating them was satisfaction enough. The more I write, the more compelled I am to write, as if an unknown force was prodding me."

Dr. H.'s encouragement was another turning point in my life.

I found myself comparing writing to painting. My need to write was my brush, the journal my box of paints. How was I to use them? It was time to stop doing only portraits of myself and my family. I wanted to broaden my vision, to include the landscape of my life. I had to learn how to transmute my experiences so that my work would have structure and dimension.

At the age of forty-seven I wanted to go back to school, but Joe's response to this idea was predictable.

"I can't see it, this foolishness. I could understand if you wanted to learn a skill like stenography or bookkeeping or even sewing. But writing? I work so hard for you, why can't you be content? What are you looking for?"

"Joe, I appreciate all you give me, but you do it for yourself as well. Sometimes I'm jealous because you enjoy your work. You have pride in yourself, in what you have accomplished. I have nothing except keeping house and raising the children. I've finally found work which makes me feel worthwhile too. Maybe it is foolishness but I want to try. If I don't try there will only be living through you and the children."

I spoke bravely, but in the back of my head I heard the voices of my mother and my mother-in-law. "If a man makes a good living and the family is well, then what are you complaining about?"

I wondered what would happen if Joe suddenly began to write, slyly taking notes, buying books and paper and typewriter ribbons, reading when he should be sleeping, wanting to go to school, having a life I could not share. Would I put my hands on my hips and say, "You must be crazy. How can you suddenly become a writer?"

It is unfair of women to expect immediate acceptance and tolerance from their men when they undergo a metamorphosis as I did. Joe felt bewildered and possibly threatened. He would say, shaking his head in puzzlement, "I didn't marry a writer, I married an ordinary girl."

I beat down guilt as one would beat down an igniting spark. I felt guilty toward my mother, my mother-in-law, my husband and my children. I felt guilty for writing at all, even more for writing about them as if I were exhibiting our lives. But the living creature was emerging. If I didn't fight for what it wanted, it would deteriorate into grayness.

We compromised. Instead of going to school, I enrolled in a correspondence course. I had taken the first step in nurturing that living creature.

For an assignment I wrote about an incident involving Bev and me when she had taken an overdose and was hospitalized. I sent the story to the *New York Times*. Instead of getting a rejection slip my story was accepted and published on the Op-Ed page of the newspaper. A few months later it was reprinted in the *Reader's Digest*. I made seven hundred dollars. I knew how hard it was for a beginner to break into print. It was as if I had won the lottery.

Receiving money was another turning point. I shall never forget the look on Joe's face when I showed him the checks. I saw a glimmer of respect for my work. If someone was willing to pay me for this "nonsense," then perhaps it wasn't nonsense after all. Others too seemed to assume that getting money made me a professional writer. I received offers from several publishers to write a book based on my story. I could not do it. There was too much about writing itself that I had yet to learn.

I knew now what I must do. A lonely correspondence course was not enough; I had to go to school — with or without Joe's consent. I wanted to learn the craft of writing.

I enrolled in courses at the New School and entered a new world. At home I thought of myself as an eccentric middle-aged woman wanting to write, when she should be content dwelling in the core of her family, basking in her husband's success. At school, however, I met many women like myself. I was not eccentric; I was only alone because I had no one at home who was like me, who shared my needs.

Critics of creative-writing courses say that good writing cannot be taught, that it is an innate talent. They may be right, but for me school took away my feeling of isolation. At home, if I talked about my writing problems to Joe or my friends, I sensed they were thinking, "Anne is involved in an unreal world while I'm involved in the real world because I work. I'll pretend to be interested."

Guiltily, I felt that writing and school were not an avocation but a private vice.

My life has become polarized since I've been going to school. I live on two levels. On one level I continue to be a housewife and mother, still scurrying in prosaic circles. I still worry about Bev. I still wish that Joe were tuned in to me. I still wish I could run an efficient household.

But on another level I am an explorer, an adventuress, mapping new courses for my life. I do not find it necessary to shut myself off from the world in order to write. My world generates my creativity; I carry "a room of my own" in my head.

I do not yet have the discipline to sit at my desk at an appointed hour each day. I do not know how to seek out my ideas. I must wait till my thoughts come to me. My mind is an uncharted sea. I am like a beachcomber waiting for the waves to wash up shells of ideas. The creativity works independently of what I would like it to do. I cannot force it. I must be patient.

Perhaps it is premature to call myself a writer. However, I cannot otherwise describe the sense of excitement, of anticipation, when I am at my typewriter. I even procrastinate before beginning to write because I enjoy the feeling of being pregnant with ideas and want to prolong it. When I have completed work to my satisfaction, when I've put on paper words that say what I feel, I am at peace with myself and with ·my family and with my world. For a few days my head is blissfully empty. Then gradually the waves roll in again and I must pick and choose from the glittering shells.

I don't know how other women juggle their lives to nurture family and muse. A man will find someone to wash his socks and prepare food and keep the children quiet, but women are conditioned to perform these time-consuming tasks for themselves — and for others. There was only one Alice B. Toklas.

How does a woman deal with the physical and emotional minutiae of her days and yet find time and energy to sit at a desk and spell out her visions? Perhaps I ponder foolishly. The strong compulsion to write, driven by the living creature, may overcome the obstacles.

*F*or more than three centuries, American women in their middle years have devoted the bulk of their time and energy to meeting the needs of their husbands and children. Whether as partners in a household economy, housewives and child-care specialists, or paid members of the labor force, middle-aged women have worked to ensure the well-being of their families while ignoring or subordinating their own desires. The current upsurge of interest in women's issues, coupled with the demographic changes that have altered women's lives in the twentieth century, has laid the groundwork for a new version of female middle age in which individual growth and personal gratification are realistic possibilities. Nevertheless, the majority of American women in their forties and fifties still conduct their lives in accordance with the traditional pattern.

The contrast between men and women in this life stage is striking. For most men, the middle years of the life span represent the pinnacle of achievement. Socialized to regard work as their primary source of identity, males assume that the accumulation of skills and experience over the years will, as a matter of course, lead to enhanced status and wealth by middle age. Success in the workplace is customarily accompanied by feelings of self-confidence and control. Yet, the sense of mastery typical of middle-aged men is not commonly experienced by women of the same age. Forced to play an auxiliary role for most of their adult life, women do not equate the passage of years with progress. The prospect of middle age instead portends only the lightening of family responsibilities. Women in their forties and fifties who are primarily concerned with personal goals have been exceptional until recently.

A collective profile of the four women whose middle years have been analyzed in this chapter reveals, first of all, that they were situated on different rungs of the social ladder. Elizabeth Saltonstall was near the top, Ellen Wheaton and Anne Lasoff on middle rungs, and the Negro Nurse at the bottom. Although all were American-born, only Elizabeth Saltonstall and Ellen Wheaton were white Anglo-Protestants. The Negro Nurse was black and presumably Protestant, and Anne Lasoff was Jewish. The ethnic diversity of the group was not matched by its geographical distribution, since all the women came from the eastern part of the United States: Elizabeth Saltonstall from Massachusetts, Ellen Wheaton and Anne Lasoff from New York, and the Negro Nurse from Georgia. With the exception of Mrs. Saltonstall, all resided in urban areas. None of these middle-aged women had more than a high school education. Anne Lasoff was a high school graduate, Ellen Wheaton attended a female seminary, and Elizabeth Saltonstall was more than just literate. The Negro Nurse had little, if any, formal education, since she was already at work by the age of ten. What all these women had in common besides their nativity was their commitment to their families. Elizabeth Saltonstall, Ellen Wheaton, and Anne Lasoff were wives and mothers, and the Negro Nurse was a widow with three children. Inclusion of middle-aged women who were single or Catholic would undoubtedly introduce other dimensions to our study, but an examination of the experiences of these four women goes a long way toward elucidating the central issues of this life stage for women.

Middle age constitutes a logical vantage point for looking back on one's life. As women review the past, they are able to discern, some with greater clarity than others, the distinctive pattern of their lives, its benefits as well as its limitations. A woman can readily see that the path she has taken not only diverges from that of her husband, but is a far narrower path, bounded by home and family. Whereas her husband's career path permits him to travel in new directions, testing and proving his abilities, her own domestic route prevents her from venturing far afield and exploring her own potential. From another perspective, however, staying close to home allows her to furnish welcome support to her children and her husband. Whether the advantages of domestic life outweigh its constraints depends on the individual woman. However, the ambivalent feelings experienced by so many middle-aged women are traceable in large part to conflicting responses to the differential assignment of social roles.

For women who marry and have children, the middle years as a rule coincide with the stage in the family cycle when children no longer demand constant attention. A mother can sit back and appreciate her offspring and take credit for their upbringing. Middle-aged women, in essence, reap the rewards that follow from the conscientious performance of the maternal role.

The experiences of Elizabeth Saltonstall and the Negro Nurse illustrate the special relationship between middle-aged mothers and their older children. Although the circumstances of their lives differed radically, both Mrs. Saltonstall and the Negro Nurse manifested deep concern for the welfare of their daughters. Each mother wished to aid and encourage her children as they moved toward maturity. The theme of self-sacrifice is especially prominent in the case of the Negro Nurse, a hard-working woman whose entire life was given over to providing support for her youngsters. Mrs. Saltonstall was not as single-minded in her dedication to her daughter, but she acted to promote the young woman's best interests whenever possible. Both women regarded their children as a source of satisfaction and pride. Having these children made their lives meaningful.

Leaving a mark on the world through the agency of others is not enough for some women. However great their vicarious pleasure from the accomplishments of children and spouse, such middle-aged women harbor a residual longing for personal achievement. In retrospect, they view their youthful decision to marry and care for a family in a critical light. Portraying themselves as thwarted individuals whose talents have not been recognized, they seek to articulate new goals at this pivotal juncture in their lives. Although this midlife reorientation does not necessarily entail a total rejection of the roles of wife and mother, it does signify an unwillingness to keep husband and children at the center of their existence.

It must be emphasized at this point that innumerable middle-aged women have never confronted these questions. Moreover, many of those who have expressed dissatisfaction with the confines of their role have been unable to transcend the limitations of time and place. The latitude of choice enjoyed by contemporary women was virtually unknown to women of past centuries. Comparing the experiences of Ellen Wheaton and Anne Lasoff underlines the importance of historical context in analyzing the life patterns of American women. Both middle-aged women aspired to something beyond family responsibilities. In fact, both had an interest in writing. But the century that separated the two made a profound difference in the outcome of their aspirations. Despite her clandestine literary ambitions, Ellen Wheaton knew that her chances of ever writing for an audience were remote. Her only real option was to continue along the path of marriage and family.

Anne Lasoff, however, arrived at middle age in an era when women were actively striving to expand their horizons through education, employment, and personal development. While her young adulthood was spent in a fashion reminiscent of Ellen Wheaton's, as a full-time mother, wife, and housewife, Anne Lasoff seized the opportunity at midlife to reevaluate her individual needs and establish personal goals. Yet it took a traumatic family event to precipitate the alteration in her attitudes and behavior.

Few present-day women in their forties and fifties possess Anne Lasoff's urgent desire to remake their lives. By middle age, a woman's identity has so crystallized around family roles that it is extremely difficult for her to carve out a new understanding of herself. To do so requires a degree of detachment not easily attainable in a society still strongly influenced by sex-role definitions formulated in the nineteenth century. Notwithstanding the tenacity of customary prescriptions, the example of Anne Lasoff and others like her suggests that it is possible for women in their middle years to defy social pressure and set their own courses for the future.

Bibliography

Bart, Pauline B. "Depression in Middle-aged Women." In *Woman in Sexist Society: Studies in Power and Powerlessness,* edited by Vivian Gornick and Barbara K. Moran. New York: Mentor Books, 1972, pp. 163–186.

Bart, Pauline B., and Grossman, Marlyn. "Menopause." In *The Woman Patient: Medical and Psychological Interfaces,* edited by Malkah T. Notman and Carol C. Nadelson. Vol. 1: *Sexual and Reproductive Aspects of Women's Health Care.* New York and London: Plenum Press, 1978, pp. 337–354.

Elliott, Grace Loucks. *Women after Forty: The Meaning of the Last Half of Life.* New York: Henry Holt, 1936.

Fried, Barbara R. *The Middle-Age Crisis.* New York: Harper & Row, 1967.

Fuchs, Estelle. *The Second Season: Life, Love and Sex for Women in the Middle Years.* Garden City, New York: Doubleday, Anchor Books, 1978.

Gorney, Sondra, and Cox, Claire. *After Forty.* New York: Dial Press, 1973.

Harris, Janet. *The Prime of Ms. America: The American Woman at Forty.* New York: G. P. Putnam's Sons, 1975.

Jacobs, Ruth Harriet. *Life After Youth: Female, Forty — What Next?* Boston: Beacon Press, 1979.

LeShan, Eda J. *The Wonderful Crisis of Middle Age: Some Personal Reflections.* New York: David McKay, 1973.

Neugarten, Bernice L., ed. *Middle Age and Aging.* Chicago: University of Chicago Press, 1968.

Neugarten, Bernice L. *Personality in Middle and Late Life: Empirical Studies.* New York: Atherton Press, 1964.

Neugarten, B., and Datan, N. "The Middle Years." In *American Handbook of Psychiatry,* edited by S. Arieti. 2nd ed. New York: Basic Books, 1974, 1: 592–608.

Reitz, Rosetta. *Menopause: A Positive Approach.* 1977. Reprint. New York: Penguin Books, 1979.

Rubin, Lillian B. *Women of a Certain Age: The Midlife Search for Self.* New York: Harper & Row, 1979.

Simon, Anne W. *The New Years: A New Middle Age.* New York: Alfred A. Knopf, 1968.

Smith-Rosenberg, Carroll. "Puberty to Menopause: The Cycle of Femininity in Nineteenth-Century America." In *Clio's Consciousness Raised: New Perspectives on the History of Women,* edited by Mary S. Hartman and Lois W. Banner. New York: Harper & Row, 1974, pp. 23–37.

Troll, Lillian E. *Early and Middle Adulthood.* Monterey, California: Brooks/Cole, 1975.

Weideger, Paula. *Menstruation and Menopause: The Physiology and Psychology, the Myth and the Reality.* Revised and expanded. New York: Delta Books, 1977.

FIVE

Old Age

Old women constitute a visible and vocal segment of American society today. More sizable than ever before as a result of dramatic improvements in female life expectancy during the twentieth century, the current group of women over age sixty-five, comprising 13.9 million in 1977, has attracted the attention of researchers, policy makers, and fellow citizens. The aging of the American population in general, as well as the increasing disparity between female and male rates of survival, has made the experience of old age a particularly timely topic for women. As more and more women reach their sixties, seventies, and eighties, the ways past generations of American females have coped with this life stage assume special interest and merit close scrutiny. This chapter focuses on the final life stage, old age, and explores the experiences of elderly women over the course of American history.

Old age, like other life stages, cannot be defined in an absolute or universal way, since ideas about old age are culturally and historically determined. The conditions of old age and the attitudes toward old people have changed over time, and individual experiences of this life stage need to be evaluated not only in terms of contemporary theoretical criteria but also within a historical framework.

Conceptualizations of the last stage of the life cycle recognize more than one standard for measuring old age. The most basic definition of old age is obviously a chronological one. Asserting that anyone over age sixty-five is an old person, although arbitrary, facilitates the compilation and analysis of statistical data and is essential for the formulation of public policy. However, the identification of sixty-five, or any comparable age, as the commencement of old age does not take into account the complexity of the aging process. Persons age at different rates and to use such a monolithic category to denote old people causes us to disregard the diversity of human conditions encompassed within this comprehensive classification.

Expanding our conception of this life stage to include factors that are less susceptible to precise measurement will help us to understand the multi-faceted nature of female old age.

Biological research reveals the limitations of a chronological standard for defining old age. Aging is a gradual process that entails certain physiological changes but involves certain continuities as well. The attainment of the age of sixty-five does not coincide with any specific biological landmark for either men or women. Nor does it necessarily mark the boundary between capacity and incapacity. It has been demonstrated that the mental and physical abilities of women remain intact well into old age, including the ability to function sexually. While physical problems are more common in old age, the incidence of severe disability is great only in persons over age seventy-five. Many women over sixty-five function as well as their younger counterparts, even though these older women may have experienced some diminution in powers. A biological definition of old age underscores the variability of the last stage of life.

Additionally, physiological changes must be viewed in light of prevalent cultural norms. In contemporary America there exists what has been termed a "double standard of aging." While older men are assessed according to a variety of criteria, including wealth and power, older women tend to be judged primarily on the basis of appearance. Since appearance is virtually synonymous with sexual attractiveness, the more youthful a woman looks, the greater her appeal. Thus, the distinctive appearance of older women with wrinkles, gray hair, and age spots has a negative connotation in modern America whereas in cultures in which older women are valued for qualities other than looks, these signs of age might produce entirely different and positive reactions. The cultural meaning attached to the physical manifestations of aging is far more important to contemporary American women than the physiological changes themselves. Strategies such as cosmetic surgery, hair dyeing, and the adoption of trendy fashions all enhance the appearance as well as the self-esteem of older women. Disguising the imprint of time has become imperative for women in a society in which the normal outward signs of the biological process of aging are deprecated.

Another dimension of old age emerges from a sociological perspective on aging. Old age, in this conception, occurs when a person loses his or her significant roles.

> Old age is not merely another turning point in the life cycle — a transition from one social status to another, as is the case in all earlier stages of life. It is a time of life when the individual becomes permanently detached from the two institutional structures — the nuclear family and the occupational system — that give form and meaning to adult existence in modern times.[1]

---

[1] Zena Smith Blau, *Old Age in a Changing Society* (New York: New Viewpoints, 1973), pp. 12–13.

The loss of significant roles is associated with retirement and widowhood, with retirement presumed to be the predominant male experience and widowhood the predominant female experience. Given recent demographic trends, women can expect to outlive their husbands, and therefore widowhood is indeed more typical for women than for men. However, recent statistics on female patterns of participation in the labor force indicate that women's lives are increasingly becoming geared to the work cycle. Today's women are working for longer periods of their lives than their mothers or grandmothers did, and predictions are that women will continue to spend greater amounts of time in the labor force. Therefore, retirement from a job now constitutes a watershed in the lives of women as well as men. Whether the role lost is wife or worker, or both, the key point of this sociological definition relates to the loss of meaningful roles in old age and the consequent psychological effects on the individual. The sense of purpose that accompanies the performance of useful social functions disappears when a person is stripped of these duties. Unless substitute roles, such as grandparent or teacher or volunteer, can fill the void, the consequences may be devastating.

A final perspective on old age focuses on the psychological development of the individual during this life stage. Certain problems of adjustment typically confront persons in late life. They arise from the stresses associated with this period of life — the decline of physical powers; the loss of meaningful roles; the incapacitation and death of one's spouse, close relatives, friends, and peer group members; and a deteriorating economic position. To cope with these stresses, aging persons attempt to adapt to their altered circumstances as effectively as possible by drawing on existing sources of support as well as establishing new channels through which material and emotional sustenance may be derived. Ideally, old people possess the inner reserves to deal with these challenges. However, countless old people are unable to keep struggling against adversity and instead assume a passive stance toward the world.

Persons approaching the end of the life span are also concerned about the issue of finality. The realization that death is imminent spurs old people to face ultimate questions relating to the meaning and purpose of one's life. Whether conceived of as preparation for death or as the culminating act of life, a compelling task of old age is putting one's life in order. This process may entail mundane matters such as disposing of material goods, completing pending business, transferring authority, and making provisions for some permanent legacy to future generations. On a more abstract plane, it will involve efforts to reconcile personal conflicts and tie up the loose ends of one's life. Retrospection has been shown to be of great value to old people in this search for meaning. What is termed the "life review" — unsystematic reminiscing about past experiences with the goal of mastering unresolved problems — has been found to be an effective means of both consolidating one's identity and achieving a significant measure of inner peace.

In dealing with the issue of finality, old people usually come to accept the fact that they no longer have a future. As they organize their lives around the present moment, they learn to appreciate the rewards of immediate gratification. Old age can be a time of growth for some individuals, and outstanding creative acts at this time of life are indeed possible. Given security and a feeling of well-being, an old person can continue to unfold his or her potentialities well after the age of sixty-five.

Aging does not take place in a vacuum. Individual experiences of old age, as of other life stages, are rooted in a historical context. Over the centuries, the constants of individual development have been arranged in different configurations. Before proceeding to an examination of the characteristic patterns of female old age, it is therefore necessary to outline the history of old age in America.

In numerical terms, old people constituted an insignificant segment of American society through the nineteenth century. The dramatic upsurge in the population of elderly citizens has occurred only in the twentieth century. While only 4 percent of the American population was over age sixty-five in 1900, today more than 10 percent is, and this figure is predicted to increase for the remainder of the century.

Despite the presence of elderly citizens throughout the course of American history, old age was not a well-defined life stage until the last three decades of the nineteenth century. Before this time the relatively few people who reached old age were regarded as integral members of their communities and not subjected to restrictions premised on age. Prevailing images of the elderly were essentially positive, although they were not universal. In the late nineteenth century, a negative conception of old age crystallized in response to the imperatives of a modern industrial society. Old people were represented as unable to function in a rapidly changing world, lacking the resources to cope with the demands of everyday life. Stigmatized as nonproducers, old people were forcibly isolated from the mainstream. Once segregated, they were vulnerable to discriminatory treatment. Popular attitudes and public policy became mutually reinforcing in setting old people apart and devaluing their contributions to society.

Negative stereotypes of old people have persisted until the present, even though the over-sixty-five age group has enlarged markedly since the turn of the century. However, in the last forty-five years the role of government, as well as of the private sector, in regard to the aged has changed notably. Since 1935, when the Social Security Act was passed, the federal government has assumed an increasing amount of responsibility for the welfare of old people. The institutional network that has emerged in subsequent decades has decisively altered the framework of old age in America. Landmark legislation such as Medicare, the Older Americans Act, and Supplemental Security Income symbolizes the federal government's expanding commitment to the nation's older citizens. Additionally, state and local agencies provide assistance to the elderly. In spite of this proliferation of programs, critics charge that governmental policy toward the aged is still inadequate; one major grievance is the level and conditions of financial support. Advocacy groups such as the Gray Panthers are engaged in political activity aimed at improving the quality of life for the country's old people.

The private sector has also endeavored to satisfy the needs of the aged through old age pension plans sponsored by corporations and unions as well as through the investment of private capital in retirement communities and nursing homes. Diverse and occasionally innovative programs have been initiated by private nonprofit organizations, sometimes with the aid of government funds, to deal with the problems of the elderly in such areas as housing, transportation, legal services, and recreation. Moreover, studies of the aged conducted in a number of academic disciplines and supported by both private and public sources have greatly expanded our knowledge of the last stage of life.

Thus, growing awareness of the concerns of America's old people has stimulated the development of institutions, services, and research projects to advance the interests of the aged. Further gains on all these fronts may ensure that old age is indeed a life stage worth reaching.

W omen in early America did not survive to old age in great numbers. With female life expectancy at birth at about forty years in the eighteenth century, the majority of women were likely to die before completing all the responsibilities of bearing and rearing children. Reaching the period of life past the age of sixty, when all the children had grown up and left the family home, was an uncommon experience. Nevertheless, those early American women who did survive beyond age sixty had a more secure place in society than their far more numerous counterparts today.

Old age was viewed in a relatively favorable light in seventeenth- and eighteenth-century America, so most old women were accorded respect for their longevity rather than penalized for it. Exceptions, of course, existed, and the lot of aged female slaves or poor old women of any background was clearly undesirable. In an economy in which production was largely centered in the home, adult women of all ages contributed measurably toward the maintenance of the family. Unless debilitated by a physical condition, old women carried their share in the ongoing work of the household. Similarly, their participation in the affairs of the larger society remained undiminished. Valued as repositories of knowledge because of their extensive experience, elderly women constituted a precious human resource for preindustrial communities. Far from being cut off from purposeful activities, women in early America continued to play a vital part in the life of their families and communities during their sixties, seventies, and even later.

Martha Moore Ballard of Augusta, in what is now the state of Maine, whose diary entries for the year 1797 are reproduced here, is exemplary of these vital older women. Mrs. Ballard, like many other elderly women in the seventeenth and eighteenth centuries, enjoyed an unbroken marriage. Although at the age of sixty-three her child-rearing responsibilities were finished, she remained in close contact with her grown children, who resided in the immediate vicinity. Her extended family circle, composed of her children as well as her grandchildren, was central to her everyday life.

Mrs. Ballard performed many and varied chores around her house, ranging from preparing food and repairing clothing to making soap and candles, gardening, and taking care of animals. She was often called upon to entertain visitors in her home, and she was active in local church affairs. But Martha Ballard's most important community function was her occupation as a midwife, a role traditionally filled by older women in early American communities. Mrs. Ballard's skills in delivering babies and treating the sick and injured were highly valued by her neighbors. The diary accounts of her professional calls suggest the arduous nature of her work and testify to her durability and strength. She depended on other local women in her work and was in turn respected by them. Whether or not they were midwives, women like Mrs. Ballard remained productive members of their communities well beyond the middle years of their lives. In early America, the transition from middle to old age, while it coincided with the figurative emptying of the nest, entailed only a minimal amount of discontinuity in social roles. Martha Ballard did not renounce her work as household producer and midwife in her old age, nor was she expected to do so.

Yet Mrs. Ballard was not oblivious to the passage of years. In her diary entries of 1797, she carefully noted her 63rd birthday, her 43rd wedding anniversary, and the delivery of her 700th baby since 1778. Her consciousness of her advanced years is revealed in her comments on her 63rd birthday. Aging, to her, implied that death was impending. Her traditional posture of resignation in the face of the inevitable was buttressed by a Puritan religious outlook that stressed inner preparation for death. Mrs. Ballard was not noticeably concerned with the outward signs of aging. She commented dispassionately on her own illnesses and injuries, but she did not link them specifically to a decline in powers resulting from old age. Ultimately, the state of her health and the timing of her death were beyond human control; what mattered most was her spiritual condition. Mrs. Ballard, as other old women of her era, would have offered a providential interpretation of her longevity, attributing her survival until old age solely to the grace of God.

— 23 —
Martha Moore Ballard

1797. JANUARY 1. SUNDAY. Rev. Mr. Stone performed exceeding well this day.

2. Mr. Ballard been surveying for Esq. Cony and Bridg.

3. Mr. Ballard went to Mr. Coney's store — he purchased a small shovel and tongs — cost 9s. 6 p.

6. I was called to see Mrs. Burtun at 1h. 20m. morn. I spent the forenoon with her and went to visit Mrs. Thwing — was called from there at 2h. p. m. by reason of Polly Burtun's being burnt in a most shocking manner by her cloaths takeing fire. Shee being in the chamber with her brother Billy. We used every measure for her relief, but all in vain. She became a victim to death.

7. I was at Mr. Burtun's — his only daughter expired at 11h. 30m. morn, her death ocationed by her being burnt. A distresed family they are. The mother expecting soon to be sick. I tarried this night. Mrs. Burtun is allmost overwhelmed with sorrow. God grant her his gracious aid in this visitation. Mrs. Cocks and Dutton assisted to lay it out.

8. I spent this day with the afflicted family of Mr. Burtun. Their child interred after the public service was ended. Mrs. Pierce expired last even.

9. I was called to see the wife of Isaac Hardin at 2h. 11m.

10. I came from Mr. Hardin's after breakfast. I wrode in a sled with Mr. Briggs to the Coart house. Went to see Mrs. Burtun.

11. Old Mr. Luke Lambart called here to see us.

12. I was called about noon to see Mrs. Ficky who was in labor and was delivered of a daughter at 3h. p. m.

13. I bo[ugh]t 7 ozs. snuff and paid for 1 oz. which I had of Mr. Carter last Friday — cost 2s. 3p.

15. I was called at 6h. morn, from Mr. Burtun's to Mr. Kimbal's to see his lady who was in labour and was delivered at 4h. 30m. even. of a son.

17. I was called at 2h. morn, to see the lady of Gen. Sewall who was in labour and was delivered at 11h. 30m. of a son. Mr. Plantain from Sharon sleeps here. Birth 3d, received 9s. 7p.

19. Mr. Joy's sister burnt to death.

21. I was called by Mr. Linkorn to see his wife at 8h. evening. Left my company to wait on themselves.

22. Mrs. Linkon was delivered of a daughter at 4h. morn. The infant appeared destitute of life for some time, but revived, and I drest it, and left that and the mother as well as could be expected.

SOURCE: Charles Elventon Nash, *The History of Augusta First Settlements and Early Days as a Town Including the Diary of Mrs. Martha Moore Ballard (1785 to 1812)* (Augusta, Maine: Charles E. Nash, 1904).

25. I was called to see the wife of Isaac Hardin, at 2h. 30m. morn. I was called for once and again, after I was there, to go and see a Mrs. Gage, but could not be spared. Mrs. Hardin was delivered at 1h. p. m., of a daughter, her 9th child. I left her and infant cleverly [satisfactorily], and arrived at home at sun sett.

27. I bot at Mr. Carter's 2 shawls, at 4 shillings, 6 pence each, which I gave to son Town's daughters. I called at my daughter's. Also 9 pence worth of gingerbread. We had a lamb come this day.

28. Mr. Ballard was at the Fort. Informs that Theophilus Hamlen's youngest child is burnt badly.

31. Mr. Ballard has been to the fort, brot 10 lbs. cotton which he had at Cony's store at 2s. 10p. per lb.

FEBRUARY 1. I have done my house work and nurst the lamb. It seems likely to live.

2. I was called at the first h. morn by Wm. Brooks, Esq., to see the wife of John Brooks who was in labour and was safe delivered 3/4 hour after 4 of a daughter — her first born. Mrs. Bond and Williams were called as assistants.

5. I was called when at breakfast to see the lady of Capt. Guild who was in labour and was safe delivered at 10h. 30m. of a fine daughter — her second child, both females.

7. I was called between 10 and 11h. even. to see the wife of Timothy Brannard. I should have wrote Rheuben. Mr. Flaid attended me.

8. Mrs. Branard was delivered of a fine son at 6h. morn. I left her and infant as well as could be expected.

12. SUNDAY. Cleared up at evening. Mr. Pollard came to his son's and conducted me to his house. I went from there to meeting, forenoon, was called at intermition to Mr. Burtun's wife who was delivered at 3h. p. m., of a fine son, and is cleverly.

17. A young man by the name of Huse came here to work. I have been doing house work.

18. Mr. Ballard bot me a pair of leather sleppers of Mr. Bond; price 7 shillings.

19. I was called to see Mrs. Pollard at 4h. morn. She was delivered at 5 of a daughter, her 4th child.

20. I have seen 63 revolutions of the sun. It seems as if I could not labor much longer, as I have done. May God grant me grace to endure with patience what I have to sufer.

21. Ezra Town and son Ephraim took breakfast. I gave each of them 6s. to purchase them bibles with. Dolly spun me yarn for candle wicks. I was called to see the wife of Samuel Davis who was in labour and was delivered of a son at 7h. 30m. even.

22. My tallow caught fire and alarmed us much. My daughter Lambard fainted by reason of her surprise.

25. I was called by a Mr. Morrill to see the wife of Mr. Ebenezer Hewin at 3h. morn. She was safe delivered at 5h. of a daughter — her 4th child.

26. SUNDAY. Was called at 4h. m. to see Mrs. Finny who was in

labour and was delivered of a daughter at 5h. 30m. The infant survived about one hour and expired without any apparant distress. It seemed to be struck with mo[r]tification. I put on the grave clothes.

27. Was called at 4h. 40m. to go to see the wife of Moses French who was in labour and was safe delivered at 8h. 30m. evening of her 4th daughter.

28. Mr. Wm. Moore conducted me home from Moses French's, Readfield. I gave him 2s. 3p. to pay Mr. Dinsmore for the use of his sleigh to conduct me to the patient above mentioned.

MARCH 1. I was called to see Mrs. Heartford at 10h. last evening. She was delivered of a daughter, her first born, at 1h. 20m. this morn.

2. Mr. Holman was here from Livermore.

4. My son Jonathan is 34 years old this day. May he, as in years, increase in virtue.

11. I was called at 11 even. to see the wife of Benja. White, who is in labour.

12. I was with Mrs. White who was delivered at 3h. morn, of a fine son.

14. I was called at 2h. morn, to Doctor Colman's to see his lady.

15. Mrs. Colman was safe delivered at 4h. 30m. of a fine daughter, her 5th child. I sett up with her this night.

16. Mr. Ballard is gone to survey for Freeman Hinkley.

17. We have been runing lie [lye] and boiling bones and bakeing. Cyrus went to mill to the Hook.

18. Mr. Ballard went to survey for Mr. Smith the blacksmith.

20. Mr. Ballard sett out at 9h. morn., for Monmouth, to survey for a Mr. Bishop.

22. I was called at 5h. p. m., to see the wife of George Thomas. She was safe delivered at 7 of a son, which weighed more than the lite side of Mr. Densmore's stilyards would weigh. I left my patients as well as could be expected.

24. I have been carding tow [short or broken fiber used to make yarn, twine, or stuffing]. Polly catched a basketfull on fire with the candle and burnt them.

26. SUNDAY. The ice on the river breaking up. There was no preaching at the Fort. I was called at 11h. forenoon, to see Mrs. Pillsbury who is sick with the rash. Her husband sick, allso. I watcht.

28. Came to Mr. Pillsbury's; find her very ill, — in a kind of delirium. They informed me she had been much so through the night past. It is my opinion the use of the bark was in some measure the cause.

29. I tarried with Mr. Pillsbury till near night. Old Mrs. Kenny advised to giv her a syrup of vinegar and onions, and a decoction of gold thread and shumake berries. It was done and she seemed revived.

30. My brother Ebenezer Moore dined here. He informed me that Mrs. Pillsbury expired this morn.

31. Mr. Ballard and myself and Cyrus attended at the house of Mr. Pillsbury. His wife's remains were intered in the burying-ground of Doctor Cony.

APRIL 2. Mrs. Copeland delivered of a daughter this evening by Pishon.

3. Clear. At son Town's [in Winslow]. He went to town meeting.

9. SUNDAY. Snowed last night and this day. Mr. Town found it almost knee high as he was conducting the ladies home; it seemed like winter indeed. I feel anxious for my daughter, but God's time is best, may he discover his goodness to her.

10. Cold indeed. The snow flies; doleful weather for those who are watching lumber on the river.

13. Son Town called me out of bed at 1h. 5m. morn. I find my daughter very ill. She was delivered of a daughter and all performed which her labour required at 1h. 20m. No women arived till after all was performed but dressing the infant. This her 11th child.

15. I sett out for home at 9h., morn. We crost the ferry in this town at 2h. 30m. Was informed there that Mrs. Briggs has been delivered of twins since I left her, and that they are dead; and that the wife of Shubal Pitts was delivered of a daughter at 9h. this morn.

16. SUNDAY. I went to meeting, afternoon; Mr. Gillit performed.

20. I was called at 1h. morn, to go to Mr. Atkins'; his wife being in labour and was delivered at 4h. morn, of a fine son, which weighed 9 1/2 lbs.

23. SUNDAY. I went to hear Mr. Stone, afternoon.

26. The Packet went past here upward. Mrs. North and daughter were on board.

27. Mr. Ballard sett out to lott out township between the river and Penobscott.

28. A South wind. There were a number of vessels went up yesterday and this day.

29. I have rackt chips and wound quills and done something about my soap.

MAY 1. I was called at 5h. morn to see the wife of Mr. Phelps. She was delivered at 10 of a fine daughter. I called in to see Mrs. Guild — find her and family well. I was at Mr. Lord's.

2. Sally spun as we could not keep fire in our loome roome.

4. We all attended worship at the Fort. The Rev. Mr. Stone discoarst from Isaiah 66c. 2nd verse.

7. SUNDAY. The ordinance of the Lord's Super administered. Mrs. Jones joined the church.

11. I planted winter squash and beens and houghed about my currant bushes and put my cloath in lie.

15. I put my cloath out to whiten. Ruel Williams and Sally here to tea.

20. Mr. Ballard returned from surveying. He went to the Hook to be shaved, and lost his watch.

21. SUNDAY. I was called to see the wife of Capt. Samuel Hussey; found her delivered of a 4th son, by the help of Mrs. Cocks. I was conducted home by water. Mr. Ballard went and redeemed his watch for one dollar.

22. Mr. Ballard been to a meeting about the bridge.

23. Mr. Lambart and the girls went to exhibition at Hallowell. Mr. Ballard gone to Dresden, on a road with others.

24. I was called to see my daughter Pollard, at 1h. morn. She was safe delivered of her 3d daughter at 4. I was called from her to see the wife of Abraham Davenport; she is in labour.

25. Mrs. Davenport was delivered at 40m. after midnight of a son, her first child. Her case somewhat singular, but I got thro with safety thro the Divine aid.

31. Mr. Ballard went to Winslow on a reference. I was called to see the wife of Charls Cox who was in labour, and safe delivered of a fine son, at 8h. evening.

JUNE 1. I was called between 5 and 6h. morn, from Mr. Cox's to see the wife of Mr. Martin who is at her father Isaac Clark's. I proceeded as fast as I could but found her put to bed by the help of Mrs. Ingerham. I purchased a pair shoes of John Brook's — price 7s. 6p. paid the cash.

2. Was called to see Sally Waid who is unwell. She seemed revived when I arived.

10. Mr. Ballard and Hoiet went to the Bolton place to work. I have done my morning work and at 8h. went to cut clover for my swine when I by some means misplased a bone in the great toe of my right foot. I soon became so lame I could not walk. At that critical moment son Lambart came in — he assisted me to get to my bed where I remained till he called Doctor Page to my assistance who rectified the misplaced bone and I was able to walk into the other room. I paid the Doctor 3s. and went about my work.

11. SUNDAY. I was called on at 9h. morn, to go to Savage Bolton's by Isaac Cowen. Met a message for me to go to Mrs. Carter's. I went and delivered her of a daughter — a second daughter — I then went on for Bolton's — had two falls from my hors[e], lamed my hand and bruised my face, but went on. Misplaced a bone in my left hand by a fall from my hors.

12. I left Mrs. Bolton by her consent in the care of Mrs. Mosier who seemed fond of tarrying. My hand pains me much.

13. Gen'l Petty, Esquire Farewell here this morn. Mr. Ballard went to the [H]ook with them on business.

15. Doctor Page came about noon and sett a bone which was broke in my hand by a fall from a hors last Sunday.

16. I was called at 10h. morn to see the wife of John Page, who was in labour and was delivered at 12 of a son, her first born.

19. Old Mr. Pollard and his wife left this town this afternoon.

24. Son Town and Ezra took breakfast here. They informed that a child of Alex Smyles' was drowned last Monday. Mrs. Livermore and her daughter Pickford called here.

25. SUNDAY. Augustus Ballard came here. He was at meeting at the Hook. They met in their meeting house.

26. Our men went to son Jonathan's; they raised a barn fram[e] for him.

27. TUESDAY. I was called at 9h. morn. to Sidney to see the wife of Bezar Trask, who has been in labour since Saturday noon. She was safe delivered at 4h. p. m., of a son. Her case was preternatural, but thro Divine goodness mother and infant are likely to do well.

JULY 1. Mr. Ezekiel Page's house took fire in the roof this forenoon. I was w[he]eling my cloth and discovered it too. Mr. Dingley, our young men, and men on three boats ran to their assistance. They extinguished the fire and returned.

2. SUNDAY. Our young folks went to Pittston to church. Mr. Ballard and myself to the Fort. The ordinance of the Super administered. A young gentleman who was a stranger performed. He delivered two excellent discourses.

4. I was called at 2h. 30m. morn to see the wife of Mager Benj. Stickney who was in labour and was safe delivered at 2h. 7m. p. m. of their 3d son and 5th child. Mr. James Bridg and Hannah North were united by the mariage covenant.

6. Mr. Town informs that a child was drowned at Canaan and one belonging to the widdow Runels was hanged by rising from bed and geting the head through between the back of a chair which the mother had sett to prevent its falling of the bed.

8. Mr. Lambert took a man by the name of Hamelton for thieft and committed him to goall [jail]. He has taken from several people about the Fort and sundry articles. May he sincerely repent and God graciously pardon him. O, how I pity his bosom friend if he has one.

9. Was called at 3h. p. m., to see the wife of Capt. William Springer, who is in labour. She was safe delivered of a very fine daughter at 10h. evening.

10. I called at Shubal Hinkley's for what he owed me for assisting his wife with her last child. The hors I was on ran into the shead and throwed me of, breaking my specktakles and allmost my limbs. I feel the efects of my fall very much. Have not been able to sett up very much. Old Lady Cony here.

11. Mr. Ballard sett out for Wiscassett to attend coart as a witness. I have felt more comfortable than I did yesterday.

12. Mr. Ballard returned from the Point. Mrs. Carter's infant expired.

13. Mr. Carter's infant was intered this afternoon.

15. I was called to see the wife of Mr. Eads, who was in labour, and was safe delivered of a fine son, between the hours of 4 and 5.

16. SUNDAY. My family all attended worship at the Fort, forenoon, except myself. I was there afternoon. A gentleman by the name of Stone performed.

19. I have made a new milk cheese — changed milk with Mrs. Joy. I had my puter [pewter] can 28 times full in my cheese.

21. Rev. Mr. Stone took tea with us.

22. Allen Lambart is one year old.

24. We went to Mr. Livermore's to see Alpheus who is confined with a broken leg.

25. I was called this morn about day to see the wife of Jerey Kimbal, who is in labour and was delivered about the middle of the day of a fine son — first son and 3d child — which weighed 12 lbs. This is the 700th birth I have assisted at since June, 1778.

26. I was called to see Mrs. Waid who was in labour, 5h. 30m. Was oblidged to walk, broke one of my shoe heels on my way and was much fatigued. Found her very ill; and delivered her of a daughter — her 7th child about 6h. morn. Had just put her to bed when Mr. Roby called me to see his wife where I was detained all day. I called to see Mrs. Cumings afternoon and slept at Gen'l Sewall's.

29. I was called to see Mrs. Hamlen at 4h. p. m., find her very ill. She was safe delivered about 5 of a daughter her 5th child.

31. I was called at 2 hours, morn, to see the wife of Mr. Thompson; find her in labour. She was delivered of her third child, a daughter, at 4h.

AUGUST 2. I was called about day dawn to see the wife of Eliab Shaw. She was delivered of a daughter — her 8th child at 9h. even. He came with me as far as the bridge over Bowman's brook.

3. A man by the name of Edson dined here, who is on his way to Sandage [Sandwich] and expects to see my brother Jonathan. Cyrus informs me that Old Mr. Pierce expired this day before noon. May we all attend to the call — Be ye allso ready.

4. My husband and I attended at the interment of the remains of our brother Pierce at 3h. this afternoon. There were three sons and three daughters, — two sons and one daughter by affinity; four grandsons. Mr. Ballard and myself, followed as mourners. Called to see Mrs. Eads' infant, it is unwell.

10. Mr. Ballard returned from Vassalboro. He was informed at the Ferry that Mr. Thwing had a child drowned in the well. I could wish it might prove a mistake. Alas. It proves a fact. God support the parents in their affliction, and be better to them than 10 sons, is my petition.

12. Mr. Ballard and I attended the funeral of Mr. Thwing's child, Samuel, afternoon.

13. SUNDAY. Thankfull took a ride with her beloved after tea.

16. Mr. Ballard sett out to go to Mount Vernon to survey.

17. I was called to see Mrs. Gill at 9h. morn, find her very unwell.

18. My patient seems very feeble the forenoon; her illness came on at noon, and she was delivered at 1h. 30 m. p. m. of her first daughter and 4th child. Mr. Ballard very unwell. I applied burdoc leaves and rhum warm, to his neck and shoulders.

20. SUNDAY. I attended at worship. Was called at the close of the sermon by Mr. Roby to see his wife who was in labour. She was delivered soon after I arived of a son.

21. Some heavy showers with thunder. Nathan Bridg called, in the shower.

24. I was called at 9h. even. to see Mrs. Joy who was in labour. She was delivered at 10h. of a daughter — her 3d child.

27. SUNDAY. Mr. Ballard and I went up to son Pollard's. His wife and

children are unwell. I should have tarried all night had I not expected I might be wanted to attend some one in greater distress.

28. I was called at 7h. morn, to see Mrs. Black who was in labour. She was safe delivered between 8 and 9 of a very fine daughter. I tarried till after dining there. Left her and infant cleverly as could be expected. Mr. Black bestowed 12 shillings as a reward.

29. I was called at 5h. 30m. morn. to see the wife of Capt. Gershom Cox, who is in labour. She was safe delivered at 7h. morn, of a fine daughter, her second child, both of the same sex.

31. Cyrus and the girls went to gather blackbury's on the hill.

SEPTEMBER 1. Mr. Bunker Farwell expired this night at 10h. very suden.

3. SUNDAY. The wife of Joseph Stackpole was admitted to full communion with the church here. Sacrament of the Super was administered.

5. I was called at 3h. morn, to go to see the wife of Andrew Goodin, who is in labour. I arived there at 4. She was safe delivered at 12 and 40 m. of a fine daughter. I left her and infant cleverly at 4h. p. m.

6. Mr. Ballard at the Hook, forenoon, surveying for Mr. Isaac Clark. We attended a lecture, afternoon. The association met at the Rev'd Mr. Stone's lodgings. A rainbow in the west at 9 hour this evening.

7. Mr. Ballard sett out to survey for Mr. Reuben Fairfield.

8. Was called, afternoon to see Mr. Whitwel's infant, who is unwell with a cold. I applyed a plaster to the stomach and onions to the feet; and gave a syrrip of mullin. It soon revived. The midle pier of the Kenebec Bridg was finisht, and there were 7 discharges of the field piece, and 3 cheers.

11. Old Lady Tounsin of Sidney here.

15. Mr. Ballard been makeing a plan for Jessy Blunt.

16. I have been mending napsacks, and makeing preparation for Mr. Ballard's going on the business of surveying.

17. SUNDAY. I mended Mr. Ballard's coat, forenoon. Went to meeting afternoon. I saw a girl take a fan out of Mr. James Page's seat and put it in her pocket. I informed Mr. Page who went to the seat she was in and she delivered it up after denying she had seen it. I did not know her name. Rev'd Mr. Stone informed us he proposes a visit to his friends.

18. Cyrus saw old Mr. Hamlen who left Oxford a weak since. My friends all well there [Luis] Hamlen arived this day with his wife.

20. My daughter and I walkt down to the Common, afternoon, to see companies who met there for review, Cyrus with us. Thankfull and Hepsy went to see the militia parade.

21. I was called at 4h. m. to see a Mrs. Getchel at the Hook who was in labour with her first child. Her husband at sea. She was delivered at 11h. of a fine son.

24. SUNDAY. I attended worship at Hallowell. John Rice's child baptised by the name of Betsy.

28. I was called at 1h. 40m. morn, to see Mrs. Gow. She was safe delivered at 4h. 40m. of a fine son, her 3d child.

29. Was called at 1h. 35m. p. m. to see the wife of Mr. William Straton of Hallowell, who was in labour, and was safe delivered at 2h. 15m. of a daughter, her second child. Cyrus brot 12 bushels apples home from the Bolton place.

OCTOBER 1. SUNDAY. Mr. Ballard went to meeting at the Hook, and attended at the interment of Joshua Learned who has lately resided at the farm of Mr. Charles Vahun at Hallowell. He expired the 29th ult.

2. Mrs. Thomas Densmore was safe delivered at 4h. 30m. this morn, of her 9th daughter and 12th child.

3. Mr. Ballard went to New France. I have been doing things about house, and tended my thread to whiten.

5. A gentleman by the name of Stone sleeps here. He is from Townsend.

6. I was called at 3h. morn, to see the wife of Isaac Savage the 3d. She was in labour, and was delivered at 4 of a daughter, her second child.

7. It is 20 years this day since I left Oxford.

8. SUNDAY. My family except Cyrus and I attended worship at the Hook. I did not feel so well as to go, but made a chees.

14. Capt. Osgood here; gave a Mr. Barrow a deed of land. Mr. Ballard and myself were witnesses to the sineing and delivery. This is 20 years since I first set my feet on the Kenebeck shore. It was at Mr. John Jones' landing below the Hook, where I spent 1 year and 17 days; then removed to his mill at Boman's brook.

15. SUNDAY. Mr. Ballard went to see John Davis, Esq'r.

16. Mr. Ballard sett out for East Andover, at 7h. this morn.

18. Mr. Tombs of Pittston here.

21. Thankfull Godfray workt for me, forenoon. John Moore came and conducted her to his father's, at Pittston, afternoon.

22. SUNDAY. We went to meeting, but Mr. Stone was not returned. Allin Lambart is 15 months old this day.

25. I was called about 6 hours, to Moses Parmer's to see his wife.

26. Mrs. Parmer was delivered of her first child, a son, between the hours of 12 and 1, morn. I went from there to Mr. White's; find his wife delivered of a son and cleverly. I walkt from Capt. Coxes to White's; and back to Mrs. Hussey's. Then crost the river with Mr. Bullin and walkt from Mr. Shepherd's to Parmer's. Then wrode a colt home, on which woman never was before.

29. SUNDAY. After meeting Mr. Stone spoke from St. John, 3 chap. 19 verse.

31. Rev. Mr. Gillit called here. Mr. Allin, the Clothier called and I paid him what was due for dressing our cloath. Ezra Allin left account of taxes. It is now 11h. even.

NOVEMBER 3. Mr. Ballard and I attended lecture; there were but a small number there. I removed my rheu and camomile from where they were into the garden. Little Jack Ballard said, if it should die you will know better next time.

4. Son Jonathan came here — took dinner, then conducted his little

ones home. May God bless and prosper them and make them ornaments in their day to religion that they may be useful members of Society when I am here no more.

6. I was called at 25m. after midnight to see the lady of Mr. James Child who was very unwell thro the day. I tarried with her thro this night.

11. It was this morn, not yesterday, I went to Mr. Lambart's. She was ill all day. She was safe delivered at 8h. 45m. even. of a fine daughter — her 2d child.

12. I was called from son Lambart at 3h. this morn to see Mrs. Child who was in labor. She was safe delivered at 6h. 45m. of a fine son — her 5th child.

13. Mr. Ballard set out this day to go to view land between this river and Penobscott with a man by the name of Bond — he is from Vermont State.

18. The ice runs in the river. Capt. William's lady put to bed yesterday with a son. Dr. Cony operator. I am informed she is not so well as could be wisht.

19. SUNDAY. Son and daughter Lambart gave their infant up by baptism, the name Dorothy. We brot little Allin home with us.

20. I have spent the day nursing Allin Lambart; he has often called for his pah and mah but has not cried much.

21. Clear and very pleasant sun, but a cool air. The Kennebeck Bridge was dedicated. Mr. Ballard and son Cyrus attended. David Wall, James Savage and Asa Fletcher were burnt some by the cartradges takeing fire through carelessness. Mr. Lang of Pittston sleeps here.

22. Mr. Ballard been surveying for Mr. Ezekiel Page.

26. SUNDAY. Snowed. Mr. Ballard went to meeting. There [were] six persons only there forenoon. I was called at 7h. even. to see Mrs. Bond who was in labour. She was safe delivered about midnight of a fine son which weighed 11 1/4 lbs. It is her 10th child.

30. This day is observed as a day of Thanksgiving. My children who reside here were to super with us, except Moses Pollard who rather chose other company.

DECEMBER 10. SUNDAY. The text, Proverbs 10th c., 23d vers.

13. Mr. Ballard surveying for Mr. Thomas.

14. I was called at 9h. evening, to go and see the wife of James Moore of Readfield. I arived there at 11.

17. Mrs. Moore was safe delivered at 3h. morn. of a son, her eighth child.

19. It is the aneversary of my marriage, and 43 years.

23. I was called to go to Isaac Cowen's, Sidney, at 9h. evening, arived there at evening.

29. At Seth Pitts' and Cowen's.

*A*merica's old women constituted a diverse group in the nineteenth century, as in other centuries. Coming from different class, racial, ethnic, religious, and regional backgrounds, their life experiences varied substantially. Yet one thing they had in common was a reliance on their families to support them during their last years. For women whose families possessed sufficient resources, this presented little problem. But for the many old women who lived near the subsistence level in the nineteenth century, the onset of old age was a cause for anxiety. Before the 1930s, government assumed virtually no responsibility for the welfare of old people, and private charitable organizations played only a minimal part in alleviating the distress of the aged poor. Therefore, elderly women were especially vulnerable when their husbands were unable to guarantee them financial security during times of economic crisis. Whether accustomed to a lifelong struggle against poverty or victimized by a sudden reversal in family fortunes, such women often had to compromise their self-respect to survive.

The case of Bethiah Pyatt McKown of St. Louis, Missouri illustrates the impact of economic uncertainty on the quality of life for women in old age. Mrs. McKown's plight is graphically detailed in the following excerpts from a series of letters she wrote to her eldest son, John D. McKown, between 1860 and 1865. Bethiah McKown was born in Baltimore, Maryland in 1798 and married James Brison McKown there in 1817. The couple had ten children, moved to Missouri about 1838, and were resident in St. Louis by 1840. Although James McKown seems to have prospered as a measurer of buildings and onetime owner of a blacksmith bellows factory, on the eve of the Civil War, the McKowns were in a precarious financial situation, barely managing to maintain their home. After Mr. McKown had a stroke and was unable to work, the previously welcome contributions from the couple's grown children became essential for survival. Following the death of her husband, Bethiah McKown, then in her sixties, was forced to share her house with one daughter's family, and she later moved into the home of another daughter. Dependent on the generosity of her sons-in-law for living space and sustenance, the elderly widow became accustomed to importuning her offspring for money, clothes, and household goods. With nowhere else to turn for support, Mrs. McKown of necessity adopted a subservient posture toward her children.

Yet it would be a mistake to assume that Mrs. McKown surrendered control over her own life when she found herself subject to the mercies of her children's goodwill. Although outwardly she exhibited the appropriate attitude of pious resignation, Bethiah McKown never succumbed to a passive acceptance of her fate. She realized that as a mother she possessed considerable leverage over her sons and daughters, and she was determined to take advantage of her status. The evidence in these letters suggests that Mrs. McKown deliberately attempted to arouse her children's sympathies for her condition while at the same time fostering a competition between them with regard to the magnitude of their contributions to her welfare. Convinced of her pivotal role in family affairs, Bethiah McKown used her communications with her children as a means of ensuring her economic well-being as well as preserving her sense of self-importance.

As a woman who derived satisfaction from the niceties of appearance, Bethiah McKown could not help but look at herself with a critical eye as she crossed the boundary of old age. Her numerous references to the external manifestations of aging — loss of memory, failing eyesight, and chronic physical illness — imply that she was self-conscious about aging. She was careful to recount to her son comments that had been made concerning her youthful appearance, implying that not looking her age was obviously desirable. Mrs. McKown's remarks lead us to speculate that an uncritical acceptance of the natural course of aging was no longer predictable by the 1860s, when attitudes toward the elderly were ambivalent at best. Mrs. McKown's outlook on old age reflects this ambivalence.

Like that of Martha Ballard, Bethiah McKown's understanding of old age was predicated on a religious world view. Living in an era when survival to old age was still exceptional, Mrs. McKown considered spiritual preparation for the end of life a matter of paramount importance. Her preoccupation with her own and her children's salvation is evident at a number of points in her letters. However, there is another strand concealed in these letters that is lacking in Martha Ballard's writings. Bethiah McKown perceived that advanced age was becoming more of a liability than an asset in modern America. Her sensitivity to the handicaps under which old women labored in her generation was clearly sharpened by her own deteriorating position. But the validity of her insight is confirmed by subsequent developments. Widowed and impoverished in the midst of a national crisis, Bethiah McKown mobilized the resources available to her and survived. More importantly, she was able to salvage her pride.

—— 24 ——
Bethiah Pyatt McKown

ST. LOUIS DEC 9TH 1860

My dear Children

Yours of the 29th inst came safely to hand three days ago, and it gave us great pleasure to hear that your family and James's were well, with the exception of your dear little Mary, who I hope by this time has much improved in health, I think you came to a wise conclusion not to give her any more medicine, for I believe the Alopathic [a system of

SOURCE: James W. Goodrich, ed., "The Civil War Letters of Bethiah Pyatt McKown," *Missouri Historical Review* 67 (1973). Reprinted by permission.

medical practice that combats disease by treatments that produce effects different from those produced by the disease treated] medicine kills ten times more than it cures We all have very severe colds, your Father is very unwell at this time altho he has gone to church, *where I should have been*, if it had not been raining, we have had very fine weather for the last week not a bit of frost and not unpleasantly cold, altho for the week previous it was extremely cold and unpleasant with frequent spells of snow. The times were never so hard in St Louis as they are now, money is scarce and labour is scarcer, hundreds of industrous men are out of employment and the amount of distress in this City never was so great; as yet, your Father has made out to live, but if three days pass without his not having some measuring to do, he trembles for fear of his not being able to support his family. We have two boarders who pay us $32 per month for their board not apiece but for both and washing. William [McKown] pays $3 per week, and the ballance your Father has to make up by *the labour of his own hands;* it costs $22 for our rent per month, and to our servant we pay [$]9 so you see we have not much to go on, and if your Father's business should fail I know not what we would do, but we hope for the best and trust on that Almighty arm that has always sustained us, for vain is the help of man, do not think I write thus to reproach you, indeed I do not, for I know if you had anything to spare from the support of your large family *we,* would have a share. We are glad to hear that you have so much work to do and that James has a good share with you, his sleepyness in the morning, was always his only fault, and it seems to grow with his years, and I am afraid he will never outgrow it. tell James and Samantha [McKown] I will write to them, if they write to me. We have heard from Mr. [Joshua T.] Bradley he is at St Paul [Minnesota] with his daughter but not doing any thing yet, I suppose it will fall to your Father's lot to keep his family this winter, tis too bad, but it is for our own Sally who is the beloved of us all and while we have a mouthful we will share it with her.... you have no idea how many of our old acquaintances have died within the last year tell James that Al Baldwin, Jordan Targee, William McCamant and young Charles Pond are dead. When we see so many falling around us that we have been intimate with, it bids us all to be ready for in such an hour as we know not our summons will come, and whether prepared or not we will have to go, my Children are you prepared to meet that summons, *if you are not,* I pray God that you may set about it right away, for now is the accepted time, and I say to you one and *All* delay not, remember that it is our daily prayer, if we meet no more in this world that we may meet where parting shall be no more forever. I have nothing new to tell you only that Joseph McKown has gone to the scene of disturbance in Kansas with the St Louis Brigade. I have not seen any of your sisters but Sarah [Bradley], since I received your letter but I will tell them to write to you, when I see Margaret, and when I write to Harriet and Bethiah. William is so busy that he hardly gets time

to eat his meals now that Joseph is gone, there is no one in the Store but Nat [Nathaniel H. Clark] and him and I tell you William sees hard times.... Farewell my children may God bless you forever is the prayer of your affectionate Parents James B & Bethiah P McKown.
[P.S.] I knew the names of all the children as far as little Kate who was the babe when we left Marshall I understood that you had one named Laura Fairfax, and I have her name down in our family Bible all the rest I recollect especially my little Grandson Charlie give my love to Jimy, Aurthur and the other little boys and tell them to make haste and learn to write so that [they] can write to Grandpa and Grandma little Charly McMurkie writes to us every time his mother writes. I forgot to tell you that the 11th of Dec which is the day after tomorrow is our 43d wedding-day I hope you will drink to our health on that day not in Liquor but in a glass of pure water once more farewell my sons and daughters.

B P McKown

ST LOUIS MAY 29TH 1861

My dear Son
    Yours of the 1st came to hand three days ago, we were very glad to hear from you once more. It is with sorrow we hear of your straitined circumstances, on your own account as well as ours, but the same fate seems to have fallen on all our dear-ones, so that we can truly sympathise with you, ...
    Your Father makes out to pick up a little now and then, barely sufficient to keep us from *starving,* and that little we have to share with Sarah and her family, her husband [Joshua T. Bradley] is *doing nothing,* and your Father is supporting him he seems to have no energy to try to get any thing to do. I think your Fathers is a hard fate our money is in a sad fix the Missouri Banks issue nothing under $5 and you must have gold or silver for change and *that,* you have to pay 15 per c[en]t for, Illinois money is far below par we had $3 yesterday of that money, and all we could get for it was $1.40 c[en]ts, this is a terrible state of things. I see nothing but ruin and starvation, and when it will end God only knows, ...

ST LOUIS MAY 18TH 1862

My dear Son
    Yours of the 30th of April, came to hand in due time, ... I am quite *well,* and also to tell you that your dear Father is much better, altho extremely feeble, he is now able to take a walk, and is as well (in my opinion) as he will ever be, there is no perceptible improvement in his hand and arm, so that he is extremely helpless, I still have to dress, undress, comb his hair and cut his victuals for him, and you can form

no idea what a care he is without you were near him all the while. yet through all his illness, and my own, I have been enabled to do all for him, and minister to all his wants. I am much surprised to hear that you had written to me twice previous to your last letter, it was the first I had had, since the 22nd of December. I have frequently sent you papers which you do not acknowledge the reciept of, and I would send you more, but my dear son, I have not the means to pay the postage, all our means of earthly support is cut off, by your Fathers affliction, and I do not believe he will ever be able to do any business in all his life again, we have a very comfortable home with Sarah and Mr Bradley, that is food, shelter and washing, and as yet we are comfortable for cloathing, but they will not last for ever, but I will not anticipate want of cloathing,... but I rely on that omnipotent hand (that clothes the lilies of the field) to clothe us....

ST LOUIS JULY 1ST 1862

My dear Son

It is with pleasure I acknowledge the reciept of your letter dated June 23d, it came to hand last night, and I hasten to answer it,...

Your Father and Mr B. [Bradley] have taken the [loyalty] oath but your *brother*, will not under any circumstances, I wish I could see you I have so much to tell you that I *cannot*, write. Nat's here pursuing the same business he has always *done*, Margaret is packing up to go to Boston she is to start the day after tomorrow he is not going with her, they are *both* *devoted* soul-and body to the *UNION* cause; Bethiah & Charles are in New York, they are *vica versa*, they have been living there for nearly three years, Charles is following the same vocation he did here; Harriet and William [Matlack] are living at Sparta Illinois; William is working in the harvest field, he says any employment to make a living. they have a fine garden and raise all the vegetables they use besides all their meat and lard. Mr B[Bradley] is in the paymasters office and Sarah says tell brother John *after a while when she gets better*, she will write. William [McKown] is in a wholesale dry goods store, his health is very poor, all the rest are well; as to your Father I think he is as well as he will ever be, his health is only tolerable, his limb's a good deal better; but his hand is in a manner useless, he can neither dress, undress or wash himself or comb his head, he is as much care as an infant and in his manner of his expression he is a wreck of what he was, it would make you sorry to see him. We are very glad to hear that you are all well, and so well and comfortably supplied God grant you a continuance of the same....

William sends his love to you *All*, and says he will write to you I have nothing new to tell you times are pretty dull. I dread to think of the coming winter, the Negro's are coming in by the hundred; and the famine in Ireland will bring the poor Irish in by scores, but this awful wicked war is killing off so many that it will make room for the number

334 □ *Old Age*

of emigrants that are daily landing on our shores. I am in perfect health you never saw me as fat in your life. . . .

Tell Virginia I had a letter from cousin Harriet Rowles and Aunt Priscy is alive and well yet. you did not say one word about James when you write tell me all about him. Oh how I do want to see you all, but I fear I never shall meet you on earth again, and if i[t] should please our heavenly Father that it should be so, try and so live my dear children that we may all meet at God's right hand where we shall meet to part no more and where there are pleasures forever more. I must now bid you adieu. your Father and sisters and brothers all join me in love to you Virginia and all your children particularly *my little Charley* tell me when you write how many children you have, what are their names from little Kate down, and how old the youngest is. And now my dear Son, may the choicest of our heavenly Father's blessings rest on you and yours, and in that day when he comes to make up his jewels may you *all* be — found among the brightest in his starry crown. So will ever pray your affectionate Parents James B & Bethiah P McKown

ST LOUIS APRIL 27TH 1863

My dear Son

It is with pleasure I acknowledge the reciept of yours of the 15th inst, . . . I have not left the city since the death of your dear-Father, nor will I do so, without notifying you of my intention. William Matlack has been here he has been up for four days, he left for *home,* yesterday morning, . . . he wanted me to go home with him and spend the summer, but I thought I would no[t] go before the first of June I, do not want to go, unless, Mr [Joshua T.] Bradley, either concludes to stay in this house or has, moved, and got fix'd in another, my furniture is all I have *left,* out of your dear Father's property, and I want to know *that is safe,* before I go any where, I would sell all I have but enough to furnish . . . one room, but in doing *that,* I would have to *strip Sarah,* and *that,* I cannot bear to do, she is a kind, affectionate child, and is a great comfort to me, and I cannot bear to afflict her, she has a hard enough time of it at any rate her husband will never say what he intends to do only that he will not stay here, and when Sarah goes and finds a house, he wont go and look at it, and so we have to live in uncertainty all the time, I would like to tell you all my grievances but I will forbear hoping I may yet see you again. . . .

ST LOUIS OCT 31ST 1863

. . . On last monday morning when Nat [Clark] came home to dinner, he said he had been all the morning with William, I ask'd him who he meant, he said William McKown, Oh said I you are joking, he said *no, he was not,* he had been to the Provost Marshall's with him he took the Oath, and gave bond in a 1000 dollars. *Nat went on his bond he,* sent him *off*, and he was as glad as any of us to see him home again he [Clark] is a strange being, Samantha was sick and out of money, and he sent her $5 altho he would not let her come into his house, if he was my own child, he could not be kinder to me than he is, such is the Man, I have . . . an elegant and plentiful home, and do not want for anything, Bethiah sends me $5 a month regularly. . . .

God bless you your loving Mother B P McKown

[P.S.] I am glad you are all safe

ST LOUIS FEB 29TH 1864

My dear Son

Your affectionate, and ever welcome letter of the 16th inst, came safe to hand, and *as usual*, was read by all of us with great *interest* and *pleasure*. . . .

I have not entirely recovered from my recent illness, the dregs of it (I believe) are still in my system, I suffer very much (at times) with spasms in my stomach! which when it leaves me, my stomach is so sore I cannot bear my hand on it, for the last two weeks I have been a good deal troubled with the Rhumatism, but dear child, the weight of years are upon me, and ailments must be expected by me, so I will not complain, you know I am naturally a cheerful disposition, and try to make my complaints as few as possible especially while I am surrounded by so many blessings, my heavenly Father has given me the best, and most affectionate of children, truly "The lines have fallen to me in pleasant places yea, I have a goodly heritage," I do not *often*, need anything, *little things*, such as *Stamps*, Envelopes or Paper I get out of, but some kind hand always supplies them, your sister Bethiah supplies me frequently with money, so that I am as well clothed as any lady of my age in St. Louis, but there is one thing I shall need before long, and which (with my slender means) I shall not be able to supply, and *that is Sheets* for my bed, every other article of bedding I am sufficiently supplied, with your dear Father always attended to every thing of that kind and always kept up a supply, but he was sick so long, and my Sheets were so much used that what I have are very *thin*. There is one request I have to make of *all* my children, and that is that you will try and save as much of your means as will put a Head and Foot stone to your dear Father's grave if *I*, had the means I would do it very soon, but *as it is, if it is ever done his children*, will have to do it. . . .

ST LOUIS APRIL 23D, 1864

My dear Son

Your long look'd-for and most welcome and affectionate letter of the 9th inst, came safe to hand, I need not tell you how much pleasure it gave me for your own heart will tell you how much your letters are appreciated, altho they are like Angels visits *few, and far between*. I have nothing new or interesting to tell only of the good health of all your brothers and sisters as far as heard from. . . .

I am sorry to tell you that my health at this time is far from good, I am greatly distress'd at times with Neuralgia of the Stomach, which when it comes on me completely prostrates me I have been confined to my bed (five days out of the last eight) *today*, I am entirely free from pain, tomorrow, I may be so distress'd with pain, that I may not be able to raise my head so insidious, and sudden are the paroxisms of this dreadful disease, but I thank my Heavenly Father, that when I am free from pain, that my spirits are as bouyant and cheerful as if youth and continual health were mine, he has bless'd me with a contented *mind* which, when contrasted with what I have come through in the last few years of my life, is an amazement to myself. You speak of my sister Ann's silence to you and Virginia now I will tell you why I think she does not write oftener, in the first place, she is not gifted in letter-writing and it is on that score great labour for her to write I do not think she is wanting in affection but she has a poor way of shewing it to those who are far away from her, and in the second place, her health is very poor, I spent the day with Mary Cary and Julia Arbuthnat a week or two ago, and they told me that they were much astonished to see how much more active I was than their Mother, she is 61 this day and Julia says she looks at least ten years older than me, I shall be 66 the 13th of next month, making almost five years difference in our ages, she has lost her spirits and is low-spirited and gloomy all the time; your uncle James has urged her to meet your uncle Isaac [Donaldson], your Aunt Elizabeth and me in Dayton, [Ohio], but she says she dont want to go. I shall write to your aunt Elizabeth today to know if she cannot be prevailed on to join us in this family gathering, Elizabeth will go, and Isaac and I will leave St Louis together on the 3 of June if nothing happens to prevent your uncle James has been to see your aunt Caroline, and it is all arranged for this family gathering, which in all probability will be our last meeting, until we meet at the Judgement bar of God, and I earnestly pray that we may *All* meet *There, an unbroken family* and hear the welcome plaudit of welldone good and faithful servants enter ye into the joy of your Lord. You will wonder how I am to bear the expense of my journey to Ohio; I will tell you, your sister — Bethiah has sent me the money to go with, but as it will take every cent of what she sent, I want *you to send me $2*, I do not want to go away without any money in my pocket. I hope you will not think hard of me for making this request of *you*, I have no one else to ask, if you cannot send me [$]2, try and send me [$]1 so that I shall not be penniless in a strange place. . . . Your loving Mother B P M

ST LOUIS DEC 26TH 1864

My dear Son

Yours of the 19th inst (together with your daughters) affectionate letters came safe to hand, and were *indeed*, welcome Christmas gifts, I was glad to hear that you were *all*, safe and well! Oh how many happy remembrances did yesterday bring to mind when *I*, like *you*, could gather all my dear-ones round me, your dear Father the gayest of the gayest amongst us, now we are all separated, and *he, the most beloved of all*, "Now to the dust gone down." Christmas in a domestic point of view is any thing but a happy day with me, but when I think it is the natal day of the Saviour of mankind, I feel that (*I*, with all the human *race*) have reason to rejoice, for did it not bring life and immortality to pass, and makes us know that if we have faith in Christ if we meet no more in this world we *can meet*, where parting shall be no more forever. I am astonished to know that you have to use Spectacles so soon I think your dear Father did not use them before he was 50, but *I*, have been wearing them ever since I was 35. I have your Father's Spectacles, but as *yet*, I cannot see through them, but if I live to be as old as he was they will be of use to me. I am in good health and retain all my faculties as well as usual, but *memory*, and that is only that I forget names. (Mr [Stephen] Edgell who you may remember) told me the other evening, that he believed I was as young as ever, said *he*, you are none of your dry up and blow up woman, his remarks made me laugh, but of this I have cause to be very thankful that now when I am nearly 67 I am yet able to communicate by letter: with all my loved children and friends, and I thank God for this blessing. . . .

ST LOUIS JAN 16TH 1865

My dear Son

Your affectionate letter of the 4th inst came safe to hand and as usual gave me great pleasure. . . .

My dear Son I now have to say something to you about myself For the *last three years*, your Sister Bethiah has remitted to me $5 monthly and regularly, for the last two months she has *omitted it* for what cause I know not unless she is no longer able to do it; that sum has supplied me comfortably, I had a good supply of clothing when your dear Father died *that*, and what Bethiah gave me supplied all my wants, but as cloaths will not last *forever*, so it is with *mine* I am getting *ragged*, Nat thinks he does enough when he gives me a home, and so he does, and I am very grateful to him for so doing I never have ask'd one cent from any of my children but now I have to do it, and to you my eldest son I ask this boon will you when you write again enclose me what you can spare, I do not *wish to ask for much nor will I ever ask again, but I will leave* it to your own *generosity* to *help to supply my necessities* William will be able in a short time to do somthing for me too, he got sadly in debt while he was with Nat but I think in a month or two he be able to do somthing for me. I want you to answer this speedily and not think hard of this the first request of your *Widowed Mother....* accept the best love from all to all. your loving Mothe[r] B P McKown

W hile it is tempting to attribute the travails of Bethiah Pyatt McKown solely to the destabilizing effects of the Civil War, the larger truth that emerges from a study of her case is that widowhood, poverty, and dependence on grown children constituted a common pattern for old women in nineteenth-century America. The almost total reliance of elderly married women on their husbands for financial support placed them in a position in which they suffered greatly when their husbands failed to provide for them. Too old to support themselves, and frequently ignorant of family finances, women caught in the web of widowhood and poverty were virtually powerless to ameliorate their condition. The result was forced dependence on children or other relatives and, as a last resort, the stigma of involuntary enrollment in an institution for the indigent.

For women in more stable economic circumstances, however, old age could be a time for personal growth and fulfillment. The following selection from the oral history of Maria Dean Foster Brown of Fort Madison, Iowa, covering the period from 1888 to 1895, when she was in her sixties, offers a vivid contrast to the portrait of Bethiah McKown at a parallel stage in her life a quarter century earlier. Although her husband's financial ineptness resulted in straitened circumstances for the couple after the depression of 1893, Mrs. Brown was never faced with the specter of poverty or want. Her experience illustrates a major alternative pattern for female old age: unbroken marriage, financial security, and independence.

Maria Brown was born in 1827 and died in 1929 at the age of 101. Clearly exceptional in the length of her life span, Grandmother Brown, as she was known, is representative of women of her generation in other ways. Married at the age of eighteen in 1845, she bore eight children, two of whom died in infancy. Her childbearing period stretched from the age of nineteen to almost age forty-three and her child-rearing responsibilities continued throughout her middle years. Taking care of her husband, her children, and the household, first in Ohio and later in Iowa, thus filled the life stages of young adulthood and middle age. During this period, her individual development was attuned to her family's expectations of her appropriate behavior. The departure of her youngest child from the family home in 1888, when she was sixty-one, signaled the commencement of a new life stage for Maria Brown, a time when her own needs became more central to her existence.

As she reviewed her life history for her daughter-in-law in the 1920s, Mrs. Brown disclosed the ways her life had changed during the first seven years of her self-perceived old age. First, the role of wife assumed greater salience for Mrs. Brown once the household was reduced to just the aging Brown couple. Daniel Brown's curtailment of his working hours enabled the couple to spend more time together, attending church, entertaining, and traveling. The companionship of her longtime partner enhanced Mrs. Brown's pleasure in these activities and seems to have sparked a renewal of intimacy between the Browns. Despite its imperfections, their marital relationship remained vital into the couple's later years and continued to be a source of satisfaction for Mrs. Brown.

The maturation of her children did not mark the completion of Maria Brown's obligation as a mother. Nevertheless, the nature of motherhood alters without the presence of children at home requiring supervision. Direct and immediate intervention in the lives of one's offspring is no longer possible, and a mother must adjust to this situation as best she can. As a consequence, Mrs. Brown was forced to develop a new understanding of her maternal role. Her grown sons and daughter continued to occupy a special place in her life, and she was always ready to advise and support them. Yet Maria Brown realized that the primary emotional bonds between mother and children are normally supplanted by new ties forged between adult children and their siblings, their spouses, and their own children. As partial compensation for her losses, Mrs. Brown acquired new responsibilities as a grandmother, and her grandchildren soon commanded her attention and affection. The passage of time had reshaped family needs, and one of the tasks of Maria Brown's old age was to adapt to her altered position as mother and grandmother.

As Mrs. Brown's family duties contracted, she found it possible to devote more time to activities that brought her personal satisfaction, such as reading and participation in the Ladies Aid Society. Since the early part of the nineteenth century, volunteer work in the community had been regarded as a legitimate outlet for women of comfortable means whose family and household responsibilities no longer filled the bulk of their time. Despite its limited impact on society, such volunteer work provided older women with opportunities for individual development through the exercise of power and the sharing of common female concerns in a congenial atmosphere. Most importantly, involvement in community service enabled mature women to define a sense of identity apart from their families. For Maria Brown, the Ladies Aid Society represented a forum in which she could discover her unique abilities as a person. This was perhaps the most important challenge of her old age.

A modicum of financial security and the absence of serious health problems underlaid the relatively tranquil and enjoyable early years of Maria Brown's old age. Declining physical powers were not yet evident, and even after Daniel Brown's financial reverses the Browns were not forced to depend on their children for subsistence. Under these favorable conditions, Maria Brown was free to establish new priorities as a wife, a mother, and an individual, thereby ensuring that the initial phase of her old age would be a time of renewed growth.

25

Maria Dean Foster Brown

Well, Jennie went, after a while, to Kansas City, where she met her Charl and began living happily ever after. And when he had mastered his stenography, Frank went to Kansas City also, found employment in a bank, and prospered.

Lizzie and Gus were both married now and in homes of their own. Will and Charlie had been married a long time. Only Herbert was left me. And he began to talk of going to Kansas City, too. Frank, who had always looked out for Herbie and shared everything with him, wrote to encourage him and urge him to prepare himself to take a place in a business office. And so Herbert began to pore over Isaac Pitman's pothooks, too.

One morning — it was the fifth day of May, 1888 — he went away. He was just a little past eighteen years old — my last baby. I stood at the door to watch him go down the street. I cannot *tell* you how I felt. It was a lovely spring morning, but I felt as if the end of the world had come. No children in my home any more! The last one going from me. Oh, oh, oh! And yet I would not have held him back!

□

When Herbert, my youngest child, left home, I realized that old age was really upon us. . . .

I used to think often of that poem of Longfellow's — how true it is — called "The Hanging of the Crane," which tells of the young people starting to housekeeping, the babies coming one by one, their growing up, their leaving one by one, and then, at the last, the man and woman left together in the house, just two, as they had started.

Here after all our tug and strain, Dan'l and I were left alone in the old house. Of course, Frank and Herbie kept coming back from Kansas City, — for Christmas and their summer vacations, — but it wasn't the same as when they really lived with us.

Dan'l and I enjoyed going peacefully together to the Presbyterian church those years. I went faithfully to the Ladies' Aid Society, too. . . . One year I was president of it, the only time I ever held a public office. . . .

I was in good health in those years and my housekeeping was simpler than it had been for a long time. I found time to read a book occasionally. About that time I read the *Prince of the House of David, Pillar of Fire, Ben-Hur, A Man without a Country* — all fine books. And I commenced to take the *Christian Herald* then and to read Talmadge's Sermons every week. . . .

SOURCE: Harriet Connor Brown, *Grandmother Brown's Hundred Years 1827–1927* (Boston: Little, Brown, 1929). Copyright, 1929, by Harriet Connor Brown. Reprinted by permission.

Maria Dean Foster Brown

Dan'l and I had some nice trips together during those years when we were first alone.... One time he said to me: "How would you like to go up to St. Paul this week? The boat gets here Thursday night." He never had to ask me twice. I was always ready to go whenever *he* was. So that night I heard the boat whistle at Nauvoo and roused Dan'l. We went about midnight. Just across from us at the breakfast table next morning sat a company of young folks from St. Louis. Going up the river for pleasure. "My wife's a fine dancer," Dan'l told them. Then they got hold of me and teased and teased me to dance with them. But I wasn't going to show off. All the way up we had the loveliest time. Good company. Fine fare. The Captain invited us to dine with him! And then, on reaching our destination, more pleasure. In Minnesota, we liked to visit the falls of Minnehaha....

In '93, like everybody else, we went to the World's Fair at Chicago.

It was wonderful how they thought of all the things they assembled there. I wanted to see everything I could set my eyes on....

Two years after the Columbian Exposition, Dan'l and I went to the exposition at Atlanta. That was a very special occasion for us. We went to celebrate our fiftieth wedding anniversary....

It came on the twenty-third day of October, 1895, and we were having lovely weather. The day before, Dan'l and I hitched the pony to the phaeton and went out to the woods for autumn leaves. We trimmed the house with them — yellow and green and red and brown....

As it was, the house looked beautiful. We provided a good supper. The only special thing I remember was pressed chicken, prepared in a way that I made up myself. We issued no invitations. We just put a notice in the paper that we wished to entertain our friends and that all would be welcome. That brought everybody, and nobody's feelings were hurt through being overlooked. Of course our children were all there and that was the important thing for us; all of them with partners, except Frank and Herbert, who were still unmarried.

Among the guests was our old neighbor, Charlie Doerr. He was, you know, a justice of the peace. He made Dan'l and me stand up in front of him, and he married us over again. And, by the way, I had a new wedding ring. I had worn the old one out. It broke in two. For a while I went without one, and then Dan'l said it didn't seem natural to see my hand moving among the cups and saucers without a ring upon it, and so, one day, he brought me home a new one....

The boys wanted to make us the nicest present they could think of. The Fair was on in Atlanta, Georgia. They thought we would enjoy it. They gave us a pass and money for all expenses.

I had to hurry up and get some clothes. I had a gray dress and cape that were very becoming. When we reached Atlanta, we went around together at first. One morning I suggested to Dan'l that we go separate ways, meeting at noon for dinner together.

I struck the Alabama exhibit. Everything there was so beautiful — the clothing they manufactured, the cloth they made it out of, the fruits displayed. At noon, I said to Dan'l: "I want you to visit the Alabama exhibit with me. There is a lady there, a Mrs. Russell, who was very kind, and who showed and explained everything to me." She made him welcome, too, and showed him everything. Then she invited us to go to a fine hotel with her and to visit a wonderful fruit farm the next day. Going along, I said to her, "This is our wedding trip!" "That's worth knowing," she answered. At the hotel a party of young people were dancing. Mrs. Russell and her husband took us about and introduced us to everybody, and they made a great deal of us.

A guest chamber with bath was assigned to us. We enjoyed it all, the beautiful bed, the lovely bath. But I worried. "She told everybody that we were on our wedding journey. I wonder if she thought we were just married," I said to Dan'l. But Dan'l said: "Let it go so. We *are* bride and groom." ...

Altogether, that Atlanta trip was just wonderful — the most satisfactory present our children could have given us. We had that treat as a bridal pair. We went through it beautifully, like newly-weds. I had a nice-looking dress and a gold chain. Dan'l walked with a gold-headed cane. He put on as much style as a French dancing master....

And so we had a few care-free times together again, Dan'l and I, almost like our courting days, in the few years that followed the going away of our last child. But we had our children on our minds all the time. Whenever they were unhappy, it was impossible for us to be happy.

□

Gus was running the paper mill in those late eighties and early nineties. He had married Sue Hesser and was keeping house not far from us....

As the years went by, Gus had considerable to worry over — as had Dan'l and I — in connection with the paper mill. At one time, after about ten years in the paper business, I thought we had come to the end of all our financial worries, and that an easy old age was assured us. Dan'l had got control of the paper mill and was making money. But about 1893 he sold out to the Columbia Paper Trust. He was offered cash or stock. I pleaded with him to take the cash, but he took the stock. It never paid a dividend.

Oh, how I wanted him to take the cash — how I wanted it! That meant security. That was something real. I just could n't stand it to have him pass that by and risk nearly all we had in an unknown thing. I said to him: "I've worked hard all my life and have n't seen much return for it. I'd like to have a good bank account once, have some cash for all my years of labor."

But he said, "Why, what could we do with it, Mother?"

"Do with it! Why, you like to travel. We could go to Europe. Think of it! We could build over this old house. We could spend a little."

But Dan'l had never cared to spend. That did n't appeal to him a bit. He would n't listen to me. Nor to Herbert, who came home twice from Kansas City to try to influence his father to let the Columbia Paper Company's stock alone. But Dan'l took the stock, saying to me, "When they pay us out, we'll go to Europe." Oh, I loved every bone in his old body, but, just the same, I have to say that Dan'l Brown was not a good financier. His penny-wise, pound-foolish ways and his strict integrity did not make him one. Just think! He practically gave away the whole thing, after we had all saved and scrimped for years to accumulate the money that bought control of the mill!

After the crash came, Dan'l was out of the paper business forever. He put practically all he had left into the purchase of a shoe store. He took in Lizzie's husband to assist him in that, and there he stayed during his remaining days. It gave him the kind of background he had always seemed to like — a village store where neighbors came and went. But it was slim picking for two families.

A profound change in public attitudes toward the aged occurred in late nineteenth-century America, resulting in a pervasive set of beliefs attesting to the inferior abilities of the elderly. Foreshadowed earlier in the nineteenth century, this negative conception of old age was firmly in place by the turn of the century. Old people of this era, unlike their predecessors, were faced with massive prejudice. Characterized as being prone to physical and mental deterioration, the aged were assumed to be weak, impotent, and obsolete. The portrayal of old people in such stereotypical ways undercut their value to society. Consequent discrimination against the elderly took diverse forms, ranging from forced retirement to overprotection and coddling. Nevertheless, one thread united such actions — a lack of faith in the capacity of old people to function in modern society.

Documenting this major attitudinal shift is far simpler than assessing its impact on an individual's experience of old age. Although marred by a contrived literary format and intermittent moralizing, the *Autobiography of an Elderly Woman*, published in 1911, sensitively conveys the feelings of an old woman at a time when the aged were considered superfluous. The protagonist is a fictional composite, an elderly New England widow who lived in a small town surrounded by her grown children and her grandchildren. She reacted vigorously against her constricting social environment. Untroubled by financial concerns, she still perceived the onset of old age negatively. Her reflections articulate the sentiments of the many women in similar circumstances.

Excluded from meaningful and productive roles in her community, sheltered and protected by her own children until she was virtually immobilized, the Elderly Woman was understandably angered at the prevalent conception of old people as essentially useless. The kindly, yet demeaning, treatment she received from her offspring proved so frustrating that she concluded that a kind of role reversal had occurred in her family. In her old age she had been reduced to a childlike state of dependence.

The particular episode she describes and analyzes here with such acuity illustrates the manner in which elderly women were barred from performing ordinary tasks. Disguised as solicitude, such prescriptions for deliberate inactivity betokened a decline in status. Once labeled old, a woman was no longer respected as an autonomous person with the capacity to order her own life. Regarded as an incomplete person, she lost confidence in her sense of self. The stripping away of responsibilities, as well as rights and privileges, that accompanied the advent of old age, caused her to feel devoid of worth.

Elderly women in every generation have faced hardships, as the case of Bethiah Pyatt McKown has shown. But the ego-damaging experience recounted here is not so much an instance of material deprivation as one of psychological deprivation. This elderly woman's loss of credibility in the eyes of the world threatened her fundamental identity. To her, a seemingly trivial incident symbolized a whole series of onslaughts on her self-esteem.

26

An Elderly Woman

I can remember the very day when I *realized* that age had claimed me at last. There is a great difference between being a thing and realizing it. A woman may say a hundred times that she is ugly; she may be ugly; but unless she realizes that she is ugly, it will make very little difference. It is the consciousness of our defects which undoes us, — and so with age.

This great readjustment began with the most trivial of events. I happened to see a little dust on the table and around on the bric-a-brac — it seems to me that dusting is a lost art — and I was just wiping it off. I was enjoying myself, for I belong to a generation which was taught to work with its hands and to delight in doing its work nicely, when I heard Margaret's step on the stairs; she is my youngest daughter, home on a visit. My first impulse was to sit down and pretend to be reading, but I resolved to brazen it out, — after all, there is no reason why I should n't dust my own bric-a-brac in my own home if I choose.

She came into the parlor.

"*What* are you doing, darling?" she said.

"I am dusting the vases on the mantel," I answered, and I tried to keep any note of guilt from my voice.

"Why could n't you have called Annie?" she asked me, with tender reproach.

"I like to stir around myself sometimes," I said, and for the life of me I could n't help being a little defiant.

"Well, then, why could n't you let me do it? You might have called me," she went on in the same tone.

"I told you I like to do it."

"It is n't good for you to stand on your feet so much. Give me that duster, mother. You'll tire yourself all out."

"I get tired *sitting*," I broke out.

"I always have said that you ought to take more exercise in the open air." By this time she had taken away my duster. "Why don't you go out and take a little walk? Come — I'll go with you."

Presently she had finished dusting, but I saw ever so many little places that I should have to wipe up later on, furtively. I should have enjoyed finishing that dusting myself.

"I'll run up and get your things," said Margaret.

Now, I cannot abide having any one trifle with my bureau drawers, and it is n't because I'm old enough to have middle-aged sons and daughters, either. Ever since I can remember, I have put my things away myself. I keep my bonnets in the little drawers and my gloves and veils

SOURCE: [Mary Heaton Vorse], *Autobiography of an Elderly Woman* (Boston and New York: Houghton Mifflin, 1911). Copyright, 1911, by Houghton Mifflin Company. Reprinted by permission.

— my everyday ones, that is — beside them; and I know that I shall never be able to find anything again once Margaret has been among them. Besides that, I do not like going to walk. Walking aimlessly for exercise has always seemed most futile to me; a feeble stroll that has no objective point, not even the post office, annoys me more than any other way of spending my time. I have never walked except when I had something to walk for, and I don't intend to begin at my time of life.

"I don't think I'll go to walk, dear. I'm going out this afternoon —"

Now, though I said this indifferently enough, in a tone which did n't invite discussion, yet I braced myself inwardly; I knew what was coming.

"Oh, mother darling," my daughter cried. "You're not going to that lecture, with your cold, in that drafty hall! And you always catch more cold in a crowd! You won't go, will you?"

"Well, well —" I temporized.

"You won't go — promise."

Then the door-bell rang, and I made my escape to my own room and locked my door after me. I knew well enough what would happen, — how Margaret would tell the others at dinner that I was going out, and how they would protest. And I made up my mind, as I often have before, that since I am old enough to know what is best for me, I would go to that lecture, let them talk as they might; so I got ready for the battle, resolving for the hundredth time that I would not be run by my children.

As I sat in my room plotting — yes, plotting — how I should outwit my daughter, it came over me what a funny thing it was that I should be contriving to get my own way, for all the world like a naughty, elderly child, while my daughter was worrying about my headstrong ways as if she were my mother instead of my being hers.

How increasingly often I hear as the years go on, not only from my own children, but from other people whose mothers are already old: "Mother will not take care of herself!" And then follow fearsome stories of mother's latest escapade, — just as one tells how naughty Johnnie is getting and how Susie kicks her bedclothes off, — stories of how mother made a raid on the attic and cleaned it almost single-handed when all the family were away; stories of clandestine descents into the perilous depths of the cellar; hair-raising tales of how mother was found on a step-ladder hanging a window curtain; how mother insisted on putting down the preserves and pickles, — rows and rows and rows of shining glasses of them, — herself, and how tired she was afterwards, as if putting down the preserves tired only women who were past middle age. And a certain indignation rose within me as I remembered that I can visit my own attic and my own cellar only by stealth or with a devoted and tyrannical child of mine standing over me to see that I don't "overdo." For the motto of all devoted sons and daughters is: "Nag mother to death, if necessary, but don't let her overdo."

Well, what if I should overdo? Before one is old, one is allowed to shorten one's life unchecked; one may have orgies of work undisturbed. And I, for one, would far rather shorten my life by overdoing than have it lengthened out by a series of mournful, inactive years...

...I thought how a similar warfare is being carried on all over this country to-day, wherever there are elderly mothers and middle-aged sons and daughters, — the children trying to dominate their parents with the end in view of making them take abnormal care of their health, and the older people fighting ever more feebly and petulantly for their lost independence. Not only struggling to have their own way, not only chafing at the leading-strings in which their watchful, devoted children would keep them, but fighting, too, for the little glimmer of youth that is yet left them.

For all this care by one's children means but one thing, and that is — age. While you slept, old age came upon you. You count the number of your years by the way your daughter watches your steps, and you see your infirmities in your son's anxious eyes; and the reason of all this struggle — why our own attics and cellars are forbidden ground to us; why our daughters take our dusters from us and tenderly nag us — is that they are valiantly, if tactlessly, striving to delay by their care the hour which they know must come, while we try to ignore its approach.

We like to kill the days, which sometimes crawl past us so slowly, with an illusion of activity, and we do not like to be reminded day by day, hour by hour, that we are old, that there is no work we need do, no "ought" calling us any more; that our work in the world is being done by other people and our long vacation has already begun.

As I sat alone that evening and soberly went over the events of the day, I clearly realized the meaning of Margaret's taking away my duster. I realized that there was no work in the world that I ought to do but take care of myself. I realized that I was old, and from that day, though I often forget it, the world has looked a little different to me; my point of view has, in some subtle way, shifted.

One of the consequences of the delineation of old age as a distinct life stage is that the boundary between middle age and old age became more precisely demarcated. By the early twentieth century, compulsory retirement had emerged as the benchmark of old age for men. Accustomed to thinking of themselves as workers, American men, upon reaching the mandatory retirement age, were suddenly and decisively separated from their jobs. The loss of their primary source of identification and meaning created a profound discontinuity in men's lives. Filling the void left by retirement from work was in many cases an insurmountable task.

During the twentieth century, and particularly since World War II, market work has also become central to the life experience of American women. More and more women spend time in the labor force and they work for longer periods of their lives. The smaller size of families and the concentration of births in the early years of marriage, coupled with the increase in female life expectancy, have enabled women in twentieth-century America to have far more continuous work histories than ever before. Female and male work cycles have begun to converge in recent years as work has taken on greater importance in patterning women's lives. Increasingly, retirement from a job marks the beginning of old age for women as well as for men.

A woman in her sixties who had combined career and family was not an anomaly by the end of World War II, when Lucy Sprague Mitchell confronted the issue of retirement. A distinguished educator, as well as a wife and the mother of four children, Lucy Mitchell was a forerunner of the many older women — married, divorced, widowed, and single — who have pursued jobs or careers since that time. Much could be written about her accomplishments as a teacher, writer, and administrator, but what is of interest in this context is Mrs. Mitchell's detailed record of her thoughts upon realizing that she had reached old age. In the following selection from *Two Lives*, the intriguing double autobiography of herself and her husband, Wesley Clair Mitchell, she reproduces a personal memo written in 1945, when she was sixty-seven, in which she took stock of her life and career and faced the prospect of a decline in her productive capacities. Although Lucy Mitchell, as a professional woman, represents the most privileged segment of the female labor force, her identification of the termination of work as the critical issue of the transition to old age is pertinent to all older women workers, whether engaged in routine jobs or specialized careers.

At the time she composed this memo, Mrs. Mitchell was still actively involved in a fulltime career in education. Her husband, whom she called Robin, was deeply immersed in his own work as an economist. The Mitchells' four grown children had left home and were on their own, and there were already a number of grandchildren in the family. Lucy Mitchell and her husband lived in an apartment in New York City and spent weekends and holidays in their country home in Stamford, Connecticut. In this remarkable document, Mrs. Mitchell presents a lucid and systematic analysis of the options open to her in old age and outlines a life plan for her last years. In the process, she discloses her beliefs about the appropriate responses to the course of aging.

Lucy Mitchell recognized that advanced age imposed certain limitations requiring people to adapt to their altered condition. Those who chose to ignore the imprint of years were failing to meet the challenge of old age. She rejected what she conceived of as deceitful solutions — disguising one's appearance or persisting in a job in spite of one's inability to perform it adequately. Acknowledging that she had arrived at a point in life at which some change was inevitable, she insisted on defining the changes that would take place.

Using the analogy of adolescence, Mrs. Mitchell set forth an interpretation of old age as the culminating life stage with a potential for growth all its own, a growth premised on a diminished capacity for action but a continuing sense of identity and a powerful drive toward completion. Evaluating her own life in terms of this model, she methodically plotted a course for her remaining years that would enable her to finish her most important projects before her death. Although this plan necessitated painful decisions to renounce accustomed responsibilities, Lucy Mitchell was determined to marshal her limited resources most effectively so as to achieve her primary career goals. Lucy Sprague Mitchell's confidence in her ability to control the future direction of her life typified her rational attitude toward life and death.

—— 27 ——
Lucy Sprague Mitchell

During the war years I had kept on the strenuous job of the Bank Street Workshop in a public school — which seemed to me a kind of climax of my long years of work. Nevertheless, for some time before I felt that it was necessary, I had begun a gradual withdrawal from some of the responsibilities I carried at Bank Street. Executive work I was more than ready to give up: I had never enjoyed trying to keep some of the wheels at Bank Street oiled. Though it was a price I was willing to pay, it sidetracked me from work of my own. But teaching had always meant more to me than it did to Robin. I loved teaching in and for itself. It was as important a part of my life as research was to Robin, for my writing had sprung largely from ideas kindled as a teacher. Yet I realized that I no longer carried a life filled with scheduled activities with my old buoyancy or efficiency, and the time when I should *feel* old was much in my mind. It was time, I felt, to "tidy up." So the summer that I reached sixty-seven, I once more followed my incurable habit of talking to myself on paper when any problem troubled me. I wrote out a sort of argument to and for myself and a planned program of future work. I called it:

MY SECOND ADOLESCENCE: SUMMER, 1945

Now I have entered a new stage in life. It is time for me to begin to tidy up. No one knows better than I that the kind of life I have lived is no longer appropriate or possible. I have been going through my old files of manuscripts, cleaning out the messes that always accumulate in a hurried life, and sorting into a pile the incomplete pieces of work

SOURCE: Lucy Sprague Mitchell, *Two Lives: The Story of Wesley Clair Mitchell and Myself* (New York: Simon & Schuster, 1953). Copyright 1953 by Lucy Sprague Mitchell. Reprinted by permission of McIntosh and Otis, Inc.

which represent invested time, thought and energy. That kind of tidying up is a necessary chore for one who likes to finish up a job neatly. But it is only the first step in the tidying up process. As far as it is possible, I should like to tidy up my professional life and hand over to others in good condition the jobs I care most about. It is time for me to decide what I shall do during the relatively few years left for constructive work. What do I really care most about? What are the "musts" that it is up to me to finish neatly? That is the positive and easiest side to the problem that I face in my present stage of life.

There is a negative side which is not as easy to face. Before I can decide what I shall do, I have to decide what I am now able to do. At this stage of life a new role means giving up, not merely taking on. Intellectually, it may be easy to decide what to give up. But it is not easy emotionally. No period of radical adjustment is easy. I feel it imperative to think through what adjustments are necessary, what I can no longer do, before I can work out and accept a new role. This need has turned me introspective. Thinking about growing old has made me feel queerly adolescent. I think I know why.

All the world knows what a hard job it is to grow up. The stage of growing up called adolescence had been learnedly and sympathetically treated in hundreds of volumes, and ignorantly treated in millions of homes. Adolescence is based on physiological changes, primarily glandular, which trail with them emotional changes toward oneself and one's place in the family and in the big world outside the family. Though the acute climax of adolescence usually strikes a girl suddenly, childhood has been a sort of preparation. Every girl arrives at adolescence after years of being called upon to make adjustments to unknown and untried things and people, of being called upon to learn a new way of living in which she gives up one familiar, comfortable support after another and looks to herself for decisions. Throughout adolescence — and that may be for years — her absorbing questions are, "What shall I do? What am I able to do?" These questions involve a new sensitivity in her relations to people, a combined trust and distrust in herself. They involve a searching for her real interests and an evaluation of herself in relation to possible jobs. Her problem is complicated by the fact that she is dealing with two largely unknown quantities — herself and the world to which she has to adjust in a new role. It is hard to make this adjustment to a new stage of life. We know that children have a hard and an emotional time growing up.

At the other end of life lies another hard job of making an adjustment to growing old. Millions of people live through this growing-old stage and yet the world has spent little effort in trying to understand it or to help them to make their adjustments. Different as it is, this stage has enough elements in common with adolescence to be called a second adolescence. Like young adolescence, this second one is based on physiological changes, including the glandular, which trail with them emotional changes. Both are periods of deep introspection. A woman approaching seventy (or younger or older) is called upon to give up the familiar and loved activities which have been her support through middle life. Again her absorbing questions become, "What shall I do? What am I able to do?" And once again, these questions involve a new sensitivity in her relations to people and to possible jobs. But now she is dealing with two largely known quantities — herself and the world to which she must adjust in a new role. Intellectually, she knows she must make this adjustment to a new way of living. But now that I have reached the stage of second adolescence, I know that one has a hard and an emotional time growing old.

The world has a cruel expression for this stage in an individual's growth which seems to deny that this stage can be growth at all. People say, "She has failed in these last years." Failed? Need this stage of life be a failure? Failure implies that she is not accomplishing what she tries or should be trying to do or to be. The question is not whether a woman who is growing old can do what she did in the vigorous swing of youth or middle age. She and everyone else knows that she cannot. This constitutes no "failure" on her part unless she tries to continue the pattern of her earlier years. That is where failure lies at either end of life — in trying to continue inappropriately young patterns of living. Growth at either end of life means successfully adapting to new and real conditions, fitting one's activities and responsibilities to the highest level of one's powers. It is a happier and more accurate expression to say one grows old, rather than that one "fails."

As I look around at my contemporaries or near-contemporaries — to see how they are meeting the absorbing questions of the stage of life we are facing — "What shall I do? What am I able to do?" — I see many who are trying to maintain their younger patterns of living. I think of one friend, some years younger than I, who is trying to *look* young. Rouged cheeks, ruby nails, frivolously short skirts, conspicuous hats perched on dyed hair, strident, gypsy scarves tied around wrinkled neck — all the tricks meant to deceive except face-lifting, which she can not afford. The falseness is pathetic and offensive as is all repudiation of reality. Truly she is failing. She is refusing to be her age, to *grow* old. Her failure is on a trivial plane. She cramps only herself by trying to hang on to the looks and clothes of younger years.

I think of another friend some years older than I who is trying to hang on to responsibilities and leadership of her younger years. She is failing, and her failure, like all failures, carries pathos with it. But it carries more than that, for her failure is not on a trivial personal plane. She is cramping not only herself but the very things she has cared about, the very things she has worked for and built up. She is a social burden demanding for herself a job she can no longer do. She has not met the challenge of her stage of life: "What am I able to do?" Her failure to adjust to a new way of living, a new role, is a devastating tragedy for herself and for the people and things she touches. She has ceased to adapt, to grow. Truly she is failing.

Now that I have definitely reached the stage of life when I cannot follow the vigorous patterns of middle life, I want to try honestly and with as little dramatic exaggeration as I am capable of, to face the question, "What am I able to do?" as a basis for deciding the imperative practical question, "What shall I do?" If I have not the ability to make new adjustments, to develop a new role for myself which is consistent with my present, not my past powers, then I am through. I shall have stopped growing. And it would be bitter for me to fail in this job of growing old, to be insensitive to the quality of my own work, insensitive to the needs of what I have cared for, worked for, helped to build up. It would be disappointing to me, but in a different way, to leave what seem to me valuable pieces of work unfinished which I alone can finish. First, then, the negative approach — what must I give up, no longer try to do? Second, the positive approach — what must I try to get done, what must I concentrate on in order to leave as tidy a life as I can?

I try to think of myself as a worker. I have always been a hard worker. I have loved a full program with little "time off." I have always carried complicated schedules easily, holding many threads of interest without confusion or neglect. And now? I can still work and work hard but I am no longer efficient without time off. What is more, I long for times off and I enjoy them — a new experience for me. Writing my garrulous autobiography is one evidence that I like time off! Under time pressure or schedules or many details, I now feel abused, worried, I neglect — all new experiences to me. In saying this I am comparing my present self with my past self, not myself with slow tempo people. I think I still click at a faster speed than the average person and require less time off than many of my younger friends. A slowed-down job for me might seem a full job to some people. But that is not the point. The point is that I am not as efficient or as happy in *my* old pattern as I was. I have no choice unless I wish to "fail." I must give up activities in which I no longer function according to my standards of work and I must give up responsibilities in situations that I care about where I think younger people are better equipped than I to carry them. And I must make the decisions for myself. I cannot expect my friends to tell me I am not as efficient as I was.

I then went over my activities and responsibilities one by one. I decided I was no longer equipped to be "a leader" in the Bureau, though I should continue as a "member of the co-operative Bureau group" more as a consultant. I argued that

A leader must be in a ferment of thinking and planning. He must live in his work. I once was a leader in the Bureau and I know. The Bureau has been the focus of my professional life for thirty years. I think I care more rather than less about what the Bureau has stood for . . . because I have lived with it long enough to test its value. Yet my mind no longer seethes with plans for the Bureau. I am no longer a leader. So be it.

I also assessed myself as a teacher.

. . . Teaching situations always used to stimulate me to fresh thinking. Now I often find myself hunting around for memories of what I once said. I find I quote myself! A quoter, a human victrola record may have some uses, but he is not a real teacher. A genuine teacher responds to the immediate situation in a new creative way. I have been a real teacher and I know. . . . I am no longer a real teacher. So be it. I will stop teaching. I will not "fail" as a teacher.

I did, however, give myself two years in which to cut down my teaching so that the work I had carried should not be embarrassed by my stopping suddenly. In the Workshop situation, too, I decided I must give up the active work in the classrooms with children but must continue for another year or two, "Planning the afterschool meetings with the teachers, giving talks on content material and above all writing reports and working with the Board of Education Committee on Curriculum Revision." As a final negative I decided to give up speaking in public, with a final "So be it!" Then I turned to planning future work.

So much for the agonizing negatives, the things I must give up. What are the positives besides workshop and reduced teaching for the next year or two? What am I able to do? *Writing* — that still lies within my powers. Writing does not have to be strictly scheduled — even when there is a time limit, I respond easily. I am happy when writing almost anything. I like to use words, to fit them closely to an idea. I have never thought I was a really good writer. Still, I get by. Moreover, I think I write as well as I ever did. I am always kindled by a new writing job — even a prescribed bulletin on mental hygiene! Writing looks to me like an exciting job which will keep me tied in with the active work I have loved and which I shall see going forward through others.

Now comes the question of evaluating the many possible writing jobs. I cannot possibly expect to finish all the writing I have begun — fourteen manuscripts lie in the pile taken from my files — to say nothing of the writing planned — at least four more books. The books, begun or planned, fall under three headings: 1) Writing about children and schools for them; 2) Writing for children; 3) Writing content material of use to teachers, particularly in human geography. Each one starts my heart beating fast and wheels whirling in my head. I can trust neither of these symptoms. I must stick to my original purpose of tidying up my life. Which kind of writing is most intrinsically *mine?* Which is most needed and least likely to be done by someone else?

When I think along these lines, I unhesitatingly choose writing about children and schools for them. Among my papers lies an outline for a general book on curriculum building which would sum up my long experience of teaching both children and teachers, what I believe in special school techniques in language, geography and social studies. It would be sort of an educational credo that I have evolved. It would take a long time to organize my material and to write such a book. This book seems to me my first "must."

After that I evaluated the other unfinished manuscripts in my files and the plans for future writing after the first "must" should have been accomplished.

All the other manuscripts which I thumb through and the other plans for books, though each one is tempting, hold less promise for the things I care most about. What are these things? Children — to give them rich and good lives at all stages of their growth, lives which will help them to grow up into understanding people, eager to tackle the problems of this complicated interdependent modern world. And children mean schools and teachers. They mean homes and parents. Children mean the future as well as the present. Children and through children, education, and through education, the world. That has been consistently the basic aim of my work. It is still my aim at this stage of my life. The world of my generation is gone. So be it. The world of my grandchildren's generation, however, needs more than ever the power to think clearly and to understand differing "other fellows." Even the atomic bomb cannot shatter the world's need for education. Indeed, education more than ever seems the only hope of a world where men wield this new power for destroying or for building good lives for themselves and for the other fellow.

I have worked through the pressing personal questions, "What am I able to do?" and "What shall I do?" and have come out with what looks like a possible program for my stage of life, small yet satisfying as my tiny contribution to education. I have even worked up considerable enthusiasm for this program. I'd like to begin on it this minute! I shall as soon as I can free myself by getting others to take on jobs which I am now inappropriately carrying. Then I can grow old busily and contentedly watching my grandchildren's generation grow up under the new pressures of a new world while I try to tidy up my life.

Tidying up my life did not work out as I had planned, however. So many strange and unexpected happenings interrupted my neat, rational program of work that I told Robin I had entered "the one-hoss shay" period of suddenly falling apart. It was, however, two physiological accidents, not my age, that prevented my carrying out the two-year tidying up program I had planned for the immediate future.

*A*n old woman in contemporary America is likely to be a widow, poor, and socially isolated. This is not to say that there are not many old women who remain married, are well off financially, or are integrated into the social life of their communities. It is to state that the particular constellation of widowhood, poverty, and isolation has been prominent in recent decades. Since the 1930s, there has been a preponderance of females in the aged population. In 1974, for instance, there were 100 women over age sixty-five for every 69 men. Women regularly outlive men nowadays, and the substantial gap between female and male life expectancy is predicted to widen in the future. When we recall that it is customary for women to marry men older than themselves, it is not difficult to understand why the majority of women over sixty-five are widows. In light of the fact that the fastest growing segment of the aged population today is the over-seventy-five group, perhaps an even more striking statistic is that 71 percent of women over age seventy-five in 1970 were widowed.

The implications of these demographic findings for the quality of old women's lives are varied and profound. They concern economic circumstances, living arrangements, social relationships, and psychological adjustment. Widowhood, the most common condition of women over age sixty-five, usually has negative economic consequences. Unless their husbands have left them sizable assets in real estate, savings, or insurance, elderly widows find it hard to get by on Social Security payments and Medicare. The Social Security system works to the disadvantage of aged widows, many of whom receive benefits only by virtue of their husbands' work records. Not having accumulated sufficient time in the labor force to qualify for full benefits of their own because they have spent most of their adult lives as housewives, these women are discriminated against by a system that devalues their contributions to society. The burdens of living on a minimal fixed income in a time of raging inflation cause some older women to seek employment to supplement their meager incomes. Even then they are forced to live frugally to preserve their resources for an unexpected crisis, such as a catastrophic illness. Although many elderly widows manage to make ends meet, some cannot help but slide under the poverty line. They, as well as many destitute old women, are totally dependent on public assistance for survival. Subject to rigorous scrutiny by welfare authorities and frequently denied the most elementary pleasures, these old women lead desperate existences at the edge of life.

The loss of intimates normally sustained in old age makes human contact especially important for elderly women. Being widowed and poor may appear to present sufficient obstacles to this, but an additional factor, the nature of her living situation, plays a significant part in determining an old woman's opportunities for meaningful social interaction. Although open to the criticism that they tend to segregate old people from the rest of society, residential settings in which the elderly are clustered together, such as housing projects, nursing homes, and retirement villages, offer old women a chance to form satisfying social ties with their peers. On the other hand, an old woman who lives in a neighborhood in which all age groups are represented, whether she lives alone or with family members, may find herself in an isolated position, estranged from the ongoing life of the community and lacking the companionship of her peers. Typically, poor old widows spend their last years in this latter sort of environment. Bereft of friends with whom to share their joys and sorrows, they retreat into their own private worlds, enveloped by an overwhelming sense of loneliness and despair.

Hannah Lambertson (pseudonym) of Fruitvale, Washington, in the Yakima Valley, was a very old woman who was widowed, poor, and socially isolated. When she talked to Dorothy Gallagher in 1973 and 1974, she was in her late nineties, crippled, and afflicted with failing eyesight and hearing. Yet the record of these conversations, an excerpt from which is reprinted here, discloses a vital intelligence and a resilient spirit. This unusual testimony allows us to penetrate the inner life of a woman whose old age was clouded by adversity, a woman who had suffered beyond measure, and who, in spite of everything, had endured.

The conditions of Hannah Lambertson's life were simple. She lived alone in a small, sparsely furnished house in an isolated rural area, supported by state old age assistance funds. Weekly visits from family members punctuated her otherwise monotonous daily routine. The overriding theme of her existence was loneliness, a circumstance she dealt with as best she could. Her substitutes for human contact were a television and a pet. Although she treasured her independence, she yearned for some sort of companionship and secretly dreamed of mingling with people in the busy everyday world.

Hannah Lambertson accepted her mode of life philosophically, readily admitting to her poverty and expressing gratitude for the government assistance she received. She resented the humiliation and constriction of personal liberty that the welfare system imposed on its beneficiaries, and she wished that she could work and support herself. Yet her vision of work emanated from a deeper source of anguish, the feeling that she no longer had anything to contribute to the world, that she was, as she put it, "in the way." This perception led her to question her very being: Why had she lived so long? What was the purpose of her life? As she reminisced about past occurrences, she pondered their meaning in the broader context of her life and tried to fit together the pieces of her history. She chose to represent herself as a sufferer, full of self-pity, and identified herself with the biblical Job. Clinging to a religious world view, yet skeptical of its validity, Hannah Lambertson unflinchingly confronted the central existential dilemma.

—— 28 ——
Hannah Lambertson

[Tom] died in 1960. I been alone now fourteen years.... When I was a widow the first time, I had my daddy and .my brother; then, when Mr. Aiken died, I still had my daddy. Now I've got no one. I'm a pauper. Don't that make Charlie mad when I say that! "You're not a pauper," he says. "Anything you get over the counter you pay your taxes on it." I say that don't make any difference. I'm not living on my own. And I have to have those snoopers from welfare. They come in your house; they go look in your cupboards and everywhere else to see what you have. They have no right to that at all. One woman, she cut my pension six dollars. She says, "You can eat spinach. Spinach is good eating." Well, I don't *like* spinach. One time I thought I got a raise in pension. I got a check for a hundred fifty-five dollars and four cents. But what it was, I had to buy my own food stamps. Before, the state was buying my stamps. I never asked the state for anything. I have never found fault if they cut me, and I've never said anything when they raised me. But you know what

SOURCE: From pp. 97–102 in *Hannah's Daughters: Six Generations of an American Family 1876–1976*, by Dorothy Gallagher (T. Y. Crowell). Copyright 1976 by Dorothy Gallagher. Reprinted by permission of Harper & Row Publishers, Inc., and Julian Bach, Literary Agency.

Hannah Lambertson

hurts? Folks are ashamed of you. They look down on you. They'll take you to the back alley to go into a store. They look down on me because I'm on welfare. It's a mighty good thing. It's better than the poorhouse when I was young. I'd work if I could, but I've got to the age where no one will hire me.

You know, my people, on my mother's side, are royalty-descended. And my kids, on my first husband's side, are royalty-descended too. Talk about royalty! It's a pipe dream. Old clothes given to me. Living on the state. Isn't it a joke? *I* call it a joke.

It's Job I'm descended from. I've had a few of Job's troubles. I appreciate how patient he was with all his sufferings. I have to be like Job and keep my mouth shut. I'm not angry, but I'm heartsick.

I had a bad fall last spring, you know. My legs just went out from under me and I lay there crying for help. That cat just sat at my head and yowled. Well, the neighbors found me and then May come out to take care of me. Next day May broke her wrist, and she said she couldn't take care of me and my dog. She had that dog put to sleep. You know what my dog's name was? Utell. That was like what my grandmother named her dog. She named him Guess, and every time somebody'd come to the house and ask what the dog's name was, she'd say Guess. Oh, they guessed all kinds of names. One time the caseworker came to my house. "What's your dog's name?" she said. "Utell," I says. "*I* can't tell," she says.

Well, I betrayed Utell. I'd taken care of her so tenderly for so long, and she just trotted off with May like she was going somewhere. I betrayed her trust. May's hard as nails.

I don't want to live on my children for anything. I've got lots of relatives that are millionaires. But I'm nothing to them and they're nothing to me. I don't go around whining and telling them who I am. Maybe they'd believe me and maybe they wouldn't. Lots of heartbreak in this life. It's an awful test. I call myself Job sometimes and I'm not giving my God up. When he sees fit to lift this curse, I'll be better off. But when that will be, I don't know. Last time I cried, I couldn't shed a tear. I've cried enough tears to swim in, but they won't come anymore.

I know I was well bred. Well educated. All the niceties of life. That's my grandmother's doing. She raised me that way. But that don't mean anything. That don't spread your bread. I'm old and only in the way right now. I *am* in the way. And I know I am by the things that are said to me. But what can I do about it? Oh, I have self-pity so much it doesn't do any good to mention it.

I've always been sorry I didn't have some kind of trade. So I could have been something. Instead of being over the washboard, scrubbing the floors. All those I worked for been dead many, many years. One woman, she was a beautiful woman, she's dead many years. I guess her children are dead now too. I'm still here. Why? I don't know *why!* Does God have something for me to do? We're not here for nothing, you know.

I want to tell you something. My first husband had gone to the hospital — it was some years ago, I don't remember when. But I didn't know this; I didn't know anything about him since he left me. But starting in June, I felt something stumbling against my bed. Ruby tried to tell me it was just the trucks going by, but something made me pray for Earl. And that November I just had to drop everything and pray and bawl and pray and bawl. I didn't even know he was sick. I didn't know what it was all about till we got the obituary that said he died in November. He came back to me after leaving the way he did.

I'm talking too much. Nobody to talk to. Nobody comes. I've told you everything I know about my life. It's been work, work, work and move, move, move. There's nothing remarkable ever happened to me. I was just like any other kid, wandering around by myself, going to school and coming home. And when I married I just tagged around wherever my husband went.

My daddy's buried in Yakima. My mother's buried in Michigan. My brother's buried in the foothills west of Auburn. I don't know where I'll be buried yet. I hope it'll be far away from this place. I want out of here so bad it makes me sick. Cry, cry, cry. You know, I wished I lived somewhere near Tacoma, or someplace. I'd get a housekeeper. I don't need one to do my work, just for companionship. And I'd have a car and when she'd be going out to do my trading, I'd say, "Me wanna go too." Sounds just like a baby, don't it?

Life is funny, very funny. And yet it's serious, very serious. I can't understand why the world should go the way it does.

G rowing old has a different meaning for every individual. Prior life history, economic circumstances, physical condition, family ties, religious outlook, and, of course, personality all play a significant part in determining the contours of a person's later years. Yet there is one defining characteristic that cuts across all these lines and in large measure shapes the last stage of life: gender. Although basic features of the aging process such as physical decline, the loss of major social roles, and the confrontation with the imminence of death affect both men and women, the precise form in which these issues are experienced is clearly influenced by gender identity. Being old and female is not the same as being old and male.

In this chapter, through an in-depth examination of the last portion of the lives of six women, widely separated in time and place, we have sought to understand the special concerns of women in this concluding stage of life. Admittedly, neither this group of women, nor any group of six women, can constitute a cross section of aged females in America. Still, the women whose final years have been subjected to scrutiny here represent a variety of backgrounds and life experiences.

Although they were all white, Protestant, and American-born, these old women differed in a number of other important ways. With respect to social class, they ranged from working class to upper middle class, with Hannah Lambertson situated at the lower end of the class spectrum and Lucy Mitchell toward the top. Martha Ballard and Maria Brown were located in the middle of the scale and Bethiah McKown beneath them. The fictional composite figure of the Elderly Woman must, of necessity, be omitted from this analysis. In terms of geographical location, these women spent their last decades in various parts of the country, Martha Ballard in New England, Lucy Mitchell in the Mid-Atlantic region, Maria Brown in the Midwest, Bethiah McKown in a southern border state, and Hannah Lambertson in the Pacific Northwest. Mrs. McKown and Mrs. Mitchell resided in urban areas — St. Louis and New York City — the others were inhabitants of small towns. Although the women were all literate, only one of them, Lucy Mitchell, had an advanced education. In fact, none of the others even had the equivalent of a high school education. All of the women married and bore children. But two women practiced a specialized occupation in addition to being housewives: Martha Ballard, the midwife, and Lucy Mitchell, the educator. In short, the old women whose lives we have examined can legitimately stand for countless other aged women. Although the voices of black, Catholic, Jewish, and foreign-born women have not been heard in this chapter, the six women to whom we have listened have told us a great deal about the experience of female old age in America.

One point that emerges from this study is that the placid external appearance of female old age often belies substantial inner turmoil. Old people since the nineteenth century have been forced to contend with the common belief that the slowing of physical powers leads to mental and emotional stagnation. Since female socialization throughout the life cycle emphasizes passivity and submissiveness, one might think it would be easy for women to reconcile this discrepancy between external and internal states. Women are trained not to express dissatisfaction with their condition. However, the restrictions imposed by old age far exceed those engendered by sex-role definitions. Confining one's activities to the domestic sphere is not on a par with a proscription of all useful activity. Conventional depictions of elderly women that focus on their patience, forbearance, and serenity conceal a depth of emotion rarely acknowledged.

The contradiction between a tranquil outward demeanor and a spirited, if not passionate, inner life is disclosed most vividly in the testimonies of the Elderly Woman and Hannah Lambertson. Barred from functioning as productive members of society, these women experienced acute mental anguish. Although the Elderly Woman had the advantages of financial security, physical mobility, and frequent social contacts, she was not much better off than the severely crippled Hannah Lambertson. Hannah's poverty, as well as her physical incapacity, literally chained her to her chair, and there she sat, raging inside at her impotence. But the Elderly Woman was, at least figuratively, in the same position, her genteel style of life doing little to ameliorate her feelings of frustration and bitterness.

American females have been socialized to be dependent as well as passive. The centrality of marriage in women's lives is taken for granted, as is woman's subordinate role in the marital relationship. Women have been taught to rely on their husbands for sustenance as well as leadership. Yet one of the deepest ironies of the female experience is that vast numbers of American women find themselves alone at the end of their lives. Having spent most of their adult years in a dependent position, these widows must learn, often at an advanced age, how to be independent, if not self-sufficient. Having dutifully submerged their identities in those of their mates, they are suddenly encouraged to articulate their individual needs and desires. In brief, they must attempt to undo the lessons of a lifetime.

All of the women discussed in this chapter outlived their husbands, but only three of them were widowed when we encountered them — Bethiah McKown, the Elderly Woman, and Hannah Lambertson. Hannah Lambertson was clearly a survivor, a woman who had learned to do what was necessary to get by. With three marriages behind her, she had come to realize the futility of depending on anyone but herself. Although not unmindful of the satisfactions of close personal ties, Hannah had steeled herself to the harsh realities of her solitary existence. Her years of back-breaking toil bore witness to her ability to support herself. Yet despite her independent spirit, Hannah was ultimately forced to rely on others for her basic needs. Still, her dependency was a result of physical debility, not psychological conditioning.

The fictional Elderly Woman's vague past history compels us to forego detailed analysis of her situation. Bethiah McKown, however, provides us with a classic example of a woman accustomed to leaning on her husband over the course of a lifetime and then, all at once, deprived of his support.

Her response to her predicament, as might be expected, was to turn to her grown children for aid. Lacking both the material resources and the practical experience essential for being autonomous, Bethiah was left with a paucity of options. In employing her only asset, her moral authority, to remind her children of their familial obligations, she resembled scores of other widows forced to become supplicants to their offspring to guarantee their own security. Although her sense of control over her own life was largely illusory, there is no doubt that the crisis of widowhood opened Bethiah's eyes to the benefits of independence.

Throughout American history, the standard script for female lives has envisioned woman's primary role as that of childbearer and child nurturer. Even though women have, in innumerable instances, contributed vital income to their families, in addition to performing all required domestic duties, society has always singled out the reproductive function as the central source of meaning in female lives. Yet by the time a woman reaches old age, this primary rationale for her existence has vanished. She has completed the task for which she is valued by society — bearing and rearing children — and her involvement in family affairs is minimal in comparison with that of former years. Thus, in another ironic twist, the culminating phase of a woman's life is, by social definition, devoid of purpose.

With recent improvements in female life expectancy, the absence of viable models for the last portion of the female life span poses a serious problem. In this connection, it is pertinent to inquire how women of former generations were able to sustain a positive self-image during their final decades of life. The examples of Martha Ballard, Maria Brown, and Lucy Mitchell suggest that those women who have learned to channel their energies into pursuits apart from the family are most successful in coping with the attenuation of family roles in old age. With long careers behind them, Martha Ballard, the midwife, and Lucy Mitchell, the educator, had only to plan ways of cutting back on their work without completely surrendering it. Maria Brown, on the other hand, deliberately had to seek out new activities to occupy her time. Her club work, insignificant as it might have been, provided her with personal rewards. The testimonies of these women remind us that old age can indeed be a time of affirmation.

Bibliography

Achenbaum, W. Andrew. *Old Age in the New Land: The American Experience since 1790.* Baltimore: Johns Hopkins University Press, 1978.

Bell, Inge Power. "The Double Standard: Age." *Trans-Action* (November–December 1970), pp. 75–80.

Blau, Zena Smith. *Old Age in a Changing Society.* New York: New Viewpoints, 1973.

Butler, Robert N. *Why Survive? Being Old in America.* New York: Harper & Row, 1975.

Fischer, David Hackett. *Growing Old in America.* New York: Oxford University Press, 1977.

Gross, Ronald; Gross, Beatrice; and Seidman, Sylvia, eds. *The New Old: Struggling for Decent Aging.* Garden City, New York: Doubleday, Anchor Books, 1978.

Hall, G. Stanley. *Senescence: The Last Half of Life.* New York: D. Appleton, 1922.

Hareven, Tamara K. "The Last Stage: Historical Adulthood and Old Age." *Daedalus* 105 (Fall 1976): 13–27.

Hochschild, Arlie Russell. *The Unexpected Community.* Englewood Cliffs, New Jersey: Prentice-Hall, 1973.

Kalish, Richard A. *Late Adulthood: Perspectives on Human Development.* Monterey, California: Brooks/Cole, 1975.

Lopata, Helena Znaniecki. *Widowhood in an American City.* Cambridge, Massachusetts: Schenkman, 1973.

Smith, Bert Kruger. *Aging in America.* Boston: Beacon Press, 1973.

Sontag, Susan. "The Double Standard of Aging." *Saturday Review* 55 (September 23, 1972): 29–38.

Spicker, Stuart F.; Woodward, Kathleen M.; and Van Tassel, David D., eds. *Aging and the Elderly: Humanistic Perspectives in Gerontology.* Atlantic Highlands, New Jersey: Humanities Press, 1978.

Troll, Lillian E. "The Family of Later Life: A Decade Review." *Journal of Marriage and the Family* 33 (1971): 263–290.